THE VALUES IN NUMBERS

The Values in Numbers

READING JAPANESE LITERATURE IN A GLOBAL INFORMATION AGE

Hoyt Long

Columbia University Press
New York

Columbia University Press
Publishers Since 1893
New York Chichester, West Sussex
cup.columbia.edu

Columbia University Press wishes to express its appreciation for assistance given by the Wm. Theodore de Bary Fund in the publication of this book.

Library of Congress Cataloging-in-Publication Data
Names: Long, Hoyt J., author.
Title: The values in numbers : reading Japanese literature in a global information age / Hoyt Long.
Description: New York : Columbia University Press, 2021. | Includes bibliographical references and index.
Identifiers: LCCN 2020037666 (print) | LCCN 2020037667 (ebook) | ISBN 9780231193504 (hardback) | ISBN 9780231193511 (trade paperback) | ISBN 9780231550345 (ebook)
Subjects: LCSH: Computational linguistics. | Quantitative research. | Japanese literature—20th century—History and criticism.
Classification: LCC P98.5.S83 L66 2021 (print) | LCC P98.5.S83 (ebook) | DDC 410.285—dc23
LC record available at https://lccn.loc.gov/2020037666
LC ebook record available at https://lccn.loc.gov/2020037667

Cover design: Noah Arlow
Cover image: Natsume Sōseki, *Bungakuron* (*Theory of Literature*), 1907, bk 1.

CONTENTS

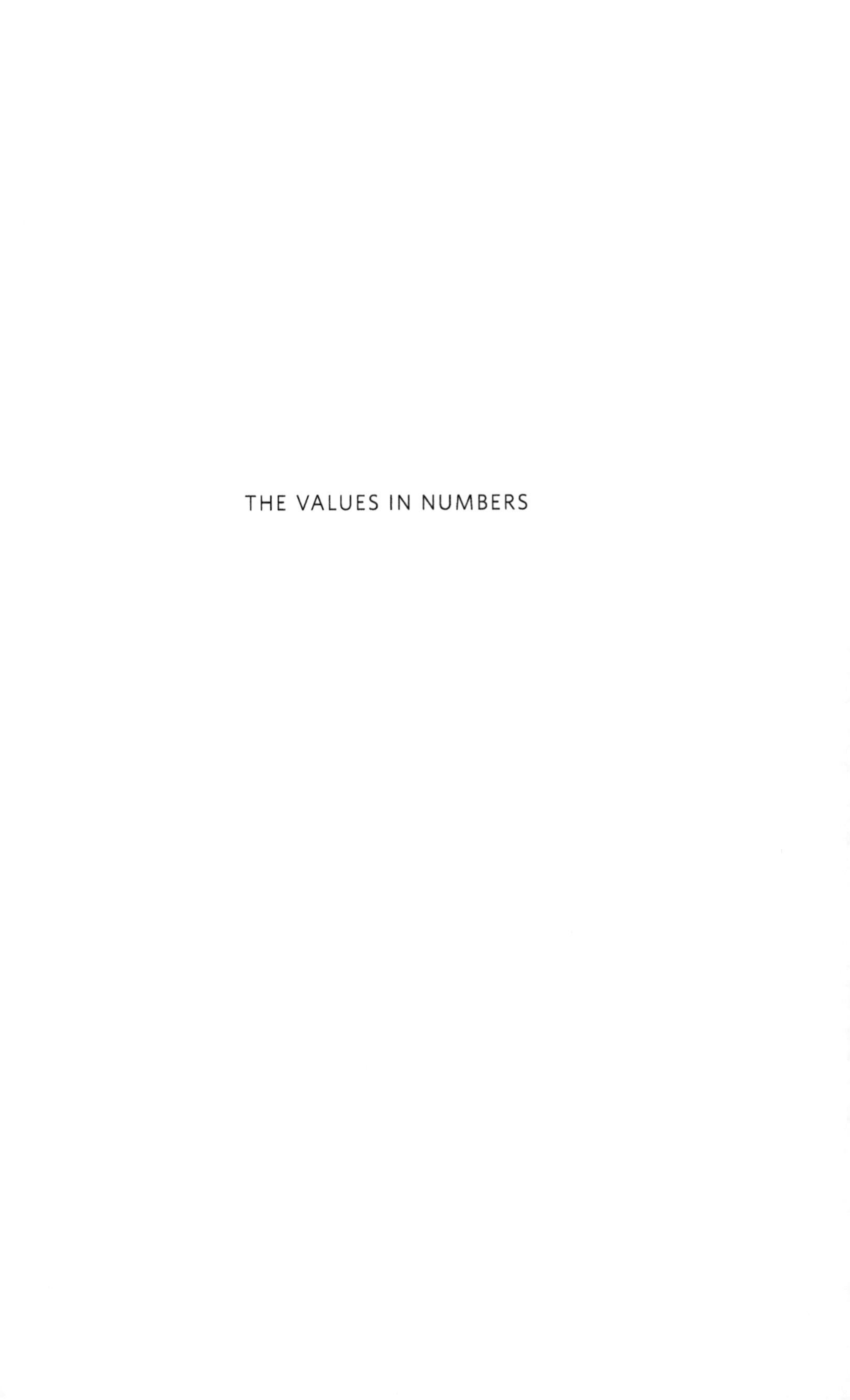

THE VALUES IN NUMBERS

Introduction

UNCERTAINTY IN NUMBERS

The history of thought is the history of its models.

—FREDRIC JAMESON (1972)

Counting cases and deducing averages is not how a man accomplished in the knowledge of the world gets to the bottom of the motives underlying human actions in their extraordinary diversity.

—B. J. I. RISUEÑO D'AMADOR (1837)

On April 25, 1837, a debate was held at the Académie de Médecine in Paris on the role of statistics in medicine. The stage had been set two weeks before when Jean Cruveilhier, who held a chair in the Paris Faculty of Medicine, called for a discussion on the matter. Medical academicians such as Cruveilhier had reason to be anxious about the use of statistical methods in medicine. The past few years had witnessed the emergence of new statistical ideas such as Siméon-Denis Poisson's "law of large numbers" and Adolphe Quetelet's "average." The former supposed that the ratio of an event to the whole varies less and less with the number of events measured, while the latter was built on the assertion that the greater the number of individuals observed, the more their individual particularities "fade from view and give way to general facts."[1] Although still in their infancy and hardly agreed fact even in the field of statistics, these ideas caused a stir as they began to circulate to other fields of knowledge such as demography, law, and now medicine.[2] In calling for a more sustained debate, Cruveilhier believed with the majority of his colleagues that there was really no debate to be had. Medicine "was not the kind of discipline that dealt in numbers and measuring instruments. It was, rather, a science of observation and *expérience*." Imposing numbers on the study of life ran "contrary to the eminently variable and elusive quality of the phenomena found in living bodies." What he called "the inflexibility of numbers" was simply incompatible with the need for medicine's methods, its very forms of knowing, to correspond to the mobility of life.[3]

When the debate finally got underway, it was the Spaniard B. J. I. Risueño d'Amador who stole the show as "the champion of antistatistical thinking."[4] His signature rhetorical move was to portray his adversaries as having lost their way, trading one kind of medical certainty—carefully cultivated through a physician's observations and experiences with particular patients—for the illusory certainty of counting. Illusory because, as he framed it, the counting and calculation of averages was a "mechanical procedure that made the majority of cases equivalent in effect to the totality," denying access to human actions (and illnesses) in their "extraordinary diversity." To use numbers was, simply put, a refusal to know variability in itself. Harking back to a tradition that referred to medicine as "the art," and which believed medical knowledge was guided by certainties found in the sensations of its artists, Risueño insisted that "the only kind of knowing able to grasp living variability was the 'individual genius of the artist,' who encountered and observed each patient as a particular case." Should medicine go the way of numbers, it would not only turn this art into "a lottery," but risk "neglecting the minority" that is obscured by averages and offer a false remedy to the inherent uncertainty of medical knowledge.

When it was their turn to respond, the defenders of numbers were quick to express their own reservations about the idea of a "normal" (average) anatomy or patient. But the problem was that the idea had been misinterpreted and misrepresented by detractors. When it was understood as a measure for identifying the range of variation in a set of observations, not a single value that erased variation, it became a useful conceptual tool. A physician could potentially generalize a treatment for patients whose symptoms fell within a given range, rather than treat every individual as absolutely unique. Few were convinced by such counterarguments, however. As the debate ended, Risueño's colleague M. Double dealt a final blow to the "numerists." Averages were but a theoretical fiction because clinical experience taught that no average anatomy or pathology, no average patient, truly existed. "I am put in mind, if you will forgive the comparison, of a shoemaker who, having measured the feet of a thousand individuals more or less, comes up with an average and makes shoes only according to that imaginary pattern."[5] The joke being, of course, that such a shoemaker is no shoemaker at all. Numbers, for the moment, were out for the count.

If this debate seems far removed from medical practice today (would we trust a doctor who placed all his authority in personal artistry?), its rhetoric will be all too familiar to anyone following recent debates in the North American academy on the value of numbers for literary study. At times, it seems that literature has become but the newest site of resistance to statistical thinking in ways that recapitulate the conceptual binaries and epistemological divisions on which Risueño and his peers depended: fixity versus flexibility of interpretation, artistic versus mechanical procedure, and attention to variability versus projections of equivalence and uniformity. It is difficult not to hear echoes of Risueño and his colleagues in the verbal jabs directed at present-day numerists who have traded the illusory certainty of statistical averages for that of computers and artificial intelligence. Their methods substitute "brute optical scanning" of texts for the symphony of human reading, which instead savors texts through "random redirections of inquiry" and "the natural intelligence of the brain making leaps."[6] Rather than observe and experience texts firsthand, they are like "people who turn on the internet to find out what the temperature is instead of opening the window to discover it is both cold and raining outdoors."[7] They drastically reduce "literary, literary-historical, and linguistic complexity" in a discipline that is "about *reducing* reductionism" and, in so doing, often "confuse what happens mechanically with insight."[8] In bringing numbers into a field of knowledge with which it is utterly incommensurate, they are like the clueless shoemaker who has somehow forgotten what a foot is. "Bad readers," to borrow a phrase from Merve Emre, for our digital age.[9]

Today's "bad reading" may look like yesterday's "bad medicine," but with hindsight it is hard not to conclude that time is on numeracy's side. The debates of the 1830s look quaint in light of how entangled numbers are in medical practice today. Yet "equivocation between the qualitative and the quantitative," which was also a moral debate about "good" medical practice, is rehearsed anew every time doctors wrestle with the impacts of new technologies on how the human body is constituted as an object of knowledge.[10] Conversely, if current debates in literary study now make it seem that this equivocation is being rehearsed for the first time, they are in fact part of a longer dialogue repeated, with variations, at least since this study was institutionalized as an academic discipline in the late-nineteenth century. The dialogue surfaces, among other places, in Victorian-era physiological theories of reading; the nineteenth-century rise of German philology; I. A. Richards's statistical studies of vocabulary; the early quantitative stylistics of Caroline Spurgeon and Josephine Miles; Russian formalism; the consolidation of New Criticism against Cold War advances in machine reading and translation; histories of the book; and sociological studies of reading.[11] In all of these cases, arguments for or against the value of numbers unfolded before the specter of new economies of information and new technologies, which were seen to be transforming, for good and ill, the institutions and infrastructures of knowledge production. Numerical thinking in its ever-changing guises acted as a flash point around which epistemological divisions between quantitative and qualitative modes of reasoning were either disrupted or entrenched. The cycle of debate repeats with every major infrastructural shift in the organization and production of knowledge, every technical innovation promising to transform how information is accessed. At each turn, rhetorical tropes are updated to bolster prescriptive claims about what it means to read literature.

The Values in Numbers is a book about this ongoing equivocation in literary studies as much as it is a contribution to its potential futures. I am interested in how we arrived at the current standoff and the ways in which it is both similar to and different from previous times. I pursue these interests through two distinct theoretical frameworks. The first is organized by a history of science perspective that looks behind the moralistic claims about *whether* or not literary study should involve numbers. These claims are inescapable and no doubt necessary to how we preserve (or try to alter) the boundaries of established knowledge practices. Furthermore, there is no avoiding the fact that the ontological status of a text, like a patient, differs with respect to the models through which it is thought. When these claims reinforce hard methodological or disciplinary divisions, however, they occlude the messier conceptual traffic flowing between them. When disciplinary truth becomes a function of how much one can isolate qualitative reasoning from quantitative, or vice versa, their entanglement as modes of knowledge making is obscured, and so too are the social practices and human actors that create and maintain the division between them. Artifacts of historical convergences, of institutionally situated compromises and negotiations over values, become the "facts" on and against which claims of disciplinary truth are forged.

This principle is born out by the notion of the average, or normal, that was at the center of the 1830s medical debates. Peter Cryle and Elizabeth

Stephens point out that in the field of medical history the "normal," buttressed by the statistical thinking of Poisson and Quetelet, is typically critiqued for "its repressive and standardizing function," as if this were its sole cultural function and its only claim on reality. It is taken as a description of the world, formalized by the calculation of averages, but an ideologically dubious one because of the facts it asserts. Investigating the longer history of the idea, however, reveals that the "normal" was understood from its inception as both average and ideal, a calculation and a value. It was a fact in the making, one that could be used to assert a norm ("the average man") to which all people, made equal through a calculation, should conform. Yet it could also be used to individualize and differentiate, making visible the gradations by which individuals deviated from that norm. As Foucault wrote, it made "it possible to measure gaps, to determine levels, to fix specialties and to render the differences useful by fitting them one to another."[12] The interpretation and cultural functions of the normal were thus up for negotiation, susceptible to the full range of political uses (and abuses) that humans might dream up.

This negotiability was apparent at the very moment its meaning was up for grabs in the French medical debates. Critics of counting accused proponents of committing to the theoretical fiction of the average and treating it as empirical reality. Defenders, however, were well aware of this fiction, acknowledging that no illness ever manifests in exactly the same way. Although an illness is not invariable, countered the young physician P. F. O. Rayer, "sometimes its variations are contained within fairly narrow limits." These ranges of variation, when treated as individual units, become useful for planning treatment for multiple patients at once. Conversely, a doctor can vary treatment in cases where patients have "some condition that deviates too visibly from the average man." The average was a useful fiction both for grouping patients with similar symptoms and for identifying outliers whose symptoms fell within a different range of variation and thus necessitated a different response. Aside from the counting, Rayer rejoindered, was this process really any different from the "average image" of an illness that doctors built up in their own minds when planning therapy? Refusing to recognize these conceptual benefits, and opposing all statistical thinking by insisting that every patient was absolutely unique, was effectively to imply that "no two facts ever resemble each other, that medical practice never takes the same form twice, and that theory is never entitled to assimilate one to the other."[13] Variation understood as absolute difference steers disciplinary practice and theory toward the nonsensical, and the doctor becomes a shoemaker who crafts every shoe as though it were his first and last.

One lesson to take from this example is that underneath the debate's moral register was a shared intellectual terrain in which concepts like individuality, difference, similarity, and pattern were being questioned and debated through distinct models of thought. When they weren't talking past each other, debaters were using these supposedly incommensurable modes of reasoning to navigate the same conceptual space, figuring in their own way the difference of things. In the process, and this is a second lesson to draw, they reveal their own models of thought as the outcome of particular investments by communities and conventions of practice and, consequently, as open to negotiation and interpretation. The "facts" of a discipline are at once the solid basis on which its sense of reality is built but are also a locus of values whose certainty is relativized at the point where these facts intermingle with those of other disciplines.[14] It is with these lessons in mind that I seek an analytical space in which the conventions of literary study can be renegotiated in tandem with the statistical facts and models applied to texts in our current global information age. Having myself spent a decade writing a book firmly rooted in the disciplinary conventions of literary studies, and now a decade more exploring how quantitative methods can supplement these conventions, I contend that there are more suitable metaphors for what it is to ply this space than the misguided shoemaker or machine reader.

The second theoretical framework organizing *The Values in Numbers* is a corollary to the first, which is that disciplinary, historical, and social location matter when considering the values of numbers and the politics that inform their use. This is apparent to anyone who has read the spate of monographs exemplary of the most recent quantitative turn, which reflect the varied ways that location shapes arguments for quantitative methods even when there is consensus that literary studies is better off reckoning with these methods than not.[15] I add to this dissonant chorus a voice situated firmly within the concerns of area studies and the questions that arise when literature becomes entangled in geopolitics and cultural and linguistic difference. If these questions seem secondary to those of why and how to read literature with numbers, we should remember that a now canonical origin point for such arguments—Franco Moretti's call for "distant reading"—was sparked by such questions and, although rarely noted, by the history of modern Japanese literature. In "Conjectures on World Literature," Moretti writes that the original conjecture he sought to test, and around which his concept of distant reading was developed, was inspired by a remark Fredric Jameson made in his foreword to Karatani Kōjin's *Origins of Modern Japanese Literature*. Namely, in "the take-off of the modern Japanese novel, 'the raw material of Japanese social experience and the abstract formal patterns of Western novel construction cannot always be welded together seamlessly.' " Finding this same configuration of local content and foreign forms occurring in places like India and Brazil, Moretti wondered where else this potential "law of literary evolution" held true, setting in motion his program to read distantly, where distance means "*a condition of knowledge*" that brings into focus units other than the text: "devices, themes, tropes—or genres and systems."[16]

Andrew Goldstone has shown that as this program advanced, and as its methods became more overtly quantitative, distant reading was dissociated from the comparative problems that had originally motivated it, its typical object increasingly organized by "the national and linguistic specializations of most literary scholars." Where it was once a problem of reading across a diverse system of literatures, it became a problem of the great unread, "of what *cannot possibly be read*" within the assumed unity of a single system.[17] In this book, I wrestle with how to weld these problems together so that comparison *and* scale can be simultaneously addressed through quantitative approaches. I explore the possibilities for reading with numbers in national contexts beyond the dominant context of English literature and also for reading between contexts and their respective cultural and linguistic histories. In doing so I shuttle between nested conceptual divisions: numbers and literature at one level, Literature and literatures at another. This movement produces its own unique set of questions as quantitative methods and models designed for the study of English literature are ported and adapted to other literary and linguistic contexts, exposing in the process how contingent they are on specific interpretative practices and archival infrastructures. When we expose the presence of white space between words, for instance, or the ability to read across centuries, as artifacts of English's linguistic and imperial history rather than technological givens universally applicable, how does this change the current conversation around numbers and their relation to literature(s)?[18]

A related concern is the question of whether quantitative approaches inherently reinforce the category of national literature, as the fate of Moretti's distant reading program would suggest. If we understand numerical abstraction to be predicated on the construction of analogous units and categories—on the reduction of linguistic, aesthetic, or cultural variation to comparable units—then it seems intuitive that quantitative methods would privilege the nation as a comparative unit ready to hand. But is there reason to believe they do so to a greater or lesser extent than strictly qualitative approaches? How much of this perceived tendency to privilege national literature is a function of ingrained disciplinary structures, rather than quantification itself? Here I push against the idea of a natural affinity between numbers and nation by showing how an insistence on comparable units can productively trouble received narratives of national literary difference, in part by projecting the equivalence of objects where entrenched value systems see only hierarchy. I insist that there are times when the flattening of difference through numbers is useful for rethinking the relation of literatures. This insistence is born of the fact that *The Values in Numbers* perpetually floats in-between the different systems of literature and numbers, world and national literary imaginaries. Karatani, in his afterword to *Origins*, suggested that the Cartesian cogito is "a process of doubt that the 'difference' between diverse systems ineluctably produces." If so, then this is a book doubly in doubt. Just as Karatani argued for doubt as a useful epistemological position with which "to expose the way in which we take what has been historically produced as natural, the contingent as necessary," I rely on doubt, and the uncertainties generated from the collision of knowledge formations, to denaturalize some of the contingent stories told about literature both *with* and *without* numbers.[19]

In order to shuttle between these diverse systems, I have organized the book by a set of themes (Facts, Archive, Genre, Influence, and Discourse) and subthemes (Difference, Sample, Repetition, Judgment, and Character) that serve as both conceptual bridges between these systems and points of complication or differentiation. Each theme and subtheme performs this dual role, providing ways to think across the epistemological divide between numbers and literature while localizing this thinking in field-specific debates about Japanese literature's relation to literatures elsewhere, particularly debates around national canon formation, the evolution and transnational circulation of novelistic forms, and colonial literary relations. I have also organized the book as a methodological primer, deliberately weaving into its thematic frameworks a gradual introduction to quantitative methods. This includes attention to the models of thought built into these methods and their contingent intellectual histories. The methods increase in complexity with each chapter, and so too the amount of data to which I apply them, allowing me to address the theoretical assumptions and interpretive decisions that go to construct these new instruments of "fact" making at different scales. These instruments, as I will make clear, are as unstable and open to negotiation as the average was for doctors in the French medical academy. And just as its place in the future infrastructure of medical practice was uncertain at the time, so too are the futures of some of the new instruments introduced here, even within the disciplines from which they are borrowed. How stable they become in literary studies will depend in large part on how much they are shared and invested in by communities of users. To this end, the code and data used in writing this book are made available so the results can be checked, reproduced, and reinterpreted by others seeking to make their own contributions to the future infrastructures of literary study.[20]

I begin the book with a genealogy of moments in which the perceived value of numbers for reading Japanese literature came under new kinds of theoretical pressures. Chapter 1, "Facts and Difference," uses these as sites for reading the institutional, technical, and epistemological contexts from which an appeal to quantification came to seem necessary and urgent. With each moment, I examine the reasoning and motivations that drove critics and scholars to place texts in new comparative spaces of relation and equivalence using the quantitative methods available to them. For novelist and critic Natsume Sōseki, mathematical formalisms offered a way to circumvent imported hierarchies of literary value that situated Japanese literature as out of sync with Euro-American aesthetic tastes. In *Theory of Literature* (1907), Sōseki drew on late-Victorian physiological theories of reading to propose that the empirical and formal properties of texts could be correlated with measures of emotional response. In the 1930s, Hatano Kanji shifted this readerly focus toward writers, combining his academic interests in psychology, linguistics, and sociology to develop a theory of style. His methodology involved categorizing and counting lexical and grammatical features to differentiate the stylistic uniqueness of authors from a larger normative background. In the 1950s, counting gave way to inferential statistics and a group of scholars working at the cutting edge of Cold War information theory and psycholinguistics. Their methods scaled to many dozens of texts, thus enlarging the background against which texts could be formally compared and dissolving well-worn categories of analysis such as author and work. This dissolution reached a new apogee in the 1980s with the critic Komori Yōichi. His work from this period, echoing Moretti's writing from the same time on the sociology of forms, injected stylistics with an interest in the historical evolution of discourse as shaped by social and cultural hierarchies. In each case, numbers were a way to figure and propose facts of textual difference that ran counter to established facts and methods of interpretive practice.

This genealogy uncovers the process by which facts from one domain (e.g., that the average is a meaningful representation of a set of disparate measurements) are carried over and adapted to another that has its own set of facts and conventional wisdoms about how different objects relate. At each moment, the process involved testing the kinds of facts that would be allowed to have purchase in literary analysis or be rejected by prevailing disciplinary norms. This was as much about deciding what numbers could mean as it was about the meaning and value of literary texts. By routing this genealogy through Japan, we also see how this process was joined to global intellectual currents through shared technical infrastructures and economies of information and was shaped by local context and the asymmetries inherent in these infrastructures and economies. The tangible outcomes of this process, short-lived and fragile though many were, expanded the possible entry points for reasoning about literature with numbers beyond the labels that describe it today (i.e., distant reading, cultural analytics). At the same time, we find in these outcomes some of the methodological building blocks (e.g., tables, word counts, feature selection, sampling, descriptive statistics) that undergird current computational approaches. A final task of this chapter is to explain some of the epistemological assumptions about texts and textual relations that enter into, and are supported by, these foundational elements.

Chapter 2, "Archive and Sample," is devoted to one of the statistical ideas that has made the current quantitative turn at once so promising and so contentious: sampling. Of all the reasons given for why this turn to numbers is qualitatively different—advancements in artificial intelligence and statistical methods for processing natural language; a media environment that demands enhanced digital literacy; the transformation of university education by neoliberal ideology—it is the increasing availability and access to large digital corpora (the promise of scale) that most animates the argument for numbers.[21] It is contentious because this apparent availability is highly uneven in terms of what has been digitized and how, and because these corpora trouble how we think about the relation of part to whole, individual observation to general pattern, in exactly the ways French doctors were troubled by the supposed certainty of averages and the law of large numbers. How many cases were enough to generalize a principle or law? Did individual healths, in all their variety, really add up to some average, background health?[22] New scales of evidence brought with them new epistemologies for thinking about the relation of part to whole, but it also forced doctors to articulate those implicit in their practice. In this chapter, I focus on this same dynamic as it plays out between practices of statistical sampling necessitated by large text collections and ideas of the case study found in literary studies. Drawing on work by Katherine Bode, Alan Liu, John Guillory, Lauren Berlant, and more broadly from the fields of content analysis, book history, and critical data studies, I provide a set of theoretical and methodological suggestions for how to constitute and reason about the relation of part to whole.

I frame these suggestions through an archeology of the largest digital collection of modern Japanese literature available to scholars, Aozora Bunko. Akin to Project Gutenberg, it represents the effort of hundreds of volunteers to digitize out-of-copyright works in all genres, and since its inception in 1997, it has grown to include more than 16,000 titles (about 40 percent of which are classified as fiction). Although it is an impressive archive, it is difficult to pretend that it captures the whole of "modern Japanese literature," or even some sufficiently representative part. It is both archive and sample, built from a logic of selection that is a combination of contemporary taste, the residue of earlier canonization processes, and the realities of copyright law. Rather than write it off as somehow "incomplete," however, a move that would withhold the possibility of reading computationally any but the most extensively digitized literatures, I try to reason about its "incompleteness" through bibliographic traces that provide similarly incomplete perspectives on a whole that is always ideational. These traces include foreign literary translations in prewar Japan (thirty thousand titles), twentieth-century literary anthologies (forty thousand titles), and Japanese literature as reproduced in high school textbooks (thirteen thousand titles). Each provides an alternative sample against which to figure Aozora's alignment or divergence along lines of time period, genre, gender, and other dimensions. Methodologically, this analysis of multiple kinds of samples allows me to introduce several helpful concepts related to practices of sampling, as well as a variety of measures and data visualization techniques for exploring bibliographic data sets.

Chapter 3, "Genre and Repetition," is the first of three case studies that use sophisticated methods of computational text analysis at increasingly larger scales, from dozens of works in this chapter to thousands by the last chapter. With respect to unit of analysis, there is an inverse progression from entire documents to passages and finally to sentences and words. Genre has been a frequent topic of study in the current quantitative turn, and scholars Mark Algee-Hewitt, Andrew Piper, Ted Underwood, and others have pioneered methods for determining how well regularities in literary language (textual evidence) align with categorizations applied to texts by various institutional mechanisms (social evidence). Machine learning methods, which learn a set of associations between these two kinds of evidence, have proven especially useful for testing the models of genre developed by specific communities of readers against computational models of texts that excel at identifying discursive or structural regularities. The genre taken up here is the "I-novel" (*shishōsetsu*). Scholars and critics have seen it as foundational to Japanese literary modernity and yet impossibly hard to define by fiction's most common elements: plot, character, and narrative. It is a fictional genre that isn't. Rather than trying to resolve this productive ambiguity, which is integral to how this self-oriented mode of writing has been read, I argue for computational models as a means to confirm and confound the conceptual frames that past readers have used to evaluate the I-novel both as, and against, genre.

I do this by creating a computational frame through which to relate texts to one another—a frame organized by measures of lexical repetition. These measures are chosen for their potential to capture more complex features associated with the I-novel by scholars (e.g., vernacularization, use of Western grammatical patterns, focused psychonarration that devolves into representations of madness), although they also have their own complicated histories in the field of psycholinguistics and the search for quantitative indicators of mental aberration. Keeping these histories and the secondary literature in view, I combine these measures with others to build a simple model of repetition as style and to explore the degree to which this style is expressed in noted I-novels and in popular fiction, against which the status of the I-novel as art has often been predicated by writers and critics. The model allows me to read stylistic tendencies at large, showing that repetition is useful for capturing part of the difference that I-novels have represented for past readers. At the same time, the model makes it possible to identify individual I-novels that express this tendency in exaggerated ways and popular works that employ this tendency against genre expectations. By moving from existing scholarship to a scaled-up reading of an entire genre and back to close analysis of texts, I provide a road map for the kinds of hermeneutic circles around which quantitative arguments tend to revolve: develop measures for stylistic features; build corpora to test how discriminating they are; relate texts according to their tendency to express these features; and close read individual texts to see where the model's evaluations align or diverge from other critical judgments. Here the model helps to retell the history of the I-novel, and of the irreducible subject as guarantor of artistic value, through the compulsion to repeat.

This history, as is well known, was not strictly bound by the nation. The I-novel emerged from the confluence of multiple interlocking systems of difference—linguistic, aesthetic, cultural—and this particular generic configuration would be repeated in China just a decade after its ascent in Japan. Chapter 3 toys with the possibility of following this trajectory using a model of repetition as style, whereas chapter 4, "Influence and Judgment," is devoted to the question of what such computational models can contribute to an understanding of the transnational circulation of literary forms and the stories we tell about the (im)possibility of influence across cultural borders. It asks this question with respect to the late 1920s, when the rise of global literary modernism sparked yet another round of attempts in Japan to recompose the written self and redefine fiction's relation to society. A critical vector of disruption was the stream-of-consciousness narrative technique, which arrived as a new generation of writers was vying for attention and just as the literary market was being transformed by new scales of economy. The stories told of its arrival, by participating writers and critics alike, fluctuate between praise for its transformative potential and successful overturning of calcified models of the literary subject (i.e., the I-novel), on the one hand, and firm convictions that it was a technique solely misunderstood or, like a rash, superficial and short-lived in its effects on the national literary body, on the other. This fluctuation parallels stories told of stream of consciousness as a world historical form, but also the theories we have for how these forms move in general, being things that can both travel the world and never go anywhere. These various stories and accounts amount to competing acts of literary judgment about literary influence, to which this chapter adds an alternative account informed by what I call *algorithmic competence.*

The aim of chapter 4 is once again not to supplant other kinds of linguistic or literary competence with an algorithmic one. Rather, it is to provide a point of reflection on the models and conventions of thought implicit within these other competencies, whether the local stories of the success and failure of stream of consciousness or the global theories of world literature that offer competing structuralist (e.g., Moretti, Pascale Casanova) and poststructuralist (e.g., Emily Apter) interpretations of cross-cultural and cross-linguistic textual relations. Each is underwritten by conceptions of textual equivalence and difference that are socially, historically, and culturally located. Computational models are no less biased in this regard, but the particular ways they bring texts into comparative relation can put pressure on the temporal, geographical, and aesthetic lines that circumscribe other acts of judgment. Methodologically, I construct this alternate perspective by shifting from an analysis of discrete features to an analysis of multiple features in combination, demonstrating how to build more complex models for classifying narrative forms and for potentially tracking their diffusion within and across national literatures. I show how one can create a model of a fuzzy and ambiguous form like stream of consciousness in one language and translate it to another to see where it holds up or breaks down. This double translation, from diffuse narrative technique to abstract model, and from one linguistic context to another, inevitably constrains how we think about the technique itself. But I argue that these constraints are not a priori aligned with any one kind of account of world literature and can indeed, by virtue of these constraints, throw new interpretative light on past acts of judgment and the constraints of scale and evidence that shape them. In particular, they open avenues to rethink the reception of modernist fiction in Japan, and writers' expansion of models of psychonarration, as a process of selective appropriation of common formal elements in varied combinations.

The final chapter, "Discourse and Character," turns from the interaction of narrative form with individual psychology to focus on discourse as it interacts with social psychology, specifically the representation of racial and ethnic others. Models of self-projection in the I-novel and high literary modernism give way to models of essentialized difference in all manner of prose fiction published between the rise and fall of Japanese empire, from 1890 to 1960. Race has been a central focus of Japanese literary and historical studies for over two decades as scholars have sought to understand the impact of imperial and colonial relations on cultural images of imperial selves and colonized others. Drawing on this rich body of scholarship, I use computation to address one of its enduring questions: How did individual writers come to know, appropriate, or subvert the dominant discourses of racial and ethnic othering that presumably pervaded the social institutions and media environments in which they wrote? The question begs another that is often less directly addressed: How do we confirm the broad contours of racializing discourse in ways adequately responsive to the scale of inquiry such confirmation requires? At root, this is a question about the dynamic between individual utterance and a general discursive system addressed by Edward Said in *Orientalism*. A host of postcolonial theorists, including Ann Stoler and Mary Louise Pratt, have followed suit in an effort to render visible the "vocabulary" and "grammar" of racializing logic under conditions of empire. By connecting their linguistically framed models with recent methods for modeling semantic relations in large bodies of text, I offer a new route for thinking about racial discourse across multiple scales.

The chapter's subtheme, character, acts as a conceptual and literary bridge for moving between these scales. At the widest scale, I use the racist and essentialist notion of "character"—the idea that individual bodies can be categorized as the sum of distinct biological and cultural traits—to identify patterns of stereotypical language across nearly two thousand works of fiction and a collection of more than nine thousand magazine articles covering the same period. In both corpora I identify clusters of semantically related terms that tend to co-occur with one set of racial or ethnic identifiers (like

"Korean") versus another (like "Japanese"). For instance, I find that words related to the voice (e.g., shriek, scream, cry, yell) are much more likely to appear around terms for "native" or "indigenous" than around terms for "Japanese." The end result of this exploration is a set of semantic grids that trace the broad contours of racializing discourse in these corpora, allowing one to see how the character of racial and ethnic others varied with identity categories and with different genres of writing. These grids subsequently provide a way to zoom back into individual texts to show how these broad discursive trends hold up or break down in discrete instances and, more important, at the level of fictional characterization. Drawing on theories of character from Deidre Lynch, Alex Woloch, and Phillip Brian Harper, as well as from Japanese writers, I identify major and minor characters in a subset of colonial fiction to see how global semantic clusters adhere at the local level of a work's character space. What I find are works that utilize words related to the voice to index their "native" character's relative degree of assimilation to Japanese ethnic identity. Close readings of these works illustrate how quantitative methods provide new ways to situate individual aesthetic strategies (i.e., those pertaining to racial characterization) in more general discursive patterns. The constraints of reading at larger scales (e.g., abstraction of textual meaning, reliance on the empirically observable, algorithmic bias), I argue, can be used to illuminate, not undermine, theories of difference crucial to the study of cultural history.

The argument that computation can assist in theorizing difference may incite the same kinds of antistatistical backlash with which this introduction began. It goes to the heart, however, of my attempt to recognize that numerical reasoning has a politics that is not as clear-cut as its detractors imply. By which I mean, to return to the average, that this reasoning involves both calculations as well as moral values, mathematical formula as well as theories and interpretations of the world and its complexity. Numbers, and by extension statistical thinking, can amplify as much as flatten difference between the things they measure; can break down and dismantle normative categories as much as construct and reify them. What these calculations come to stand for depends on the theoretical and social uses to which they are put and the degree of institutional investments made in them. Yet as in the French medical debates, the critique of numbers in literary studies has focused on their capacity to reduce particularity and variation and to replace the expert judgment of the human reader. We must, of course, be critical of how this reductive capacity becomes imbricated in structures of power and oppression: the underwriting of eugenic thought by nineteenth-century statistics; the erasure of laboring bodies who produce the data on which numbers depend; the magnification of race, class, and gender inequality by today's machine learning algorithms.[23] But attending to the politics of numbers also means opening up the "facts" they support to debate by recognizing the historical processes by which disciplinary and other communities came to agree on these facts. Rather than flat out rejection, we open up to negotiation the theoretical fictions poured into them and position ourselves to imagine what other fictions they might support.

Nearly two hundred years later, the average is now a fact of medical practice, and indeed of everyday life, in ways its detractors could not have foreseen. Will any of the statistical abstractions and quantitative models of thought now being applied to literature feel similarly nonnegotiable two hundred years from now? There is reason to be skeptical given that literary studies has long proved resistant to welcoming such abstractions into its disciplinary communities. Those that do gain momentum as instruments of fact and meaning making tend to be treated as the property of other disciplines (e.g., linguistics, sociology, psychology) or skirted off and tucked safely away in subfields (e.g., stylistics, book history, humanities computing, cultural analytics). In this sense, attempts to bring numbers to literary history and criticism have perpetually been "science-fictional" in the way that Karatani's *Origins* was science-fictional in the eyes of Jameson: their new abstractions model the form of a critical reality "that does not yet exist, but which it would be interesting to experience."[24] *The Values in Numbers* is another in this long series of attempts to convince literary scholars that such abstractions are interesting enough to model a critical reality wherein they can supplement or be combined with the qualitative abstractions we use to support existing disciplinary facts. They are interesting not as substitutes for other models of thought or guarantors of certainty but for the productive doubts they generate about how and what we know of the literary past. As the numerical abstractions of today gain currency in other disciplines, and as the science fictions of artificial intelligence become science facts woven into the very fabric of our information society, literary scholars should have a say in negotiations over the new facts and realities these abstractions generate with respect to language, culture, and the creative arts. This will mean taking seriously the models of thought supporting them and following the lines of conceptual traffic that link them to the models we consider our own. Doing so will not only better position us to vouch for the certainties of qualitative reasoning, it will also give our reading minds more freedom to wander the vast interpretative space between idiosyncratic genius and calculating machine.

Chapter One

FACTS AND DIFFERENCE

> In science in the making (or "hot" science), truth is still a wager, a subject of debate; only gradually, when science cools down again, are certain results encapsulated, becoming "recognized facts," while others disappear altogether.
>
> —ALAIN DESROSIÈRES (1993)

By Desrosières's definition, it seems a terrible category error to call literary studies a science in the making, or a "hot" science. For literary critics and historians, truth is never not a wager. Textual meaning is always subject to debate and interpretation and varies with its contexts of production and reception. This, arguably, is one of the "recognized facts" of the field, just as the "extraordinary diversity" of individual patients was a recognized and inviolable fact of French medicine in the 1830s (see introduction). In both cases, these facts were a bulwark against numbers and their perceived incompatibility with studying individual variation. The facts changed in medicine, of course, as the debate over statistical methods heated up under the weight of "an avalanche of printed numbers that occurred throughout Europe" beginning in the mid-nineteenth century.[1] In contrast, recent debates in literary studies over the use of quantitative and computational methods suggest that the facts have changed little there. When Desrosières writes of "science in the making," he is writing specifically about statistics, which he historicizes as an evolving, ever-shifting consensus about the truths for which numbers are allowed to stand. Literary study, in contradistinction, often seems to be guided by an enduring consensus about the truths for which numbers are not allowed to speak.

There is every reason to be constantly vigilant about the uses and abuses to which numbers are put, especially when they cool down into recognized facts. Yet sustaining the notion that numbers are incompatible with literary studies relies on two fundamental misperceptions. First, that the truth of numbers, and quantitative methods generally, is not itself a product of historical debate and contestation. Second, that literary critics have only ever invoked this truth when appealing to the objective certainty numbers presumably provide. This chapter complicates these misperceptions by tracing a genealogy of past moments in which numbers have seemed necessary and useful to the study of literature in Japan and elsewhere, reading them into the longer history of (statistical) science in the making. The value of Desrosières's history of statistics—what he calls a "concrete history of abstraction"—lies in its reversal of the traditional relationship between history and statistics by showing how the modes of statistical thought that operate in a given moment are "themselves related to the arts of doing and saying studied by general history."[2] It replaces the question of the objectivity of numbers with that of *objectification*, which is to tell the history of how particular interpretations of numerical abstractions gain their reality by becoming the object of institutional and infrastructural investments, by becoming conventionalized.[3] Numbers are a vehicle for the realities projected onto them by users, cooling down to become recognized fact only after an involved process of deliberation and consensus making. This projection occurs at the point where numbers bring disparate objects into new spaces of equivalence (i.e., make them comparable along a limited set of dimensions) and, in so doing, facilitate the construction of new "facts" of similarity and difference via numerical interpretation. Over time, and with continued investment, these facts begin to stand in for reality itself.

I bring this historicizing impulse to prior quantitative turns in literary studies to at once acknowledge that numbers are and always have been political, but also to recast these prior turns as moments when the truths of literature with respect to numbers became a wager. These turns, emerging in dialogue with wider global currents, include physiological approaches from the turn of the last century, early studies of style in the 1930s, statistical approaches from the 1950s, and historical stylistics in the 1980s. Although the technical, intellectual, and institutional contexts differ in important ways, in each case I find a concern with shifting scales of information and with the problem of how to reconcile established knowledge practices and critical norms in light of such new scales of evidence. These concerns were naturally shared by other disciplines responding to their own avalanches of data, and literary scholars and critics looked to them for hints on how to handle the problem of relating and comparing internally varied objects to infer broader regularities or patterns of difference. Rather than view them as blindly borrowing quantitative methods from elsewhere, however, I situate them as actively creating equivalence spaces wherein new facts of literature could be generated, thus challenging established interpretive conventions. They were trying to imagine methodological infrastructures that, under the weight of more evidence, could support new "facts" of difference between texts, authors, genres, and national literatures. To trace how some of these facts became recognized, while others were abandoned, helps to illuminate the past politics and practices of reading literature with numbers. It also, as will become clear by the end, puts into relief the truths that are at stake in deciding to read with numbers now.

LITERATURE AS FORMULA

The first moment in my genealogy centers on novelist and critic Natsume Sōseki, whose turn to numbers stemmed from his own personal battles with information overload. In the preface to *Bungakuron* (*Theory of Literature*, 1907), he describes his struggle as a student in London to master English literature, or even to decide how to study it. Sent at the behest of the Japanese government in 1900 to acquire expertise in the subject, his first inclination was to try a brute force approach in which he grabbed "every work related to English literature that [he] could get his hands on," flipping randomly through as many pages as he could. Pausing to compare the number of books he had read with those yet to read, he realized he had "to make a drastic change in [his] approach to studying."[4] A few years after his return to Japan in 1903, Sōseki tried to communicate this lesson to his students at Tokyo Imperial University. In a seminar on eighteenth-century English literature, he warned that "it is certainly no easy task clearly and accurately to evaluate the dozens or hundreds of writers who appeared within a span of one hundred years. Even among Western scholars, there are many who, beyond the confines of their own historical specialty, have yet to look at works that even ordinary people have read."[5]

In both instances, Sōseki confronts the problem of how to extract and communicate general principles in a way commensurate with the scale of the object being addressed. He seems unwilling to place his trust in existing authoritative sources and feels compelled to read everything in a systematic way. Why? If the impulse is familiar to us now, when so much of the archive seems just a few keystrokes away, was it shared by his students and contemporaries? *Bungakuron* was itself born of this impulse, and in part was an attempt to theorize literature as a "material object of research" with the aid of mathematical formulae and measurement.[6] Karatani Kōjin has said of the work that "there was nothing inevitable about its appearance in Japanese (or even Western) literary history . . . [it] was a flower that bloomed out of season and therefore left no seed . . . an abrupt and solitary [vision] which [Sōseki] himself must have found disorienting."[7] In truth, its flowering looks timely when connected to its sources of pollination. These sources lay at the confluence of theoretical and institutional currents from sociology, psychology, and the natural sciences. Sōseki drew on and synthesized ideas about collective consciousness from the Spencerian school of Social Darwinism; on ideas about individual consciousness as a flow or stream of instantaneous moments from the work of William James; and on thermodynamics as a model for understanding social change and complexity.[8] If these influences are well known, less attention has been given to the sources shaping his thoughts about language and his proposed ideas for how to quantify its material properties and cognitive effects. Yet it was the very enumeration of linguistic properties that would allow Sōseki to imagine a comparative space existing in parallel to, and apart from, existing norms for evaluating literature. He came to see these norms as far too myopic for the new regimes of disciplinary knowledge being forged around him.[9]

"Scientific languages," as historians of science remind us, "are not born, they are made, and made with a good deal of effort."[10] For Sōseki, that effort was aimed at constructing a form of "taste" divorced from those that presumed a universal standard of evaluation but were biased by historical and social location—"by the history, social legends, particular institutions, and customs belonging to a given society."[11] He recognized that authoritative claims about proper taste were always historically and culturally relative. If used as the basis for comparing works from different times and places, one risked ceding critical authority to those with social and political power, leaving those in weaker positions of power (like the Japanese) to be judged on someone else's aesthetic terms.[12] Sōseki told his students that it was difficult and rare to achieve a "necessary correspondence" between different aesthetic tastes such that they might obtain the status of a universal truth. Where correspondence could be achieved, however, was by adopting a "critical" stance that responded to the "arrangement of materials" in literary texts—to their "order, length, and structure"—and not to personal likes and dislikes. Even if "a foreigner and a Japanese should reach opposite conclusions" about a work or set of works, each could at least claim the validity of their conclusions by pointing to a shared set of empirical observations as their basis.[13] They could point, in other words, to some agreed upon facts. By appealing to a quantitative and descriptive language that separated the appreciation of literary content from the critical analysis of its form, one could create a truly comparative history of world literature. Establishing shared measures of value meant separating out observation from evaluation.

The idea that a more neutral critical practice, mediated partly by numbers, could create a common ground for thinking across linguistic and social divides was not a solitary vision at this time. That Sōseki was open to methods more familiar to the instrumental sciences reflects at one level his institutional setting. For his generation, "science . . . was but one field in the production of knowledge that was to be evaluated for its rigor, persuasiveness, and ability to constitute and grasp its object."[14] The idea of the modern research university was itself being constituted at this time through the evaluation, planned and mandated by the state, of Western scientific discourses deemed essential to modernization and to enhancing Japan's status in the international scientific community.[15] A case had to be made for the study of literature too, and *Bungakuron* represents an effort to situate this study vis-a-vis the natural and social sciences.[16]

At another level, Sōseki's vision, particularly its emphasis on comparison, resonates with ontological practices common to nineteenth-century statistics. When this emerging science was picked up in Japanese intellectual circles in the 1860s, it appeared in the form of statistical tables that compiled and placed in a uniform space all manner of political, economic, and social information about the countries of the world.[17] This mode of arranging and presenting knowledge sparked, as it did in Europe and elsewhere, a "statistical fever" among early Meiji intellectuals and government officials.[18] Responses to this fever varied, but tables were particularly compelling for intellectuals such as Fukuzawa Yukichi (1834–1901) because they expanded the field of vision of the world by placing nations into a shared framework for assessing their differences. Moreover, they relied on a powerful assumption that empirical observations about a state and its society, taken en masse, could identify macrosocial regularities (even moral ones) governing that society and predicting its destiny. Fukuzawa was especially taken by the latter notion in *Bunmeiron no gairyaku* (An outline of a theory of civilization, 1875). He saw it as a way to measure and think about the "change of the human mind" (or the "spirit") of a nation over time, something that could not be discerned "from one event or one thing."[19]

Statistics was instrumental in allowing the difference between and within nations to be construed as a function of a nation's relative civilizational progress. The comparative thinking it enabled can also be discerned in ideas about differences across national languages and literatures.[20] In 1907, soon after Sōseki's departure from Tokyo Imperial University, Haga Yaichi, a professor of national language studies (*kokubungaku*) employed in his former department, offered his own vision of what a more scientific and systematic study of literature must entail. It should, he argued, "discover the threads that link one work to another" by isolating the key dimensions that define an individual work—specifically, time, place, author, and genre—and use them as the basis for objective comparison.[21] It should ask how works differ along these dimensions and determine which features stand out as characteristic for a given time, place, or body of works. In his mind, philology (*bunkengaku*) would be essential to identifying the features (e.g., rhetorical style, vocabulary, phrasing, sound, rhythm) along which this cross-national and cross-temporal comparison could be carried out.[22]

Haga's views echo Hippolyte Taine's sociological formula of "race-milieu-moment" as the key determinants of literary history and reflect a methodological paradigm common to the emergent practice of literary history in this era.[23] Parallel debates about the necessity of objective comparison were taking place among Haga's colleagues in linguistics, although with an opposing emphasis on the importance of national particularity. Prominent figures including Ueda Kazutoshi and Hoshina Kōichi insisted that the narrow, ahistorical, and nation-centered focus of classical language studies be abandoned for the modern, scientifically oriented linguistics of Europe. As Hoshina described it in 1910, the "principles and rules" of this new academic field could be "applied to analyze a language of any country." Its methods were diachronic and comparative, making it possible to "treat all of language equally, regardless of its kind, the time in history it was used, and the region where it was used."[24] The implicit tension between an inward facing, narrowly focused methodology and an outward facing, explicitly comparatist one animated the organization of linguistic study in Japan over the next several decades, as it did Sōseki's contrast between locally situated aesthetic evaluation and universally legible units of comparison.

Thus we can discern parallels between statistical thought in the mid-nineteenth century and Sōseki's proposed "critical" stance, specifically in the new comparative frameworks it afforded and the conviction that studying individual cases was inadequate for dealing with "entities or phenomena too numerous or too remote to be understood separately."[25] Methodological similarity, however, is distinct from the many and varied theoretical uses to which statistical thinking was put. The politics of when to use numbers is as fraught as the politics of how to use them, and to what ends, as historians of statistics demonstrate.[26] Sōseki, unlike Haga, did not wish to reify the text as a stable historical artifact and national cipher defined by a selection of core determinants. Nor was he eager to assert and reify hierarchies of civilizational difference.[27] Rather, Sōseki took the very act of reading and its relation to consciousness as his starting point, eventually arriving at a multilevel approach combining a generalizable theory with an inductive method for finding evidence to support this theory and to go beyond the study of individual cases. This method is where numbers finally enter into his theory of literature, but the theory provided the necessary framework for their interpretation.

At the highest level, Sōseki proposed to capture the experience of literary texts, what he called the "form of literary substance" (*bungaku-teki naiyō no keishiki*), by a single mathematical expression: F + f. The formula represents a combination of social and psychological factors that add up to the manifestation of a text in the reader's consciousness. It expresses not what is *in* a text, not its content or formal properties, but rather the outcome of its being filtered through an individual's perception at the moment of reading. Or more precisely, the accumulative effect of this filtering in the process of reading. Like James, Sōseki understood consciousness as a series of waveforms, such that reading could be imagined as a linear sequence of F + f equations resolving themselves at each instant and in relation to what lay immediately before and after. The "F" in the equation "indicates impressions or ideas at the focal point of consciousness, while f signifies the emotions that attend them."[28] At its base, the content of F depends on sensory input from the material world, although it extends all the way to abstract philosophical ideas and thus varies in its level of concreteness. Little f, in turn, varies "in direct proportion to the degree of concreteness of F" (e.g., the closer F is to material sensation, the more emotion will accompany it), and also important, literary substance is only possible when this emotional element is attached to some F taken from "the myriad social objects."[29]

Simple as the F + f formula appears, the open-ended nature of the parameters means that it can generate an infinite number of noncomparable solutions. Not only can the content of F and f vary at each instant and in relation to other instants, their values can also be measured at different temporal and social scales. Temporally, large F represents consciousness of an impression or idea at a single instant, over many days and years, or across decades. Socially, it can stand for individual consciousness or for a larger group consciousness. Similarly, little f is understood as the composite of a range of sensory inputs and emotions that also changes over time, expanding or contracting as a text unfolds in narrative time or as general attitudes toward literature shift across historical time. Both F and f thus represent the set of all possible F's and f's and add up to something like the zeitgeist of a period.[30] What a text means, or how it is appreciated, derives from the infinite combinations of F + f that are possible in a specific time and place and for a given individual, not from any single standard of aesthetic value applied universally or at a given level of F (e.g., the nation).[31]

As I will show, Sōseki was not content to rest with such irresolvable indeterminacy. Even at this most abstract level, however, it is important to note that his proposed formula was less like a flower out of season than like a flower out of place. It appeared at the cusp of a transition in English literary criticism that, as Nicholas Dames describes it, saw a physiological novel theory (one that "took reading itself . . . as its central data" and "which employed an experimental science") replaced and forgotten by an early twentieth-century theory that abstracted the novel from "the matrices of response it evokes . . . in order to [see it as] a spatialized form dedicated to epistemological processes [that allow] us to *know* something or someone."[32] That is, from an object of physical and emotional stimulus to an object of thought. Like Sōseki's theory, the "physiology of the novel" treated the novel as "a temporal form directed toward a receptive consciousness which in turn was shaped, at least in part, by the exigencies of that form." It was concerned not with what a novel *is* but with what a novel *does*.[33]

It was also meant to be value neutral; to be "positivistic, experimental, relatively nonjudgmental about the habits, tendencies, or social effects of the expansion of literacy, largely neutral on the merits of various novelists and novelistic schools."[34]

Sōseki intersected with the network of actors and ideas traced by Dames at several points. He was well versed, for instance, in the "philosophical-psychological vein of rhetoric" that dominated mid-nineteenth-century Victorian discourse on language. A key contributor to this discourse—psychologist, philosopher, and occasional literary theorist Alexander Bain—had a tremendous influence in Japan.[35] In Dames's account, Bain occupies center stage with the "intellectual polymath" G. H. Lewes and his influential *Principles of Success in Literature*. This work, originally serialized in 1865, was part of Sōseki's personal library, and he consulted it in preparing his *Bungakuron* lectures.[36] *Principles* describes a set of fundamental laws, materialized in specific rhetorical techniques, that predict the success or failure of a literary work for a given readership. Lewes's guiding assumptions were that

> any effective or valuable literary theory must . . . take into account facts of response, precisely "psychological" or cognitive facts of response, as a way of explaining which features of a given genre are pertinent and unique. . . . Matching a valid general profile of a given style of reception to an equally valid general profile of a literary genre's typical form, and explaining each with reference to the other, becomes the working definition of an advanced critical practice.[37]

Some of the core contributors to physiological novel theory were equally invested in the study of rhetoric as a valid index of a writer's mentality and consequently an indicator of the physical responses likely to be induced in a reader. Indeed, much of their work was published in manuals of composition and rhetoric, to which Sōseki himself was indebted.

It was through rhetoric that Sōseki sought to establish a correspondence between reader response and literary form, thus isolating the elements and principles driving the F + f equation at its most atomistic level. "Once we have in place a means of accounting for the manner of increase and decrease in this single element F, we will then proceed to examine the manner of shift of the small f that accompanies this fluctuating large F.

In this way, after clearly determining the nature and interaction of these two elements, we will first be able to talk of quantitative changes (*sūryōteki henka*) in the material of literature."[38] But how to measure this interaction? And how to establish a correspondence between this interaction, which produces the "form of literary substance," and the stimulus to which it is a response (e.g., the actual words on the page)? In his 1907 lecture to his students, Sōseki pondered how to express the "formless and odorless" emotions aroused by literary works in "tangible characters or signs." It is easy to do this with our perception of hot and cold, he suggested, which we express in degrees on a thermometer. But what expressions are available for the emotions aroused by texts? Here he told his students to proceed by both dissecting the emotions prompted by a work—understood as "a continuous string of numerous words and characters"—and the narrative "facts" to which these emotions correspond. In both cases one must account for the "order, distribution, strength, tempo, development, ebbing and flowing" of these emotions and facts. "When we dissect our emotions like this and simultaneously dissect the facts that provoke our emotions, we can make pairs between those that align with each other."[39]

Pairs, in other words, could be found between the reader's formless emotions and measurable differences in the facts of a text. The assumption that such pairs exist, and that they may be consistent, is the critical bridge to numerical analysis, which Sōseki tries to cross in book 4 of *Bungakuron*. He does so in the context of a comparison of Realist and Romantic (or idealist) schools of writing, exemplified for him by the work of Jane Austen and Charlotte Brontë, respectively. Adopting a formalist approach, he breaks down the categorical distinction between Realist and Romantic writing into a combination of two variables: thematics and expression. The former relates to the material of the work, its selection and arrangement of topics; the latter relates to the rhetorical techniques used to intensify or dull the latent emotional content of this material (what Sōseki refers to as f). Depending on the type of rhetorical technique utilized by a writer (e.g., emphasis, ornamentation, metaphor, personification)—which are described in detail in the first six chapters of book 4—the intensity of emotion attached to a thematic is heightened or diminished. Along these two axes of thematics and expression, Sōseki imagines a range of possible intensities (relying again on the thermometer analogy) that combine to produce a spectrum of styles from whose end points Realistic and Romantic writing get their identity (figure 1.1).

	取材法	表現法
浪漫派	120	120
	110	110
	100	100
	90	90
	80	80
	70	70
	60	60
寫實派	50	50

FIGURE 1.1. Possible combinations of thematic (*shuzaihō*) and expressive (*hyōgenhō*) intensities in literary works. Romantic (*roman-ha*) works fall at the upper end of the spectrum, and Realist (*shajitsu-ha*) works at the lower end. *Source*: Natsume Sōseki, *Bungakuron*, 1907, bk. 4.

The numbers within the columns represent the comparative quantity of emotion that arises in the readers of various schools as they play out across the techniques of thematics and expression. Occupying the lowest row, realism takes as its theme the objects of daily life. The objects of daily life do not often give rise to an extraordinary f. Let's provisionally assign a quantity of 50 to this f. Because they refuse from the start any gloss or ornamentation, the expressive methods of the realists will also occupy an f in the bottom ranks, and we've reflected this by assigning a value of 50. As one moves up the scale in intensity of theme, one increases 10, then 20 degrees, finally reaching 120. The numbers 120 and 50 are arbitrary and simply designate relative level of intensity.[40]

There are several noteworthy things about this formulation. First, Sōseki states just prior to this that the combination of thematics and expression can generate "a variety of hybrid forms" such that one might find a romantic thematics joined with realist expression or vice versa.[41] Thus, in his table, the columns represent two independent scales. Nevertheless, by aligning them in this tabular form, he creates an equivalence space that allows for passages to be directly compared along just two dimensions. This space recalls the spaces of comparative thought opened up by the tabular form in nineteenth-century statistics, although he creates it by stabilizing particular units of analysis (i.e., discrete passages) with a numerical value. Yet, if this value is presumably tied to some method of measurement, Sōseki offers no description of how to get from words to numbers. How does he arrive at the number 50? Or 120? These values are meant to reflect the relative concreteness or abstractness of thematic material and the kinds of rhetorical expressions used, but no mechanism is given for mapping these textual features to a specific value. The table is a quantitative fiction.

Like Lewes, Sōseki's wave model of consciousness led him to confront how to isolate the elemental textual units corresponding to each moment of consciousness, and from there how to analyze the effects of their interaction across successive moments. It was the problem, in effect, of formalizing the relation between fragment and whole, unit and process, to map literary form to reader response in a principled way. His proposed solution was to break down the text into thematic and expressive units and map their combined emotional effects onto a continuous, thermometer-like scale. Lewes, in contrast, relied less on explicit quantification and more on metaphors taken from vivisectionist experimentation, chemistry, and psychophysics. Sōseki too seems to have found these metaphors useful, particularly as a way to prevent essentialist readings that might mask the multidimensionality of texts with superficial labels. He decries this tendency among contemporary critics and suggests a potential remedy in another lecture from 1908 on "The Attitude of a Creative Artist" (Sōsakuka no taidō). There he argues that a truly detailed differentiation of romantic and naturalist works would acknowledge

> not only the countless transformations born in the space between the pure objective attitude [of the naturalists] and the pure subjective attitude [of the romantics], but also the countless secondary transformations resulting from

> the ties between each of these first transformations and every other to create hybrid forms. Seen thus, an author's work can no longer be roundly labeled "Naturalist" or "Romantic." Rather, one has to dissect the text and carefully identify each element, saying that this spot has a Romantic quality in this particular way, while this spot has a Naturalist quality in this particular way. Moreover, one can't simply stamp the label "Romantic" or "Naturalist" on these spots but must explain how much of the other category is mixed in and at what ratio.[42]

Here we find the metaphorical language common to Lewes and other physiological theorists, but also a quantitative imagining that maps the complex interaction of rhetorical elements to a ratio or amount. The latter puts Sōseki in conversation with a much closer contemporary, Vernon Lee, who carried the mantle of physiological novel theory into the twentieth century and, just as it was being forgotten, gave it a decidedly numerical cast.

Lee's work originally appeared in English periodicals in the 1890s but was revised and edited in book form in the 1920s. Her particular insight was to turn the long held focus on textual units from higher-order stylistic or narrative techniques, as in Lewes and Sōseki, toward "the minutest elements to which literary style can be reduced, namely, single words and their simplest combinations."[43] In *The Handling of Words*, Lee randomly sampled five-hundred-word passages from six authors and tabulated the frequencies of different parts of speech. These counts, listed ahead of each passage, became the starting point for close readings that "[brought] to light remarkable and suggestive differences in the use to which those words (and the small fry of auxiliaries, conjunctions, prepositions, etc., perhaps most of all) were put" by different writers. Although Lee recognizes, in the end, that her "statistical experiment" is bound to fail given the limited sample size and a failure to control for the biases of subject matter, she maintains the belief that "the pattern in which an individual author sets his words, connecting and co-ordinating them in a way peculiar to himself . . . exerts its own special power over the Reader, because it has elicited in that Reader's mind conditions, or rather activities, similar to those which have produced that pattern in the mind of the Writer." The reader responds because specific patterns of language excite the mind in consistent, intersubjective ways, drawing on "the Reader's stored-up images and feelings . . . to produce a particular effect."[44]

As with Sōseki, Lee's attempts at quantitative reasoning remained a thought experiment that would be left for others to try to put into practice. But the manner by which she tried to extend Lewes's and Bain's theories into a focus on a text's minimal units and their patterns of interrelation, as well as her insistence on the novel's susceptibility to measurement, help us see Sōseki as occupying a similar transitional position between Victorian physiological theory and the new practices of quantitative reasoning that it inspired.[45] Sōseki's search for a correspondence between literary form ("the arrangement of materials") and reader response was further animated by a desire to construct measures of difference not beholden to culturally and historically situated hierarchies of value masquerading as universal truth. This desire compelled him to see texts as atomistic formations that revealed themselves, upon dissection, to be sequences of thematic and expressive tendencies that react and combine in the process of being read. For Sōseki, this was a means to subvert the practice of labeling texts with qualitative categories such as "realist" and "romantic" in ways that obscure their multidimensional and processual quality under a single term and leave the critic to treat them as uniform, solid lumps.[46] It also neutralized the idea that one category is inherently better; they merely occupy different positions on a common scale. "As to which of these two orientations to expression and thematics will captivate you, it is a matter of the times, your age, your gender, and ultimately your innate preference."[47]

For Sōseki, the advantage of pursuing a quantitative measure of the emotional valence of a text was clear. Not only did it remove from consideration the biased response introduced by a reader's own cultural position but it also separated out content from form in a way that made texts of different linguistic and literary traditions comparable on a single scale. Or at least this is what motivated his analytical strategy. There was a trade-off, of course. In eliminating one kind of universalizing hierarchy (that the aesthetic proclivities of one tradition should dictate those of other traditions), he substituted another; namely, that the typical modern reader, wherever he or she may be from, would consistently exhibit the same emotional response to similar combinations of expression and thematics. Absent a consistent pairing, for instance, between a preponderance of nouns in a passage and a "cool" emotional response by readers, Sōseki's thermometer would be of little use as an instrument of comparison. The kind of objectivity he sought depended on a critical assumption about the universality of human physiological responses to rhetorical forms. It was an assumption he was never able to test because, like Lee, Sōseki offered no method by which to translate between the counts of words and the different responses they elicit. Had he done so, he would have to show evidence of how generalizable this translation was across different social and temporal contexts. It is that very project that I. A. Richards would take up in England just a few years after Sōseki's death. Ironically, his attempts to scientifically isolate the smallest unit of aesthetic experience led Richards from the novel to poetry, and from a large-scale interest in literature as social technology to small-scale practices that made "full attention" to the text the sine qua non of literary study.[48] As physiological novel theory gave way to close reading, the seeds of Sōseki's own numerical turn came to be nurtured in Japan by a focus on writers, not readers, and on more precisely defined linguistic features, laying the ground for a quantitative stylistics.

MAKING LITERATURE COUNT

It would be some time before the seeds cast by Sōseki's quantitative imaginings bore fruit. They went largely untouched, in fact, until 1935, when they were tended to by Hatano Kanji (1905–2001) in *Bunshō shinrigaku: Nihongo no hyōgen kachi* (The psychology of style: evaluating Japanese expression). Like *Bungakuron*, it wove together psychology, sociology, and the study of rhetoric, although its reference points had been updated: from associationist to gestalt psychology; from Spencer's social Darwinism to the sociology of Durkheim; from the study of composition and rhetoric to structural linguistics and stylistics. Hatano saw Sōseki's treatise as part of a late-Meiji surge of interest in rhetoric and psychology as frames for literary analysis, one that included Shimamura Hōgetsu's *Shin bijigaku* (New rhetoric, 1902) and Igarashi Chikara's *Shin bunshō kōwa* (New lectures on writing, 1909).[49] Since that time, however, the study of *bunshō*, which Hatano understood as rhetorical style, had sorely waned, only recently attracting renewed attention in Japan and overseas. Most notable in Japan was the publication of Tanizaki Jun'ichirō's *Bunshō tokuhon* (A primer on style, 1934), which combined a history of rhetorical style with analysis of its principal elements. It had already sold tens of thousands of copies.[50] In light of this resurgence, Hatano saw an opportunity to reimagine the study of bunshō as a "technical science" that could "accurately measure the individual effects of personal language" in the creation of written, and specifically literary, texts.[51]

Hatano's appeal to science and measurement, although not framed through Sōseki's global comparative lens, was also invested in dislodging entrenched aesthetic hierarchies in response to a new information environment. In Hatano's mind, rhetoric was such a popular topic of late because modern life led to increasing social differentiation and, as a result, to a desire by individuals to develop language that best expressed the uniqueness of their own thoughts and ideas. The study of bunshō was for Hatano the study of how people were learning to cut through all of modernity's rhetorical noise to make themselves heard. Trained as a psychologist, but with interests in language and literature, Hatano criticized past studies of rhetoric for their inadequate attention to the "sociality" (*shakaisei*) of language, a consequence of their ties to associationist psychological theory and the fixed hierarchies of stylistic value it encouraged.[52] Such hierarchies obscured the contextual nature of language as material form, which was at once the idea, taken from gestalt psychology, that individual utterances are determined by the total array of interpersonal and linguistic conditions from which they emerge. There are echoes of Sōseki in this attempt to turn style into historical and social fact by isolating certain formal qualities but also of certain Russian Formalists who, by the late 1920s, turned attention to the problem of literary evolution after an initial emphasis on literary language as an autonomous, internally coherent form.[53]

Hatano's interest in the relation of utterance to societal language was inspired by Swiss linguist Charles Bally's science of "stylistics," translated as *bunshōron* by Kobayashi Hideo, a linguist and soon-to-be key interlocutor for Hatano.[54] Central to Bally's stylistics was the idea of studying "the expressive resources of a whole language" to give "a systematic description of its peculiarities at the level of *parole*, linguistic expression, rather than the underlying obligatory grammar." Bally "emphasized the *affective* uses of language, the musical and rhythmic qualities, the varieties of possible expression and the constant imbrication of utterance with 'life.'"[55] To Hatano, Bally's attention to the context (*bamen*) of expression, and his theory that individuals dynamically adapt internal associations of words to these contexts, marked a critical break with associationism and its lack of attention to the volitional and affective dimensions of language.[56] But Hatano left unresolved the question of how individuals negotiate a common set of expressive resources to convey the uniqueness of their life experience. Hatano was precisely interested in how individual utterances were "socialized" (i.e., shared with others), and he sought to reconcile his interest in unique expression, and authorial agency, with his reading of Durkheim, for whom society is a set of regulating systems (e.g., religious rites, customs, language) by which people gain a "collective image" of themselves and through which they share thoughts, feelings, and actions.[57] To convey personal experience through language requires appealing to this collective image and drawing on linguistic symbols and rhetorical techniques that affect others precisely because they are shared.

To better understand this expressive process, Hatano looked to literature because he believed this process was different for writers than for the general public. Most individuals were wholly constrained by the collective language of society, but writers were more deliberate and creative in deploying rhetorical techniques. Citing social psychologist Kurt Lewin, Hatano saw the original purpose of these techniques as conveying the "tension system" (*kinchō taikei*) one feels in relation to a specific event or context.[58] Lewin theorized behavior as a function of the interplay of person and environment—a dynamic field (or "life space") of interdependent needs, goals, beliefs, sensations, and other psychological tensions.[59] Re-creating this complex field such that it could be shared with others was, for Hatano, the primary goal of communication. Naturally, it is impossible to re-create the totality of this tension system owing to the constraints imposed by language (e.g., the inability of language to replicate sensation or materiality). What interested Hatano, however, particularly as it concerned artistic production, was how artists transformed these constraints into "forms" (*keishiki*) that generate their own unique tension systems and emotional effects, partially compensating for the failure to convey a total experience or context. Akin to how painters had transformed the constraint of the picture frame into its own unique form, writers have transformed linguistic constraints into an abundant collection of forms on which to draw and innovate. "When thinking about rhetorical technique," Hatano concluded, "the two questions we have to consider are how a total context is recreated and how a writer, in the process of this re-creation, overcomes the constraints of doing so and renders [these constraints] beneficial. The former question pertains to life's emotions, the latter to emotional forms. The psychological study of style, at root, is the study of how life's emotions are expressed through specific emotional forms (language). In one respect, this is nothing other than the study of the characteristics (*tokuchō*) of language."[60]

It was to study these characteristics that Hatano turned to numbers. If writers condensed individual experience into discrete "forms" linked to unique psychological or emotional contexts, and if these forms manifested as empirical, measurable features, it stood to reason that one might isolate the different "force fields" expressed by writers by observing variation in these features. Assuming these features truly correlated with distinct kinds of force fields, quantification was a way to capture and categorize these correlations across multiple textual instances. It was a way, as for Sōseki, to project textual objects into a space of equivalence where certain kinds of difference could be more clearly ascertained. Vernon Lee, it turns out, was his inspiration for constructing such a space, and his case studies parallel her method of tabulating simple features such as the ratios of different parts of speech. Through this new space Hatano hoped to differentiate the stylistic forms (*bunshō no keitai*) present in literary texts and establish an association with the creative attitude of each writer and the psychological responses induced by his or her style.[61]

Hatano's openness to Lee's ideas owed a lot to his institutional and disciplinary location. Graduating from the psychology department of Tokyo Imperial University in 1932, it was former mentor and leading scholar in educational psychology, Kidō Mantarō, who invited him to write on "Japanese stylistics" (*kokugo bunshōron*) for a book series on "Japanese Phraseology" (*kokugo hyōgengaku*).[62] A second mentor, Matsumoto Matatarō, had recommended Lee's *The Handling of Words*.[63] Matsumoto was a leading figure in the field of experimental psychology and played a key role in shaping it according to the international norms of scientific practice.[64] Several of his students made significant contributions to the new field of intelligence testing and measurement in the 1920s, creating a key pathway for the introduction of modern statistical methods in Japan. One of them, Tanaka Kan'ichi (1882–1962), even authored a primer on statistical methods as applied to the field of education in 1928, a text that Hatano may have used in his classes.[65] At the time, statistical method was in the midst of an "inference revolution," led by statisticians R. A. Fisher and Karl Pearson, that added to the descriptive statistics of the nineteenth century new techniques for measuring and expressing the uncertainty of hypotheses in light of observed data.[66] This revolution was not absorbed by the discipline of psychology until after 1940, however, so the methods on which Hatano could have potentially drawn still lacked an attention to statistical modeling, sampling, and experimental design.

If Hatano's institutional location meant that knowledge of descriptive statistics was close at hand, he had no template for applying it to language.[67] Nor did his direct mentors offer much encouragement, telling him the task was too difficult and that he should stick to topics for which there were established methods.[68] Hatano's solution was to start with a simple case study—a comparison of the writing styles of Tanizaki Jun'ichirō and Shiga Naoya—in which the counting of basic characteristics would mediate between the interpretative practices of literature and psychology, respectively. From the literature side, Hatano based his case study on existing criticism about the difference between Tanizaki's and Shiga's bunshō. An essay by Fukada Kyūya had praised the detached and minimalist technique of the latter over the former's rhetorically florid attempts to represent the senses. Hatano wanted to test whether this qualitative evaluation corresponded to empirical and irreducible differences in stylistic form—what he called the "character" (*seikaku*) of their writing.[69] He wanted to translate into numbers a set of categories that critics had already arrived at qualitatively. In linking an essential character to each author's writing style, he was also quantifying a then dominant hermeneutic in Japanese letters in which biography served as the overriding arbiter of textual meaning.

From the psychology side, Hatano put forth a working hypothesis based solely on what he observed in two passages highlighted by Fukada (table 1.1). He proposed that stylistic differences between Tanizaki and Shiga amounted to a difference in the intended role or purpose of their writing. "In the case of Tanizaki, his depiction of events or things invariably makes language (*gengo*) the subject of the account. In contrast, while Shiga uses words to narrate events or things, the words are only a medium—at the center are always the thing or event itself. An event is expressed directly as the thing itself, the words doing no more than point to it."[70] Hatano expanded on this distinction to suggest that Tanizaki's and Shiga's writing represent different "tension-systems" created in response to experiencing an event or thing. "While Tanizaki's tension-system adopts an expressive form that is social and based in *logos*, the intentionality of Shiga's writing is directed at 'objects' (*mono*) and not at social transparency. The former is concerned with how to socialize his depiction [of an object]; the latter

TABLE 1.1
Stylistic comparison of two passages

Tanizaki Jun'ichirō (from "Ashikari")	Shiga Naoya (from "Yamagata")
Otoko mountain, with the round and full moon at its back just as it was in that painting, its slopes covered with clusters of dimly lit trees giving off a velvety sheen and against a horizon where the color of dusk still lingered somewhere, stood there dark, deep, black.	It was a beautiful tree-covered mountain with a number of small streams that the locals referred to as "sawa," and upon whose waters danced the sun's light filtered through green leaves. Dark moss covered the rocks, atop which hydrangeas were blooming in beautiful profusion.

is concerned with how faithful he can be to an object. The former strives to make his own tension-system socially understood; the latter, in contrast, desires an agreement between words and objects."[71] We might imagine this as a recapitulation of Sōseki's distinction between thematics and expression, with Tanizaki on the side of excessive rhetorical ornamentation (romantic) and Shiga on the side of a sparse, object-centered style (realist). Hatano, however, substitutes a notion of style tied to literary movements for one tied to the psychological character of authors.

Up to this point, nothing about Hatano's analysis necessitates counting. Mapping stylistic to psychological categories is wholly determined by existing interpretations. Numbers become useful only when he tries to scale this mapping beyond these two short passages. They are a way to stretch the space of comparison by abstracting out the most essential lines of difference. Specifically, he isolates five characteristics that he suspects will explain the stylistic differentiation he's mapped out: sentence length (Tanizaki's were longer); the number of phrases per sentence, as determined by punctuation (Tanizaki had more); the relative proportion of different parts of speech (Shiga used more nouns); the use of figurative language (Tanizaki relied on simile and Shiga on implicit metaphor); and complexity of sentence structure (Tanizaki used more relative and qualifying clauses compared to Shiga's simple compound structure and reliance on conjunctions). Each is a purely formal, as opposed to semantic, feature, and each can be represented as the count of a thing that is or is not there. Quantification expands the space of comparison even as it constrains what can be compared.

A look at one feature, sentence length, helps expose the epistemological underpinnings of Hatano's enumerative method. He gives no justification for choosing it, nor was it an inspiration from Lee. George Udny Yule, the Scottish statistician and early pioneer of statistical studies of literature, argued for its use as a tool in authorship attribution, but not until 1939.[72] Hatano may have taken a cue from a 1925 essay by Kawabata Yasunari, who identified sentence length as a key element in building a new theory of literature around bunshō.[73] Whatever the impetus, he followed Lee's example and sampled fifty prose sentences each from Tanizaki's "Kin to gin" (Gold and Silver, 1928) and Shiga's "Ama gaeru" (Tree frog, 1924).[74] His decision to sample sentences instead of words, as Lee had done, was to avoid the problems introduced by the lack of word boundaries in Japanese, namely, ambiguity around what defines a lexical unit. This problem also steered him toward the single Chinese character *ji* as his unit of measurement, which raised problems of its own. If a sentence with a few long words has the same number of characters as one with many more short words, should we say they are equal in length?[75]

Pressing on, Hatano combined his counts of sentence length with a tabular representation and yet another essential tool from nineteenth-century statistics: the average. This, as we learned in the introduction, was the idea that one could create a "kind of whole" from multiple disparate observations of a single phenomenon.[76] Tables allowed Hatano to show the distribution of sentences of a given length in each work, ranging from sentences less than 10 characters to those between 121 and 130 characters. Averages allowed him to summarize this distribution as a single value and compute the standard deviation (i.e., a measure for the total spread of the data) for each work (figure 1.2). The resulting values confirmed his initial suspicion: Tanizaki's sentences were significantly longer than Shiga's, averaging 49.2 characters as compared to 32.1. They also reinforced what was evident from the table, namely, that most sentences from Tanizaki's text clustered around the 30 to 50 character range, with fewer and fewer appearing as one approached the maximum sentence length. In contrast, Shiga's sentences clustered at the low end of the range, sharply decreasing in number from there and not exceeding the range of 80 to 90 characters.

Hatano took these average values as evidence for his theory. The choice of longer or shorter sentences, he reasoned, corresponded to whether emphasis was meant to be put on the "nuance" (*nuansu*) of the words or on that of the objects being described. Longer sentences are language centered and thus more in tune with the rhythm of mental processes,

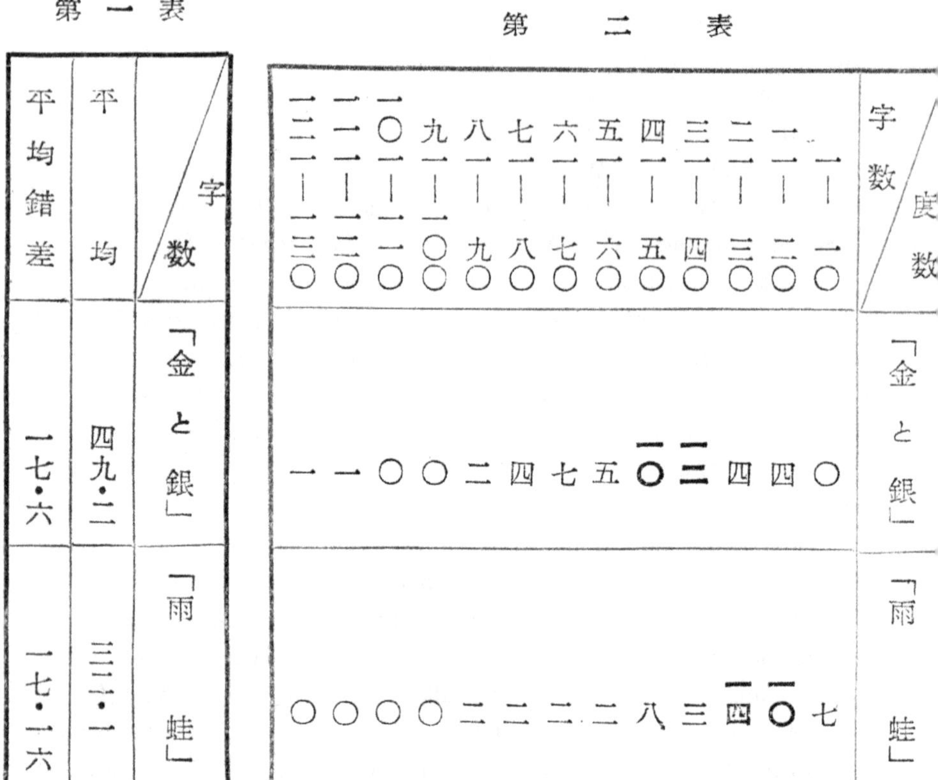

第一表

字数	平均	平均錯差
「金と銀」	四九・二	一七・六
「雨蛙」	三一・一	一七・一六

第二表

字数／度数	一—一〇	一一—二〇	二一—三〇	三一—四〇	四一—五〇	五一—六〇	六一—七〇	七一—八〇	八一—九〇	九一—一〇〇	一〇一—一一〇	一一一—一二〇	一二一—一三〇
「金と銀」	〇	四	四	**一二**	**一〇**	五	七	四	二	〇	〇	一	一
「雨蛙」	七	**一〇**	**一四**	三	八	二	二	二	二	〇	〇	〇	〇

FIGURE 1.2. Two tables from Hatano's *Bunshō shinrigaku* (1935): (*Left*) shows the average sentence length and standard deviation for two works: Tanizaki's "Kin to gin" (*top*) and Shiga's "Ama gaeru" (*bottom*); (*Right*) shows the distribution of sentences of a specified length in each work, with bolded numbers indicating the peak of these distributions. Reproduced with the permission of Shinchōsha.

whereas shorter sentences are object centered and thus responsive to the rhythm of what is being observed.[77] To this evidence Hatano added analysis of his other selected features, finding that Tanizaki's sentences have a more complex structure and use more adjectives and Shiga's are simpler and use more nouns. These new "facts" reinforce his hypothesized classificatory schema: Tanizaki's style is oriented toward language and society, what he called a "declension-type" (*yōgen gata*) style that uses more verbs and adjectives, whereas Shiga's is oriented toward things and objects, or a "substantive-type" style (*taigen gata*) dominated by nouns.[78]

At this point Hatano's conceptual machinery outruns his methodological tool kit, leaving us to reconcile the gap between the average sentence length in a sample of a single text and his claims about an author's psychological orientation to the world. What about all the other contextual variables that are surely correlated with this orientation, such as semantic content, narrative pacing, or broader stylistic trends and influences? Rather than reject the whole experiment for failing to close this gap, I am interested in how its underlying reasoning brings textual objects into a space of equivalence to which Sōseki's thermometer only vaguely alluded. In making the leap from the average sentence length to general authorial tendency, Hatano leans heavily on the idea of the average. To wit, he uses the averaging of differences across many sentences to posit regularity across a whole text, and then across the whole of an author's style. As formulated by the Belgian statistician and sociologist Adolphe Quetelet in the 1830s, the idea of the average was predicated on the notion that measurements of individuals (e.g., human height), although imperfect on their own, were deviations from a central tendency around which the individuals as a group adhered. In turn, this modal value, which was only ever an ideal, allowed the existence of a common cause, or even an ensemble of smaller causes, to be inferred (e.g., the Creator's intention), transforming this ideal into a "real object" that could be compared with other similarly constructed objects.[79] For Hatano, authorial intention as common cause allowed him to scale up from measurements of disparate sentences to new kinds of wholes and new facts of difference between them. He offered a glimpse of the analysis such facts might afford when he calculated the average sentence length of other major writers (Akutagawa Ryūnosuke, Kikuchi Kan, and Satō Haruo) to show that Tanizaki and Shiga lie at the far ends of the spectrum.[80]

The use of such basic statistical thinking to relate individual rhetorical pattern to wider discursive background was a crucial addition to the available methodological infrastructures for reading texts with numbers. Sōseki had hinted that the elements of a text could be tallied to ascertain its position on a continuous scale, and Hatano formalized the procedure by identifying discrete elements and devising ways to count and compare them. If the relationship he posited between these elements and authorial style (and ultimately reader response) feels unconvincing, overly determined as it is by his psychological theory of style and the prevailing cult of authorial identity, it is necessary to distinguish his use of quantitative method from the interpretations he gave it. The two are related but not mutually dependent. His method did summarize a text and its effects in ways that violated the supposed singularity of the relationship between reader and sentence, reader and text. It abstracted away the particulars of that unique event to produce a different kind of reality, one that scaled beyond this singular instance to grasp at the relation of individual utterances to their larger linguistic, psychological, and social contexts. To the extent that literary critics wanted to preserve the sanctity of their unique relationship to the text and to monopolize the types of knowledge this relation produced, Hatano's averaging out of differences would meet resistance, just as the idea of the average was resisted for decades by the nineteenth-century European medical community.[81] This resistance gave way, however, when disease became imagined as "a collective problem calling for general solutions."[82] Hatano's constitution of the literary text as a new kind of analytical object was similarly waiting for new collective problems for which quantitative reasoning seemed a valid solution.

At the time, however, few in Japan knew what to do with this object. Senior colleagues told him to go back to studying psychology. In contrast, two senior faculty at Tokyo Imperial University—the classics scholar and philologist Ikeda Kikan and modern literature scholar Yoshida Seiichi, famous for his work on Naturalism—were more encouraging.[83] That there might be pockets of receptivity among literary critics is not so far-fetched. In the late teens and early 1920s, for instance, critics Kikuchi Kan and Nakamura Murao had expressed a desire for objective yardsticks (*monosashi*) and fixed standards of value to help combat "standard-less impressionist criticism," or criticism biased by temporary trends and fads, although the only tangible solution they offered amounted simply to new forms of expert consensus.[84] In 1930, the proletarian critic Hirabayashi Hatsunosuke expressed doubt about the possibility of a truly scientific criticism (*kagakuteki hihyō*) because this implied the creation of a set of universally shared standards with which to evaluate artistic objects. He figured that one hundred people will respond to a work of art in one hundred different ways. No scientific criticism could overcome such divergent evaluations. Nevertheless, he did admit that scientific criticism might usefully describe the contextual differences between two works, even if this would be analogous to treating the Mona Lisa and an actor print by Toyohara Kunichika as two different species of tree.[85] Much less cynically, the scholar Tsuchiya Noboru argued in 1938 that a formalist theory (*yōshikiron*) of description was the scientific bridge needed to relate the interpretation of individual literary works to an analysis of authorial intention; by treating texts as concrete, historical phenomena with specific characteristics, one could establish a disciplinary language allowing for broader comparability.[86] Yet he too gave no methodological road map for such a theory. As the linguist Kobayashi noted in an enthusiastic review of *Bunshō shinrigaku* from 1936, Hatano's experiments in quantitative method were its most valuable contribution despite the preliminary nature of his conclusions. They opened up new intellectual territory precisely by linking a theory of expression to new practices and techniques for generating empirical evidence.[87]

LITERATURE ON A CURVE

By the mid-1950s, this territory was being settled by contributors to a third quantitative turn who looked back to Hatano and Kobayashi as progenitors of a radical new approach to style, or *buntai*. Kobayashi had redefined the notion of buntai as not just a broad categorical label for distinguishing historical forms of written language (e.g., colloquial style, epistolary style) but as akin to Hatano's idea of bunshō, a finer-grained and individualized concept of style as the outcome of a writer's negotiation with linguistic and aesthetic conventions. And yet as one contemporary critic observed, the two had pursued buntai along divergent modes of "scientific analysis." Kobayashi subjected works to a rigorous qualitative analysis that attempted to relate the critic's affective response to style with the "linguistic facts" of a work to intuit a writer's character or mentality. Although erudite and instructive, Kobayashi's analysis was based on his subjective impressions and expert aesthetic evaluation and was thus difficult to replicate. Hatano, on the other hand, relied on "statistical method" and situated stylistic uniqueness vis-à-vis comparison with other works or established stylistic norms. The ability to discriminate relative stylistic differences through objective comparison seemed more promising as a general method than Kobayashi's constrained, singular readings.[88]

Some took issue with the basic assumptions underwriting Hatano's objective procedure, such as the notion that the use of different word types conveyed anything about an author's character.[89] For proponents of quantitative methods, however, this was less a problem with numbers than with the interpretation Hatano had given them. As Yasumoto Biten, a key figure in this third quantitative moment, argued in 1963, the value of the methods "depends on the ideas that put them to use. And these ideas, whether taken from psychology, linguistics, or elsewhere, are the offspring of their *zeitgeist*."[90] The zeitgeist of this moment, it turns out, was heavily informed by the ascendant Cold War fields of information theory, psycholinguistics, and cybernetics. They brought with them a new citational network for amplifying Hatano's earlier innovations and an information/theoretic view of language as something constrained by statistically measurable principles. As George Miller, one of the leading spokespersons for this new view put it, "statistical simplification is imperative" to deal with the fact that people "say so much." It provides a "general statistical orientation to tell us what kinds of utterances are important to consider."[91] Miller investigated how information theory and probability could help "draw a statistical map of our communicative behavior" to better address the gap between what we choose to say and what a context chooses for us, where context may include audience, grammar, individual needs and experience, or the words surrounding an utterance. He was joined in this effort by statisticians such as George Yule, psycholinguists George Zipf and Pierre Guiraud, and sociologists Zellig Harris and Charles Osgood, who in the 1940s and 1950s laid the ground for the statistical study of language.[92] In Japan, their work was received by a growing community of scholars exploring the intersection of psychology and language. The community represented a disciplinary consolidation and narrowing of interpretive flexibility when compared to earlier moments of quantitative imagining about literature. Precisely for this reason, however, it proved to be a more active and robust community than those in times past.

Proof of this robustness was the publication in 1957 of *Keiryō kokugogaku* (Mathematical linguistics), the official journal of the Keiryō Kokugogaku Gakkai (Mathematical Linguistics Society of Japan). By 1960, the group boasted a membership of more than 250 scholars working in linguistics, national language studies, psychology, mathematics, and statistics. While a majority of them were university professors and lecturers, at least two dozen were researchers affiliated with the newly established National Japanese Language Research Institute (Kokuritsu Kokugo Kenkyūjo). Created in 1948 under the auspices of the Ministry of Education, it aimed to conduct scientific surveys and studies on the "language life" (*gengo seikatsu*) of Japanese.[93] Both the institute and the journal were instrumental in widening the institutional base for quantitative studies of language. Although language in general was the object around which this base organized itself, from early on literature was seen as a vital and accessible source of linguistic data. This section surveys the work of three figures who put literature at the center of their analysis, showing how they added to Hatano's existing quantitative scaffolding with newer methods and their attendant epistemologies. Specifically, I focus on methods related to sampling (how to think of the part in relation to the whole); statistical modeling (how to infer regularities from empirical data); and multidimensional analysis (how to study the interaction of multiple variables). All became key infrastructural elements for creating new spaces of equivalence and for shifting once again the possibilities of figuring textual difference.

As I will show, the creators of these spaces tended to let numbers stand in for theorization itself. This was not, however, because of a lack of awareness about the constraints statistical methods placed on the interpretation of literary style. In 1957, in the third issue of *Keiryō kokugogaku*, the linguists Matsuyama Yō and Miyajima Yoshiko wrote about "Studies of Expression and the Problem of Quantification" and argued that such studies needed to give careful thought to how "the qualitative is changed into a quantity through quantitative methods," but also to how one collects quantitative data (*dēta*) about expression and extracts conclusions from it. "This is not a simple problem of statistical technique, but one of how to handle data in a way that incorporates knowledge from this field of study."[94] On the one hand, they were concerned with the tendency in studies of expression, especially in work by Hatano and Kobayashi, to identify some formal difference or uniqueness in a work (e.g., sentence length)—the effect—and relate this to the impression desired by a writer (e.g., longer sentences imply a greater focus on language)—the cause. To establish this relation based on a single effect raised a host of other questions: Was this the right effect to be considering? What evidence could be given for its importance? Was it right to focus on discrete elements rather than on their combination and interaction?[95] On the other hand, the authors were concerned with the underlying data used to support arguments about expressive uniqueness. How can the analyst responsibly expand the empirical background (i.e., the statistical population) against which single works, or measurements, were interpreted?

Linguist and stylometrist Nakamura Akira took an early stab at the problem of expansion, framing it as a matter of statistical sampling. In 1958, he published a study of sentence and phrase length as part of an initial inquiry into the "rhythm" of Japanese prose. The essay opened with a long, flowing 371 character sentence from Tanizaki's monumental *Sasameyuki* (The Makioka sisters, 1943–1948).[96] It seems he was still the standard bearer of verbosity. Nakamura, however, wanted to know just how far outside the norm he was, and sought to realize the desire for scale latent in Hatano's original case study. This meant essentially returning, via a statistical lens, to the question raised by Sōseki about how to read any one work against a century's worth of books. How many texts should one look at to be certain of Tanizaki's degree of deviation? Against what population of texts could this deviance be confidently assessed? And how should one sample this population? In trying to relate the part to a reconceived whole, Nakamura had to demarcate the very boundaries of "modern Japanese literature." Or more precisely, what representation of it would best make visible the degree of Tanizaki's exceptionality. In fixing this expanded ground of comparability, he was also opening the door to facts of difference unavailable to Hatano's pairwise experimental design.

Nakamura ultimately settled on a sample of fifty texts. Other studies from this period also decided that between fifty and one hundred works was a sufficiently representative sample. But representative of what, exactly? From what idea of the *whole* were these works deemed a suitably representative *part*? In Nakamura's case, his principles of selection emphasized an even distribution of works over time and a healthy mix of canonical (i.e., high literary) authors. He surveyed several popular modern literature anthologies, relying mostly on Chikuma Shobō's *Gendai Nihon bungaku zenshū* (Anthology of contemporary Japanese literature), and selected two works by twenty-five authors. This resulted in five works from the late-Meiji period (1868–1912), twenty from Taishō (1912–1926), and twenty-five from Shōwa (1926–1989). Five of the authors were women. The authors do not appear to have been chosen for their involvement in specific literary movements, nor with attention to their place in existing critical discourse. He elides, in fact, much of his selection logic, giving the false sense that these are literary specimens plucked objectively from a neutral, transhistorical space standing in for "modern Japanese literature."[97] Nakamura's hope was that Tanizaki's exemplarity, if he had any, would show up as a deviation from the norms of this space. My interest here is not with the blind spots created by Nakamura's sampling method, which could be endlessly critiqued, but with the epistemological stakes of the method itself. The need to explicitly define a whole through which to understand a smaller part meant having to demarcate a text's representative context in ways not required by less quantitative modes of reading, where "discourse" or "milieu" allow the boundaries of context to be left to the imagination. Sampling is interesting precisely because it sets in motion a debate about representativeness that goes unarticulated when scale is not of methodological or theoretical concern.

I revisit this debate in chapter 2, but here I focus on the implications of sampling for how Nakamura came to think about the relation of texts and authors. In the end, Nakamura sampled twenty thousand phrases (representing eight thousand five hundred sentences) from his fifty works, extracting from each the average sentence length (measured by characters), average phrase length, average number of phrases per sentence, and a distribution of the different phrase lengths.[98] The result was a supercharged version of the tabular form (figure 1.3). Tables such as this would became a standard feature in quantitative studies of this time, making visible the staggering amount of hand tabulation and computation taking place behind the scenes. They also served as expanded spaces of equivalence in which to draw lines of differentiation. Nakamura used them to calculate how far his fifty sampled works deviated from the global average on each measure and found that the average sentence length in *Sasameyuki* was 80 characters longer than the overall average of 40.4, far exceeding any other work. Shiga's sentences, by contrast, were 13 characters shorter. Even at this expanded scale, Tanizaki still stands out. Yet this observation began to feel less consequential to Nakamura once he had the expanded table of values before him. For now he could group writers by the number of phrases used per sentence or by average phrase length (i.e., their rhythmic tendencies), allowing him to associate authors and texts based on "facts" external to received interpretive traditions that privileged authorial style and individual biography. These factors become temporarily dislodged as the common cause of textual effects because the newly generated groupings suggest other causes (e.g., narrative content, time period, and genre) potentially holding the texts together.[99] By shifting the scale of analysis from two to fifty works, Nakamura could begin to redraw the map upon which

表 5.1

作者	成立	作品	文当たり平均字数	平均からの隔たり	句当たり平均字数	平均からの隔たり	文当たり平均句数	平均からの隔たり	文当たり句数度数分布 1	2	3	4	5	6以上
泉　鏡花	1898	絵日傘	75.7	+35.7	11.2	−5.0	6.2	+3.8	3	7	9	7	6	18
	1922	竜胆と撫子	42.0	+1.6	10.7	−5.5	3.6	+1.2	9	7	7	10	5	13
夏目　漱石	1906	草枕	30.9	−9.5	13.8	−2.4	2.1	−0.3	24	16	6	2	1	1
	1916	明暗	29.5	−10.9	20.0	+3.8	1.4	−1.0	31	16	2	1	0	0
島崎　藤村	1906	破戒	36.3	−4.1	13.9	−2.3	2.4	0	14	16	5	8	5	2
	1929	夜明け前	38.2	−2.2	15.5	−0.7	2.3	−0.1	16	17	11	3	1	2
永井　荷風	1909	すみだ川	48.5	+8.1	24.4	+8.2	1.9	−0.5	24	13	5	5	1	2
	1916	腕くらべ	54.8	+14.4	26.8	+10.6	2.0	−0.4	37	9	2	0	2	0
森　鷗外	1911	雁	46.1	+5.7	15.7	−0.5	2.8	+0.4	18	17	10	3	2	0
	1916	渋江抽斎	35.0	−5.4	15.5	−0.7	2.1	−0.3	21	14	8	4	2	1
徳田　秋声	1913	爛	34.2	−6.2	13.3	−2.9	2.4	0	12	23	11	3	0	1
	1941	縮図	77.5	+37.1	16.2	0	4.5	+2.1	5	12	4	7	5	17
広津　和郎	1917	神経病時代	30.6	−9.8	16.1	−0.1	1.8	−0.6	24	14	7	3	0	2
	1919	やもり	45.5	+5.1	13.2	−3.0	3.2	+0.8	11	12	9	8	6	4
芥川竜之介	1917	偸盗	41.6	+1.2	8.1	−8.1	4.6	+2.2	0	9	9	13	7	12
	1926	歯車	30.6	−9.8	19.2	+3.0	1.5	−0.9	29	16	4	1	0	0
久保田万太郎	1917	末枯	29.3	−11.1	13.0	−3.2	2.1	−0.3	20	7	9	6	6	2
	1929	春泥	33.9	−6.5	15.6	−0.6	2.0	−0.4	36	3	3	4	1	3
志賀　直哉	1917	和解	27.1	−13.3	19.9	+3.7	1.3	−1.1	35	11	3	1	0	0
	1937	暗夜行路	27.5	−12.9	14.9	−1.3	1.7	−0.7	29	12	8	0	1	0
佐藤　春夫	1918	田園の憂鬱	44.5	+4.1	14.8	−1.4	2.8	+0.4	11	18	6	6	3	6
	1919	お絹とその兄弟	30.3	−10.1	14.3	−1.9	2.0	−0.4	14	19	8	5	2	1
菊池　寛	1918	忠直卿行状記	50.5	+10.1	16.0	−0.2	3.4	+1.0	2	15	13	7	3	10
	1921	蘭学事始	37.2	−3.2	8.9	−7.3	3.8	+1.4	2	9	21	7	1	10
室生　犀星	1919	性に眼覚める頃	43.5	+3.1	17.1	+0.9	2.4	0	5	16	16	7	4	2
	1934	あにいもうと	67.9	+27.5	21.6	+5.4	3.0	+0.6	5	15	17	7	2	4
武者小路実篤	1920	友情	26.8	−13.6	16.4	+0.2	1.5	−0.9	32	16	2	0	0	0
	1950	真理先生	24.9	−15.5	15.1	−1.1	1.6	−0.8	30	14	2	3	1	0
宇野　浩二	1923	子を貸し屋	58.0	+17.6	11.7	−4.5	4.6	+2.2	6	5	10	12	8	9
	1938	器用貧乏	58.3	+17.9	11.1	−5.1	4.8	+2.4	2	3	13	8	7	17
宮本百合子	1924	伸子	34.2	−6.6	16.0	−0.2	2.3	−0.1	11	14	15	7	3	0
	1946	播州平野	40.8	+0.4	13.7	−2.9	2.8	+0.4	6	19	20	2	2	1
谷崎潤一郎	1924	蓼喰ふ虫	63.9	+23.5	20.9	+4.7	2.9	+0.5	11	15	10	8	1	5
	1948	細雪	120.5	+80.1	15.7	−0.5	6.3	+3.9	0	5	4	11	6	24
山本　有三	1928	波	30.6	−9.8	13.7	−2.5	2.1	−0.3	19	17	11	1	1	1
	1937	路傍の石	36.9	−3.5	10.2	−6.0	3.3	+0.9	3	13	12	12	6	4
横光　利一	1929	日輪	30.7	−9.7	14.2	−2.0	2.0	−0.4	13	22	11	3	1	0
	1936	機械	92.2	−51.8	42.1	+25.9	2.1	−0.3	13	22	9	3	0	3
佐多　稲子	1936	くれなゐ	36.0	−4.4	15.1	−1.1	2.2	−0.2	19	15	8	6	2	0
	1947	私の東京地図	44.7	+4.3	15.4	−0.8	2.7	+0.3	16	21	13	4	0	1
網野　菊	1938	妻たち	53.0	+12.6	14.9	−1.3	3.3	+0.9	8	15	15	7	2	3
	1947	金の棺	57.3	+16.9	18.5	+2.3	2.9	+0.5	11	19	10	4	1	5
壺井　栄	1938	大根の葉	35.7	−4.7	17.8	+1.6	1.9	−0.5	18	17	8	5	2	0
	1953	岸うつ波	41.2	+0.8	16.9	+0.7	2.3	−0.1	14	13	14	6	0	3
平林たい子	1946	かういふ女	56.9	+16.5	21.9	+5.7	2.5	+0.1	7	24	9	7	2	1
	1950	黒の時代	52.2	+11.8	24.1	+7.9	2.1	−0.3	13	25	11	1	0	0
三島由紀夫	1949	仮面の告白	34.8	−5.6	13.2	−3.0	2.1	−0.3	13	16	8	5	3	0
	1952	真夏の死	27.0	−13.4	13.3	−2.9	1.9	−0.5	12	20	11	4	2	1
川端　康成	1954	千羽鶴	31.8	−9.6	13.9	−2.3	2.1	−0.3	16	19	6	5	1	3
	1955	山の音	26.9	−13.5	13.0	−3.2	1.9	−0.5	21	15	10	4	0	0
		総合平均	40.4		16.2		2.4		751	727	455	256	117	194
			(以上20,000句による)						(以上2,500に句よる)					

FIGURE 1.3. Data table from Nakamura's "Kotoba no bi to chikara" (1958). For each author on the left, two works were analyzed. The first three columns report the average number of characters per sentence, the average number of characters per phrase, and the average number of phrases per sentence. Values are provided on the left of each column, with standard deviations on the right. The final column represents the distribution of phrases of a given length in each work. Reproduced with the permission of Nakayama Shoten.

differences between utterance and linguistic system, part and whole, might be compared.

Unfortunately, Nakamura left it mostly to others to link this map to broader psychological or literary theories. The inclination to let the numbers speak for themselves was a characteristic of Yasumoto Biten's work too, if to a greater degree. A prominent voice in the early issues of *Keiryō kokugogaku*, he graduated from Kyoto University in 1959 as a psychology major and exhibited a strong facility with the advanced techniques for statistical inference that permeated the discipline of psychology at that time, particularly in the United States.[100] Yasumoto's methodological contributions are many, but one of the most consequential is the idea of modeling as applied to statistical comparison and prediction. In his seminal work from the period, *Bunshō shinrigaku no shinryōiki* (New Frontiers in the Psychology of Style, 1960), Yasumoto built on Hatano's studies by singling out many of the same stylistic features for analysis. These had become the accepted tools of the trade. He also built on Nakamura's work with his own sampling method. His corpus consisted of single works by one hundred authors selected from Chikuma Shobō's anthology.[101] Where Yasumoto diverged was in his attention to aligning his empirical observations of texts with statistical models. Specifically, in the case of sentence length, he sought to discern whether its distribution in works by a given author followed statistical distributions common to other natural and social phenomena, such as the normal distribution (bell curve).

This compulsion to fit empirical data about language to canonical statistical distributions ran through much of the burgeoning field of psycholinguistics. To discover such fits was at once to identify larger statistical regularities in how language operated but also to create a bridge that translated language into quantitative forms that could be manipulated and compared according to accepted mathematical procedures. In the specific case of sentence length, Yasumoto wanted to know if the frequency of sentences of a given length, when plotted as a curve, would have a central peak (indicating a majority of the author's sentences are of equal length) that gradually sloped to the left and right (indicating diminishing amounts of shorter and longer sentences). Should this be the case, he could understand this linguistic feature through one of the foundational principles of frequentist statistics: the central limit theorem. The theorem asserts that certain phenomena, such as human height, when measured across an increasingly large number of independent instances, converge to a normal distribution. Moreover, if the instances being measured are properly sampled, then the properties observed in the sample (e.g., mean, standard deviation) will approximate the properties of the larger population. That is, one can make strong inferences about the whole based on observing only a small part. This link to probabilistic inference proved a powerful motivation to try to fit observed linguistic data to the idealized world of statistical models.

To Yasumoto's delight, he found that the lengths of sentences used by an author, when transformed using a conversion table, formed a normal distribution. The distributions for different authors also tended to gravitate toward a particular length and hover around it. To each writer, that is, her own unique bell curve. Indeed, having found this normal distribution in Mori Ōgai's works, Yasumoto derived a formula for the fitted curve (figure 1.4) and suggested that Ōgai wrote "under the influence of this formula's limits."[102] Such an abstraction replaces authorial intention or social convention as common cause with the determining force of the statistical model itself. This force is portrayed as something to which every author will adhere, more or less, with slight variation. Ōgai's formula for sentence length, in other words, describes the same basic shape as Shiga's formula, or any author for that matter, even if the values that constitute each formula vary. It is precisely because their curves follow the same basic shape, however, that they can be compared in what is yet another new equivalence space. Yasumoto repeated this procedure for other features (frequency of periods; frequency of metaphor per paragraph; frequency of nouns per paragraph; frequency of color words per paragraph) to show that they too could be fit to their own idealized curves or distributions, although not always the normal curve.[103] Although this approach opened up new spaces of comparison for Yasumoto, and was meant as a provocation for thinking about the subjective limits of style, the reduction of writing to a statistical model would seem to go too far in downplaying individual creativity and the free play of subjective intention or desire. It also supplants, as was the tendency in this period, any theory of expression with the purity of statistical abstraction, as if the messiness of writing could so readily be washed out by the laws discovered in large numbers.

This tendency was again on display in Yasumoto's essay on "The Future of Kanji." Using his corpus of one hundred authors, he sampled one

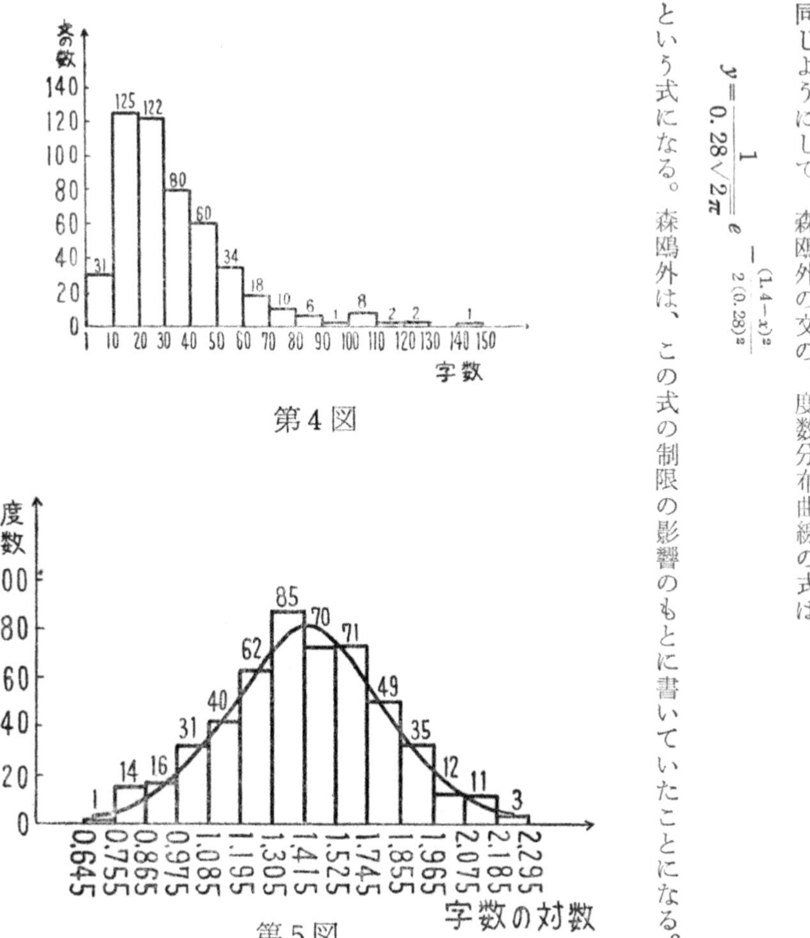

FIGURE 1.4. The two histograms from Yasumoto's *Bunshō shinrigaku no shinryōiki* (1960) represent (*top left*) the distribution of sentences of a given character length in Mori Ōgai's writing and (*bottom left*) a modified version that renders this distribution as normal. (*right*) is a formula corresponding to the fitted curve of the second histogram. Reproduced with the permission of Seishin Shobō.

thousand character passages from each and plotted the average number of *kanji* used over time. This revealed a downward trend between the years 1900 and 1955, dropping from a high of 393 kanji per 1,000 characters to just 275 by the end (a 30 percent decline). With these data Yasumoto could leverage another key instrument of inferential statistics: the prediction of an event's probability based on what is known about the past. Specifically, he predicted several possible futures for kanji based on different models: linear, exponential, and polynomial. The first assumes a constant rate of change over time, the second a gradual decay toward infinity, and the third a constantly accelerating decline. Using these, he estimated three possible futures for when kanji might disappear from written Japanese: the year 2191; never, despite their becoming increasingly rare; and the year 2031. Although this thought experiment ignores the influence of social and cultural forces likely to disrupt the idealized paths of these models, Yasumoto's point was to demonstrate how the juxtaposition of such models might spark conversation about the very nature of stylistic evolution as a social process. If the models themselves seem terribly simplistic even by the standards of his own time, the experiment was intended to show how relatively large amounts of empirical data were an opportunity for thinking with, and across, statistical models, which was in turn to reason about multiple theories of linguistic, literary, and other real-world processes.[104]

Yasumoto's models are simplistic because they are one-dimensional, based on just a single textual feature. In his doctoral thesis, however, he had considered what it would take to study the interaction of multiple features, a problem that emerged as another central concern in quantitative studies of this moment, particularly in the work of Kabashima Tadao.[105] He earned his degree in literature from Kyoto University in 1950 and spent his early academic career studying expression and style while dabbling in psycholinguistics and information theory. In 1965 he wrote *Buntai no kagaku* (The science of style) with fellow rhetorician Jugaku Akiko. Like previous work, the study relied on the twin components of a broad, diverse corpus (eighty sentences sampled from one hundred works by one hundred different authors) and the comprehensive tabulation of stylistic features. These include Hatano's canonical features but also the amount of quotation, the ratio of onomatopoetic words, and the percent of sentences containing conjunctions, each hand-counted by a team of assistants.[106] The book's guiding theoretical premise was that writers select forms of expression in response to intention and the conditions of utterance; that the forms can be loosely categorized by their "expressive orientation"; and that these categories correspond to linguistic proxies that can be measured in an objective and consistent way.[107] Correspondences are established through the close rhetorical analysis of representative passages whose stylistic traits become the basis for creating quantitative measures of distinction.[108]

This mixed-methods approach took established rhetorical categories and tried to reverse engineer measures of difference between them. For example, citing a passage from a novel by Ōoka Shōhei, "Musashino fujin" (A wife in Musashino), the authors label it "summarizing expression" (*yōyaku-teki hyōgen*) because, like a newspaper article, it provides the basic outline of an event (the who, what, when, where, why, and how) and avoids excessive detail about the event's particulars. In contrast, a passage from Satō Haruo's "Den'en no yūutsu" (A pastoral elegy) is "descriptive expression" (*byōsha-teki hyōgen*) because it focuses on particulars (e.g., the color of a bug, the length of its antennae) and is something from which one could paint a picture or imagine a scene in a film.[109] Descriptive expression is further divided into "static" and "dynamic" types. The authors then construct an "objective measure" corresponding to the feeling one gets when reading passages of each type. Focusing on different parts of speech—specifically nouns, verbs, and adjectives and adverbs—they plot the number of one group (nouns) against changes in the ratio of the others across all one hundred passages in their sample (figure 1.5). The resulting graph indicates that the ratio of nouns is slightly negatively correlated with a lower adjective to verb ratio (or MVR); the more nouns present, in other words, the fewer adjectives there will tend to be in a passage compared with verbs.[110]

At a conceptual level, these findings do not go much further than Hatano's distinction between declension and substantive type styles or Sōseki's distinction between thematics and expression. Methodologically, however, something innovative is happening. Passages from texts are being related along two different dimensions and being positioned in Cartesian space according to the mutual relation of these dimensions. Points on the lower right of figure 1.6 are passages with more nouns and a lower MVR and, thus, more "summarizing." Points in the upper left have fewer nouns and a higher MVR (a higher adjective to verb ratio) and are more "descriptive." Individual data points can be singled out in this way (e.g., A is a passage by Tanizaki, B a passage by Shiga, and C a passage by Ibuse Masuji) and subjected to closer analysis.[111] More important, the points can be seen as part of loose groupings that occupy their own distinct regions. They can be clustered based on how they express the features under analysis. As with

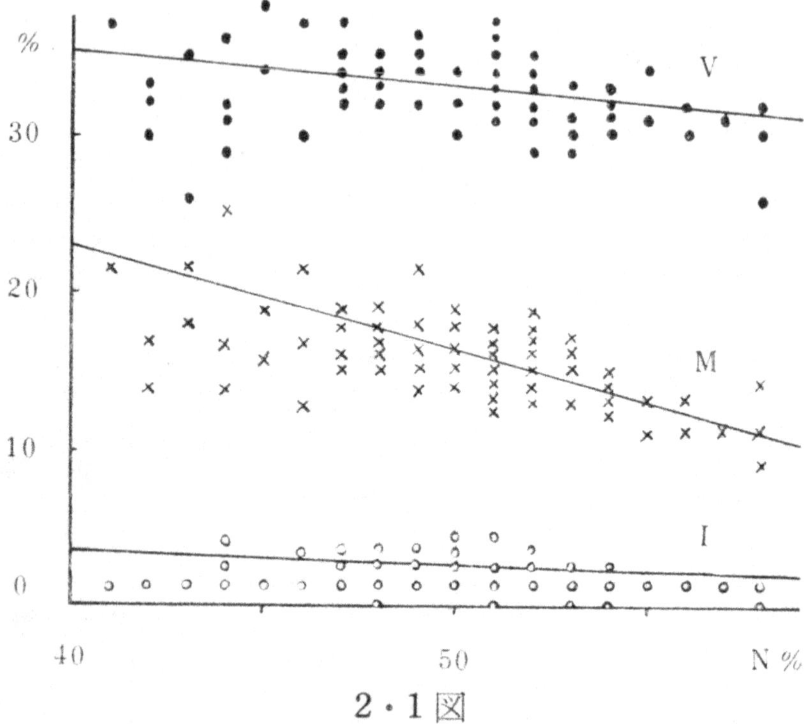

FIGURE 1.5. A plot from Kabashima and Jūgaku's *Buntai no kagaku* (1965) showing how the ratio of nouns (N) in one hundred sample passages varies with the ratio of verbs (V) and adjectives/adverbs (M). They combine the latter two ratios into a single measure called MVR (M/V * 100) and show a slight negative correlation of N with MVR. Reproduced with the permission of Sōgeisha.

Nakamura's approach, this scaled-up mode of viewing harbors the potential to destabilize text and author as primary explanans and make room for alternate interpretations of textual similarity and difference. Which texts are close to Tanizaki's? Who is stuck in the middle with Shiga? Texts and authors are placed in configurations potentially invisible to established critical lenses, prompting exploration, as Kabashima suggests elsewhere, of other possible causal mechanisms (personality, occupation, sex, background, or age).[112] The contextual factors initially abstracted away to create this space of equivalence thus come back to help sort out the figures of difference therein exposed.

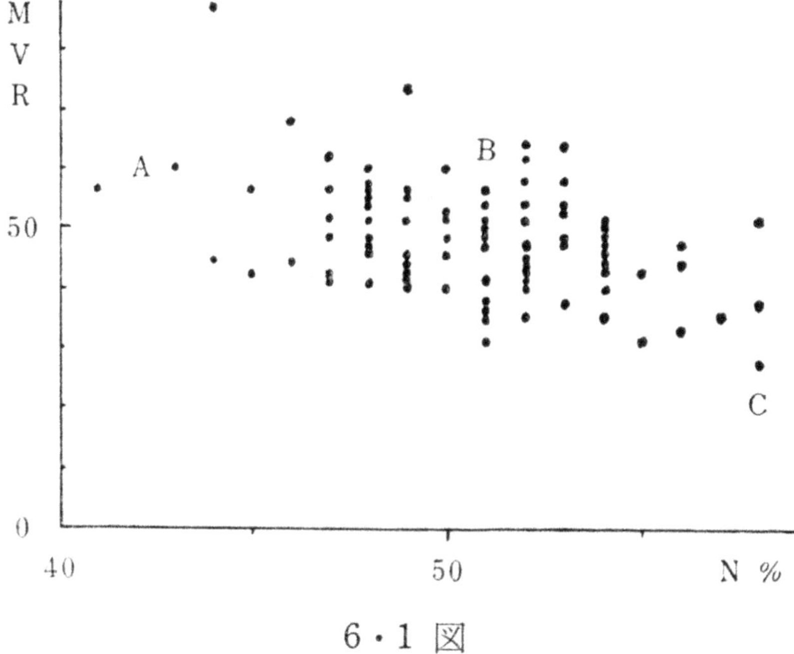

FIGURE 1.6. A scatterplot from *Buntai no kagaku* showing the ratio of nouns (N) and MVR for one hundred sample passages. Point A represents a passage by Tanizaki, B a passage by Shiga, and C a passage by Ibuse. Reproduced with the permission of Sōgeisha.

QUANTIFICATION IN THEORY

As Kabashima and others raced to build their speculative methodological machinery, they increasingly left unattended practices of interpretation more familiar to their colleagues in literary departments. Their innovations increasingly feel like solutions to problems that these colleagues did not have. Something of this disconnect is evident in the fact that quantitative work on language and literature was done within ever-narrower institutional and intellectual contexts. The equivalence spaces that Nakamura, Yasumoto, Kabashima, and Jugaku built failed to circulate much beyond their laboratories and journals.[113] Advances in quantitative method continued to be made, of course. Judging by the articles published in *Keiryō kokugogaku*, computers entered the scene in the 1970s as tools for language processing and measurement, although their immediate utility was stalled by the inability to read and parse Japanese script. Hurdles to processing language computationally were more easily surmounted where alphabetic scripts reigned, facilitating by the early 1950s the groundbreaking work in machine generated concordances by poet and critic Josephine Miles and, separately, Father Roberto Busa.[114] Even without computers, corpus linguistic research extended into semantics, discourse analysis, and probabilistic language models, building on advances in the 1950s and 1960s by linguist Noam Chomsky and sociologist Zellig Harris. When this research focused on literature, it mostly stuck to specialized linguistic topics and was limited to case studies of a few texts. If larger corpora were used, the focus remained on well-worn stylistic categories such as diction, parts of speech, and orthography.[115]

The lack of cross pollination between psycholinguistic studies and literary studies proper could be explained away as an effect of entrenched disciplinary lines that kept apart humanistic and scientific modes of inquiry. Joseph Murphy has suggested that these lines were potentially blurrier in Japan than in North America, noting that in the 1970s major critics such as Maeda Ai and Karatani Kōjin sought ways to merge mathematics and literary theory because they recognized a correspondence between the philosophical problems addressed by each.[116] On a practical level, deeper engagement across disciplinary lines may have been hampered by the technical and human resources necessary to collect, count, and analyze literature as data. If ideological bias or technical hurdles were indeed factors, it would have been in spite of broadly shared intellectual concerns because buntai was a topic on the minds of many writers and critics in the 1950s. It served as an analytical lens for immanent stylistic readings of authors and works in the manner of Kobayashi but also as a critical construct for theorizing larger scale historical and social dynamics. Expert roundtables and special issues on buntai appeared throughout the decade in journals dedicated to language and literature.[117] The October 1954 issue of *Gengo seikatsu*, for instance, carried articles analyzing the diction and orthography of several canonical authors using a mixed-methods approach as well as essays by contemporary writers who reflected on their own individual styles. Notably, the issue opened with a roundtable between the critics Itō Sei, Kamei Katsuichirō, and Usui Yoshimi that ranged across topics including choice of orthography, the use of pronouns, stylistic influence, and the historical drivers of stylistic innovation.

Itō was a key contributor to debates about style at this time and had very recently crossed paths with Hatano when the latter served as an expert scientific witness in the *Chatterley* trial of 1951.[118] One of Itō's more significant contributions was a 1947 essay on the emergence of style, "Sutairu no hassei," in which he offered a theory of style's relation to thought, as well as to society, in ways resonant with Hatano's understanding of style as the outcome of a conscious negotiation between individual psychology and the constraints imposed on it by shared stylistic conventions. Yet Itō also argued against a particularly modern conception of style as technique (*shuhō*) or method (*shudan*) deployed in a rational and utilitarian way in response to a writer's social environment or normative linguistic conventions. This view may reflect the reality of how writers had come to understand the emergence of style—and Itō admits to reluctantly holding on to this notion himself—but it also symbolized "a type of artistic malady" that turned them into objects that could be observed and measured if one abstracted out essentialized forms from the phenomena they represented.[119] Itō sought to counter the effects of this view by reimagining style as an "organic," "animate" force at work in writers.[120]

Critic Etō Jun echoed Itō's bifurcated theory of style in *Sakka wa kōdō suru* (Writers' actions, 1959). In a chapter on novelistic style, "Shōsetsu no buntai," he claimed that although buntai expressed "individuality," or *kosei*, it was not *the* expression of individuality itself. To see it thus was to uphold a narrow sense of buntai as the persistence of specific stylistic characteristics tied to a static notion of the authorial subject. This narrow sense, in Etō's opinion, had stunted the evolution of the Japanese novel and needed to be replaced by a broader sense of buntai as a set of elements reflecting the dynamic relation of the individual to the whole of social reality. Understood through this lens, a true authorial style began at the point where deindividuation became the goal of writing. Style that remained latched to the idea of the individual self was no style at all (*hibuntai-teki*).[121]

Like quantitative thinkers of the day, Itō and Etō sought to illuminate the interaction of individual utterance with wider systems of expression. Yet their theories of how style emerges, which resist any empirical demarcation of the elements of buntai, also celebrate the complexity and indeterminacy of this interaction in ways not easily amenable to quantitative accounts.

There is a tension in their arguments between a systemic approach to style and a metaphysics of style. This tension came to a head in Anglo-European critical theory in the early 1970s, resulting in a major backlash against stylistics in both its quantitative and qualitative guises. Stanley Fish issued his famous broadside against stylistics in 1972, calling into question the very idea "that one can read directly from the description of a text . . . to the shape or quality of its author's mind."[122] He took issue with the ways that linguistic patterns could be arbitrarily interpreted to fit with whatever a critic wished to say about an author's state of mind. This produced highly subjective, immanent readings of texts that explained little of how written language actually signified to readers. Just a year earlier, as part of a conference proceedings on "Literary Style," Roland Barthes framed the issue as a too narrow focus on the idiolect of the author and not enough attention to the idiolect of the institution of literature. Before one could think of style in the individual sense, one needed to think about "literary language, a truly collective writing whose systematic features should be surveyed."[123] The quantitative studies examined thus far surely exhibit this will to survey, but they mostly adhered to questions of how individual authorial style deviated from an implied normative style whose social and historical location is never clearly delimited.

Barthes saw the opposition between norm and deviation as constitutive of the concept of style. Yet if style was "a distance, a difference," as he put it, the next question to be asked was, a difference "in reference to what?" Here is where the analysis of style had to shift away from the examination of internal psychological mechanisms and toward an exploration of multiple layers of discourse—which was also toward "the conviction that style is essentially a citational process, a body of formulae, a memory (almost in the cybernetic sense of the word), a cultural and not an expressive inheritance." Or more metaphorically, "if up until now we have looked at the text as a species of fruit with a kernel (an apricot, for example), the flesh being the form and the pit being the content, it would be better to see it as an onion, a construction of layers (or levels, or systems) whose body contains, finally, no heart, no kernel, no secret, no irreducible principle."[124] This was not in itself a rejection of quantitative reasoning but a rejection of some of the uses to which it and purely qualitative accounts of style were being put. Fredric Jameson and Jonathan Culler further problematized these uses in the early 1970s. Jameson did so through a critique of the antidiachronic tendencies of Formalism implicit in the model of language developed by Saussure, but also in the early work of the Russian Formalists; Culler did so, following Barthes, by calling attention to the institutional conventions, mental codes, and functional categories external to the text that governed how literature was written and read.[125] Of perennial concern was the issue of where (and how) to draw the line between text and context.

Traditional stylistics did not end with Stanley Fish, but neither did it turn its quantitative attention in the directions that critics in the early 1970s were pointing. For the time being, this task would mostly be left to sociologists and book historians.[126] This was true in Japan as well, where stylistics continued to prefer close, qualitative studies of individual texts and authors. Although it avoided numbers, it did not necessarily avoid matters of scale, especially when it came to historical studies of style. By the late 1980s, there was a sizable body of scholarship regarding the development and evolution of literary language. This research, even when it took individual authors as case studies, was fundamentally concerned with systemic questions about the various social and linguistic influences leading to the formation of the modern written vernacular (*genbun itchi*). For instance, a volume titled *Buntai* (Style, 1989) collected passages representing different moments of stylistic evolution. An essay by the editors speculated about the features of Western languages that most influenced the "style" of modern Japanese, including punctuation, conjunctions, and words or grammatical constructions related to reasoning and argument.[127] But if the speculations hinged on assumptions about the frequency of such features, the evidence remained anecdotal.

A book on style from 1988 by Morioka Kenji, one of the founders of historical stylistics, exhibits similar tendencies. A member of Kabashima's generation, Morioka spent his career researching Japanese language education, communication, and readability measures, so he was no stranger to statistical methods. His writing on literary style and its influence on the modern vernacular, however, eschewed quantitative reasoning for a case-based, philological approach. He also expressed an acute awareness of the limitations of stylistics as it had been practiced and codified by Hatano and Kobayashi. For them, style (buntai) was conceived as a function of the author—a set of characteristics shared across multiple works regardless of differences in theme or aesthetic orientation. "In other words, an author's uniqueness will unconsciously surface in their writing (bunshō) no matter what, and the aim of stylistics is to observe this uniqueness by skillfully capturing the linguistic particularities through which it surfaces."[128] Morioka faulted the dominance of the I-novel for such a myopic view of style and, while not relinquishing the author as endpoint of analysis, argued for restoring their creative agency by attending to how stylistic choices respond to contextual differences at the level of the work (e.g., theme, setting, and plot).[129] Only by accounting for such contextual determinants, Morioka concluded, could stylistics close the existing gap between itself and literary criticism.[130]

Although Morioka looked to internal rather than external determinants, his motivations are similar to those surfaced in the early 1970s critique of stylistics. They also reflect a critical shift in Japanese literary criticism of the mid-1980s encapsulated in the "*Kokoro* debate" (*Kokoro* ronsō), which centered on Sōseki's eponymous canonical novel from 1914. At the crux of this debate was the rejection of *sakuhinron* (study of a single work) and its ultimate grounding "in an implicit worship of the author as semi-mystical, transcendent 'prophet,' a stance that mystified the actual historical position of the literary work and its author."[131] Leading this critique was young upstart and institutional outsider Komori Yōichi, who proposed reading the novel as a text (*tekisuto*) rather than as a work (*sakuhin*). As Michael Bourdaghs explains, "In using the term *text*, Komori meant in part to stress the openness of *Kokoro* to its outside both in terms of its insistence on intertextuality and in terms of its narrative incompletion. . . . By insisting that literary value lay not so much in the text itself as in the relationship between the text and its reader, Komori's stance challenged . . . the position . . . of Sōseki . . . as the guarantor of value standing behind the text."[132] This debate, which helped usher in new critical methodologies from linguistics and semiotics, is seen as "one of the culminating moments in what might be called the 'linguistic turn' in Japanese literary studies,"[133] although the genealogy traced so far shows that the ground for this turn was laid much earlier.

The timing of this turn neatly coincides with Morioka's call for something like a "literary turn" in stylistics. In 1988, Komori published an extended monograph on *Buntai toshite no monogatari* (Narrative as Style), its opening lines echoing Morioka's sentiments and also those of Barthes: "Every literary expression does not necessarily belong to the individuality or uniqueness of he who created it." Individuals may choose expressions according to their particular circumstances, or their own intentions and obsessions, but texts are also formed out of the myriad texts they cite. The text, Komori asserted, is a fabric woven from the narrative(s) latent in these cited texts and the narrative(s) they set into motion; it is simultaneously "the pattern that emerges from this fabric."[134] The convergence of literary theory and stylistics in Komori's early work provides a useful bookend to our genealogy, revisiting as it does some of the fundamental questions raised at earlier moments while prefiguring—not in method but in theory—some of the ideas animating the current quantitative turn.

In his opening chapter, Komori rejects the author as a final arbiter of meaning in favor of the discursive histories embedded within language. This requires a new methodology of reading that sees texts as being comprised of smaller units of expression that encode specific historical styles and their associated narratives. If unique authorial expression is to be found anywhere in a text, it will be found in the ways these units are juxtaposed and brought into conflict with each other. To demonstrate this methodology, Komori meticulously dissects a passage from Futabatei Shimei's *Ukigumo* (Floating Clouds, 1887–1889), considered one of the progenitors of the modern Japanese novel. The passage comes just as the novel hints at possible romantic feelings between its two main characters, Bunzō and Osei, who gaze upon the moon as it rises above the bamboo hedge outside their room. Komori identifies three sentences in the passage and breaks them down by their "paradigmatic relations" with style at the level of diction and their "syntagmatic relations" with style at the level of structure and narrative. The first sentence, owing to its diction and rhythmic pattern, is said to paradigmatically and syntagmatically call up the memory of classical Japanese poetry (*waka*); the second is read as a continuation of the waka style that, through its shift in diction, gives way to the style of Chinese poetry (*kanshi*); and the third invokes kanshi at the level of diction but Western style personification at the level of description (e.g., the moon is described as "rising" in ways foreign to the waka and kanshi style).[135]

From this single passage, Komori proposes a more general theory of how units of expression operate within a text, asserting that "when phrases (or their combination) are taken from traditional or classic literary genres, even when these phrases consist of a single word (or fragment), they call forth the memory of the entire genre. This memory is activated at the surface of the text by stylistic characteristics (*buntai-teki tokushitsu*) and their paradigmatic relations at the level of diction as well as their syntagmatic relations at the level of overall structure." These stylistic characteristics, moreover, "will activate memories of the narrative form contained in the text from which they were borrowed."[136] Komori's formulation here echoes Sōseki's atomistic approach in treating a text's most basic unit (i.e., the sentence) as classifiable according to a single, reducible trait. It also echoes Hatano's approach in treating stylistic characteristics as indexes of some greater affective association, although here they index not individual "tension-systems" but the collective memories of a genre.

If there is something *typical* about individual sentences—a set of markers that encode generic associations—it stands to reason that one could quantify the relative proportion of these markers and classify the sentences accordingly. This, at root, is the procedure Komori enacts in his qualitative analysis of Futabatei's writing. Yet right at the moment when we can imagine scaling up this analysis toward a comparative history of stylistic evolution across many sentences (and many texts), Komori opts for shifting scale along a different dimension. Specifically, he moves toward exploding the very atomistic model he has just established by substituting for it another model of how these atoms collide. When sentences associated with different genres or narrative forms interact, this revised model suggests that their original associations with that genre or narrative dissolve, forming new, hybrid associations.[137] In other words, it posits that every moment of interaction between recognized styles (buntai) is also the moment when these styles transform into something else, thus pushing the evolution of style in a new direction. On one side is a model informed by Roman Jakobson's communicative framework in which message and meaning are embedded in shared codes and contexts. Readers share these codes to the extent they recognize them through the same set of stylistic traits. On the other side is a model that, akin to Jameson's critique of Formalism's antidiachronic tendencies, posits the inherent instability and dynamism of these codes—they can be mixed within a text to form entirely new patterns or overlooked by communities of readers unfamiliar with them.

To reconcile these opposing models at the level of authorial expression, Komori turned, like all the others in this genealogy, to psychological theory. Specifically, he looked to Erich Neumann's Jungian influenced studies of aesthetics, which treat creative expression as a negotiation between the individual and society's collective unconscious. Under this theory, as Komori understood it, the "creative individual" is one who disrupts entrenched archetypal forms that have become encoded in *langue* and enframed by cultural systems. These systems are not permanent, however, and in periods of collapse, it is creative individuals who inject new forms and expressions into the collective unconscious where they potentially replace older archetypal forms (figure 1.7). Komori, following Neumann, felt that by studying this process of injection one could glimpse the underlying dynamics of cultural change.[138] In refocusing attention on the creative individual, Komori reinjects time, but also uncertainty, into his proposed new Formalism.

Against the backdrop of the "*Kokoro* debate," *Narrative as Style* suggested a method of reading that displaced the single author and work as meaningful units of analysis. They are still present, of course, to the extent that they mediate the relation of individual expression to a wider system,

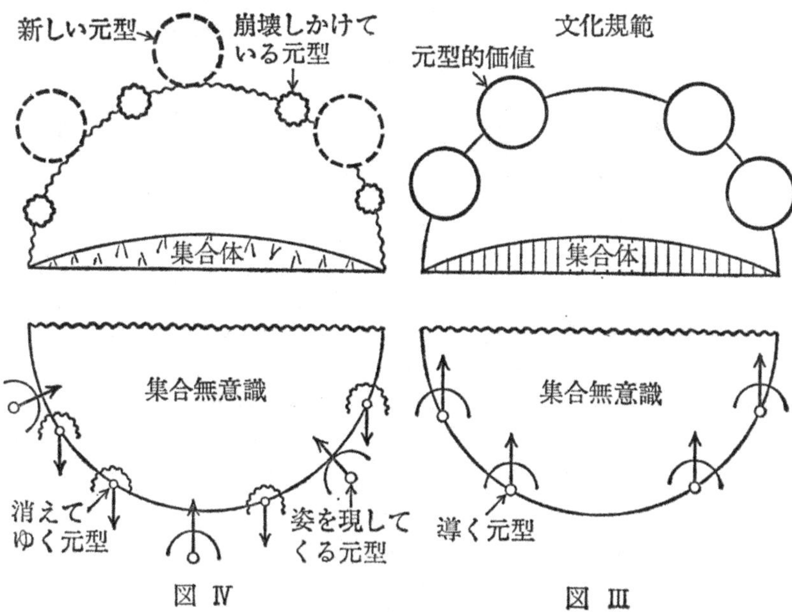

FIGURE 1.7. A schematic drawing from Komori's *Buntai toshite no monogatari* (1988) that is adapted from Erich Neumann's "Art and Time" (1954). The right-hand image illustrates cultural norms in a moment of stability, with the social collective (top hemisphere) and the collective unconscious (bottom hemisphere) sustained by existing values and forms. In the left-hand image, small circles represent either new cultural forms being generated from these hemispheres or older forms disappearing from them. Reproduced with the permission of Chikuma Shobō.

but the preferred unit of analysis is now stylistic form itself as a kind of trace of cultural change. It exists within the text and also external to it as a persistent material form that simultaneously morphs in response to narrative and historical context. Indeed, only by persisting do its differences across time and context become legible. Komori's proposed method is also a challenge to received forms of literary history that would situate their readings of authors and works within a closed national context. As he states at the outset, the entire book

> is an attempt to capture the mutual relation of Meiji-20s "modern" narrative and the formation of style using the textual dynamics in *Ukigumo* as a base model. By clarifying how the introduction of a style with Western grammatical structure changes and breaks down the traditional narrative of a man and a woman, giving birth to a new narrative form, the book also interrogates the system of "modern literature" as it has become naturalized.[139]

Implicit here is the notion that narrative form is partly determined by the circulation of stylistic forms within and across languages. From this perspective, "modern [Japanese] literature" is not a naturally closed system but a byproduct of morphological variation within a system open to outside influence.

A few years before Komori's study, Franco Moretti espoused a similar vision of what literary history might be should it shed its emphasis on "great works or great individuals" whose innovative irreducibility is celebrated by an endless proliferation of singular interpretations.[140] For Moretti, who echoes conversations from the early 1970s but also some of the Russian Formalists, the problem with this emphasis was twofold.[141] First, it privileged the *difference* of the masterpiece against an assumed but never articulated system of *convention*. Second, it downplayed the role of extraliterary phenomena such that, lacking a set of shared empirical foundations against which to validate one's claims, critics were free to assign social meaning to a masterpiece or a rhetorical form however they pleased.[142] For the history of literature to transform itself into a history of rhetorical forms, which for Moretti was to bring it into conversation with the social sciences, it would "have to start from the realization that a form becomes more comprehensible and more interesting the more one grasps the conflict, or at least the difference, connecting it to the forms around it." Moretti animates the psychological aspect of this conflict through Freud, rather than Neumann, but his emphasis on conflict and change comes close to the kinds of complex relations Komori tried to elucidate. "As well as grasping the succession of different and mutually hostile forms, literary history must aim at a synchronic periodization which is no longer 'summed up' in individual exemplary forms, but is set up for each period, through a kind of parallelogram of rhetorical forces, with its dominant, its imbalances, its conflicts and its division of tasks."[143]

Moretti, like Komori, was working in the wake of earlier formalisms and developing a critical vocabulary for thinking about literature systemically and materially without resorting to explicit quantification. In light of the genealogy traced so far, both appear in this earlier moment to be perched on the same side of the theory-method pendulum as Sōseki. That is, they have a richly developed theory for how to read complex textual relations from empirical traces of style but no method for doing so at the scale at which they imagined these relations to be operating. As Moretti said at the time regarding his proposed new sociology of forms, "Who knows whether it is a reasonable project and not just a little personal utopia (which, moreover, I am still a long way from having begun to put into practice)?"[144] It was Moretti, of course, who would swing back toward method in a decisive way. By 2000, his "little personal utopia," which was hardly his own to begin with, had evolved into a study of morphological evolution at the world scale to be carried out by "distant reading," a term which initially meant pulling together "a patchwork of other people's research, without a single direct textual reading."[145] A decade later, distant reading of morphological evolution "had itself morphed into an analysis of quantitative data," in turn giving rise to an experimental lab and a series of pamphlets by collaborators and students who were using quantitative methods to analyze everything from the length of novel titles and character networks to century-spanning trends in diction and the Bordieuan dynamics of literary canon formation.[146]

These studies are in turn part of a growing body of computational work that is redefining what it means to read at a distance, both by building on past quantitative efforts and by adopting new tools for large-scale text analysis. This growth has been facilitated by several factors that were noted in the introduction: the rise of digital archives and powerful instruments for representing complex literary and linguistic phenomena (e.g., genre, character, theme) in large collections of texts; renewed interest in materialist and sociological histories of literature; and the emergence of a media ecology increasingly underwritten by the algorithmic processing of data and one that has had profound consequences for the way humans communicate and interact. All of these factors have spurred a range of financial and intellectual investments in the new styles of quantitative reasoning on display in the chapters that follow. These investments have contributed to an institutional environment in which quantitative approaches to literature now feel like a legitimate response to specific theoretical problems, particularly ones concerning scale, the history and sociology of discourse, and algorithmic and data literacy.

Meanwhile, similar levels of investment in computationally aided research have been slower to materialize in Japanese literary studies. Nor has there been a significant transfer of investment from fields outside of literature, such as linguistics and the social sciences, despite the contributions they have made to the quantitative analysis of language and culture. Linguists, for instance, have created comprehensive digital corpora while promoting the potential applications of corpus linguistics to literature in Japan's growing digital humanities communities.[147] Book historians, for their part, have long employed descriptive statistics to evaluate trends in publishing and consumption.[148] Despite these developments, *Distant Reading*, a compilation of Moretti's earliest quantitative work, was translated into Japanese only in 2016.[149] Several technical and institutional asymmetries may explain the lack of parity with the development of computational criticism in Anglo-American English departments: digitization of nonalphabetic scripts; the related difficulty of building representative collections that span significant periods of time, one compounded by the radical transformations in written language and print media over the last two hundred years; the need for specialized resources to computationally process a language lacking word boundaries; and the smaller number of individuals in the academy with the technical know-how to build and use these resources. These asymmetries have limited the growth of computational research in ways specific to area studies fields more generally and remind us of the asymmetries long embedded in the global evolution of information processing technologies.[150]

As these asymmetries even out, should we expect quantitative methods to be warmly welcomed in Japanese literary studies? If the past is any guide, the present quantitative turn will remain science-fictional, hovering between disciplinary cliffs whose shapes are stubbornly held up by the valleys between them. But perhaps this is to look at past turns from the wrong vantage point. From within a disciplinary formation (i.e., literary criticism) that has long resisted attempts to create equivalences—to give general "form to the chaos of countless singular observations," as Desrosières describes the rationale behind modern statistics[151]—these past turns will only ever look like dead ends. We must retain a healthy and informed skepticism of numeracy and scientific thinking, drawing lessons from disciplines in which quantification long ago provoked crises of epistemology and disciplinary identity. Yet, as this genealogy has shown, past turns are less dead ends than creative gambits to build new methodological infrastructures that combine quantitative and qualitative approaches. Their intent is to expand the possibilities for constructing and communicating "facts" of difference across multiple, disparate observations, bringing these observations into newly figured comparative relation. For Sōseki this meant putting literature from different traditions on a more "neutral" field of physiological response, thus bypassing entrenched hierarchies of aesthetic value. For Hatano it meant positioning texts in a common stylistic field in order to compare their relative uniqueness against a shared system of expressive constraints. In the 1950s and 1960s, scholars sought to enlarge this field by increasing the dimensions and points of reference against which deviance from stylistic norms could be measured. Komori, for his part, conjoined something of Sōseki's atomistic approach with an attention to the sociohistorical determinants operating in conjunction with individual psychology.

In all of these cases, the motivation for creating new equivalence spaces stemmed from critical literary problems in no way alien to the intellectual concerns of the discipline, whether it be reader response, stylistic evolution, communicative context, or discourse. Yet in each case we also find a dissatisfaction with the categories of distinction (e.g., entrenched aesthetic hierarchies, authorial biography, literary work) available for addressing these concerns. The turn to numbers was a way to destabilize these categories in order to experiment with others; to think with other units of analysis and at other scales of comparison. Justification for these turns never solely revolved around claims to scientific validity or technological progress (and we have seen that scientific methods were themselves in constant flux).

They were also imbricated in efforts to negotiate the shifting social and media conditions under which texts circulated and by which knowledge about them was acquired. As Jameson noted about use of the linguistic model in the 1970s, its deeper justification could be found in "the concrete character of the so-called advanced countries of today . . . a world saturated with messages and information."[152] Today the degree of saturation feels only more intense.

Such saturation is understandably anxiety inducing, just as it was for Sōseki, and indeed as it was at the origins of the modern research university, as Chad Wellmon has described. He argues that "the research university was an institutional response to structural changes in the media environment of the eighteenth-century German Enlightenment," wherein many felt that print had reached a saturation point: "there are too many books; there is too much data."[153] To insist there were too many books, however, was really to insist "that there were too many books to be read . . . in a particular way." The lesson learned here is that "sifting out knowledge from information is always normative; that is, it always entails historical and cultural assumptions about *what is worth knowing*."[154] In the current age of information overload, we see again the same anxieties surfacing about what and how we should read. These anxieties are not confined to debates over "distant" versus "close" reading, quantitative versus qualitative methods. They are part of debates over what it means to read literature at all. What works should be valued? How should we value them? Who gets to decide these things? The wager placed on literary truth by the current numerical turn is not, as this book argues by way of example, about resolving such questions definitively. Rather, it is about exploring the communities of value that we might create in response to our present information age; about understanding what values are occluded from view in such communities; and a reminder of what we fail to see when we tether our interpretive communities to only certain kinds of recognized facts.

Chapter Two

ARCHIVE AND SAMPLE

> Quantity and quality wilt when long separated. But a danger often present . . . is the establishing of quality not upon the determination, or even upon the disregard, but upon the assumption, of quantity.
>
> —JOSEPHINE MILES (1946)

Numbers, as we learned in chapter 1, have been dancing around the study of literature since that study was disciplined and institutionalized in the late nineteenth century. That dance has become more intimate and intense, however, with the increasing availability of large collections of digitized, machine-readable texts. Their impact is most directly felt at the level of the keyword search, now a nearly unconscious part of the research process that creates a false sense of the archive (or at least a substantive portion of it) as being a few keystrokes away. Although Sōseki, living through his own information revolution, could imagine all those unread eighteenth-century works lining the shelves of modern libraries, he surely could not have imagined being able to see them all. Likewise, Hatano and his successors were confident that modern Japanese literature could be effectively sampled from literary anthologies, but they turned to sampling precisely because they lacked the means (and hands) to count everything. In this sense, their conceptions of "everything" were bound by the print cultures and information societies in which they worked. Today, when private companies such as Google and public institutions such as the Hathi Trust Resource Center or the National Diet Library are busy digitizing millions of books, the idea of "everything" seems bound only by what has not made the journey from ink and paper to strings of zeroes and ones. At the end of this journey, in its more utopian versions, awaits Borges's total library, a virtual space where all that has ever been written is hyperlinked and ready to hand.

Less idealistic accounts, however, recast the dream of a universal library and total access as a nightmare of crushing information overload. The problem is twofold, relating to both material concerns and the scalability of reading. Materially, the illusion of total access quickly dissipates with the reality that digitization produces its own constraints on the constitution of the archive. These constraints include the limited ability to reproduce print in all its historical variety and the institutional and social location of digitization projects, which effect what gets digitized and how it is made accessible to users.[1] From the perspective of reading, the constraints come in the form of the algorithms used to search and extract meaning from digital collections, without which their content remains opaque and lifeless. The short history of Google Books nicely encapsulates the gap between universalistic hubris and the reality of how digitization constrains the archive. First conceived by Google cofounder Larry Page in 1999, the project got underway five years later and by 2006 was already subject to hyperbolic speculation about the potential of "the universal library [to] deepen our grasp of history, as every original document in the course of civilization is scanned and cross-linked."[2] As Siva Vaidhyanathan has shown, however, the aspiration to totality soon fell prey to the realities of copyright law, the limits of the digital for representing the variability of print, imperfect search algorithms, competing metadata standards, and concerns about accessibility, authority, and transparency.[3] There is nothing seamless about the transition of the world's print heritage into digital form.

Attending to what is lost and deformed in this transition is important, although not at the expense of considering how the transition itself facilitates new ways of recognizing what the print archive is and was. Access to knowledge has always been partial and imperfectly mediated, buoyed by specific assumptions and ideas about what constitutes the "complete" archive or any relevant portion of it. What's true of the "canon," as John Guillory has described it, is also true of the archive. "No one has access to the canon as a totality . . . no one ever reads every canonical work; no one can, because the works invoked as canonical change continually according to many different occasions of judgment and contestation."[4] Following Derrida, we must acknowledge that these occasions are further determined by the "technical structure of the *archiving* archive," which shapes "*archivable* content even in its very coming into existence and in its relationship to the future."[5] Digital collections, in remediating the archive as imagined totality, are also occasions to critically reflect on past and present technical structures for organizing knowledge and to compare their effects on what gets noticed, what gets valued, and what gets read. This chapter explores the impact of the digital on how we think about what to read, setting the stage for a conversation about how and why to read at the scale of less than everything but more than one person could possibly manage.

At the center of this exploration is Aozora Bunko (hereafter Aozora), the largest digital collection of Japanese language literature in existence. For the foreseeable future, attempts to reason quantitatively about modern Japanese literature at the scale of more than one hundred texts are likely to begin with this collection. Comprised of nearly sixteen thousand manually transcribed and proofed texts by 2018, it is the most reliable repository for machine-readable and open-access prewar texts. This is not likely to change soon owing to the strictness of copyright protections and the challenges that Chinese characters present to optical character recognition technologies. These challenges are compounded in the case of prewar texts with their varying print qualities and diversity of script styles, which make automatic bulk digitization difficult to do with sufficient accuracy. To the extent Aozora remains the digital collection of first resort, its size inviting illusions of representativeness, it is worth investigating the institutional and social mechanisms that inform its construction and enable a particular vision of "modern Japanese literature." What representation of the archive has been produced from Aozora's unique "biography?" to use Katherine Bode's phrase.[6] No less important, what kinds of representations of past literary production can be created from its uniquely situated vision?

Both of these questions lead to the problem of sampling, which I address in this chapter as a twofold problem. The first part of the problem is that Aozora functions as a sample of the archive in the way a climate scientist might think of an ice core sample, its variegated layers of particles and dust recording, from a localized context, the effects of complex processes and systems driving global climate conditions over time. It is like a sensor that captures, in a locally biased way, some portion of the dust kicked up by the processes shaping the production and consecration of literary value. Understanding what vision of "modern Japanese literature" is preserved in Aozora is thus in part a matter of understanding how its layers of soil and sediment, light and dark, align or diverge with those found in other records of the literary past, which naturally differ with historical and institutional location. The second problem of sampling relates to its use in statistics as a set of methods, as well as theories, for drawing inferences about a population from some subset of that population. When working with digital collections such as Aozora to craft large-scale arguments about literary history, we invariably face this twofold problem of how to build a statistically useful sample from a larger, nonintentional sample whose relation to the archive is opaque because the composition of that archive—that imagined total population—is unknowable.

The problem has itself generated a productive debate about evidentiary practices in literary scholarship and the extent to which they are thrown into new relief by the scale of digital archives. In this chapter, I contribute to this debate by addressing both aspects of the sampling problem. On the one hand, I try to understand the particularity of Aozora as a sample by using a comparative method that aligns it with several large-scale traces of the bibliographic record: bibliographies of foreign translations into Japanese, the contents of omnibus literary anthologies, and a catalog of literary works included in high school textbooks.[7] By comparing these traces of the never completely knowable archive, we begin to see how Aozora uniquely captures the global processes of literary production and valuation only ever visible in such biased, partial traces. I ground this comparison in the related problem of sampling as method, recognizing it as a set of shared conventions *and* attendant theories for thinking and evaluating the relation of part to whole. To work with digital collections is to confront the practices that literary critics and historians have relied on, and those we might borrow and adapt, for reasoning across different scales of evidence.

AOZORA AND THE EVIDENCE GAP

Aozora's biography emerges out of the same confluence of forces that drove the creation of Google Books. These forces centered around various private and commercial attempts in the 1990s to make electronic books available on the internet. Two of Aozora's founding members, in fact, met via Voyager Japan, a fledgling e-book software company. Tomita Michio, who became Aozora's leading visionary and spokesperson, was a nonfiction writer increasingly frustrated with a publishing industry in the mid-1990s that saw little commercial value in out-of-print titles and that offered few mechanisms for their continued circulation. At the time, he was trying to publish a revised edition of his history of personal computing from 1985, but also a new work, *Future of the Book* (Hon no mirai), which was an extended meditation on how digitization would transform the way people read. In his frustration, he turned to Voyager Japan where he met Noguchi Eiji, a software developer who helped him develop e-book versions of his books for the Voyager platform. This platform also allowed users to download books from the internet, prompting both men to think about the possibilities of creating an online, virtual bookshelf for electronic books.[8]

In 1997 this bookshelf materialized with just seven texts, all of them acquired from a corpus linguist at Fukui University who had digitized them for the internet. They included works by Mori Ōgai, Yosano Akiko, Futabatei Shimei, and Nakajima Atsushi, foreshadowing the role that Aozora would come to play as a repository for canonical literary figures. But the original vision for the site was far more expansive—it was to be an open repository for out-of-copyright *and* self-published works. For Tomita, the digital medium symbolized a liberating force that would democratize the circulation of ideas by untying them from the constraints of static, physical books. In the preface to *Future of the Book*, he looked with anticipation to a globally networked world where books would be both ubiquitous and instantaneously accessible, as if residing in the "blue sky" (*aozora*) above. One need merely look up to see their own ideas and those of others etched, as if by chalk, in the clouds.[9] Tomita's dream of a library in the sky to which anyone had free access as a consumer *or* producer of content stands in contrast to the archival ambitions of Google Books, the profit motivations of Amazon Books, or even the noncommercial Project Gutenberg, a crowd-sourced digital library that was an inspiring model for Tomita and Noguchi that already hosted one thousand titles by 1996. As Aozora grew, however, this emphasis on production waned and the horizons of Tomita's boundless blue sky narrowed.

Although the horizons narrowed along the dimension of content, they remained broad with respect to access and ownership. Two years after its founding in 1997, the project had more than one hundred volunteers inputting and proofreading texts to be added to the collection. There was internal debate about how this labor would be acknowledged and rewarded, but there was never any question that out-of-copyright material belonged to no single entity and must forever circulate freely.[10] Ostensibly, this meant any work whose author had been deceased for fifty years and upon which there were no additional copyright claims. Beyond this single restriction, volunteers could digitize whatever they wished. The only selection oversight provided by project coordinators was a list of authors dead for more than fifty years and an inventory of which works had already been claimed by volunteers (to avoid duplicate efforts). With these minimal restrictions in place, the number of works in the collection grew from ten in 1997 to five hundred in 1999, seventeen hundred by 2001, forty-seven hundred by 2005, and to nearly sixteen thousand works by 2018. Lacking direct oversight on what to include, the operative logic of selection is effectively the cumulative contingent choices of hundreds of individuals constrained by the intersecting trajectories of biography (i.e., mortality), copyright law, and the availability of texts. Given this bottom-up, laissez-faire method of selection, what claims on representation of literary history might Aozora have? What is the sample of "modern Japanese literature" captured by the wisdom of the crowd and the materials available to them for reproducing textual artifacts? What, in the end, can such a sample tell us?

This brings us squarely back to the problem of sampling as method. The notion that a greater body of evidence naturally better represents the whole of some phenomenon is a basic tenet of quantitative approaches to literary and cultural history. It is also one of its most anxiety inducing at the level of disciplinary practice. To argue for the value of such approaches requires reckoning with their insistence on examining many texts for synchronic or diachronic patterns instead of individual works through a richly elaborated set of contextual references. This insistence cuts at the heart of literary criticism's institutional identity, which has for more than a century privileged deep and intensive interpretation of single objects in ways that preserve their aesthetic autonomy (and so too the autonomy of the critic).[11] To create and analyze a sample of texts in order to generalize from them is, some claim, "to violate the individuality of the text" or "deliberately elide the particulars that make the study of literature critical."[12] In the space between the idea of sampling and the closely read case study—a dichotomy whose vociferous defense reinforces how entrenched the latter is in literary criticism as a disciplinary formation—emerges what Andrew Piper calls an "evidence gap." This gap calls attention to the ways that we, as interpreters of textual meaning at any scale, establish "the representativeness of our own evidence" for how part relates to whole, text to context. It also exposes the disciplinary practices and epistemological assumptions that inform the defense of one kind of representativeness over others.[13]

To caricature the debate at its extremes, a primary defense of reading individual texts intensively and closely is that this is the only way to attend to all of their variation and to language's inherent ambiguities. Relating high-dimensional and highly particular objects to others in lower dimensional equivalence spaces erases their individual complexity. It denies to interpretation a "chromatic plenitude," as Jonathan Culler calls it: "A playing of all possible notes in all possible registers."[14] Defenders of computational methods, on the other hand, point out that the complexity of the particular case is invariably used to make broader claims about the nature and evolution of literary and historical discourse. It is singular and exemplary all at once. But this exemplariness is often assumed from textual evidence that represents only a fraction of everything said or written in a given period. Given the unprecedented ability to observe so much more of this background with digital methods, or so the argument goes, one should explore more cases to validate existing claims and strengthen support for generalizations made with them.[15] From one side sampling appears to undermine interpretation itself by ignoring all the variation and ambiguity that attends the individual text. From the other it looks as though literary criticism has all along been restricted to making arguments with samples of one (i.e., the case study).

Both sides ultimately rely on competing theories of how to generalize from the particular, even when this theorizing is defined in opposition to generalization itself as a form of knowledge construction. As Lauren Berlant argues, the case as genre "hovers about the singular, the general, and the normative."[16] Even when there is an appeal to the singularity concept as "that which resists being generalizable," this appeal runs "antagonistically into the prevalence of case-study narrativity in scholarship, which mobilizes a whole variety of descriptive and interpretive processes of determining likeness, generality, or patterning."[17] Conversely, the explicit construction of samples that scaled-up modes of reading demand, and the many ways proposed for explicating the relation of specific parts to specific contexts, entails its own assumptions about individual variation and difference. If methods for relating part to whole have been more formalized in disciplines outside literary studies, this formalization has always entailed its own set of narrative practices for dealing with cases. The point is not to choose one set of practices over another but to ask, citing Berlant again, "how certain norms of making a case got to be that way in a given domain of expertise" and to consider how these norms might complement one another in domains that treat one or the other as the only legitimate path to knowledge.[18]

Part of the reason the aspiration to read at greater scales rankles critics of computational methods is because the emphasis on reading more is often conflated with an ambition to read everything. The latter smacks of a positivist outlook where exhaustive representation is believed to produce absolute truth and a God's eye view of the world. The conflation is understandable given that the rise of computational criticism has coincided with the rise of data science and the hype surrounding "big data" as a means of producing knowledge about the world. As scholars in the emerging field of critical data studies have pointed out, this hype is predicated on the notion that access to vast amounts of data about human interaction provide an objectivity that obviates the need for theory.[19] Samples acquired through social media platforms are so large now that one can mistake them for snapshots of reality in toto, but size is deceiving. It obscures the biases inherent in these data sets by virtue of how the data is collected. Having access to billions of Facebook or Twitter posts creates the illusion that one is observing a whole population when one is really seeing mixtures of subpopulations based on who has access to these platforms and on their platform specific effects.[20] More generally, size obscures the reality that any large data set is also a "data assemblage" built from "systems of thought, forms of knowledge, finance, political economy, governmentalities and legalities, materialities and infrastructures, practices, organizations and institutions, subjectivities and communities, places, and the marketplace where data are constituted."[21] Rather than obviating the need for theory, these data assemblages demand critical reflection on the histories of their construction and the ways they are taken for representations *and* samples of the world.[22]

The same holds for digital collections that have been built by libraries, research centers, open-source platforms such as Aozora, or private interests—each a product of specific institutional forces, material histories, and selection practices.[23] To critique them as obvious constructions, however, requires more than writing them off as irrevocably compromised or irrelevant to the ways we already have of knowing the literary archive. Any representation of the archive, however it may be mediated, is partial. Access to digital collections and the new evidence gaps they create are an opportunity to reflect on the partiality of knowledge past and present, and to problematize anew the notion of representativeness, not an excuse to double down on the fallacies of exhaustiveness or the irreducibility of the singular case. They should provoke the creation of a more flexible and nuanced language with which to think about how much evidence is enough to make a specific generalization and, conversely, how much is too little.

Developing this language means looking outside of received disciplinary practices for relating part to whole. Within literary studies proper, the last decade or more has seen an internal interrogation of these practices and a proliferation of new or newly revived methods for turning textual evidence into interpretation and argument.[24] Although generative, the splintering of "close reading" into myriad interpretive modes has done little to disrupt the dominance of "case-study narrativity." In disciplines that have longer histories of dealing with quantity, there is a much richer, although no less contested, set of strategies for relating evidence to argument beyond the confines of the case study. Whether in statistics, where the idea that sampling could approximate larger populations took decades to establish, or in more recently quantified fields such as sociology, in which case-study and non-case-study approaches represent intellectual trade-offs rather than winner-take-all strategies, there is much to learn from how others have thought the relation of parts to wholes.[25]

SAMPLING TEXTS AND CONTEXTS

One particularly instructive field is content analysis. Although its origins can be traced to the eighteenth century, it emerged as a coherent method in the 1930s and 1940s in an effort by the empirical social sciences to respond to new kinds of information overload, namely, the rise of mass media forms (particularly newspapers) and their weaponization by the state for propaganda. Led by key figures in communication studies such as Harold Lasswell, Bernard Berelson, and Paul Lazarsfeld, content analysis was interested in how these forms shaped public opinion and were themselves shaped by specific ideologies. To understand them, however, meant being able to read large bodies of texts and images in a less impressionistic and conjectural way. They had to be read systematically to "combat the human tendency to read textual material selectively, in support of expectations rather than against them."[26]

At the time, numbers were seen as integral to achieving such systematicity and were deployed to describe the manifest content of mass communication (e.g., stereotypes, ideological messages) with the belief that such content resided *inside* the texts or images in question.[27] As the field matured, however, and found new applications in historical and literary study, this emphasis on quantification was tempered and the definition of "content" made relative to the contexts of use in which content, and its multiple potential meanings, are situated. What has continued to matter for content analysis are the problems of scale (how to read more texts than a single person can manage), systematicity (how to read for meaning in ways both replicable and consistent), and inference (how to relate the patterns of meaning observed to the contexts that can explain them). On this last point, Berelson and Lazarsfeld were clear from the beginning: "There is no point in counting unless the frequencies lead to inferences about the conditions surrounding what is counted."[28]

When we look back to the first large-scale attempts at quantitative stylistics by Japanese scholars in the 1950s and 1960s, it can seem at times that they missed this critical point, as if they were counting just to count. Put more generously, their counting led them not toward inferences about a set of text's external conditions but to inferences about more texts. Klaus Krippendorff, in his instructive primer on content analysis, makes a critical distinction between these two types of inference. The first, inductive inference, entails generalizations to similar kinds, as when the characteristics of a larger population are inferred from what one observes in a sample of that population, or even in a single case. The early progenitor of quantitative stylistics, Hatano Kanji, was making an inductive inference when he concluded that Tanizaki Jun'ichirō tended to write longer sentences after finding that the sentences in a single work were on average longer than in works by his contemporaries.

Abductive inference, in contrast, proceeds by matching particulars internal to some set of texts with particulars external to them (a hypothesis or analytical construct that best explains the observations). Logically, neither has to imply the other, and inferences about their relation can only be made with some degree of probability. This probability increases the more an analytical construct takes other conditions or variables into account. When Hatano sought to explain the tendency to write longer sentences by relating it to Tanizaki's psychopathology, he was making an abductive inference, albeit one weakly supported by empirical evidence.[29] That is, he was making a generalization based on observing a particular feature across many separate textual instances and inferring their patterned relation to another set of particulars (i.e., the writer's state of mind or creative intentions). For Krippendorff, such generalizations in content analysis aim not toward "accurate representations of the textual universe" but toward "construct[ing] a world in which the texts make sense and can answer the analyst's research questions," even if within this world certain questions become answerable and others make no sense. This world, this context, is "the analyst's best hypothesis for how the texts came to be, what they mean, what they can tell or do."[30]

Krippendorff's description of the analyst's task will feel familiar to literary critics who seek to relate individual texts to contexts. The difference is that to read many texts in a consistent way content analysts are less able to let the hermeneutic process unfold across many divergent contexts, switching from one to the next as interpretation proceeds. They can still respond to multiple contexts, but for any one they must stop and *explicitly* construct the world in which the observations recorded from a body of texts "make sense" to the inferences they wish to draw. This involves choosing the sample of texts (and then the sample of features within those texts) that best supports the sense one wants to make. Here is where content analysis as interpretive method is useful for literary critics thinking across the evidence gap opened by the digital turn. It is, first of all, explicit about the relations it constructs between part and whole, whether the relation is of feature to text or of texts to context. Second, it offers several methods for positing these relations and a language for specifying how they bias and constrain the inferences one can make with them. There is less need for such explicitness when dealing with a handful of texts, as one can hold and turn each one, like a gem, to refract the light of one context and then another. Each text becomes the lens through which these contexts (aesthetic, discursive, political, historical) hold together and are made to support interpretative claims on the object. Try generalizing these claims across many more texts, however, and it becomes impossible to hold them all up simultaneously to so many rays of light. This is where sampling becomes a valuable heuristic for generalizing about more texts over a narrower range of contexts.

In plainest terms, sampling is motivated by questions whose scope exceeds the evidence that is available or possible to observe. One samples when one cannot read everything relevant to the inferences one wants to make. And when one believes that not every unit of observation is absolutely the same, in which case it would be enough to look at a *single* instance, nor absolutely different, in which case it would be necessary to look at *every* instance. Sampling carves out a space in between these extreme ontologies, although different sampling techniques will do so based on different assumptions. The techniques of "traditional sampling theory," for instance, as developed in survey research, make several strong assumptions that rarely hold for texts in the ways they do for people: that the individuals sampled are independent of one another; that these sampled individuals are the units being counted; that every individual is equally informative on the questions being asked; and that the sample has the same distributional properties as the population it is meant to represent (e.g., the proportion of men and women in the sample matches the proportion in the population).[31] These assumptions give traditional sampling theory its statistical power, and is the power to which proponents of quantitative method in the 1950s and 1960s appealed when, as noted in chapter 1, they created their samples of "modern Japanese literature."

This power wanes, however, to the extent that sampled units are not equally informative with respect to the questions being asked. As Krippendorff argues, content analysts "have to consider at least two populations at once: the population of answers to a research question and the population of texts that contains or leads to the answers to that question." He suggests several sampling strategies for bringing these populations into alignment. One is "relevance sampling," also called *purposive* sampling, which involves selecting texts based on how well they help answer a given research question. The criteria for a text's relevance may be the use of certain keywords, or inclusion in a particular type of publication, and is left to the analyst to specify. One does not sample probabilistically to represent some "true" underlying population of texts but rather constructs the population of relevant texts and samples from this much smaller universe. The critical difference is that this universe is recognized as an artificial world and not presumed to be a stand-in for the world itself. A slightly more formalized technique is called "cluster sampling," which is useful when one can identify lists of larger groups, or clusters, from which to sample randomly or systematically one's primary unit of analysis (e.g., articles, paragraphs, sentences). These might be journals and magazines containing literary works; genre labels assigned by critics or historical actors; or well-defined aesthetic movements in which works, and authors, can be grouped. Here, sampling bias can enter in if the units of analysis are unevenly distributed across the clusters, thus making it more difficult to justify statistical generalizations. A final, more formal strategy is "varying probability sampling," which Krippendorff defines as useful when one can weight texts by their probability of relevance to a given research question. If the question pertains to the cultural influence of texts, for instance, one might consult best-seller lists, reviews, or book awards to sample more heavily from higher-ranked texts. One could also use this method to reverse known biases in normative discourse by giving greater weight to voices excluded from it.[32] These strategies illustrate some of the considerations that go into constructing the world against which generalizations about a body of texts make sense. Although more constrained than the process of selecting exemplary cases, where relevance can be defined over multiple contexts at once, the strategies are no less open to the critical subjectivity of the researcher who defines "relevance" in relation to her questions and contexts of interest. Compared to these strategies, the samples produced for stylistic analysis in the 1950s and 1960s by Nakamura and others look ad hoc and ill-defined, conflating "relevance" with inclusion in a literary anthology.

Another point of contrast from the predigital era comes from 1980, when researchers at the National Japanese Language Research Institute aimed to compile a new dictionary of modern Japanese. Their first step was to build a concordance of one hundred "representative literary works" (totaling more than three million words) from which to select example sentences for the dictionary. Like their predecessors, they first turned to literary anthologies as an index of value or importance. Instead of one anthology, however, they used fifteen, starting with Kaizōsha's sixty-three volume *Gendai Nihon bungaku zenshū* (1926–1931) and ending with Chikuma Shobō's ninety-seven volume *Chikuma gendai bungaku taikei* (1975–1979). And instead of relying on one person's expertise, they convened a committee of ten prominent scholars and writers to select representative works, including major critics Maeda Ai, Nakamura Mitsuo, and Kōno Toshirō. Each committee member was asked to select one hundred works from a master list of 1,506—the number of works included in at least three of the fifteen anthologies. At this initial stage they were performing a loose kind of varying probability sampling on a population of texts deemed representative by virtue of anthologization, and where texts received greater weight the more they had been anthologized across the previous half-century.

This led to a second round of sampling as committee members selected their one hundred works based on a complex and sometimes contradictory set of criteria. The works had to be "representative" (*daihyō-teki*) in the sense of being by "well-known" (*chomei na*) authors and having high "artistic value" (*bungei-teki kachi*); they had to be widely read in their own time or continually read up to the present day; they preferably did not contain heavy use of dialect; and finally, they could not skew toward any one author or time period. This was a more amorphous and, as a result, a more subjective kind of probability sampling carried out over multiple dimensions of value. There is also no way to know how each member chose to emphasize any one of these criteria. Any discrepancies were washed out in the final step, which singled out 139 works selected by four or more members. Chronologically they range from Sanyūtei Enchō's *Kaidan botan dōrō* (A ghost story: the peony lantern, 1884) to Ōe Kenzaburō's "Shisha no ogori" (Lavish are the dead, 1957), with the majority falling between 1901 and 1950.

Does this sample better represent "modern Japanese literature" than those created by Nakamura or Kabashima? It feels more authoritative because it draws on collective expertise and a larger data set. But the question, as a detour through content analysis shows, is too imprecise. The validity of the sample as a representation of some population gains to the degree to which the process of construction is oriented around a specific research question and grounded in a specific interpretive context. Here, the different axes on which works were asked to be ranked, and the lack of a research question, makes it difficult to assess the sample's validity on its own. Some biases have likely been evened out, but new ones have just as likely been produced. Only nine of these "representative" works, for instance, or about 6 percent, are by women.[33]

Every sampling strategy produces biases that over- or underrepresent aspects of the phenomenon being investigated and that must be accounted for in one's analysis. Content analysis offers a more principled language with which to think about these biases relative to the interpretive contexts built around our objects of study and the questions we ask of them. It is also a more explicit language that lends itself to collective critique, replication, or refinement. This is one crucial advantage of the sample just described, however vague its explanation of selection criteria. No such advantage can be ascribed to Aozora. It is a sample of "modern Japanese literature" in the way an ice core is a sample of historical climate patterns, produced from myriad unknowable selection processes, local material constraints, and its status as an online platform. It is what Krippendorff calls a "convenience sample"—a body of texts on which no sampling effort is made and which thus leaves "uncertain whether the texts that are being analyzed are representative of the phenomena . . . the analysts tend to infer."[34] This label applies to any digital archive whose size is taken as sufficient justification for its representativeness. The "bigness" of big data lures the analyst into thinking that a sample *is* the population, or that it can provide an unbiased estimate of dominant patterns within that population.

Aozora is not so large that we might naively generalize its quantitative properties to all of "modern Japanese literature." Such generalizations are rarely the point of computational literary history, and indeed the experiments to follow use a combination of more selective and purposive sampling techniques, filling in Aozora's inevitable gaps where necessary to pursue specific research questions. At other times they try to control for the effects of bias by extracting patterns across many samples to see how they hold up across these samples. Yet because the experiments still use Aozora as a starting point, we cannot ignore its particular relation to that global system of literary valuation of which it is one localized trace. What residual effects of this system do we find etched into its compound layers? In which directions do they skew? Before applying lessons from content analysis about how to sample, we need to understand what we are sampling from. What are the research questions to which Aozora is best suited, the evidence gaps it can help to narrow? This, in turn, is a chance to reflect on the partiality of other existing traces of the global system and to show how their comparison opens new ways of thinking about individual texts in relation to their many possible contexts.

AOZORA BUNKO AS SAMPLE—THE CASE OF WORLD LITERATURE

To understand Aozora as a sample of the literary past first requires subsetting out the works of prose fiction. What initially looks like an impressive number of texts (about 14,300 with duplicates removed) masks their diverse generic difference.[35] Based on the Nihon Decimal Classification (NDC) subject codes assigned to each text, almost 40 percent (5,575 texts) of the collection is fiction. Within this category, 20 percent (1,134 texts) are further classified as juvenile fiction. The next largest categories are essays and criticism (26 percent, or 3,695 texts), poetry (10 percent, or 1,425 texts), works related to theater and drama (4 percent, or 612 texts), and social science material (also 4 percent, or 611 texts). At the low end are categories such as history, letters and diaries, aesthetics, and religion and philosophy, all of which contribute 3 percent or less to the total collection. Together, the collection represents the output of 856 unique authors, including poets as old as Sappho (630–580 BCE) and writers born as late as the 1930s, with the majority (over 60 percent) of them born in the last half of the nineteenth century.

Text length is another feature that exposes the collection's diversity. For those interested in analyzing prose fiction, whether longer novels or shorter stories, Aozora's scope rapidly narrows since many of the works equate to just a few pages of printed text. At the extreme ends of the distribution are Miyamoto Yuriko's epic novel *Dōhyō* (Signposts), a semiautobiographical work from the immediate postwar, and a haiku by Hagiwara Sakutarō ("Returning from Israel, I stand alone on top of the snow"). Plotting the overall distribution by sorting the titles according to length in characters, we see that the haiku is far more characteristic of the length of texts in the collection (figure 2.1). To get a more precise sense of this, we can look at what falls in the middle of the distribution by calculating the average, or *mean*, text length. Close to the average is Hayashi Fumiko's "Shitamachi" (Downtown), a classic postwar short story that runs to twenty-three pages in the pocket-size edition (*bunkobon*). The average can be a deceptive marker of the "middle," however, given its sensitivity to outliers such as *Dōhyō*, which is 30 percent longer than the next longest text. Another statistic for indicating the middle of a distribution is the *median*, which is the point that divides the top half of observations from the bottom half. Here the median text length is about a third of the average, or as long as "Tsukiyo no denshinbashira" (Telegraph poles on a moonlit night), a children's story by Miyazawa Kenji that runs to just nine pages in its *bunkobon* edition.[36] Selecting out just the "fiction" titles and plotting the distribution of their lengths as a histogram (figure 2.2), the bulk of them still tend to be short, with the median length falling roughly

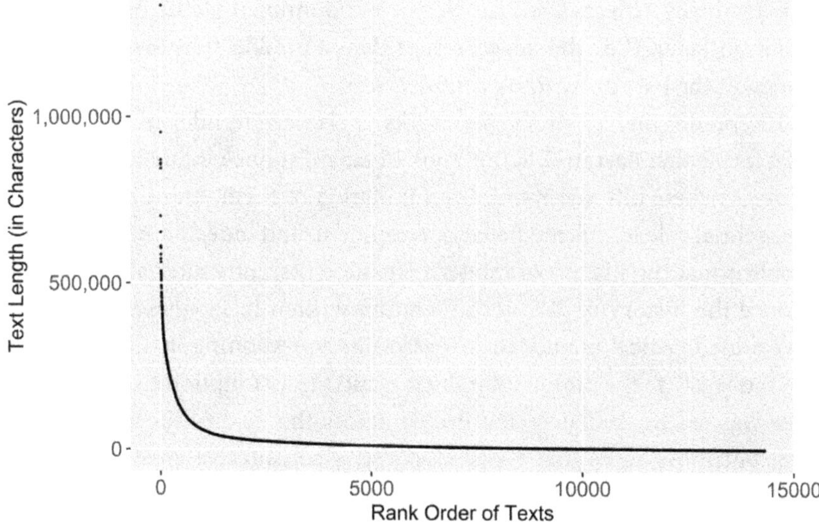

FIGURE 2.1. Distribution by text length (measured in characters) of 14,300 titles in Aozora. Titles are ranked by length and plotted from longest (Miyamoto Yuriko's *Dōhyō*) to shortest (Hagiwara Sakutarō's haiku).

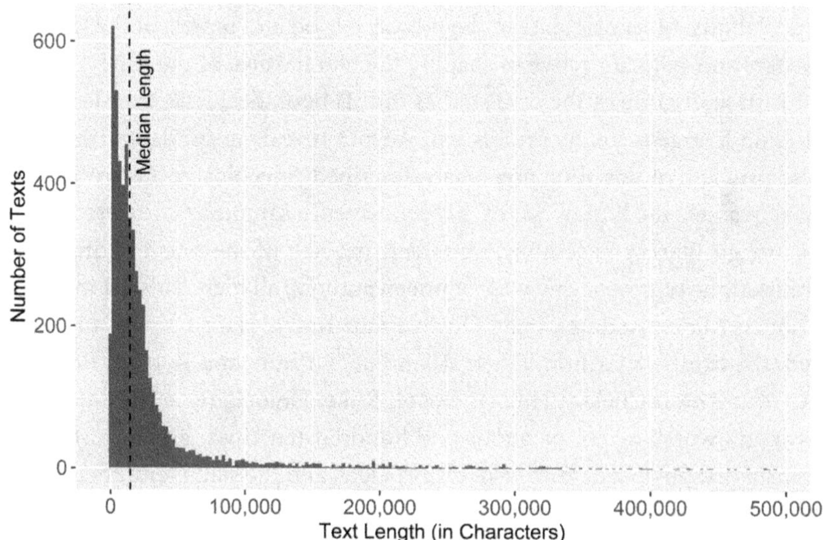

FIGURE 2.2. The distribution by length of the 5,550 titles categorized as "fiction" in Aozora. Each column represents the number of titles of a specific length. About 350 titles fall near the median length of 6,710 characters.

between "Shitamachi" (20,036) and "Tsukiyo no denshinbashira" (6,878). This tendency reflects the historically less dominant status of long form fiction in Japan (i.e., the novel) rather than a predilection toward shorter works on the part of Aozora's volunteers.

The predominance of shorter works is also a reminder of the specific local forms that narrative fiction took in Japan, at once influenced by ideas from elsewhere but never simply an imitation of them. Translation played an essential role in this mediated development, and indeed it has long been a truism that the history of modern Japanese literature after about 1890 is at once the history of "Western literature written in Japanese."[37] Scholars have added critical nuance to this assertion, questioning its narrow focus on "the West" as the dominant influence and the assumption that this influence was felt immediately and evenly across the field of literary production, but most agree that translation was a constitutive creative force of modern Japanese literature at the level of both content and form.[38] Any attempt to represent literary output of the period must acknowledge the presence of this "foreign literary hegemony," strong or weak as it was relative to other national literatures. The legacy of this hegemony is reflected in Aozora too, a collection of ostensibly "Japanese" language texts that has a sizable amount of translated works, of which four hundred fifty are literary translations. Most originate in the prewar period and represent the labor of writers and scholars active in shaping the literary field at the time.

Although none of the case studies in this book deal with translated fiction on a large scale, its presence in Aozora reveals in miniature the twofold problem of sampling previously described. Specifically, the problem of how to assess the limitations of this convenience sample as a representation of foreign literary hegemony. Consider that half of the four hundred fifty translations represent the work of fifteen authors, all men. This list includes Thomas Mann, Arthur Conan Doyle, Franz Kafka, Hans Christian Andersen, the Brothers Grimm, Edgar Allen Poe, Lu Xun, and Romain Rolland; but also Anton Chekov, Nikolai Gogol, Rilke, Baudelaire, and Dante. Half as many works again, or about one hundred ten titles, are by just three translators: poet Ueda Bin, writer Mori Ōgai, and Russian literature scholar Jinzai Kiyoshi. The influence of all of these figures is well attested in scholarship, but at this small scale, and without a research context in which to relate them, the choices underlying this particular arrangement of foreign literature feels arbitrary and random at best. How might we assess the gap between this arrangement and those we believe are a better reflection of the actual composition of foreign literary hegemony in the prewar period?

We could look to history itself and to representations of foreign literature that seemed reasonable at the time. After 1927, writers and readers in Japan would almost certainly have pointed to *Sekai bungaku zenshū* (Anthology of world literature) as one such representation. Published by Shinchōsha, this two-part, fifty-seven volume series was immensely popular and helped change the face of commercial publishing. Part of the *enpon* (one-yen) book boom that saw the emergence of a competitive market for cheap, multivolume series of modern great books, older classics, and other less high-minded collections for the masses, Shinchōsha's series emerged a clear winner, selling more than four hundred thousand complete sets compared with rival Kaizōsha's "modern Japanese literature" series, which sold just two hundred fifty thousand.[39] The series was the latest in a long process of selecting, sorting, and canonizing the mass of foreign texts available for import or translation, whether by critics producing lists of notable books; by librarians curating the shelves for an expanding network of public libraries, or by educators eager to manage "international intercourse" in the Japanese language classroom.[40] Beyond Japan, the series paralleled developments in British and American commercial publishing that from the 1890s saw the confluence of the "scholarly list" mode with the mass-market "enterprising" mode to produce what has been called a "patriarchal capitalist" mode.[41] Out of this mode came series like Routledge's "World Library," "World Classics" by Oxford University Press, and J. M. Dent's "Everyman Library for Young People," created in 1905 with the ambitious goal of publishing one thousand great works. Reducing an infinite sea of texts to a curated selection, these series were meant to educate the masses as much as to keep the lay reader "out of the grog shop or away from newspapers."[42]

The affinity of *Sekai bungaku zenshū* with this patriarchal capitalist mode is made clear in the unprecedented two-page ad that series editor Satō Giryō created in 1927 and in which he claimed that the series was equivalent in content and price to Everyman's Library.[43] This was pure salesmanship in terms of the actual number of works, but part 1 of the anthology contains many similar authors and titles (table 2.1). Dante, Goethe, Milton, Shakespeare, and Cervantes were there to represent the classics; Hugo, Balzac, Dickens, Flaubert, Maupassant, Tolstoy, Turgenev, Dostoevsky, Poe, and Hawthorne stood in for the nineteenth-century novel; Chekov,

TABLE 2.1
Authors and works anthologized in part 1 of *Sekai bungaku zenshū*

Author	**Translated Work(s)**
Dante	*Divine Comedy*
Boccacio	*Decameron*
Shakespeare	*Hamlet, Romeo and Juliet*
Cervantes	*Don Quixote*
Milton	*Paradise Lost*
Walter Scott	*Ivanhoe*
Rousseau	*Confessions*
Goethe	*Faust*
Poe	*Selections*
Nathaniel Hawthorne	*Scarlet Letter*
Victor Hugo	*Les Miserables*
Alexandre Dumas	*Count of Monte Christo*
Balzac	*Selections from The Human Comedy*
Charles Dickens	*Tale of Two Cities*
Emile Zola	*L'Assommoir*
Flaubert	*Madame Bovary*
Guy de Maupassant	*A Woman's Life*
Ivan Turgenev	*Fathers and Sons, Virgin Soil*
Dostoyevsky	*Crime and Punishment*
Tolstoy	*Resurrection*
Chekhov	*Selections*
Maxim Gorky	*Selections*
Sienkiewicz	*Quo Vadis*
Henrik Ibsen	*Selections*
Bjornson	*Selections*
Knut Hamsun	*Hunger*
Strindberg	*Confessions of a Fool, Dance of Death*
Thomas Hardy	*Tess of the D'urbervilles*
Joseph Conrad	*Selections*
D'annunzio	*Triumph of Death*
Daudet	*Sappho*
Hauptmann	*Selections*
Maurice Maeterlinck	*Monna Vanna*
Schniztler	*Selections*
Anatole France	*Thais, Crainquebille*
Henri Barbusse	*Hell*
Charles Phillipe	*Bubu of Montparnasse*
Bernard Shaw	*Selections*
John Galsworthy	*Selections*
Synge	*Selections*
Rostand	*Cyrano de Bergerac*
Romain Rolland	*The Wolf*

Gorky, Maeterlinck, Ibsen, and Hamsun, among others, added more contemporary fare.[44] Satō, like Dent, also framed the series as part pedagogical and part civilizing mission, touting it as a "giant textbook for the study of humanity" and "a necessary qualification for being a global citizen." But the masses were not the only market he and Shinchōsha were after. They knew that the works had to appeal just as much to those writers and intellectuals who would confer on them the cultural capital necessary to make them valuable. When prominent political theorist Yoshino Sakuzō authored a promotional piece in *Tokyo nichinichi shinbun* (Tokyo daily newspaper) in advance of the series' publication, he quoted a friend who, upon seeing the two-page ad, exclaimed that every title, to the very last one, was "food for the soul and a work that should always be close at hand. I want them all so bad I'm ready to rush out and get them."[45] This was a textbook for the masses as much as an ornament displaying that one had already absorbed the lessons contained therein.

The window that the Shinchōsha series provides onto historical conceptions of world literature in Japan is easily explained by Pierre Bourdieu's idea of a "dual discourse," which suggests that the democratization and mass production of a culture's "classics" is always partly an opening up of knowledge only after it has been "permitted, authenticated and ultimately cheapened by the upper strata, whether these are the aristocrats and officials who endorse the books or the professionals and intellectuals who edit and publish them."[46] But this is not the only way to read the intentions behind these choices. In her study of Oxford's "World Classics" series, Mary Hammond reminds us that a sociological frame can obscure more prosaic rationales for text selection. For the editor of "World Classics," what often took precedence over aesthetic merit or canonical recognition was whether a work was out of copyright and cheap to acquire; its length suitable to the series' format; and its content inoffensive to lower- and middle-class readers. Shinchōsha, for its part, had been publishing literary translations for a decade, and more than 60 percent of the titles in part 1 had been published in earlier formats.[47] Editor Satō was also adamant about including translations that would be highly legible to mass audiences and took extra measures to edit each translation for clarity even when it was a previously published title.[48] Such pragmatic rationales make the process by which some works are plucked from global flows to be translated and later canonized seem all the more contingent.

These contingencies raise again the question of how reasonable was this arrangement of writers and works as a representation of what was being translated and circulated prior to this moment. How arbitrary were the editor's selections? If they were partly biased by the twin interests of profit and pedagogy, how far and in what direction did they skew? Contextualizing the seeming contingency of these selections requires, as scholars of world literature and book history have shown, an attention to processes of anthologization and curricular canonization; the role of publishers in shaping market dynamics; reception as imbricated in institutional and archival histories; and the effects of translatability and aesthetic form.[49] Here I contend that the bibliographic record itself can be a means of delimiting the contingency often read into acts of selection. Contingent decisions naturally compound over time, lending a historical gravity to the value of works that becomes visible at the scale of this record, or at least the traces of it that are available to us. In the rest of this section, I show how this visibility can help to contextualize the perceived arbitrariness of the representations of world literature in the Shinchōsha anthology, but also in Aozora.

Of all the bibliographic traces assembled in this chapter, the one for translations traveled the longest route to become digital data. Scanned and hand input from two print resources, it is incomplete in parts and noisy in others due to errors introduced by optical character recognition (OCR). It also bears the peculiar histories of these two resources. The first, *Meiji-ki hon'yaku bungaku sōgō nenpyō*, covers the Meiji period (1868–1912) and provides a comprehensive list of 4,510 literary translations in all genres published in newspapers, magazines, or individual books. Entries are listed by year and categorized by the source author's country of origin.[50] A second resource, *Meiji • Taishō • Shōwa hon'yaku bungaku mokuroku*, covers 1912–1955 and is a nearly eight hundred page index compiled by the National Diet Library.[51] Each of the nearly twenty-eight thousand entries, representing works by 2,398 foreign authors, includes metadata about the author's country of origin, dates of publication, translator, and publisher. Like the Meiji index, it records literary translations across all genres but is limited to stand-alone volumes or multivolume sets, including reprints. It is thus blind to the mass of translated material published in general interest and small coterie magazines, which could shift attention more quickly to the newest literary imports.[52] Both resources are mostly blind to literature outside of Euro-America and Russia, thus reinforcing the equation of "world" with "the West," which was also integral to Shinchōsha's vision. Not one Chinese writer, for example, is included in either bibliography.

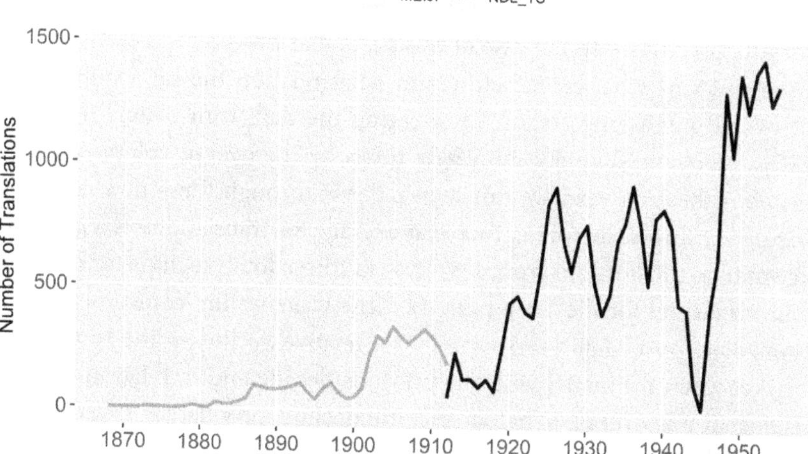

FIGURE 2.3. Counts of literary translations into Japanese from 1868–1955. The Meiji period data (MEIJI) is graphed separately from the Taishō and Shōwa period data (NDL_TS) because they come from separate bibliographic sources. The Meiji period ended in July 1912, so two data points are shown for that year; data from the two periods are not combined.

Although bearing the symptoms of a particular definition of world literature, insights can still be gleaned from these bibliographic traces. Here I concentrate on the temporal aspects of the data as they help to situate the selections made by editors of the Shinchōsha anthology. Figure 2.3 shows the raw counts of translated items by year for both bibliographic data sources. Every indexed translation is counted equally, whether it is a long form novel published as a stand-alone volume, a short story included in a collection, or a poem from an anthology. This figure already tempts us with several stories about how the field of literary production's relationship with translation evolved over this period. There is a clear story of decline as the Pacific War (along with state censorship and resource scarcity) reached its climax, although overall publication trends are needed to contextualize this decline. There are also less obvious stories about translation's rapid rise from the war's ashes and its equally rapid rise in the 1920s, peaking at about nine hundred translations just as Shinchōsha was preparing to release its anthology. One of the most surprising potential stories is that there was so much room for the translation market to grow after what looks like several years of stagnation in the teens. Did the market really contract so much relative to the years before and after? Was it because the publishing industry as a whole was in a slump?

These questions are a reminder that no data provide a sufficient explanatory context on their own. Data always beget more data (i.e., other contexts for interpretation). In the case of this particular low point in the teens, we need to know what came before and what relation the raw counts have to overall publishing trends. By merging the data with counts from the Meiji index and dividing the yearly totals by the overall volume of publications for each year, we can revisualize it through these new contexts. Figure 2.4 shows the rolling two-year average for translations as a percentage of total publications from 1883 to 1942 (these totals include newspapers and magazines for the Meiji period).[53] The visualization confirms that the immediate post-Meiji years represent a relative decline in the translation market when compared with the previous decade and in relation to publishing trends overall. What caused the decline, or whether it was felt as such at the time, is beyond the scope of this chapter.[54] We might look to the "High Treason Incident" (*taigyaku jiken*) of 1910, which put a chill on political and literary expression in these years as the government clamped down on material deemed subversive or detrimental to traditional morality. Foreign books and literary translations were seen as particularly dangerous in this light and were already subject to suppression by Home Ministry censors.[55] We might consider whether dominant aesthetic movements in these years, whether the self-centered Naturalism of I-novel writers or the

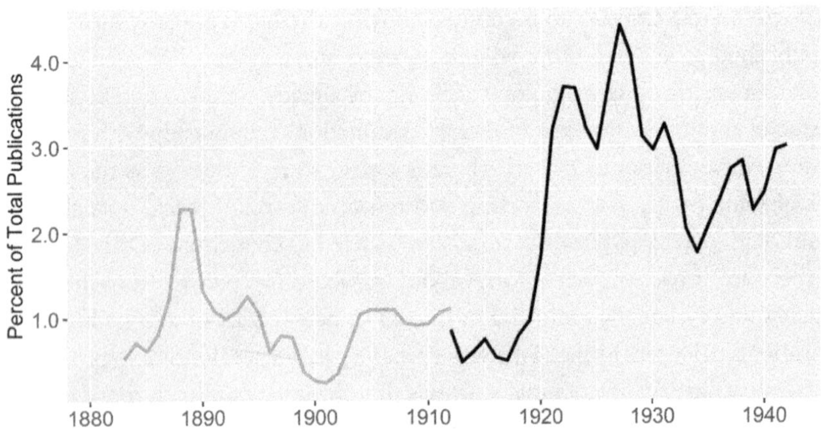

FIGURE 2.4. Literary translations as a percent of total publications from 1883 to 1942, displayed as a rolling two-year average. The total publication figures include books, magazines, and newspapers until 1912, but only books after that point.

opposing antipolitical aestheticism (*tanbishugi*) of Nagai Kafū and others, led to a general inward turn. Or perhaps translators simply shifted their efforts toward magazines and other media not captured in this data set.

The bibliographic record is only an entry point into deeper qualitative inquiry, but by contextualizing its temporal dynamics we can construct periodizations that are not discernible at higher resolutions. If literary translation entered its own "winter years" from 1913 to 1918, as the figure seems to indicate, how might this evidence add to more localized ideological, aesthetic, or institutional evidence brought to bear on our reading of individual acts of translation? Knowing, for instance, that Tolstoy, Emerson, Maupassant, and Goethe were most widely translated in these years—a period that saw the median birth year of all translated authors drop significantly, bottoming out at 1810, or roughly 108 years in the past (figure 2.5)—the next most translated author, novelist, and playwright, John Galsworthy (1867–1933), and future Nobel laureate, stands out all the more. Ōtani Gyōseki's decision in 1914 to publish twenty-three of his recent dramatic sketches, some of which bore the political consciousness of class and gender issues for which he was just coming to be known, seems all the more fresh, radical,

FIGURE 2.5. The approximate number of years into the past that translators and publishers were looking between 1912 and 1955. For each year, distance into the past is determined by subtracting the weighted median birth year of all translated authors from that year. This distance is displayed as a rolling two-year average. Around 1918, the distance was just over 100 years. In the late 1940s, it bottomed out again at 135 years (or roughly 1813). At the time that *Sekai bungaku zenshū* was being published, the distance peaks at just under 70 years, suggesting that a larger number of relatively newer authors were being translated.

and prescient.[56] As the market for translations recovered from an apparent downturn in the teens, building to a wave that crested just as *Sekai bungaku zenshū* was published (1929), we might wonder how striking its choices were in light of that wave and its aftermath. Did they reflect and reinforce past trends, or did they deviate from them, signaling futures to come?

To reframe this quantitatively, we can imagine each author's record of translation into Japanese as a temporal trend line, calculating the percentage of all translations attributed to that author for each year. Alternatively, we can aggregate the trend lines of many authors together, showing how much collective attention is given to them by the publishing market each year. With *Sekai bungaku zenshū*, for instance, it makes sense to group authors based on the part in which they were included because the editorial calculus differed for each part. Authors in part 1 were generally older, more canonical figures, with a median birth year of 1836. Authors in part 2, which began publication in 1930, skew younger, with a median birth year of 1876. Here Shinchōsha was placing bets on Jack London, Upton Sinclair, Aldous Huxley, Thomas Mann, and Leonid Leonov, who were still relatively new to the translation market. If we plot the trend lines for each group, we can then determine whether a significant change occurs at the moment of publication. Does the moment mark a break in the trend line, such that the percentage of translations noticeably drops or begins to rise? Or is the moment just one stage in a continuing trend? Determining this becomes a way to understand whether the anthology was responding to the historical gravity of past contingent decisions or setting them into motion.

It also raises a key methodological question that every analysis of temporal trends must address: how to know when a change in the data is meaningful or not. Time series analysis is the subfield of statistics devoted to this question, and from which I borrow one of the simplest methods for testing whether a "structural break" exists at a specific point in a trend line. Known as the Chow test, it tells us whether linear models fit to subsets of a sample (i.e., the trend lines before and after a specified break point) perform differently from one another and from the trend line as a whole. A significant result ($p < .05$) means that the two subsets perform differently enough to provide evidence of a "structural break" in the data.[57] I apply this test to the moving average of the percent of all translations from authors in parts 1 and 2, breaking the overall trend lines at the respective points of publication (1929 and 1932). The trend lines are shown in figures 2.6 and 2.7. For part 1, a

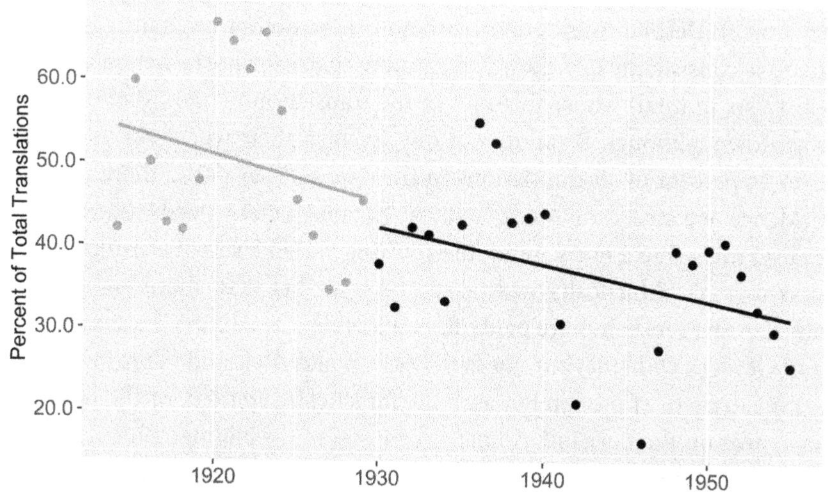

FIGURE 2.6. A scatterplot showing what percent of all translations in a given year are foreign authors who were anthologized in part 1 of *Sekai bungaku zenshū*. Simple linear trend lines have been fit to the data points prior to, and following, its initial publication in 1929. They indicate a constant downward trend from 1912 to 1955.

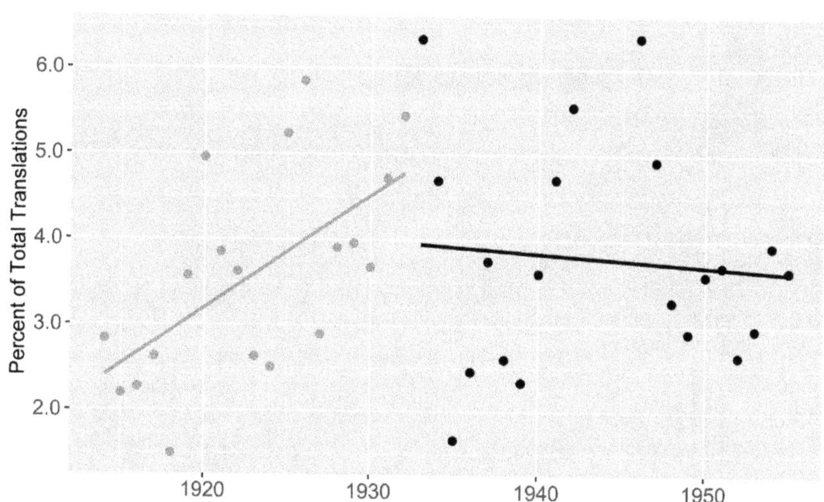

FIGURE 2.7. A scatterplot showing what percent of all translations in a given year are by foreign authors who were anthologized in part 2 of *Sekai bungaku zenshū*. Simple linear trend lines have been fit to the data points prior to, and following, its publication in 1932. They indicate a sharp upswing before 1932, followed by a period of high variability.

Chow test reveals that there is not significant evidence of a structural break (p = 0.79). Despite considerable variation at the author level, the aggregate trend is consistently downward, suggesting that Shinchōsha bet on authors (forty-six in total) whose fortunes in the translation market were on their way down, although certainly not out. By 1950 their works still make up over 25 percent of all translations in the data set. For part 2 there is more evidence of a structural break (p = .05) because a clear, steady ascent prior to 1932 turns into a noisy trend line showing varied levels of attention from year to year. Shinchōsha was taking a bigger bet with these less proven authors that seems to have paid off, incidentally, for authors Thomas Mann and Georges Duhamel but not Jack London and Aleksandr Kuprin.

What, then, of the foreign authors Shinchōsha ignored, or the ones yet to appear on the horizon? A final affordance of the bibliographic record is the ability to read the nonselection of authors as itself indicative of the standards of literary value by which the anthology editors were operating. It allows us to see this operation in inverse, as it were, hinting at how improbable it was for an author not to be anthologized given his or her presence in the larger market. Figure 2.8 shows the top fifty translated authors overall

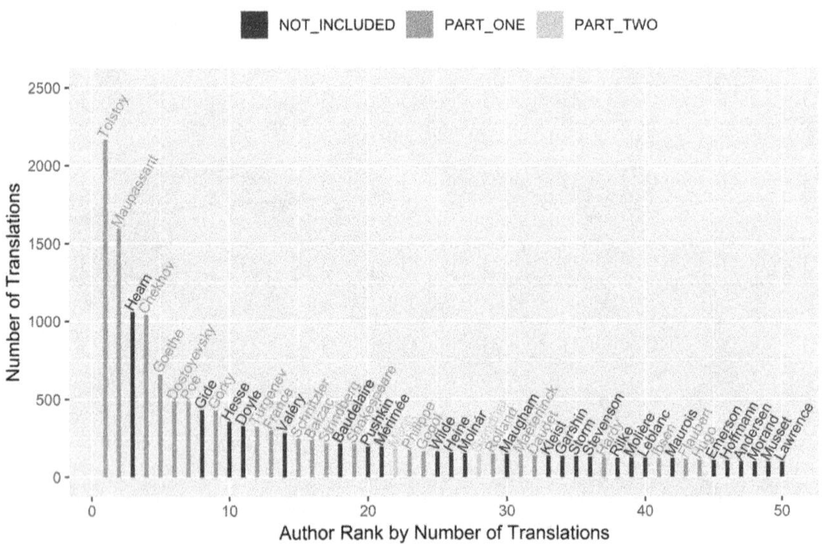

FIGURE 2.8. The fifty most translated authors between 1912 and 1955, ranked by the number of entries recorded in the National Diet Library index. Column shading indicates whether an author was included in part 1 of *Sekai bungaku zenshū* (dark gray), part 2 (light gray), or not at all (black).

between 1912 and 1955, categorized by whether an author was included in *Sekai bungaku zenshū* or not. Each omission potentially masks a more interesting story, whether about the slower uptake of writers such as Andre Gide and Herman Hesse; the ambiguous positionality of Lafcadio Hearn vis-à-vis received images of world literature; or the genre biases that kept Arthur Conan Doyle from appearing in those images.

I end with the list of translated authors with which we began. Just as the bibliographic record was used to situate the Shinchōsha anthology against a wider field of historical gravity, we can do the same for Aozora by comparing its contents with figure 2.8. Although the record provides no insight into how these authors fared after 1955, the presence of any overlap is instructive. Doyle, for instance, feels less out of place in light of how much attention his work has been given historically, but so too Chekhov, Poe, Gogol, and Mann. Rather than just a random or haphazard sample of world literature, Aozora has discernable links to the longer history of translation in Japan. At the same time, the absence of Tolstoy and Maupassant is more glaring given their dominance in the bibliographic record, which perhaps at how much attention has shifted away from these writers since 1955. In these gaps between past and present acts of selection is the chance to think about how to supplement Aozora as a digital archive to create more reasonable samples of prewar literary translation. How one does so will ultimately depend on what is to be asked of this material at greater scales of inquiry. But here we have seen how the bibliographic record can be a useful context through which to begin to evaluate our own selections against the compounded contingencies of history.

AOZORA BUNKO AS SAMPLE—THE CASE OF NATIONAL LITERATURE

Turning attention to Japanese language literature, which makes up a far larger portion of Aozora, we might expect the gaps between present and past acts of selection to be narrower, or at least less idiosyncratic. To be sure, copyright law will be a major constraint on its coverage. But unlike in the United States, where the law imposes a clear cutoff (currently all works published before 1924), in Japan copyright is applied to the author and was, until 2018, set at fifty years after death (it is now seventy).[58] It is thus harder to know exactly where the gaps widen into a sharp cliff.

Something of copyright's impact is visible if we compare Aozora's contents with the 139 works selected by the National Japanese Language Research Institute (see appendix table A2.1). Aozora contains seventy-nine of them (57 percent), although it could contain one hundred based on the current copyright status of the authors. Excluded due to copyright are authors who made their name in the immediate postwar period (e.g., Mishima Yukio, Ibuse Masuji), but also canonical figures who lived into the early 1970s (e.g., Shiga Naoya, Kawabata Yasunari, and Mushanokōji Saneatsu). But what of the twenty-one titles where copyright is not an issue? What constraints, beyond copyright, might explain their absence, and in turn help understand the gaps between Aozora's representation of Japanese language literature and those found in other traces of the print archive?

To get at these questions requires digging deeper into the anthology as archival instrument. We have already learned how so many past samples of Japanese language literature depended on anthologies as a first-order selection mechanism, including the list of 139 representative works just discussed. Contributors to Aozora have similarly relied on anthologies as the basis for their transcriptions. One important way to illuminate Aozora's relation to the print archive, then, is to ascertain the ways in which it aligns with, or diverges from, the contents of literary anthologies and the selection biases contained therein. Undoubtedly, comparison with anthologies reveals more about Aozora's representation of modern literature relative to the history of commercial publishing than to the realities of prewar literary production. Because this history is responsible for instantiating the hierarchies of value that shape perceptions of prewar fiction, however, as Edward Mack and others have argued, the comparison can help delineate Aozora's relation to the prewar print archive vis-à-vis these hierarchies.[59] How does Aozora's representation align with what publishers and editors have collectively imagined prewar fiction to be?

As a first point of comparison, consider the anthology mentioned several times in the previous chapter: *Gendai Nihon bungaku zenshū* (Collected works of contemporary Japanese literature, 1953–1958), published by Chikuma Shobō (hereafter GNBZ). This is the anthology to which Yasumoto Biten and others in the 1950s turned when looking for ways to scale up their stylistic analysis. Spanning ninety-nine volumes, GNBZ ushered in a new postwar standard for anthologies of "modern Japanese literature," replicating the success of its earlier namesake, published by Kaizōsha between 1926 and 1931. Like its predecessor, Chikuma Shobō's editors wanted the anthology to be affordable and accessible to a mass audience. They also sought to restore a vision of the modern canon purged of the ideological extremes prevalent in the war years. Editor Usui Yoshimi, the project's mastermind, originally wanted to title it *Kokumin bungaku zenshū* (Complete works of national literature), drawing on the postwar reinflection of *kokumin* as a symbol of a more democratic, more human-centered national polity.[60] Usui, a prominent critic and novelist in his own right, was largely responsible for selecting the anthology's contents, which included 1,758 works of fiction, poetry, theater, and criticism. Fiction made up three-quarters of the total. The works represent the output of 215 unique authors—half of whom have five or more works in the collection—and go as far back as Tsubouchi Shōyō's *Shōsetsu shinzui* (Essence of the novel, 1885–1886) and as far forward as postwar best sellers like Ōoka Shōhei's *Nobi* (Fires on the plain, 1952). Only 16 of the authors (7 percent) are women.

Chikuma's bet that Japanese readers would be hungry for a newly purified version of the modern canon, one that shied away from political ideology or from dealing with questions of class and ethnicity (i.e., proletarian and colonial fiction), paid off. The anthology was one of the most successful ever published, selling 1.3 million volumes and saving Chikuma from imminent bankruptcy. With its focus on high-brow vernacular fiction from the 1890s through the early 1930s—the "old literature," as Nakamura Mitsuo dubbed it in 1952—but also works by a new generation of postwar authors writing in what he criticized as the "old style," the anthology consolidated a prototypical vision of what counted as literature in this period.[61] That vision is only partially reproduced in Aozora, which contains variants for just 34 percent (600 works) of the titles in the GNBZ across all genres. For fiction alone, this figure jumps to 38 percent (503 works). The gap is narrower in terms of author overlap: Aozora contains titles by sixty-two of the authors with five or more works anthologized in GNBZ, or 58 percent. One might suspect copyright to explain the rest of the disparity, but based on the death dates of the authors in GNBZ, a remarkable 75 percent of the titles have already entered the public domain. In concrete terms, 700 works that could be part of Aozora are not. Figure 2.9 illustrates the copyright cutoff years distributed across all GNBZ titles and conveys what proportion of GNBZ's vision of modern Japanese literature could be added to Aozora right now. The portion between the dotted lines also shows how much of the sizable remainder must wait until 2055 before it can be added.

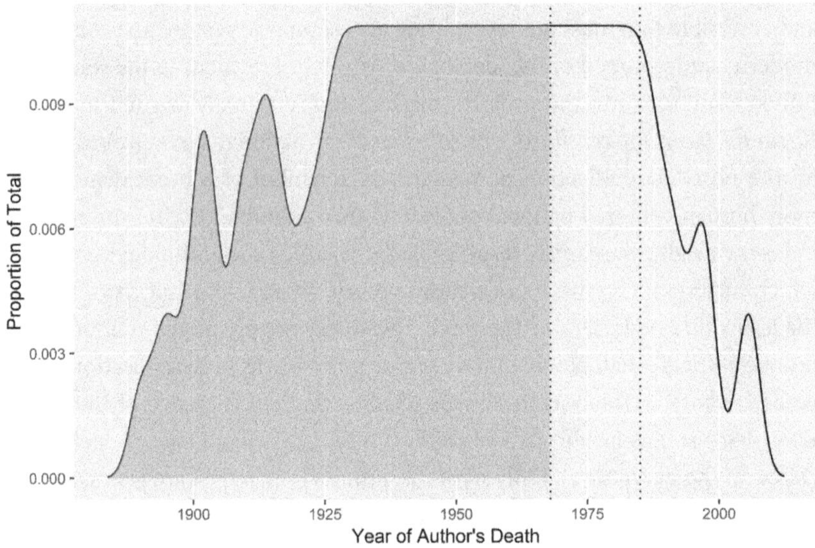

FIGURE 2.9. The proportion of titles (shaded) in *Gendai Nihon bungaku zenshū* that are out of copyright and thus could be added to Aozora immediately. The space between the dotted lines is the portion of works that will have to wait until 2055 to enter the public domain.

It is perhaps not surprising that Aozora's contents do not mirror Chikuma's very specific postwar vision. But neither does it appear that Aozora is pursuing it, at least based on the copyright status of the works in GNBZ. A few obvious targets are put out of reach by copyright, including standard bearers of the "old literature" such as Kawabata Yasunari and Shiga Naoya, but this is not the overriding constraint on what has been selected for digitization. Some authors simply do not appeal to the tastes and interests of Aozora's volunteers. Tsubouchi Shōyō and Uno Kōji, for instance, have only a dozen texts between them in the collection. When they do appeal, attention is typically given to a different set of texts than the ones selected by GNBZ editors to represent an author's oeuvre. Notably, of the one hundred authors with the most works of fiction in Aozora, almost half (forty-eight) are not included in GNBZ, a large portion of whom are writers of popular and historical fiction. Although this comparison with GNBZ yields a few important clues for uncovering Aozora's underlying logics of selection, it can only take us so far. It reveals nothing of the processes of taste making and canonization over the last seventy years that have likely made certain works and authors more susceptible to digitization. How might we capture something of the aggregate effect of these complex, evolving processes? What titles and authors would rise to the top if we could?

John Guillory argues that every attempt to present the canon, even in the form of the omnibus anthology, "remains a selection from a larger list which does not itself appear anywhere." The canon is always "an imaginary totality of works" that is never accessed as a totality because any invocation of it is always partial and contextual.[62] Anthology editors impose their biases on the process of selection even when they are ostensibly trying, as were the editors of Kaizōsha's groundbreaking *Gendai Nihon bungaku zenshū*, to be comprehensive or to capture the "noise" of an entire period. When these biases are funneled through committee, as in the creation of an anthology known to have inspired Kaizōsha's series, the *Harvard Classics*, the results can feel "more or less arbitrary," as that series editor Charles Eliot once put it.[63] Even though these decisions can seem partial or random in their moment, they can be reinforced and repeated over time. Exploring the compound effect of these decisions (i.e., which titles and which authors were anthologized most often) will never bring the canon as imaginary totality into view, but it points us to the pools and shallows where the unpredictable currents of literary judgment have tended to gather.

In 2004, the publisher Nichigai Associates produced an extensive record of these decisions by indexing the tables of contents of 1,255 omnibus and individual author anthologies. It contains nearly six hundred thousand entries by over eight thousand five hundred unique authors across the genres of fiction, poetry, and theater, beginning in 1897 with Narushima Ryūhoku's collected works (*Ryūhoku zenshū*). Figure 2.10 shows the number of discrete zenshū volumes published each year and tells us both familiar and lesser known stories: a first wave of anthologization driven by the enpon (one-yen book) boom of the late 1920s; a second wave in the mid-1950s as publishers such as Chikuma Shobō tried to reestablish a literary market lost to wartime censorship and deprivation while taking advantage of new demand from public and school libraries; and a third phase starting in the late 1960s when the market peaked.[64] The data is suspiciously sparse before 1925. Not included are several multivolume collections that were key precedents for the Kaizōsha-led enpon boom.[65] After 1925, however, the data better represents the range and volume of omnibus publications. To wit, one historical account contends that over three hundred multivolume

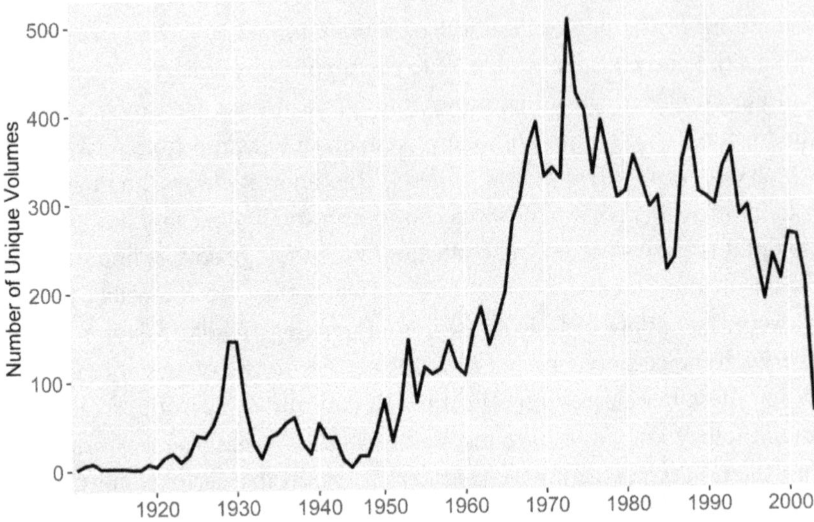

FIGURE 2.10. Number of discrete *zenshū* volumes published per year based on the Nichigai anthology data. Counts include volumes from both omnibus and individual author anthologies in all genres.

series were published at the height of the enpon boom (1925–1929). Impressive as this sounds, only forty of these were related to modern Japanese fiction, poetry, or drama. Of these, sixteen were omnibus anthologies.[66] The Nichigai index catalogs twelve of them and lacks only two of the series dedicated to prose fiction.[67]

Assessing the index's coverage of the postwar decades is more difficult owing to the tremendous increase in anthology publication. From the 1950s onward, old and new publishers alike competed fiercely for space in the expanding mass market of zenshū publication, producing dozens of variations on Kaizōsha's original concept. Takashima Ken'ichirō estimates that as early as 1953 there were roughly three hundred zenshū of all types in production, accounting for 30 percent of the total book market.[68] Lacking a comprehensive list of all these zenshū, it is hard to estimate what proportion is covered by the Nichigai index. Nevertheless, the trend line for volumes per year, split into the categories of omnibus and author anthology, reflects the current understanding of the rise and fall of the zenshū market. Figure 2.11 shows how each type of anthology contributed differently to the three waves described here and clearly indicates how quickly the

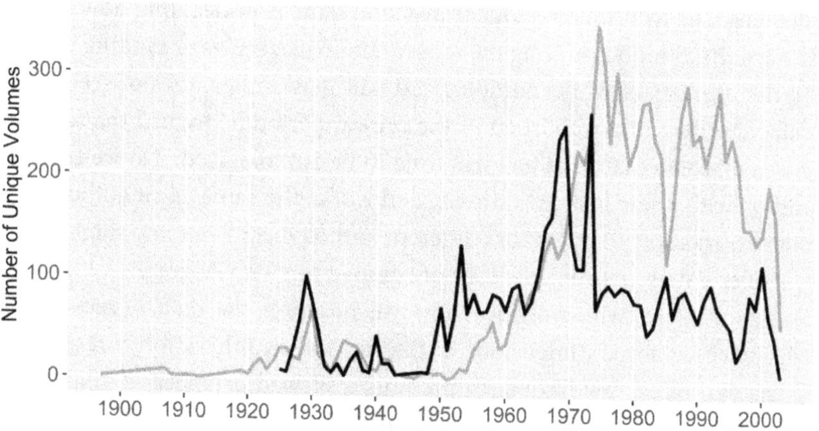

FIGURE 2.11. Number of discrete zenshū volumes published per year in all genres, broken down into omnibus (black) and individual author (gray) categories.

zenshū bubble burst in the late 1970s. A decade of speculative investment that saw publishers marketing to new middle-class homeowners and their increasingly educated baby boomer children ended abruptly with Chikuma Shobō's bankruptcy in 1978.[69] After this, individual anthologies comprised the bulk of the market, and omnibus anthologies shifted their focus to literature long left out of the canon. Whatever aggregate view of modern Japanese literature the Nichigai index offers, it will be dominated by editorial choices made before the omnibus bubble burst.

At the scale of hundreds of anthologies and hundreds of thousands of individual selections, obtaining this view is no longer as easy as examining a list of titles. First, it is necessary to limit the scope of analysis to fiction because other genres, especially poetry, are likely to follow different patterns of anthologization. Using a dictionary of modern Japanese literature, I labeled authors according to the primary genre in which they wrote. Some of the authors labeled as fiction writers by this method naturally wrote in other genres, but the aim is simply to capture those authors whose fiction was likely to be anthologized frequently.[70] This process reduced the original data set to nearly 190,000 entries, of which 38,360 come from 179 omnibus anthologies and the rest from 569 author anthologies. Although still a lot to look at, the units of analysis are now somewhat more comparable. The challenge, as with the previous translation data, is in deciding how to sort these units. Simply counting the most anthologized titles or ranking writers by the number of works anthologized will mask other ways of seeing the data. Should works published in the prewar period be treated the same as postwar works that have had less time to be anthologized? Do we treat an author with a few heavily anthologized works the same as an author with many works spread out across different anthologies? Does any single strategy offer a more reasonable basis of comparison with Aozora?

Any strategy will influence how we interpret the data because each will privilege some dimensions at the expense of others. With respect to individual titles, raw frequency presents a skewed perspective of a work's importance because it does not account for time. Works that are anthologized earlier are more likely to end up at the top just by virtue of their having had more time to be anthologized. Table 2.2 shows how this can

TABLE 2.2
Top ten titles in the Nichigai *Zenshū* index

Overall	**1920–1959**	**1960–1979**	**1980–2003**
29 - 奉教人の死 (Akutagawa Ryūnosuke)	10 - 伊豆の踊子 (Kawabata Yasunari)	24 - 野火 (Ōoka Shōhei)	8 - 押絵と旅する男 (Edogawa Ranpō)
29 - 地獄変 (Akutagawa Ryūnosuke)	10 - 忠直卿行状記 (Kikuchi Kan)	23 - 俘虜記 (Ōoka Shōhei)	6 - 風博士 (Sakaguchi Angō)
29 - 伊豆の踊子 (Kawabata Yasunari)	10 - 恩讐の彼方に (Kikuchi Kan)	19 - 舞姫 (Mori Ōgai)	5 - 流星 (Inoue Hisashi)
29 - 野火 (Ōoka Shōhei)	9 - 奉教人の死 (Akutagawa Ryūnosuke)	18 - 奉教人の死 (Akutagawa Ryūnosuke)	5 - 山月記 (Nakajima Atsushi)
28 - 枯野抄 (Akutagawa Ryūnosuke)	9 - 地獄変 (Akutagawa Ryūnosuke)	18 - 阿部一族 (Mori Ōgai)	5 - ハムレット (Hisao Jūran)
28 - 舞姫 (Mori Ōgai)	9 - 嵐 (Shimazaki Tōson)	18 - 鼻 (Akutagawa Ryūnosuke)	5 - 風琴と魚の町 (Hayashi Fumiko)
28 - 鼻 (Akutagawa Ryūnosuke)	8 - 蜃気楼 (Akutagawa Ryūnosuke)	18 - 友情 (Mushanokōji Saneatsu)	5 - 屋根裏の散歩者 (Edogawa Ranpō)
27 - 阿部一族 (Mori Ōgai)	8 - 玄鶴山房 (Akutagawa Ryūnosuke)	17 - 暗い絵 (Noma Hiroshi)	5 - 死後の恋 (Yumeno Kyūsaku)
27 - 山椒大夫 (Mori Ōgai)	8 - 秋 (Akutagawa Ryūnosuke)	17 - 山椒大夫 (Mori Ōgai)	5 - 利根の渡 (Okamoto Kidō)
27 - 坊っちゃん (Natsume Sōseki)	8 - きりしとほろ上人伝 (Akutagawa Ryūnosuke)	17 - 聖家族 (Hori Tatsuo)	5 - 喪神 (Gomi Yasusuke)

Note: The top ten titles are listed by count overall and for the specified date ranges. Author names are given in parentheses.

obscure works that were just as successful in their own time. In the first column are the top ten most frequent titles (and their authors) in the data set overall. Subsequent columns list the top ten titles for the periods 1920–1959 (the first and second zenshū booms); 1960–1979 (the peak bubble for zenshū production); and 1980–2003 (after the collapse of the omnibus anthology market). With the exception of Ōoka Shōhei's *Nobi*, the overall counts are biased toward prewar works. A couple of these works take an early lead in the first period and maintain this high pace of anthologization in the second. But it appears that the second period is really driving the process of consecration. Six of its top ten titles are included in the overall list. In the third period, we see the impact of the postbubble market for zenshū in the form of lower overall counts, but also a set of authors absent from any of the other lists. This is not due to the relative newness of these titles because all are prewar or immediate postwar works. Rather, there appears to be a marked shift of attention in this final period away from "pure" literature and toward popular genre fiction, precisely the kind of thing that was missing from the vision that GNBZ set into motion.

Because raw frequency obscures the advantage afforded to works anthologized earlier, we need a way to normalize for time so that we can compare works on a time-neutral playing field, just as we would normalize a city's crime statistics relative to its population. The easiest way to do this is to turn the raw counts into a ratio, dividing a work's total number of inclusions by the years since it was first anthologized. In this way, a work anthologized ten times over sixty years will have half the value of one anthologized ten times over thirty years. We can also normalize time by giving more importance to works anthologized intensely over a short period but that did not gain a foothold in the canon. Dividing frequency by the first and last years of anthologization provides us with such an "intensity" measure. Table 2.3 shows the top titles as determined by these two measures. Even from this small sample, it is clear how different are the stories that each ranking tells. Ōoka's *Nobi*—the harrowing account of a soldier's final desperate days fighting in the Philippines and a sustained meditation on the dehumanizing effects of war—rises to the top of the Time Normalized list. It shares this space with several award-winning works from the 1950s, namely, Yasuoka Shōtarō's "Kaihen no kōkei" (A view by the sea, 1959) and Yoshiyuki Jun'nosuke's "Shūu" (The rain shower, 1954), but also Kawabata

TABLE 2.3
Top ten titles across multiple measures and data sets

Overall	Time Normalized	Intensity
29 - 奉教人の死 (Akutagawa Ryūnosuke)	29 - 野火 (Ōoka Shōhei)	9 - 洪水 (Inoue Yasushi)
29 - 地獄変 (Akutagawa Ryūnosuke)	27 - 俘虜記 (Ōoka Shōhei)	3 - 雨 (Kitahara Nobuo)
29 - 伊豆の踊子 (Kawabata Yasunari)	25 - 墨東奇譚 (Nagai Kafū)	3 - 半身 (Osargi Jirō)
29 - 野火 (Ōoka Shōhei)	22 - 驟雨 (Yoshiyuki Jun'nosuke)	8 - 補陀落渡海記 (Inoue Yasushi)
28 - 枯野抄 (Akutagawa Ryūnosuke)	23 - 桜島 (Umezaki Haruo)	3 - 天魔 (Ikenami Shōtarō)
28 - 舞姫 (Mori Ōgai)	20 - ガラスの靴 (Yasuoka Shōtarō)	3 - オツベルと象 (Miyazawa Kenji)
28 - 鼻 (Akutagawa Ryūnosuke)	24 - 雪国 (Kawabata Yasunari)	3 - 疎林への道 (Kojima Nobuo)
27 - 阿部一族 (Mori Ōgai)	22 - 灰色の月 (Shiga Naoya)	3 - 無心状 (Ibuse Masuji)
27 - 山椒大夫 (Mori Ōgai)	18 - 海辺の光景 (Yasuoka Shōtarō, 18)	3 - 水溜り (Niwa Fumio)
27 - 坊っちゃん (Natsume Sōseki)	18 - 花影 (Ōoka Shōhei)	3 - 創作余談（抄） (Shiga Naoya)
LRI	***Textbooks***	***Aozora***
暗夜行路 (Shiga Naoya)	180 - 山月記 (Nakajima Atsushi)	こころ (Natsume Sōseki)
或る女 (Arishima Takeo)	169 - 羅生門 (Akutagawa Ryūnosuke)	銀河鉄道の夜 (Miyazawa Kenji)
墨東綺譚 (Nagai Kafū)	164 - こころ (Natsume Sōseki)	吾輩は猫である (Natsume Sōseki)
無限抱擁 (Takii Kōsaku)	142 - 舞姫 (Mori Ōgai)	人間失格 (Dazai Osamu)
浮雲 (Futabatei Shimei)	70 - 城の崎にて (Shiga Naoya)	走れメロス (Dazai Osamu)
田園の憂鬱 (Satō Haruo)	63 - たけくらべ (Higuchi Ichiyō)	ドグラ・マグラ (Yumeno Kyūsaku)
蟹工船 (Kobayashi Takiji)	61 - 富岳百景 (Dazai Osamu)	羅生門 (Akutagawa Ryūnosuke)
五重塔 (Kōda Rohan)	55 - 三四郎 (Natsume Sōseki)	坊っちゃん (Natsume Sōseki)
あらくれ (Tokuda Shūsei)	51 - 武蔵野 (Kunikida Doppō)	山月記 (Nakajima Atsushi)
檸檬 (Kajii Motojirō)	46 - 檸檬 (Kajii Motojirō)	蜘蛛の糸 (Akutagawa Ryūnosuke)

Note: In the upper half of the table are the top ten titles in the Nichigai *Zenshū* index based on three separate measures (raw count, time normalized count, and intensity). In the lower half are the top titles as ranked by the Language Research Institute survey; by overall count in the high school textbook data set; and by number of times accessed by Aozora users.

Yasunari's canonical *Yukiguni* (Snow country, 1947). Literary giants of the prewar period have been entirely displaced by their immediate postwar counterparts. In the Intensity column, in contrast, we find familiar authors alongside mostly unfamiliar works—one-hit wonders that flashed brightly before fading, including Inoue Yasushi's "Kōzui" (Flood, 1962), anthologized nine times in just three years (1966–1969).

We can imagine other normalization strategies using contextual variables such as sales data, which would allow for ranking titles by the commercial success of each anthology. My intent, however, is simply to point to the many possibilities for transforming frequency into relation in a data set. Each forking path through the data entails different assumptions about how its objects relate to one another, and each produces visions of the literary universe with varying degrees of overlap with the vision in Aozora. Works with high intensity, for instance, are likely to recede more quickly from the cultural imaginary and be less ready to hand for Aozora's volunteers because they were less frequently reprinted. Works with more staying power in omnibus anthologies are likely to be more susceptible to digitization. At the same time, if we go by the time normalized measure, they are also more likely to be works still in copyright. In fact, Aozora contains one hundred of the top one hundred fifty works by raw count (67 percent); sixty-nine of the top one hundred fifty by the time normalized measure (46 percent), owing to the increase of in-copyright titles; and a mere thirty-two of the top one hundred fifty by the intensity measure (21 percent). (Recall that the overlap with the LRI list was 57 percent.) These numbers enhance our understanding of how Aozora aligns with the different aggregate visions projected by the Nichigai index and how well it could address research questions relevant to such visions.

Another perspective on Aozora's degree of alignment is provided when we use authors as the unit of analysis. Here too we might be inclined to sort authors by the number of total works in all omnibus anthologies. But this would privilege authors anthologized earlier, treating every work, no matter its length or genre, as equally informative of an author's stature. If we suppose that brevity raises the chance of a work's anthologization, raw frequency will further advantage authors who mostly wrote shorter works.[71] In truth, long novels were not necessarily avoided by omnibus editors, and some publishers made them a selling point while developing printing formats capable of cramming more text on every page.[72] Moreover, just having a greater number of short works is no guarantee of their inclusion, or of the same ones being selected over time. Assessing the impact of length on anthologization will require a study of its own, not to mention precise data on page length, but it is clear that we need a way to both control for time and to acknowledge that the sheer number of works anthologized obscures other factors. The question of "how much" needs to be qualified, at the very least, by the question of "how often."

A popular measure from bibliometric studies, known as the Hirsch index (or h-index), does precisely this. Devised as a method to quantify the impact of a scientific researcher's output in terms of breadth of citations in academic journals, the measure has become an oft maligned symbol of the devaluation of academic labor under neoliberalism and the rise of a new class of administrative bean counters in the university. Outside of its political uses and abuses, however, the index is an attempt to quantify the amount of an author's productive output by how widely it is cited by peers in that field. Applied to the anthology data, such that selection by an editor is seen as a kind of citation, the h-index transforms raw counts into a relational framework in which how an author is anthologized matters more than how much. Mathematically, the h-index works by taking all published (e.g., anthologized) titles, ranking them by their number of citations (e.g., inclusion in an anthology), and counting down from the first position for as long as the rank is greater than or equal to the citation count at that rank. The rank at the last position where this holds true is the h-index. For instance, the author with the highest h-index in the Nichigai data set is Akutagawa Ryūnosuke (h-index = 21). This means that twenty-one of his most anthologized works have been included in an omnibus zenshū at least twenty-one times. To normalize for time, we can divide this value by the years since the author's first work was anthologized. This "m-index" puts authors of different generations on more equal footing.

Table 2.4 lists the top twenty authors as determined by each metric, with total counts followed by the h-index and m-index values. Comparing these lists, it is clear how much the raw counts privilege writers most active in the prewar period. This view of the literary universe will feel all too familiar to students of modern Japanese literature, with the giants of late-Meiji fiction well represented (e.g., Mori Ōgai, Izumi Kyōka, Higuchi Ichiyō, Natsume Sōseki) and so, too, their dominant Taishō and early-Shōwa period successors (e.g., Akutagawa, Shiga Naoya, Kawabata Yasunari, Tanizaki Jun'ichirō). The h-index measure shuffles the order of some of these names but replaces only four of them with new authors: Kajii Motojirō, Yokomitsu Ri'ichi, Nagai Tatsuo, and Umezaki Haruo. The differences are instructive, however. In the case of Kajii, for instance, we

TABLE 2.4

Top twenty authors across multiple measures and data sets

Overall Count	H-Index	M-Index	Textbooks	Aozora
Akutagawa Ryūnosuke (1283)	Akutagawa Ryūnosuke (21)	Akutagawa Ryūnosuke (0.26)	Natsume Sōseki (592)	Natsume Sōseki (17M)
Shiga Naoya (838)	Shiga Naoya (16)	Kajii Motojirō (0.2)	Shimazaki Tōson (400)	Akutagawa Ryūnosuke (16M)
Mori Ōgai (821)	Kunikida Doppō (15)	Shiga Naoya (0.2)	Akutagawa Ryūnosuke (357)	Miyazawa Kenji (14M)
Kunikida Doppō (694)	Mori Ōgai (14)	Dazai Osamu (0.2)	Mori Ōgai (330)	Dazai Osamu (13M)
Dazai Osamu (658)	Kajii Motojirō (13)	Kunikida Doppō (0.19)	Shiga Naoya (246)	Yoshikawa Eiji (4.4M)
Kawabata Yasunari (587)	Dazai Osamu (11)	Mori Ōgai (0.18)	Miyazawa Kenji (240)	Yumeno Kyūsaku (3.9M)
Ibuse Masuji (522)	Ibuse Masuji (11)	Ōe Kenzaburō (0.15)	Nakajima Atsushi (208)	Mori Ōgai (3.5M)
Shimazaki Tōson (483)	Hori Tatsuo (11)	Inoue Yasushi (0.15)	Dazai Osamu (174)	Nakajima Atsushi (3M)
Hori Tatsuo (473)	Yokomitsu Ri'ichi (10)	Nagai Tatsuo (0.15)	Higuchi Ichiyō (174)	Sakaguchi Angō (2.8M)
Inoue Yasushi (443)	Higuchi Ichiyō (10)	Ibuse Masuji (0.15)	Ibuse Masuji (159)	Kajii Motojirō (2M)
Higuchi Ichiyō (432)	Nagai Kafū (10)	Hori Tatsuo (0.15)	Tanizaki Jun'ichirō (135)	Kitaōji Rosan (1.7M)
Nagai Kafū (408)	Tanizaki Jun'ichirō (10)	Shimao Toshio (0.15)	Kawabata Yasunari (120)	Niimi Nankichi (1.7M)
Masamune Hakuchō (403)	Masamune Hakuchō (10)	Yoshiyuki Jun'nosuke (0.15)	Abe Kōbō (116)	Edogawa Ranpō (1.5M)
Izumi Kyōka (401)	Kikuchi Kan (10)	Yasuoka Shōtarō (0.15)	Kajii Motojirō (102)	Shimazaki Tōson (1.4M)
Kikuchi Kan (367)	Kawabata Yasunari (9)	Umezaki Haruo (0.15)	Hori Tatsuo (92)	Kobayashi Takiji (1.3M)
Tanizaki Jun'ichirō (362)	Natsume Sōseki (9)	Sakaguchi Angō (0.14)	Kunikida Doppō (86)	Izumi Kyōka (968K)
Mushanokōji Saneatsu (345)	Tokuda Shūsei (9)	Tamiya Torahiko (0.14)	Kōda Aya (86)	Kikuchi Kan (965K)
Natsume Sōseki (334)	Inoue Yasushi (8)	Yokomitsu Ri'ichi (0.13)	Inoue Yasushi (80)	Arishima Takeo (962K)
Tokuda Shūsei (318)	Nagai Tatsuo (8)	Mishima Yukio (0.13)	Itō Sei (80)	Hori Tatsuo (886K)
Ishikawa Jun (310)	Umezaki Haruo (8)	Ōoka Shōhei (0.13)	Shakespeare (80)	Higuchi Ichiyō (779K)

Note: The first three columns list the top twenty authors in the Nichigai *Zenshū* index along three separate measures: overall count, h-index, and m-index. Figures given correspond to the values for each measure. The Textbooks column lists the top twenty authors by raw count in the high school textbooks data set. The Aozora column lists the top twenty authors according to the number of times any of their works were accessed between 2009 and 2017.

learn that, despite his relatively low overall count, he fares much better than others when accounting for how many of his works have been repeatedly anthologized. Although his and Yokomitsu's presence at the top is not unexpected, that of Nagai and Umezaki *is*, especially given how little scholarly attention their early postwar fiction has received. When controlling for time, their presence grows even stronger and so, too, does that of other canonical writers who made their name after the war, including Ōe Kenzaburō, Sakaguchi Angō, and Mishima Yukio. In the last slot of the m-index column is Ōoka Shōhei, whose much lower ranking across all these measures indicates how much his presence in omnibus anthologies is dependent on a few highly anthologized works.

These lists are just one way of assessing authors' popular and scholarly reception in the postwar period. They provide narrow windows onto an imaginary totality that no one had direct access to—a totality filtered through the bits and pieces that made it onto the reference shelves of public and school libraries or the newly outfitted middle-class interiors born of Japan's postwar recovery. These windows could be used to justify the construction of a corpus that sampled authors based on their relative positions in these lists, but this would also mean surfacing their underlying assumptions and linking them more concretely to specific research questions. Here the windows are useful to the extent they reveal the compound effects of cumulative editorial choices on the authors who are heavily sedimented into the archive. In particular, they allow us to compare the result of these effects with the compound vision available through Aozora. A direct comparison is more difficult without some measure of relative attention (e.g., which authors are most often viewed on Aozora), a problem I take up shortly. But some insight can be had by looking at the authors best represented in Aozora's fiction (excluding juvenile fiction) in terms of number of titles archived in the collection. Figure 2.12 shows the top twenty authors and their representation relative to the top fifty authors overall. A few names are familiar from previous lists, but the majority are not.

In fact, nearly half fall into the category of popular genre writers, many of whom are the same authors most frequently anthologized after the bursting of the zenshū bubble: Edogawa Ranpō, Yumeno Kyūsaku, Hisao Jūran, and Okamoto Kidō. Although not excluded from the earlier omnibus anthologies, they appear with much less frequency or are segregated into their own anthologies dedicated specifically to "popular" (*taishū*) literature

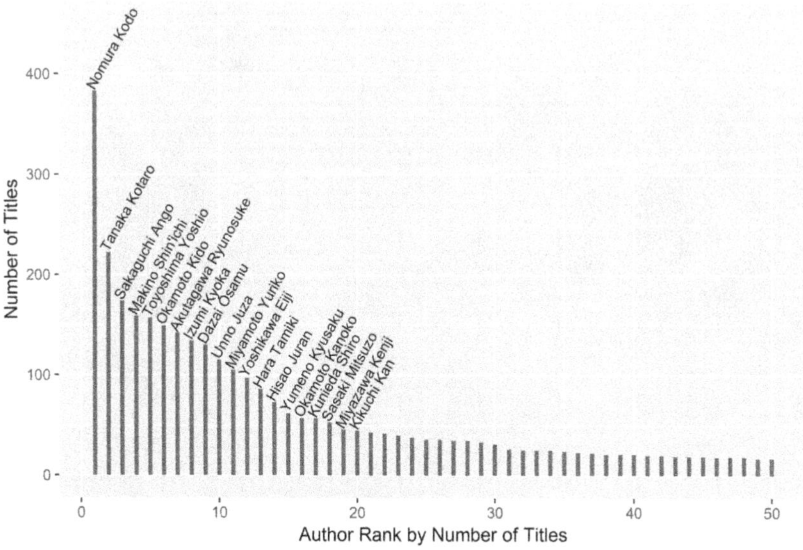

FIGURE 2.12. The twenty authors with the most fiction titles in Aozora. For reference, the graph shows the counts for the top fifty authors in the collection.

or one of its subvariants, including detective, historical, fantasy, horror, and science fiction. The impulse to create such a two-tiered market goes back to the original zenshū boom of the late 1920s and is part of the very bifurcation of the field of production that this boom, and related developments in the print culture industry, helped reinforce. Within anthology publication specifically, however, the level of overt investment in popular fiction has fluctuated over time. Indeed, calculating the moving average of the number of volumes dedicated to variants of such fiction, we find that investment bottomed out precisely during the postwar bubble before rising again in the 1980s and 1990s to constitute most of what remained of the omnibus anthology market (figure 2.13). In this respect, the predominance of popular authors in Aozora serves as a corrective to the canonization of mostly prewar authors, and mostly "pure literature" (*junbungaku*), in the second and third waves of zenshū production. If Aozora partly represents the results of this canonizing process, it also fills in some of the areas buried by or expunged from these earlier waves.

A final point that must be addressed is the dearth of female authors, which is in keeping with their near total omission from any of the lists

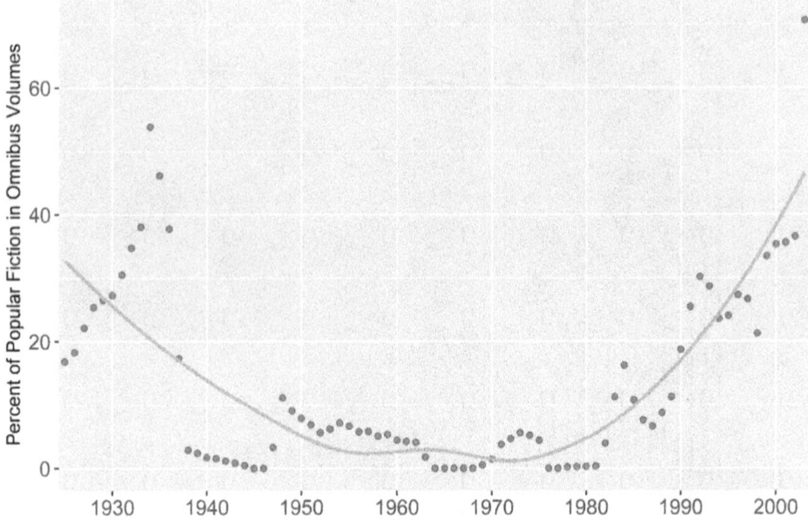

FIGURE 2.13. The moving five-year average of the percent of volumes dedicated to popular fiction out of all omnibus fiction anthologies. A loess curve has been fit to the data to show the general trend.

generated so far. Within the subset of Aozora works classified as fiction (again excluding juvenile literature), the proportion of texts by female identified authors is less than 9 percent, which is slightly worse than the 10 percent for omnibus anthologies and the 12.5 percent for individual author anthologies. These low figures mask an even more alarming pattern in the anthology data, however. When the proportion of titles by female authors is calculated as a moving average over time, it stays close to 10 percent well into the 1990s (figure 2.14), rising only with the publication of several omnibus series dedicated to women writers. It is no surprise that the processes of canon making in Japan are biased against fiction by women. It is shocking, however, just how strong and consistent the bias is within this sector of the literary publishing market. To what degree it reflects the actual demographics of writers at any given point since the 1930s is a question requiring further study.[73] Most pertinent here is the fact that with respect to gender Aozora reflects all too well the status quo. When we see a figure repeat itself like this across such varied samples—these different sensors of literary value's global dynamics—it signals how systematic these dynamics are and how digital archives can compound the biases of their print forebears. In constructing samples from these archives, we must attend to these

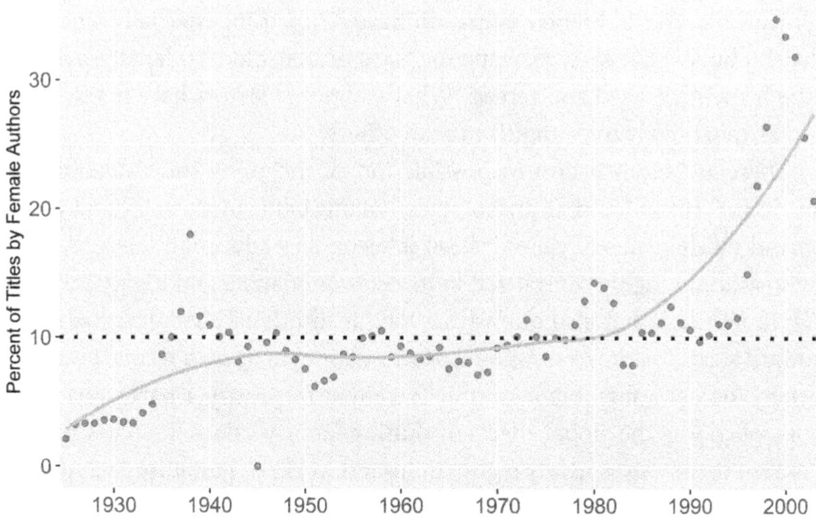

FIGURE 2.14. The moving five-year average of the percent of titles by female identified authors in all omnibus fiction anthologies. A loess curve has been fit to the data to show the general trend. The dashed line indicates the 10 percent threshold, which is rarely crossed until the mid-1990s.

biases and decide whether to counter them by oversampling the effected subpopulation or address them as historical artifacts of real underlying biases.[74]

We must also attend to inflection points where these biases even out. Figures 2.13 and 2.14 indicate that the zenshū bubble's collapse ushered in a different vision of the omnibus anthology and its ideal reader. The consecration of national canons was a less profitable venture than appeals to popular taste or attempts to compensate for voices long pushed to the margins of such canons. In the case of popular genre fiction, the postbubble anthology market and the communities of reading it likely fostered in the 1980s and 1990s is well reflected in the logics of selection informing Aozora's construction. In the case of writing by female authors, however, the uptick we see in omnibus anthologies does not transfer to Aozora in any global way. It may be that the pool of female authors from which Aozora's volunteers can draw remains constrained by copyright law. Thus, even as the demographics of authorship have changed over the past half-century, the gender imbalance in the pool of out-of-copyright authors has not.[75] Nevertheless, knowing that Aozora does not reflect the increased attention given to female writers in literary anthologies raises a question about what global processes of literary valuation have stepped in, especially since the zenshū bubble collapse, to shape the ways prewar modern Japanese literature is memorialized and reread. What additional factors have made some works more likely to be digitized than others?

There are surely a host of possible forces, including the availability of works in forms other than anthologies, but one of the more stable and widespread mechanisms of canonization is secondary education. Here we find an institution highly centralized in its decision making and highly influential in its reach, but also one with a long institutional memory that tends toward stasis. Before examining Aozora's fiction on its own terms, I want to briefly look at a final bibliographic trace that records in a narrower, more controlled way the global effects of shifting literary values. It comes from a data set that indexes nearly eighty thousand works of literature included in almost seventeen hundred high school textbooks published between 1949 and 2007.[76] The data set is useful as another reference point for situating Aozora in relation to the always imaginary totality of works from which it draws. Pedagogically, it is an opportunity to consider what can be done with a more refined and institutionally specific bibliographic data set and to devise a way of comparing its vision of modern Japanese literature with others. Up to now we have relied on calculations of percentage overlap or observations of differences across the topmost layers of each core sample. As these samples proliferate, however, we need to measure their differences in ways reflective of their overall composition.

Of all the bibliographic data sets analyzed in this chapter, the textbook data set is by far the cleanest and easiest to navigate. Purchased as digital data directly from the publisher, it comes as a highly structured text file easily converted with a Python script into a database. Each entry consists of the title of a work and metadata (e.g., textbook title, publisher, date) for every textbook in which that work was included. Reliable as it may be as a data source, however, one still needs historical and institutional context to turn it into something useful. It is important to know, for instance, that literary texts are taught within the framework of language education, and that the latter is periodized to reflect Japanese linguistic variation over time. Thus nearly half of the textbooks in the data set are devoted to classical forms. Removing these leaves about 13,000 entries included in 842 textbooks and attributable to 2,752 authors. It is also useful to know that textbooks, which are produced by private publishers, have since 1949 been subject to approval by the Ministry of Education and that approval alone is not a guarantee of widespread adoption. Any new textbook confronts a curricular infrastructure (e.g., lesson plans, examinations) built around all that has come before. In this sense, this data set is a record of editorial choices made in the interest of winning state approval and with an eye to those texts in which instructors and school boards have already invested resources. Finally, prose fiction is generally included in textbooks in a redacted or condensed form. Titles should thus be understood as references to a work in part, not in whole.[77]

This bibliographic trace provides insight into a system of valuation that rewards stasis and continuity, not dynamism and innovation. Indeed, when examining just the raw counts for each title, it quickly becomes apparent that the system's feedback mechanisms have rewarded the same four works over and over again (see table 2.3). These titles dominate the representation of modern Japanese literature in high school textbooks and are collectively referred to as *teiban* (standard) texts. Benefiting from institutional processes set into motion in 1951 for Nakajima Atsushi's "Sangetsuki" (Tiger-poet), and in 1957 for the other three, these teiban texts gradually accrued ever more value, appearing in 20 percent of modern language textbooks approved in 1975 and, except for Mori Ōgai's "Maihime" (dancing Girl), in 40 percent of those approved in 2007.[78] After the teiban texts the raw counts fall quickly, dropping to just nine for the one hundredth most frequent work, Umezaki Haruo's "Sakurajima" (Cherry island). Looking across the other lists in the table, it is notable that only "Maihime" and Kajii Motojirō's "Remon" (Lemon) appear in any other top ten. The degree of overlap increases after aggregating raw counts by author (see table 2.4). Sōseki is now at the top, a position he holds in no other list. Yet he is followed closely by familiar names—Akutagawa, Ōgai, and Shiga, who sit near the top of all the rankings. Nakajima Atsushi, unsurprisingly, is not far behind. But the absence of his name in the anthology rankings reveals how skewed is the perspective offered by the textbook data on this particular count.

We did not need this textbook data to identify the teiban texts, although it does clarify the magnitude of their monopoly on literary attention in the high school classroom. These data become useful in making visible the cumulative efforts of publishers to steer this attention elsewhere. What is going on below the fixed surface of the teiban texts? Does it correspond at all to the processes shaping Aozora? The relative paucity of prose fiction works included in high school textbooks between 1949 and 2007 makes the question of archival overlap much less relevant. Although there are nearly thirteen thousand titles overall, the bulk of them occur with such infrequency, and in publications with such disparate reach, that it is hard to imagine them informing the cultural imagination to the same degree as works in anthologies. Of the top one hundred most frequent titles found in textbooks, excluding poetry and nonfiction, 87 percent of out-of-copyright works (fifty-five titles) can be found in Aozora. If overlap is not as useful a metric of comparison here, reader habits certainly are. Since 2009, Aozora has published monthly reports of how many times each work is accessed by users. The last columns of tables 2.3 and 2.4 provide the rankings of titles and authors based on these data. To give a sense of the difference in magnitude here, Sōseki's *Kokoro* was accessed more than four million times from 2009 to 2017, compared with two million for Nakajima's "Sangetsuki." In all, Sōseki's works were accessed more than seventeen million times, compared with 778,822 times for Higuchi Ichiyō, who holds the twentieth spot.[79]

Immediately apparent from the list of most accessed titles, which includes the top three teiban texts, is that the high school literary canon has a significant influence on user traffic to Aozora. These texts likely rank so high because teachers and their students find it useful to read them online. But what of the other most frequently accessed titles and authors? Should we expect more overlap between what generations of high school students have been assigned and the preferences of Aozora's users, or between the latter and the aggregate decisions of generations of anthology editors? Given the different time scales, institutional contexts, and media platforms that have produced these rankings, the chance of overlap seems low. Even so, it is worth considering how to compare such lists in a holistic fashion to account for more than just the entries at the top. Several methods are available for measuring the correlation of ranked lists of items, but here I choose a modified Kendall's tau statistic to determine how closely matched the top fifty authors are across the five lists. Figure 2.15 shows the resulting values for each pair of lists, with darker tiles indicating higher correlation. The main insight to be gleaned from the figure is that Aozora is more closely aligned with the anthologies than with the high school textbooks, and that the latter have little overlap with anthologies. Despite the prominence of the teiban texts, curricular choices are on the whole not a good predictor of the authors read most often by Aozora's users.[80]

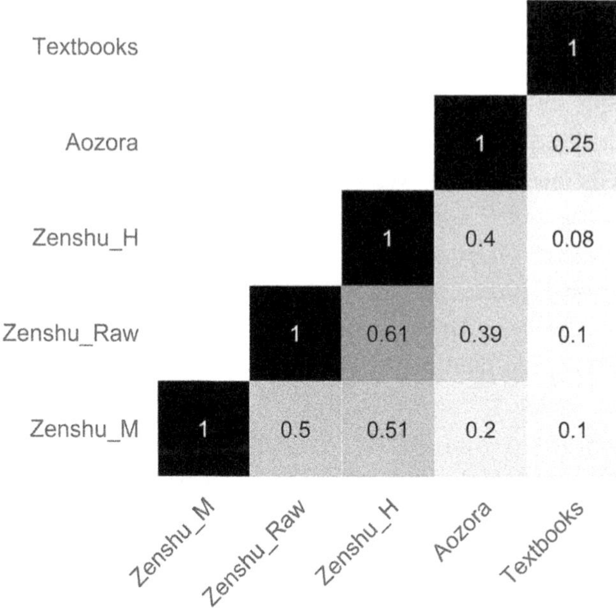

FIGURE 2.15. A matrix showing the degree of correlation between ranked author lists as measured by a modified Kendall's tau statistic. Darker tiles indicate higher correlation. The lists are comprised of the top fifty authors in postwar high school textbooks, Aozora access rankings, and the anthology data as determined by three measures: h-Index, raw frequency, and m-Index.

With this correlation matrix we have pulled back far enough to take in the many core samples of modern Japanese literature thus far unearthed. Lists of titles have been reduced to ranked lists of authors and further transformed into ordered numerical strings whose correlation can be measured statistically. It is, no doubt, a disorienting perspective, as individual texts and authors recede into their respective core samples like microscopic particles buried within layers of packed ice and soil. Our first inclination might be to rip these layers apart, liberating each particle from this single binding context to expose it again to light from multiple interpretive angles. But it is worth holding our focus for a moment on this reductive view, itself just one possible outcome of a series of conscious interpretive choices and statistical manipulations. Its purpose is not to provide a singular understanding of Aozora's relation to the print archive but a provisional map of the rifts and valleys that form where its representation of Japanese language literature collides with other situated knowledges of this archive.

At the very highest scale, which is also the lowest resolution, we have a means to understand how Aozora is informed by different histories of textual selection and valuation as they have unfolded across several intersecting aesthetic, commercial, and educational contexts. Its own biography is woven out of these earlier instruments of archival memory even as it begins to weave its own patterns. We know that Aozora captures several bright patches of the foreign literary field, albeit in rather disconnected bits and pieces. It hews closely to prewar authors canonized in anthologies and textbooks, although it does not always direct attention to the same canonical titles. It stitches together an expansive section for popular genre authors who previously left faint marks in these same anthologies and textbooks. And finally, we know it adheres all too well to the patterns by which women writers have been marginalized in archival memories.

Going forward, this multiperspectival map will need to be expanded and revised with other bibliographic traces. Those analyzed thus far should also be further explored as potential resources for constructing samples of all kinds, which means identifying the population of questions to which these samples might lead to meaningful inferences. Do the most anthologized works in a given period, for instance, share certain formal or stylistic features? What features distinguish works popular in one period versus another? These are not the questions asked in this book, which is more invested in the prewar field of literary production and in questions specific to the intricacies of that moment. To get at these questions requires targeted supplementing of Aozora as a convenience sample, using traces of the archive more fine-grained than what the bibliographic traces used in this chapter provide. Yet these traces will continue to frame our global understanding of the distinct perspective that the Aozora collection offers, one that will loom larger as the scale of evidence grows from a few hundred texts in the next chapter to several thousand by the last. As a prelude to this progression, it is worth a brief look inward at Aozora to roughly delimit, through its finitude, the population of questions to which it lends itself.

AOZORA AT THE LIMITS

My excavations of the bibliographic record have drawn on several techniques for describing and visualizing the contours of a data set and for refining the set of research questions a collection of texts can address. Applying them to the

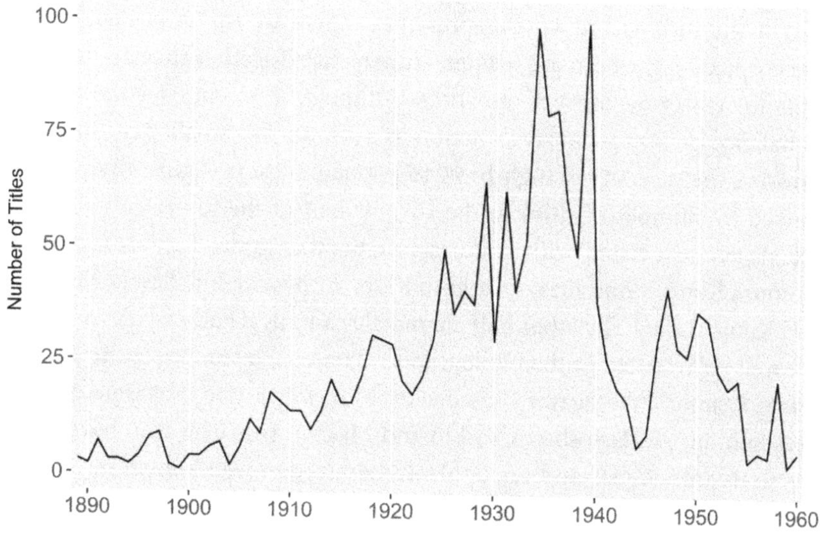

FIGURE 2.16. Number of titles per year in the Aozora fiction subset corpus. This graph represents 1,753 of the total 1,867 titles for which dates of first publication could be verified.

Japanese language fiction in Aozora, and more narrowly to those works that exceed the mean text length of the collection (e.g., equal to or longer than Hayashi Fumiko's "Shitamachi"), several intrasample constraints become apparent.[81] Plotting this corpus subset by date of first publication shows that most fall between 1908 and 1954 and are highly concentrated between 1925 and 1940 (figure 2.16). Outside of this period, there are fewer than a dozen texts per year, making analysis of longitudinal trends beyond this time frame unreliable. Conversely, trends within this time frame are likely to be driven by the mass of texts that form the graph's middle peaks. A second point is that this mass, which builds from the early 1920s and crests in the late 1930s, roughly parallels a steady upward trend in overall book publication at this time, at least as indicated by the *Shuppan nenkan* data cited previously.[82] Yet these same data show that a publishing boom of equal magnitude occurred between 1897 and 1910, a period woefully underrepresented in Aozora. Even if we grant that literary publication made up a smaller share of the total during this earlier boom, the dearth of late-Meiji fiction reinforces again that this corpus is best suited to questions whose historical horizon begins around 1910.

Within this horizon, the range of suitable questions will be further limited by the authors and works represented. There are 174 unique authors in the corpus, 19 of whom are women (11 percent). Together they are responsible for 126 (7 percent) of all works. Although it accentuates the gender imbalance present in Aozora's fiction as a whole, this smaller corpus does preserve the diversity of high-brow to popular authors (figure 2.17). When ranked by number of titles in the corpus, half of the top twenty authors are closely associated with historical or popular genre fiction, including Nomura Kodō, Unno Jūza, Okamoto Kidō, Yoshikawa Eiji, Sasaki Mitsuzō, and Kikuchi Kan. The other half are mostly canonical authors whose works are well represented in the bibliographic data sets, including Izumi Kyōka, Dazai Osamu, Akutagawa Ryūnosuke, Mori Ōgai, and Natsume Sōseki. Less familiar are Toyoshima Yoshio and Makino Shin'ichi, who have fared worse in anthologies and textbooks but who were well known in literary circles of their own time and have amassed devoted followers since. This relative diversity at the level of genre and audience bodes well for analyses that want to account for the breadth of literary output in the interwar period and, like much recent scholarship, aspire to blur the historical divisions

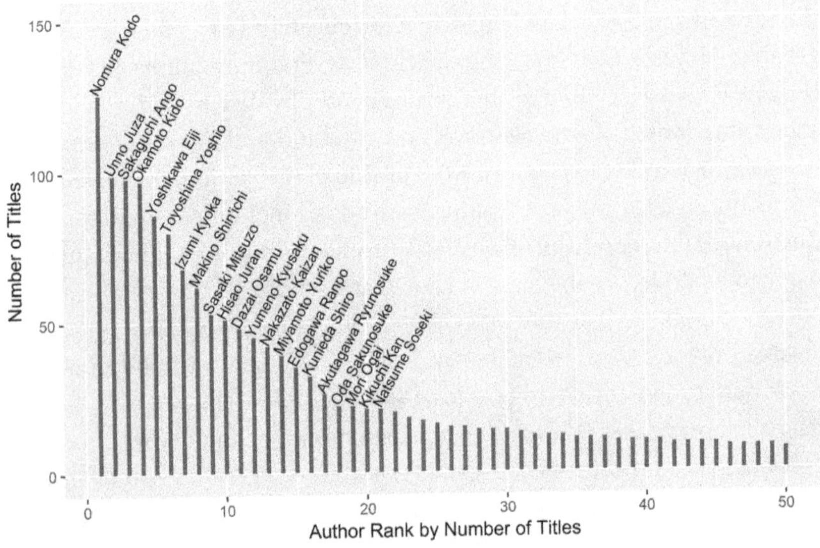

FIGURE 2.17. The twenty authors with the most titles in the Aozora fiction corpus subset. For reference, the graph shows counts for the top fifty authors in this reduced corpus. Kikuchi Kan and Natsume Sōseki are tied with twenty-one titles each.

between "pure" and "popular" literature actively being constructed and contested in these years. The chapters that follow leverage this diversity to test and perturb such divisions at the level of style, form, and discourse.

To do so, however, an additional set of constraints must be accounted for. If it appears that there is diversity at the level of author and genre, there is more homogeneity at the level of work, at least for certain well-represented popular authors such as Nomura Kodō and Okamoto Kidō. Of the 126 works attributed to Nomura, for example, 114 are installments in *Zenigata Heiji torimono hikae* (The casebook of Zenigata Heiji), a series that began in 1931 and ended in 1957 with nearly 400 episodes of varying length. Each new episode continued the ongoing adventures of Edo-period detective Zenigata and his trusty associate Hachigorō. Okamoto, incidentally, had pioneered this subgenre in the late teens with his *Hanshichi torimono chō* (The casebook of Hanshichi), of which sixty-two installments are in the reduced corpus. Further inspection reveals that many of the historical fiction writers are represented through a limited number of serialized titles. This is not true for writers of detective and science fiction such as Unno Jūza and Hisao Jūran, but even so more than four hundred works in the corpus belong to a larger series. Given the mostly episodic nature of these series, such that the narrative content varies from one installment to the next, it makes little sense to treat them as single works. Still we must be cognizant of the sampling biases introduced into large-scale analysis by the overrepresentation of works from a single series or author. By not controlling for these biases through the creation of more balanced samples, we might describe as a general trend (i.e., the increased use of specific words) what is really the local effect of serial repetition or authorial style.

These biases, along with the generic and temporal ones already noted, demarcate this collection's "outer limits." Much of this chapter has focused on how to delineate these limits through comparison with other large-scale core samples of the print archive. Although awareness of these limits is crucial to thinking about the kinds of literary historical questions this particular digital sample can address, the point of such awareness is not to defend (or critique) this corpus as a (mis)representative list or static canonical sample. On the contrary, this awareness is meant to lead us away from myths of absolute fidelity or plenitude—because there is no such thing as a complete picture—and toward the "relational mode of reasoning" that such large collections afford.[83] Relational because this corpus can be subdivided and rebalanced to create different kinds of samples through which to analyze a particular phenomenon; because its limits point us to where it could be supplemented with other texts and other kinds of evidence to expand the population of questions it can address; and finally because it can itself be related to other samples and case studies to confirm or complicate the evidence they provide about large-scale literary trends.

On this last point, consider how the Aozora fiction corpus allows us to revisit and replicate some of the investigations of literary change introduced in chapter 1. Yasumoto Biten's analysis of the change in mean percentage of kanji characters within literary texts, when redone with this corpus, shows a similar downward trend between 1900 and 1955 (figure 2.18). In absolute terms, the results show a decline from roughly 200 kanji per 1,000 characters to about 150, as compared with his estimated drop from 393 to 275. In relative terms, however, this 25 percent decline is close to his 30 percent. On the one hand, some caution is warranted given that most of the change in our sample occurs at its ends, where the amount of data is sparser. On

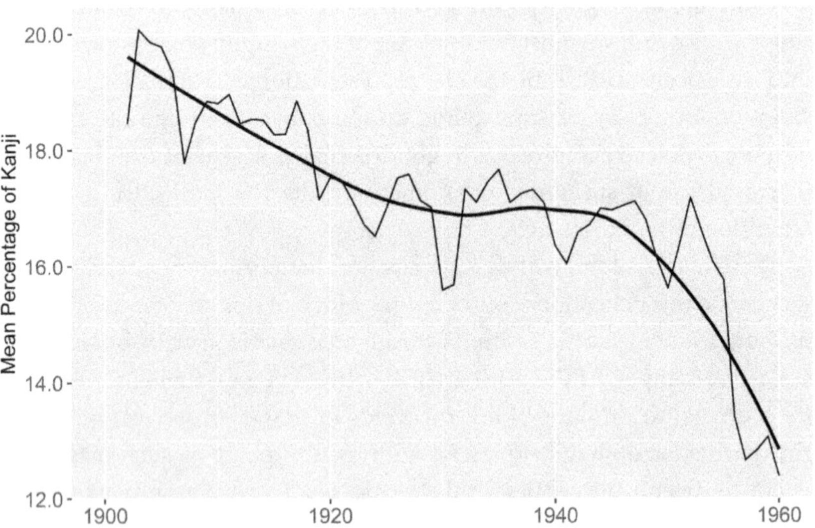

FIGURE 2.18. This graph uses the Aozora fiction corpus subset to reproduce Yasumoto's analysis of how the mean percent of kanji characters decreases over time. A loess curve is fit to the data to better illustrate the general trend.

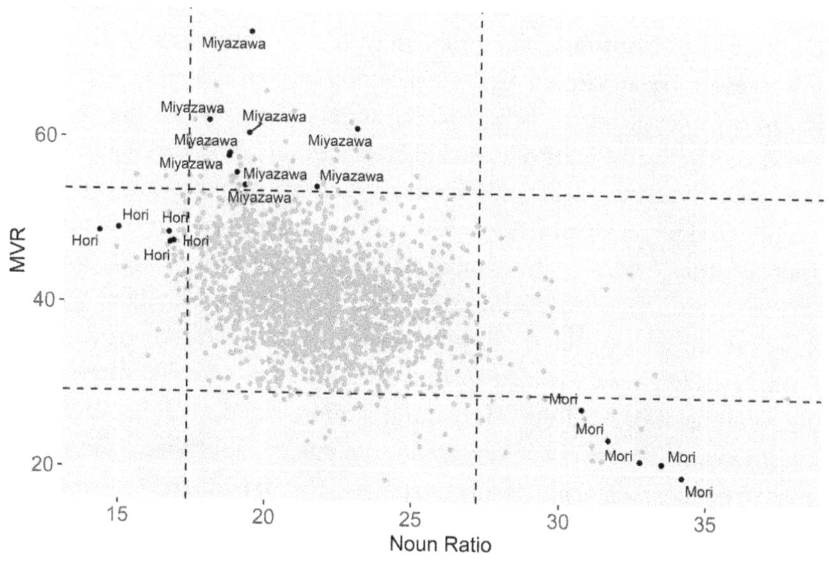

FIGURE 2.19. This plot reproduces Kabashima and Jugaku's comparison of noun ratio and MVR (figure 1.6) using the Aozora fiction corpus subset. Dashed lines indicate the 2.5th and 97.5th percentiles for each variable. Points outside these lines can be viewed as outlier texts.

the other hand, that the trend is approximately reproduced adds evidence to the claim that the decline was a real background change and is thus a meaningful context in which to situate individual works.

Similarly, we can re-create the plot that Kabashima Tadao and Jugaku Akiko made to explore how noun proportion in a literary passage is related to MVR, or the ratio of verbs to adjectives and adverbs. Figure 2.19 plots the part of speech counts for the corpus.[84] The dashed lines indicate the 2.5th and 97.5th percentiles for both variables, outside of which fall outlier texts relative to the distribution of noun ratio and MVR values overall. This plot replicates their finding that an increase in nouns is negatively correlated with a lower MVR score (e.g., fewer adjectives and adverbs when compared with verbs). Zooming in closer, it brings new outliers into view because of the wider comparative context. Whereas Ibuse and Tanizaki previously stood out as the most "summarizing" and "descriptive," respectively, now it is the historical fiction writer Mori Ōgai who is most "summarizing," the children's author Miyazawa Kenji who is most "statically descriptive," and the modernist stylist Hori Tatsuo who is most "dynamically descriptive."

The emergence of these new outliers in the much larger Aozora corpus snaps back into focus the problem of the "evidence gap" with which this chapter began. Recall that Kabashima and Jugaku were extending Hatano's earlier effort to distinguish the styles of Tanizaki and Shiga using sentence length and parts of speech. Hatano, in turn, was seeking to verify the qualitative assessments of a literary critic for whom the styles of Tanizaki and Shiga were distinctive types. With each expansion in comparative scale, each narrowing of the evidence gap, a new figuration of difference is achieved, and so too are new ways of reading the exceptionality or typicality of specific texts within the larger trends described by these figures. Shiga is displaced by Ibuse, who is displaced, finally, by Ōgai. Should we treat the last figure as more definitive because it is more exhaustive than previous ones? Exhaustiveness in and for itself—that unattainable limit point where everything has been read—is no guarantor of fact or truth. It is only ever an imagined whole, an instrument of fact making that requires "political and cognitive" investment before it can be collectively acknowledged as fact.[85] In a series of shifting figurations of difference such as those sketched here, it is easy to privilege scale as the final determinant of truth. But knowing of Aozora's various misalignments with the bibliographic record, it seems more prudent to recognize scale as an ongoing, unfinished negotiation over what counts as part and whole; over how much of the whole needs to be seen in order to see enough; and over all the ways the gap between part and whole might be narrowed to establish meaningful variation or typicality within larger unities.

It is the same negotiation alluded to by Josephine Miles in this chapter's epigraph, where she observes that the "establishing of quality" of a poem or other aesthetic object is often predicated on assumptions of quantity, the latter of which go unverified beyond the level of "general impression." But these "touchstones in art," these "rarities" singled out as being the most unique or particular along some dimension, also turn out to be fragile because of "their variability from reader to reader." Miles felt it was time "to give some proportion to the description" of poetic quality by understanding that poetry is "all that is in it as well as the best that is in it."[86] If literary critics no longer frame the exceptionality of artistic objects in terms of "quality," we have found other ways to justify a continued focus on "rarities" and the interpretive flexibility that such singular cases allow. The case study continues to be valuable precisely because it does not subordinate the "chromatic plenitude" of a text to the kinds of abstraction that comparison of many texts requires. Comparison invariably entails a narrowing of the dimensions through which texts are described, especially as the space of comparison expands.[87] Their internal coherency and localized meaning fragment, subsumed by higher-order structures and relations that can occlude, as Stanley Fish put it, "the protean and various significances which are attached, in context and by human beings, to any number of formal configurations."[88]

Reading for particularity is indeed one of the cornerstones of literary studies as a discipline and should remain so. But in practice, as Miles suggested decades ago and as others have repeatedly pointed out, even the most focused readings of particularity never wrest themselves entirely from comparison or assumptions about relative quantity. Case studies hover, as Berlant reminds us, "about the singular, the general, and the normative" even when privileging the irreducibility of the individual case or, as Alan Liu says of the New Historicist anecdote, celebrating it as random access into historical processes always everywhere indeterminate. As soon as there is a move to generalize beyond that case—to claim that it is exceptional, typical, or symptomatic of some greater whole—then a kind of quantitative logic comes into play. One has to make assumptions and choices about the relative significance of all the possible contexts that might impinge on a text's meaning (e.g., biographical, historical, discursive, political, readerly). Case-study narrative may try to represent this narrowing of context as driven by the indeterminacy of the text itself, but this only highlights for Liu a paradoxical desire for "random determination or determined randomness"—a desire to at once transcend the constraints of history while also reading through them and selecting those most relevant to one's interpretation. Subtending this desire is a series of selections on context that is something like a database query.

> Here is a key incident. It has a microdesign that feels like it may be part of a broader pattern. What does the whole data set of history look like if we filter it through that microdesign (in SQL, e.g., "SELECT author, work FROM history WHERE keyword = 'nature' OR keyword = 'Napoleon' AND year > '1802' ")? What other "hits" might be returned leading toward pattern recognition—that is, the recognition of "episteme," "mentality," "structure," "power," etc.?[89]

If this reads as a parody of historicist method, the humor works in part because of the degree to which the digital archive and keyword search already mediate so deeply the ways that scholars go about constructing the relation of part to whole, text to context. Access to more evidence, and faster ways of searching across this evidence, have forced anew the centuries old confrontation between different modes of generalization—those latent in the study of singular works and those renewed (or made possible) by changing archival infrastructures. Old as the confrontation is, it feels heightened now because of how embedded these new infrastructures have become in scholarly research practice when compared with the numerical tables, concordances, and mainframe computers of earlier eras. For some, it has become harder to ignore all the evidence we have available for the "establishing of quality," especially with respect to contexts and scales of description that, for all the affordances of the closely read case, cannot be captured through that practice alone. But to say that we should pay more attention to this evidence is not to cast aside those affordances, nor to hand over the burden of interpretation to scale in and for itself and the algorithms that render this scale knowable. As I have demonstrated, the evidence gap can be narrowed with numbers from many directions, and in many ways. Moreover, these methods, which can be thought of as attempts to construct or model the representativeness of parts in relation to wholes, are themselves protean and variable and subject to interpretation at every step of the way.

To recognize this is to recognize some of the points of continuity across the case-study and non-case-study opposition. I have addressed these continuities through the language of sampling and selection, which transposes the language of "representativeness" into a different key. It is a language that, whether in its statistical and social-scientific registers or in its more humanist variations, encodes epistemologies of generalization—of how we think about the diversity of individual parts within and against the unity of larger wholes. To the extent that literary historians are compelled to address larger bodies of evidence, even and especially when these are known to be partial and incomplete, it is this language we must learn and adapt to our own critical ends. This means drawing on the resources and practices of content analysis and other disciplines, and it will certainly involve continued debate and negotiation over how and when to sample—of how and when to construct wholes external to and exceeding individual texts.[90] That it involves such negotiation, and thus requires scholars to make explicit the "representativeness" of their samples against the piles of archival debris that history leaves in its wake, should be welcome news wherever there is a desire to pry open the black boxes through which critical judgment often operates. The digital archive is a chance to rethink, once again, the various meanings of the individual text and what textual interpretation stands to gain (and lose) from projecting this multiplicity into discrete dimensions across expanded scales of relation.

Chapter Three

GENRE AND REPETITION

> Writing about the shishōsetsu is not unlike . . . peeling an onion, skin after skin, in a vain attempt to get at the "core"; there is something inherently elusive about the entire project.
>
> —EDWARD FOWLER (1988)

Histories of modern Japanese literature find the *shishōsetsu* (or I-novel) a difficult subject to avoid. In revisiting this history through numbers, this book is no different. So many histories of Japanese literary modernity, and East Asian literary modernity more broadly, begin as histories of the narrativized self.[1] This is reason enough to start a quantitative exploration of this history at the same place. But the I-novel also appeals because of its slippery ontological status. The genre remains an archetype of a specifically "Japanese" adaptation of the novel form, which then became a model for Chinese and Korean writers.[2] It is also a genre that "critics have debated for well over half a century but . . . failed to come up with a workable definition."[3] Susceptible, like any genre, to the constant warping of its boundaries by critics who question which texts should and should not belong, each new generation is tempted to find lines of division that can explain why these particulars add up to a categorical difference with novels written elsewhere and otherwise. Both defying and demanding definition, the I-novel is an ideal starting point for considering how reading for difference in literary history gains from the scaled-up comparisons and model-oriented thinking that quantitative approaches afford.

Attention to genre also moves us beyond the author-focused stylistics that, as seen in chapter 1, have long oriented quantitative approaches to literature in Japan and elsewhere. In its apparent persistence across time and space and across a multiplicity of texts, genre is an object that feels well suited to the wider comparative lens that numerical abstraction and computational modeling provide. In its historical and social variability, however, genre also helps dislodge any pretense that such modeling is purely objective or divorced from interpretation. On the contrary, genre highlights the affordances of models, and predictive modeling in particular, for mediating between a too deterministic focus on the singular features of a genre (that it must include X) and a too arbitrary assertion that genre is held together only by the intentions of an ever-shifting community of readers. What has been said of science fiction ("there is no such *thing*") and of literature more generally ("literature is not") has also been said of the I-novel ("a literary and ideological paradigm by which a vast majority of literary works were judged and described").[4] Challenging such denials of empirical reality, but also recognizing that genre is an inherently social construct, scholars Ted Underwood and Andrew Piper have used predictive modeling to explore points of alignment and divergence between textual and social evidence. That is, between the linguistic regularities and family resemblances discoverable in a set of texts and the categorical judgments and generic distinctions that have been applied to these texts by communities of readers over time.[5] Computational models of genre are useful not for solidifying these distinctions but for investigating the stability or incoherence of the texts they describe.

In the case of the I-novel genre, communities of readers first began to cohere around it in a series of literary debates in the mid-1920s. Its earliest critics treated it as a passing fad, one that had writers gravitating to narratives tightly focused on a single interiority, usually that of the author. These "mental state novels" (*shinkyō shōsetsu*), as critic Nakamura Murao called them in 1925, propped up by a "herd psychology" that led writers to prize the banalities of their everyday lives over the realistic depiction of characters, were for him and others a sign that the development of literature in Japan was at risk of being warped. Writers were so smitten with the mental state novel that they could no longer evaluate its aesthetic merit objectively, nor its proper relation to other novelistic forms, in particular, its relation to what Nakamura called the "authentic novel" (*honkaku shōsetsu*) that was exemplified for him by Tolstoy's *Anna Karenina*. Although more challenging to write because of their elaborately constructed fictional worlds, these novels were closer to the "true path of literature" in his estimation. By 1927,

Hirabayashi Hatsunosuke lamented how far writers had deviated from this path, adopting an improvisational mode that attenuated creativity and effectively meant "no polishing of plots, no careful selection of material, no reflection on the thoughts and actions of the characters, and no necessity."[6] Plot, character, and even creativity itself were being sacrificed to the expression of personal interiority as the ultimate criteria of artistic merit.

For defenders of the I-novel, it was precisely the artifice of authentic novels that made them inferior. It bound them to the whims of the marketplace, making them popular in the sense of trivial and "vulgar" (*tsūzoku*). For critic Kume Masao, writing in 1925, the novels *War and Peace*, *Crime and Punishment*, and *Madame Bovary* were just grand tsūzoku novels, "just something to read." The artifice lay in their author's willingness to enlist the other (i.e., fictional characters) to express themselves, which was to deviate from the essence and foundation of all art: the self.[7] That same year, writer Uno Kōji chimed in to argue that mental state novels can better express the author's self because they do so more directly than authentic novels. In trying to define them formally, he followed Kume in citing their lack of interest in others. Practitioners like Kasai Zenzō, for whom the form was a means to unify life with art, could not afford to write about "lady something-or-other, workers, geisha, old tales, or vendettas." But Uno also singled out style, specifically the "remarkable style" of Mushanokōji Saneatsu, as a unique feature of the I-novel. For him, the genre originated in Mushanokōji's naive, childlike style and its innovative deployment of "colloquial" language. Here too, though, he stressed its lack of artifice, claiming it was not a conscious creation on the author's part. "He just followed his instincts and naturally wrote in this way."[8] In 1927, Tanizaki Jun'ichirō and Akutagawa Ryūnosuke famously turned this debate about artifice and value to matters of plot, the former complaining that the Japanese novel (i.e., confessional fiction) most lacked a "capacity to construct."[9] He much preferred Stendahl and historical fiction.

These snapshots show how the I-novel came to be recognized within a matrix of conceptual divisions that, as Jonathan Zwicker has argued, were already emergent in the 1890s. Divisions between foreign and domestic fiction, "between commercial literature and art for art's sake, between money and art, between plot and what?"[10] Precisely. If not plot or character, if not artifice or technique, then *what*? This *what* lay at the heart of attempts in the 1920s and after to differentiate the I-novel as a genre that both is and is not. Although critics and later historians have spilled a great deal of ink positioning the I-novel along the dimensions of literary value and national character, they have also attempted to enumerate its distinctive linguistic and stylistic features or else deny that it has any common characteristics at all. I do not propose to settle this debate, but rather to mediate its extreme positions with the equivalence spaces and comparative frameworks that computational modeling affords. Neither is it my intent to isolate *the* pattern that characterizes the I-novel, or to define a model that represents all works assigned this generic label. Any pattern found is conditioned by the materials and methods used to discover it, and so too the interpretations it is given. Robert Darnton's caution about the pursuit of history applies to genre too. It involves too vast a range of variables "to be reduced to common denominators. In struggling with them, the [literary] historian works like a diagnostician who searches for patterns in symptoms rather than a physicist who turns hard data into firm conclusions."[11] My interest in this chapter is in how our diagnoses change when we track a narrower set of symptoms across a wider range of cases.

The symptom I focus on is lexical repetitiveness, or redundancy. There are many ways to model the belief that I-novels represent a coherent genre. Here I opt for a set of measures that capture heightened redundancy in writing. This quality has historically been linked to several higher-order linguistic and aesthetic qualities associated with the I-novel, including vernacular style, the influence of Western grammar, psychological realism, and mental aberration. I seek to understand how generalizable these associations are by testing the degree to which repetition and redundancy reliably distinguish a collection of I-novels from the plot-driven works against which the genre was so often set apart, namely, works of popular fiction. In other words, I test whether repetition can be read as symptom and proxy for something like a shared "mentality," one made of "unconscious grammatical patterns and semantic associations, more than clear and distinct ideas."[12] This is at once to test the relation between this mentality and arguments about what does and does not count as an I-novel. It is also to model a surface phenomenon, repetition, such that the model potentially becomes an explanation for deeper interactions between modern writers' figurations of self and the artifice, however unconscious, by which these figurations were inscribed. To the degree this explanation holds over multiple textual instances, it becomes a way to blur some of the divisions—between art and money, between the Japanese novel and novels elsewhere—that have quarantined the I-novel from the moment it was first diagnosed.

READING REPETITION

A compelling motivation for studying literary quantity is the ability to call attention to the "repetitions of language" that otherwise may be overlooked. As Piper has argued, "literature is not founded on the rare and the singular, but rather the common and the collective, the fabric of repetition from which it is made," and part of the value of computation is to be able to follow the "grooves and channels" of this fabric.[13] Which of them to follow, however, and how to do so, are much more difficult questions. In *Fiction and Repetition*, J. Hillis Miller catalogs some of the many grooves one might trace:

> On a small scale, there is repetition of verbal elements: words, figures of speech, shapes or gestures, or, more subtly, covert repetitions that act like metaphors. . . . On a larger scale, events or scenes may be duplicated within the text. . . . A character may repeat previous generations, or historical or mythological characters. . . . Finally, an author may repeat in one novel motifs, themes, characters, or events from his other novels.

Miller argues that readers interpret novels in part by noticing these recurrences, for "any novel is a complex tissue of repetitions and of repetitions within repetitions, or of repetitions linked in chain fashion to other repetitions."[14]

If repetition is fundamental to reading, it is also always an abstraction, according to Gilles Deleuze. Noticing repetition is what allows a thing or an event to acquire a fixed identity in one's mind, yet this identity is always virtual in that the noticing itself is an abstraction. Only when the infinite variations that intervene between one occurrence of a thing and another—difference, in short—are abstracted out does the very idea of repetition become possible.[15]

Such abstraction takes place when we read, of course, even in the case of smaller, more stable units of analysis (e.g., phonemes, words) observed across a handful of texts. The study of alliteration, parallelism, or rhyme are good examples of this. Abstraction becomes all the more essential as these units gain in complexity and as one observes more instances of them. Tracing the repetition of a theme, character, or scene requires bracketing all of the additional layers of context that attend such entities and vary with each instance. Yet this is essential to fixing their identity across instances and to the counting that makes their repetition meaningful—as a thing that happens more (or less) often than some other thing. Linguists who study repetition attend to this necessary abstraction by carefully articulating what is to be counted and the background against which the counts become meaningful. One recent study identifies at least ten categories of repetition for analysis, including absolute repetition (a simple frequency); positional repetition (an unexpected higher or lower frequency at a given position in a text); associative repetition (two things coinciding more often than expected in a given frame); and repetition in blocks (a thing repeated according to a lawful distribution over blocks of text).[16] It is assumed in each case that repetition makes quantitative sense only relative to existing patterns of usage, whether in terms of the thing itself, its use with respect to some context, or its use with respect to time.[17]

One virtue of computation for studying repetition is being able to count many instances of something both consistently and efficiently. This alone, however, does not help to determine *what* to count or *how* to interpret the meaning of repetition. The process is no less "virtual" then the qualitative ways we have of noticing repetition because it is no less a subjective abstraction. Repetition occurs for many reasons, including exogenous structural factors (e.g., the limitations imposed by grammar or lexical inventory) as well as intentional use for stylistic effect, to establish thematic bonds, to provide rhetorical emphasis, or to control the flow of information.[18] In constructing a model with which to compare textual regularities, we might do as Underwood has done for English literature and focus on clusters of lexical items that repeat more often in some genres than others. Consider a set of seventy texts, published largely between 1907 and 1930, that have either been designated as I-novels by scholars or are deeply associated with the genre by virtue of their author or autobiographical mode. This includes works by some of the genre's best known contributors—Mushanokōji, Kasai, Tayama Katai, Uno Kōji, Shiga Naoya, and Chikamatsu Shūkō—but also lesser known and even parodic send-ups of the genre by writers such as Iwano Hōmei, Kanō Sakujirō, Hirotsu Kazuo, Akutagawa, and Tanizaki.[19] Would we expect these works, on the whole, to employ a distinctly different lexicon than an equal-sized sample of plot-driven genre fiction from the twenties and thirties, including classic whodunits by Kōga Saburō and Unno Jūza, erotic-grotesque thrillers by Edogawa Ranpō and Hamao Shirō, and sword-laden historical dramas by the likes of Yoshikawa Eiji and Nakazato Kaizan?[20]

It seems obvious that these works, given their thematic foci and narrative modes, could be easily distinguished by comparing their diction. The most naive approach would compare the different frequencies with which any word (or lexical unit) is used as a proportion of the total number of words in each group of texts. This tends to privilege the highest-frequency words, whose frequency may only be a function of how common they are in the language as a whole rather than how distinctive they are of any one group. Another approach is to ask which words in each group are used with a frequency that is unexpected if we assume all the texts are generated from the same source language. A word that occurs with wildly different ratios in each group here becomes evidence of group dissimilarity and, thus, of the word's distinctiveness.[21] This approach, known as the χ^2 (chi-square) test, reveals that the most distinctive words in the I-novels are first- or third-person singular pronouns (myself, I, he, her) and words related to family (home, elder sister, children, mother). The popular works, in contrast, show a predilection for swords, lords, and castles, but also cases (*jiken*), detectives, and criminals. It is hardly surprising that works obsessed with narrating the self naturally tend to spend more time talking about it and its immediate social relations. An analysis of distinctive words can only take us so far in trying to capture the illusive *what* around which the I-novel's generic identity has long perambulated. But if the repetition of specific diction is unenlightening, what of the deeper structures of repetition animating these opposing populations of selves and samurai, families and detectives? What of repetitiveness itself as a stylistic trait?

The intuition that repetition, in and of itself, might differentiate works labeled as I-novels from those labeled otherwise is born out of long-running debates about the genre's coherency. Literary historians who attest to the empirical reality of the genre generally place the form's origins at the turn of the twentieth century, when a new generation of writers transformed the representational logic of Naturalism into an obsession with documenting one's inner thoughts and daily experiences no matter how shocking or mundane. By 1909, it looked to one critic like Japan had entered an "age of confession," one that would dominate the literary establishment into the early 1920s.[22] To explain this age, and the texts written under its spell, some scholars have looked to definitive shifts in narrative structure, rhetorical style, or social and media contexts, teasing out specific features that a majority of the texts share.[23] One change to which the genre is intimately bound is the consolidation of the modern written vernacular, or *genbun-itchi*, and the development of a colloquial style. Other scholars point to active experimentation with imported narrative techniques and grammatical forms from European languages that occurred in close concert with vernacularization. These imported elements (often referred to as *oubunmyaku*) include free indirect discourse and long interior monologue, but also punctuation, use of personal pronouns, translated conjunctions, inanimate subjects, personification, new kinds of analogy, inverted syntax, "persistent" or overwrought description, and the clear delineation of subject-predicate relations.[24] With respect to the latter, much attention is given to how Japanese, as a noninflected language that traditionally allowed for great flexibility in whether to specify the grammatical subject, was both leveraged and deformed by Naturalist writers associated with the turn to self-obsessed narrative.[25]

Some scholars have sought to identify the I-novel's coherency in specific linguistic determinants, and others have sought to disassemble it. They parse the multiple ideological currents running through its representative works, question its stability over time, and erode its claims to being narrative fiction in any true sense.[26] The latter strategy, made by practitioners and critics alike, often means emphasizing the genre's lack of emplottment. I-novels are tedious descriptions of "your own life and nothing else" that have "no shape, no form, no style"; "fragmented and short-winded"; "a random account of personal experience"; a "medium for intimate expression that would suffer from too much attention to structure"; or "a string of impressionistic musings."[27] In 1907, Shimazaki Tōson foreshadowed this emphasis on narrative lack when he described his shift in novelistic method from the Realist, highly emplotted *Hakai* (The broken commandment, 1906) to the more personal and self-centered *Haru* (Spring, 1908): "With *Haru* I completely stopped working out a structure and, having only vaguely in mind that I would try to paint such and such sort of character, I wrote the work without making any sort of plan."[28] To eschew structure and plot was precisely the point of the confessional mode.

There is a fine line between feigned indifference to narrative structure and the development of aesthetic techniques precisely to project its absence. Tōson's *Haru* sits right at the threshold of a moment when such techniques were coming to be valued in Japanese letters, and indeed dramatizes this shift by redistributing its narrative focus from two main characters in the first half of the novel to the individual mental anguish of the suicidal poet Aoki in the second half. As Christopher Hill notes, Aoki was one of the many "neurasthenic characters" who proliferated after the Russo-Japanese War, particularly in novels from the rising Naturalist school and in works retroactively associated with the I-novel (e.g., Tayama Katai's *Futon*, Iwano Hōmei's *Hōrō*).[29] An entire body of self-referential fiction, in fact, was dubbed the "neurasthenia novel" (*shinkei suijaku shōsetsu*), itself a by-product of an emergent consensus that psychological deterioration and mental anguish were the proper source and subject of modern art, and that artistic creativity was itself a form of mental abnormality, thus making the latter a necessary condition for becoming an author.[30]

This consensus was informed by French Naturalist writing, characterized by a movement in the "direction of disintegration and confusion"; "from order to disorder, from mental stability to hysteria and madness."[31] It was also influenced by Max Nordau's popular *Degeneration* (1892–1893), which modeled literary critique as a form of medical diagnosis and found in French Naturalist and symbolist writing the symptoms of a degenerate age: "overweening vanity and self-conceit, strong emotionalism, confused disconnected thoughts, garrulity (the 'logorrhea' of mental therapeutics), and complete incapacity for serious sustained work."[32] As Pau Pitarch-Fernandez has argued, Nordau's treatise had the effect of popularizing medical terms to evaluate, and then later to validate, a heightened aesthetic sensibility and literary genius. He likely would have read the following lines from *Haru*, describing Aoki's ceaseless meditations on his own ennui, as symptomatic of social degeneracy: "It became a habit, and even when there was no need, he thought. He thought, he thought, even worn out he still thought. There was hardly a moment when his mind was at rest."[33] By 1908, this was looking increasingly like the mark of male artistic genius.

Vernacularization, adoption of Western grammar, substitution of plot for a solipsistic focus, mental disorder—I highlight these elements because each can be connected to ideas about—and measurement of—repetition understood as lexical redundancy. Indeed, redundancy has been central to scholarly attempts to differentiate not only the modern speaking subject but also the mentally aberrant one. Defined as the repetition of certain units of language (e.g., letters, phonemes, morphemes) either due to contextual dependency or to the enhancement of message reliability, redundancy is inherent to all natural languages.[34] Languages are structured by rules and conventions that allow us to predict, for example, how likely it is that a word will follow another word or sequence of words, or to drop words implied by context. A degree of predictability, hence repetition, creates the foundation for communication and shared meaning. Yet many have argued that this built-in redundancy is even more extreme in spoken language, and in oral cultures in general. Walter Ong, for instance, argues that formulaic expressions and repetition are an aid to memory in oral cultures and that in oral discourse "the mind must move ahead more slowly, keeping close to the focus of attention much of what it has already dealt with. Redundancy, repetition of the just-said, keeps both speaker and hearer surely on the track."[35] Linguists who study conversation suggest that "repetition is at the heart not only of how a particular discourse is created [between speakers], but how discourse itself is created."[36]

If speaking is more redundant than writing, what of writing that expressly imitates the spoken word and rejects some of the conventions of literary language? Scholars have used repetition to identify the linguistic markers of colloquial style in Western language contexts, and it is reasonable to wonder if the development of this style in Japan also resulted in heightened redundancy.[37] We know that authors associated with the I-novel strove to create a reportive style that felt as immediate and transparent as speaking, perfecting the colloquial idiom to such an extent that by the 1920s it was seen as a stranglehold by modernist writers such as Yokomitsu Ri'ichi, who pushed for a new literary Formalism emphasizing the material properties of the written word itself.[38] Also perceived as a hindrance was the idiom's incorporation of Western grammatical elements, which Tanizaki decried as so much monstrous "translation-ese" and as alien to native Japanese forms of literary expression.[39] Some of the same writers credited with perfecting a colloquial style are credited with successfully Europeanizing written Japanese, and indeed the two linguistic developments (along with the imperative to confession itself) are seen by some scholars to entail one another.[40] Significantly, several of the core elements associated with imported Western grammar have been singled out for the repetitiveness they introduce to literary language. In particular, an overuse of personal pronouns and a delineation of subject-predicate relations that lead to overexplanation and unnecessary repetition of words otherwise implied by context. Tanizaki highlights these elements in his 1934 primer on style while chiding himself for his own youthful infatuation with the third-person pronoun "he" (*kare*).[41]

If the imbrication of colloquial idiom and foreign grammar give reason to suspect that I-novels will be more repetitive than contemporaneous genres, what of their predilection for intense psychological description and representation of mental disorder? Will this similarly manifest as heightened repetitiveness? Freud famously associated repetition with psychological function by interpreting acts of mental reproduction as a mechanism for resisting confrontation with unpleasant, repressed memories.[42] Yet only with the rise of psycholinguistics in the United States and Europe between the 1930s and 1950s were attempts made to empirically ground this association. Ironically, some of the most common measures of lexical repetition and redundancy used by computational linguists today are products of this moment. An interest in such measures stemmed from a desire by psycholinguists to develop tools for educational and clinical assessment such that, given a particular sample of writing or speech, researchers could easily measure things like lexical diversity. If more of the same words were repeated at higher frequency, or if many different words were being used with lower frequency, this might indicate something about the writer's or speaker's mental state.

George Zipf laid some of the groundwork for this research in 1935 when he developed his eponymous law stating that the distribution of word frequency ranks in a given sample of natural language obeys a power law. That is, the frequency of any word is inversely proportional to its rank in the frequency table, where rank is determined by ordering all words by their frequency in the sample. In theory, this means that the most frequent word will occur twice as many times as the second most frequent word, and so on. Zipf's Law is still accepted as a universal feature of natural languages, but of interest here is the psychological interpretation he originally gave it. He read it as a symptom of a deep property of mind called "the principle of least effort," which he derived from a model of communication in which speakers benefited from reducing "the size of [their] vocabulary to a single word" whereas listeners preferred to "increase the size of a vocabulary to a point where there will be a distinctly different word for each different meaning."[43] Balancing out these two opposing forces in communication would generate, under normal conditions, the smooth rank-frequency relationship that his law described. Yet the very idea that there should be a normal, or natural balancing of forces, was predicated on Zipf's investigation of deviations from this norm. Specifically, he analyzed the recorded speech of autistic and schizophrenic patients and argued that a sharper negative slope in the rank-frequency relation meant fewer words were overloaded with more meanings, suggesting a resistance to adjusting one's private language to a common cultural vocabulary.[44]

In 1938, John B. Carroll developed a diversity measure based on the observation that the growth of word diversity with text size must approach a limit. His measure focused on how often frequent words tended to be repeated in a passage, and he asserted that measures like this could help assess the relative adherence of one's verbal behavior to linguistic norms.[45] The next year, Wendell Johnson introduced the notion of type-token ratio (TTR): the number of unique words in a text divided by the total number of words. He suspected that the ratio might serve as "a measure of degree of frustration, or of disorientation," and that it could serve to quantify the phenomena of "one-track mind," or "monomania."[46] Johnson participated in several studies in the early 1940s that used his TTR measure, among others, to compare the speech and writing of adults and children, different age groups, IQ groups, sexes, schizophrenics, and normal adults.[47] These studies observed that higher IQ correlates with higher lexical diversity and higher TTR; that the college freshman's TTR is slightly higher than the schizophrenic's; and that speech on the telephone is more repetitive than schizophrenic speech. The notion that lower diversity in word use, and thus greater repetition, signaled abnormality of some sort (e.g., less education, less ability to relate to others, or extreme orality) was central to early psycholinguists' theories about language and cognition.

These measures of lexical diversity shared a mathematical relation to a measure which became highly influential in the 1950s and represented an alternate approach to the problem of repetition: entropy. Following the work of Claude Shannon and Warren Weaver at Bell Labs, and as part of the general reconceptualization of language as a stochastic (information-theoretical) process at this time, psycholinguists began analyzing not just the diversity of words but the predictability of their sequential order (their "transitional probabilities"). They refocused ideas about repetition through the twin lenses of redundancy and the efficiency of communication channels. In an information-theoretic context, the redundancy of a message (its entropy) reflects the amount of "information" in that message. Here information means the likelihood of a message based on the units available to constitute it, but also all the ways of combining these units given the rules or patterns governing their arrangement. Information, in short, expresses how many different ways a message can be constructed given these initial constraints. The most information-rich language would be one where any given word is equally likely to appear next to any other. Every word, and thus every message, in this artificial language would carry new information because each would be as random and unpredictable as the one before it. The messages would also be wholly unintelligible, which is why all natural languages have some redundancy built into them.

Like TTR, entropy and its companion redundancy have served as compelling frameworks for thinking about the psychology of language. Roman Jakobson, for instance, has theorized that language is a code whose conventions differ between inner, affective language (which tends to be more redundant) and exteriorized, intellectual language. Anthony Wilden has used the notion of redundancy to reinterpret Freud's description of psychic symptoms as revealed in multiple, overdetermined ways. The compulsion to repeat, he argues, is really a safeguard against inner mental noise.[48] Although theoretically useful, entropy has proven tricky to measure in a holistic way. Not only does it vary with text length, it also varies with the unit of analysis and the length of the sequence being considered. As a sequence grows longer, so too does the number of possible combinations with which to predict the randomness of the next item in the sequence. Entropy is thus biased by how much of a text or corpus is available to be measured and is also increasingly intractable as the number of units and their possible combinations increases. In practice, this meant that early applications of entropy to text were confined to smaller units of analysis (e.g., phonemes, letters, syllables) because one could expect to see the fuller range of possible combinations in a given portion of text.[49] It also meant that the focus remained on individual words or word pairs, such as with Gustav Herdan's use of entropy to measure how writers manipulate the variability of expression to avoid undue repetition.[50] When confined to the individual word level, entropy simply captures the spread of the total words of a sample among the different words available in that sample. The passage with highest entropy is one in which every word is unique and different; in the lowest every word is the same.[51]

Buried within the history of the now canonical linguistic measures of TTR and entropy is a recurring assumption that repetitiveness and redundancy correspond to mental state. The fact that psycholinguists continued to pursue this correspondence, regardless of whether lexical repetitiveness or relative homogeneity of word use truly indicate schizophrenia or monomania, reinforces how intuitive this assumption was, at least since Nordau. Intuitive enough, in fact, that we can imagine writers leveraging it to project mental disorder (recall Aoki: "He thought, he thought, even worn out he still thought."). Add this to the association of repetitiveness with orality and an exaggerated use of certain imported grammatical forms and we are reminded of how overdetermined any reading of repetition will be. There is no easy way to disentangle all its possible causes using only generic measures. Nevertheless, if repetition potentially reflects the concentrated effect of all these higher-order phenomena, then it becomes a tempting diagnostic for testing whether works designated as I-novels exhibit this effect to a greater degree. Does an emphasis on one or several of these phenomena add up to a shared "mentality" across dozens of self-referential works?

MEASURING REPETITION

Having provisionally fixed the kind of repetition to count, the next step is to measure it within the corpus of I-novels. TTR and entropy measures are straightforward to implement, although they are highly correlated with text length. Thus instead of applying them to whole works, I apply them to works divided into equally sized segments (in this case one thousand words, or about fifteen hundred individual characters).[52] Averaging all the values across these segments provides a mean TTR and entropy score for each work. Standard deviation of the values tells us how widely they vary across a work. Together, TTR and entropy will help indicate which works tend to repeat fewer types of words more often. Because they treat every word as a discrete unit, however, they overlook the repetition of words or characters in their original sequence. It would be useful to know if a work is not only repeating a narrower range of words more often but also a narrower range of phrases or character sequences across its entirety. To capture such long-range dependencies between sequences of individual phonetic and Chinese characters, I use an entropy measure developed by Ioannis Kontoyiannis that can be applied to an entire work.[53] A lower score indicates more repetition of the same narrow set of character sequences.

To these I add two additional measures for capturing the narrowness of vocabulary in a work. One is George Yule's "Characteristic K," developed in 1944 to measure the repetitiveness or uniformity of vocabulary in a text. It relies on word rank and frequency for its calculation, relating the sum of all word frequencies to the number of words with a particular frequency, and was designed by Yule to be independent of sample size.[54] A second measure is an index of lexical concentration developed by French linguist Pierre Guiraud, also in 1944. "Guiraud's C" expresses the proportion of a text's cumulative word frequency which is taken up by its fifty most frequent "content" words. Here, I define a "content" word as any noun, including pronouns and proper nouns. According to Guiraud, higher values of C imply that "an author concentrates his attention on a relatively narrow range of words with full meaning," which in turn testifies to "thematic compactness, to the concentration on the main theme, [and] in some cases also to stock phrases."[55] Both Yule's K and Guiraud's C are related to entropy in that they depend on the sums of relative word frequencies but have the virtue of not requiring texts to be divided into smaller segments.[56]

When applied to the I-novel and popular corpora, almost all of these measures indicate a tendency of the I-novels to be, on average, more redundant and less lexically diverse than popular works. More precisely, when comparing the distributions of each measure using a common statistical test, the mean value for I-novels is either higher or lower to a degree that is statistically significant.[57] Average TTR and entropy, for instance, are generally lower for the I-novel texts, a fact that can be visualized with violin plots (figure 3.1). The plots illustrate that I-novels, as a group, score slightly lower on these measures compared with popular works, with a few extreme outliers pulling the distribution lower (width corresponds to the proportion of works that have the values indicated on the y axis). Interestingly, I-novels also have a lower standard deviation of TTR and entropy, indicating that they are more consistently repetitive across all one thousand word segments. Looking at Yule's K and Guiraud's C, I-novels tend to have higher values, suggesting more lexical uniformity and more compact narrative focus. One measure that shows no significant difference is Kontoyiannis's

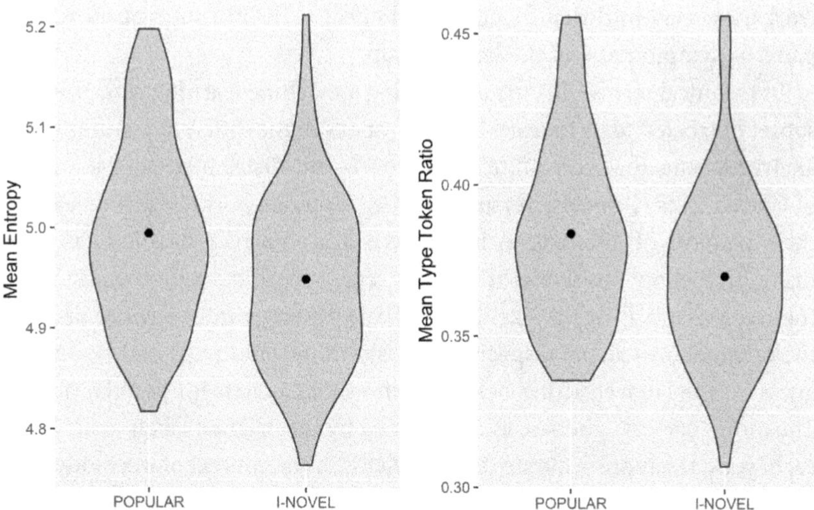

FIGURE 3.1. The distribution of values for mean entropy and mean type-token ratio (TTR) in all Japanese works classified as popular and I-novel. The width of the violin plots corresponds to the proportion of works with the value indicated on the y axis. Black dots indicate the mean of each distribution.

entropy measure; neither genre, in other words, has significantly more or less long-range dependencies than the other. Overall, however, most of the measures signal a slight tendency toward repetitiveness in works designated as I-novels.

A "slight tendency," needless to say, does not make for a convincing argument. Although the difference in distributions is statistically significant, the bulk of works in both groups mostly fall within the same range. Do all these slight tendencies add up to evidence of anything more? Before drawing any conclusions, we want to know if these tendencies, when analyzed in concert rather than individually, are any better at discriminating the two genres. We might also want to investigate which works are pulling the distributions higher or lower, and what lexical cues might hint at a tendency toward repetitiveness. In the first instance, I can leverage the kinds of predictive modeling introduced at the beginning of the chapter, whose main impetus is the ability to look at many features in combination, sometimes thousands, to determine if their relation can better explain, in a statistical sense, the social evidence (i.e., genre labels) applied to a corpus.

If entropy alone reliably distinguishes only a few I-novels from popular works, we may find that its combined effect with other measures reveals patterns symptomatic of the larger group.

In technical terms, this means training a machine learning *classifier* on a subset of labeled texts to *learn* how the values of the different features being analyzed—and that constitute one's *model*—are distributed across one set of labeled texts (I-novels) versus the other (popular works). Having learned these patterns of distribution in the texts it is shown, a classifier can then make predictions on works it has not seen, providing a probability score (between 0 and 1) of the likelihood of a work being in one genre and not the other. Scores above a specified decision threshold (e.g., 0.5) result in a guess for the I-novel; scores below the threshold a guess for popular fiction. The more "correct" guesses, as determined by the original labels assigned to each work, the more accurate the classifier is in the context of the model and labels on which it was trained. Applying this approach here, I can determine whether a model built just from the features specified so far is any good at distinguishing I-novels from popular fiction. It turns out that it is not. A logistic regression classifier trained on the data using tenfold cross validation (i.e., training ten times on 90 percent of the data and predicting on the other 10 percent) guesses the assigned label correctly only 64 percent of the time.[58] In other words, not much better than random. Moreover, using a process called "best subset selection," we know that this accuracy is the highest that can be achieved with these features, and that only three of them are needed to do so: mean TTR, Yule's K, and the Kontoyiannis entropy measure.[59]

Yet if these various measures of lexical redundancy are not good at distinguishing the I-novels as a group, they do tell us that some of these works push the tendency to repeat further than any of their popular counterparts. In the case of entropy scores, for instance, seventeen I-novels fall more than one standard deviation below the mean compared to only seven popular works. This includes the extreme outliers Mushanokōji's *Omedetaki hito* and Uno Kōji's *Hitogokoro* (Human heart, 1920), but also Hirotsu Kazuo's "Chichi no shi" (Death of my father, 1930), Shiga Naoya's *Wakai* (Reconciliation, 1917), and Akutagawa's *Haguruma* (Cogwheels, 1927). Although these works vary widely in narrative content, the one thousand word segments that contribute to their lower entropy may share something in common. In fact, when we look at the words most distinctive of the lowest entropy I-novel segments versus the highest ones, at the top of the list (after filtering character names) are personal pronouns such as *jibun* (oneself), *watashi* (I), *boku* (I), and *kare* (he); the verb stem *omou* (to think); and two forms of the conjunction *shikashi* (but, however).[60] In contrast, the most distinctive words in the high-entropy segments are mostly particles associated with reported dialogue (e.g., *yo, n, ne, nee, wa*). The former set of words stands out precisely because they recall the higher-order phenomena commonly associated with I-novels, in particular the adoption of Western grammatical elements (personal pronouns and conjunctions) and the penchant for narrating internal thought.

To determine whether general repetitiveness coincides with specific lexical items in the I-novel, we can expand our feature set and model. Are there groups of words or patterns of use that can help triangulate the tendency toward repetition with the I-novel corpus? Based on the previous clues and on intuitions gleaned from the secondary literature, the most obvious features to include should account for such things as use of pronouns, conjunctions or connective phrases, and verbs of cognition or feeling. For the first two, I create sentence level measures that give the proportion of non-dialogue sentences in a work containing a first- or third-person singular pronoun and the proportion that begin with a conjunction or connective word.[61] For the last feature, I calculate the ratio of words whose lemmatized form derives from one of the following: *kanzuru* (to feel), *kangaeru* (to think), *omou* (to think), *kokoromochi* (feeling), *kibun* (feeling), *kimochi* (feeling), and *shinpai* (concern, worry). In addition to these features, I also measure the proportion of more generic categories of lexical and notational items such as punctuation, periods, and grammatical function words (e.g., particles, interrogatives, demonstrative pronouns, copula).[62] Finally, I measure the proportion of dialogue in each work. Individually, almost all of these features have a distribution in the I-novels that differs from popular fiction to a statistically significant degree. The difference is slight in some cases (I-novels have slightly less punctuation, slightly more periods and function words) and more extreme in others (the mean ratio of cognition/feeling verbs is 1.5 times that of the popular works; the ratio of sentences with first- or third-person pronouns 1.8 times as much; and the amount of dialogue about two-thirds that of popular fiction). Self-contemplation, it seems, leaves much less time for small talk. The only feature that showed no significant difference on its own was the ratio of sentences beginning with a conjunction or connective word.

These differences point to further stylistic tendencies within the I-novel corpus, but it is equally illuminating that several of these new features correlate with measures of repetitiveness. Across all texts, measures for pronoun, conjunction, thought/feeling verb, and function word use negatively correlate with mean TTR and entropy in the range of −.42 to −.67 (perfect negative correlation is −1). This means that a rise in one (e.g., thought/feeling verbs) tends to correspond with a decline in the other (e.g., TTR), as visualized in figure 3.2. We also see from this plot that the negative correlation (as indicated by the fitted regression lines) holds *within* each genre, if to a slightly lesser degree in the I-novels. The more thinking and feeling taking place in a text, the less lexically diverse it tends to be. Such correspondences are likely to strengthen our previous model by amplifying the signal given by repetitiveness alone. In fact, when I created a classifier from the full set of features, it was far more accurate (82 percent). This time, a combination of just four features best predicts whether a work is an I-novel or not: standard deviation of TTR, personal pronoun usage, thought/feeling verbs, and use of conjunctions or connective words. These four are distributed in such

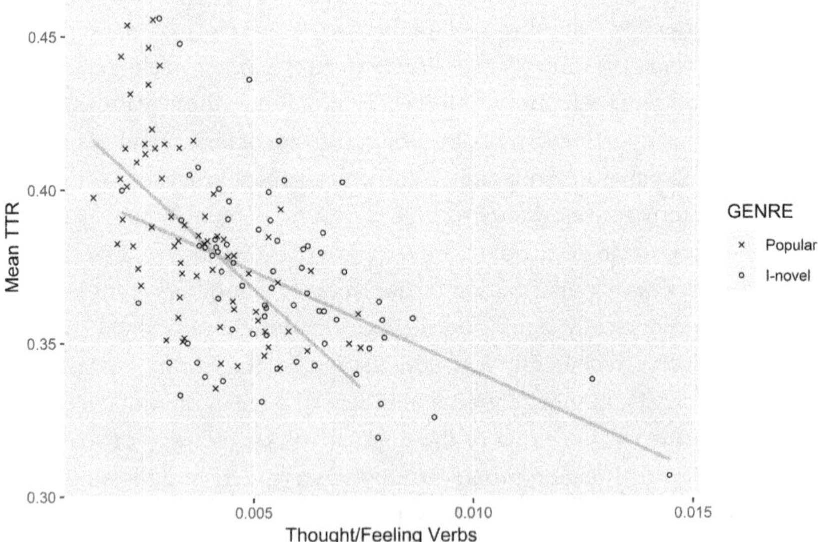

FIGURE 3.2. Scatterplot comparing values for mean type-token ratio (TTR) and proportion of thought/feeling verbs across all Japanese works classified as popular and I-novel. Linear regression lines are fit to each genre and indicate a negative correlation in both.

a way that, when analyzed in relation, they do a much better job than the previous model of separating I-novels from popular fiction.

But is it good enough? Does the model convincingly diagnose, as a surface symptom, the higher-order linguistic and aesthetic phenomena that are critical determinants of the I-novel as a genre? The first question exposes the double-edged sword that is predictive modeling, at least as used by literary historians. On one side is the need to build models that are accurate enough to convince us that the models are meaningful—that they are picking up real differences in the categories of interest and that these differences can be related to the model's features. On the other side is a constant skepticism of the limits of perfect accuracy in an interpretative context. Although we could continue to refine the model so that it perfectly distinguishes between I-novels and popular fiction, it would be so tied down (or overfit) to these 140 works that lessons learned from it would no longer be generalizable beyond them. Even more disconcerting, such a model would obscure the points of overlap and intersection we expect to find between genres whose categorical fuzziness is acknowledged from the outset. Given the few dimensions we use to probe this fuzziness, there will invariably be works in which social and textual evidence does not readily align, and these are important for understanding what the model is seeing. In the end, whether the model is not good enough, or too good, is not something the model itself can answer. This falls to critics who must evaluate a model's findings in the context of their arguments. Here, we have to decide whether the features in our second model, and the works that accentuate them, speak to a shared stylistic "mentality" that enabled and sustained the making of a literature for the self—a literature about something other than character or plot.

Part of making this decision means exploring the expanded equivalence space afforded by the model. Recall that the classifier does not return a categorical decision about whether a work is an I-novel but a probability score between 0 and 1. These scores can be used to create an equivalence space that is also a continuum. In figure 3.3, I-novels are listed on the right and popular works on the left. Works are ordered from top to bottom by their probability of being an I-novel based on our model. In one glance, you can see which works, regardless of their assigned genre label, express the model features in ways most similar to (or divergent from) the majority of I-novels. The cluster of I-novels above 0.7 makes the classifier as accurate

Fitted Probability

1.0 Omedetaki_hito Shii_no_wakaba Tbota_no_mushi Chichi_wo_uru_ko Suikyosha_no_dokuhaku Sei_ni_mezameru_koro

Ai_no_tame_ni

Shinsei Suika_kuu_hito Tojou Nakama Wakai Younen_jidai

Chichi_no_shi

Giwaku Mousou Haru_no_tori

Akuma_no_deshi

Remon

Nobuko Haguruma Fuyu_no_hae

Renai_kyokusen

Fuyu_no_hi Heibon

Ugomeku_mono

Ippon_no_hana Tandeki

Fushuu

Kodomo_no_kanashimi Tsuma_wo_kau_keiken

Satsujinki

0.8

Nouha_soujuushi

Utsuriga Kasou_jinbutsu

Fukami_fujin_no_shi

Namerigawa_hotori_nite Wakaretaru_tsuma_ni_okuru_tegami Arakure

Yakudoshi

Kusatta_kagerou

Yo_no_naka_he Sekenshi

Kumo Cisoisha

Yamanote_no_ko

Hoima_to_uguisu

Kanashiki_chichi

Shimo_kouru_yoi Jukensei_no_shuki Tasogare Tono_he Kyoran Aru_onna

Jinkou_shinzou

Shiju_yonichi Futon

Himitsu

Doroningyo Hitogokoro Den'en_no_youtsu Michikusa

0.6

Hanshichi_torimonocho_(no1) Hanshichi_torimonocho_(no3)

Ko_wo_tsurete Gouku

Kurokami

Vita_sexualis

Muki

Arajotai Chichi_no_konrei Chijin_no_ai

Haru

Hannichi Kyozo_no_chichi

0.4

Rantouba_no_tennyo

Shi_no_seppun

Tsuma Kabi Tou_seikatsusha

Ketsuekigata_satsujin_jiken Kyarakosan: Shakoushitsu

Yaneura_no_sanposha Keu_no_hanzai

Hanshichi_torimonocho_(no45)

Hasekura_jiken

Oppa_no_satsujin Kohaku_no_paipu Tantei_yawa

Yuki_no_yadori Majan_satsujin_jiken

Shosen_densha_no_shagekishu Jyonan

0.2

Kare_ga_koroshita_ka Hanshichi_torimonocho_(no2)

Shokubutsu_ningen Sei_arabe

Seigi Ougon_wo_abiru_onna Kinrou Miyamoto_Musashi: chi_no_maki Akum

D-Zaka_no_satsujin_jiken Bochi_tenboutei

Shonen_no_hi Boi

Onna_kisha_no_yakuwari

Daibosatsu_toge_(no_2) Tatsu_no_kiritsu

Tange_sazen: Part_3 Tange_sazen: Part_1 Norowaro_no_ie

Daibosatsu_toge_(no_3)

Sekigaisen_otoko Nazo_no_onna Rinpun Mayu_kakushi_no_rei

Daibosatsu_toge_(no_1)

Sabaku_no_koto Denkiburo_no_kaishi_jiken

Jimushi Naruto_hicho: kamigata_no_maki Kusa_meikyu Odoru_bijiin_zou

Tange_sazen: Part_2

Nangoku_taiheiki

Mato Dosenkai_jiken

Jingai_makkyo: yumobito

Shinpi_konchukan

Shinshu_koketsujo

0.0 Koumou_keisei Kokushiken_satsujin_jiken Ningyo_no_nazo_oiwa_goroshi

POPULAR I-NOVEL

Genre

as it is. The works of popular fiction parallel to them prevent it from being any better. All the titles above 0.7 share a tendency toward consistent levels of lexical homogeneity, repeated personal pronoun use, verbs of thought and feeling, and beginning sentences with conjunctions. The figure invites us to read them through these shared tendencies before opening them to the myriad other contextual dimensions that interpretation warrants. For instance, we might search for other shared qualities that strengthen the link between their empirical tendencies and experiments with colloquial style or foreign grammar. Or with specific representational strategies for turning interiority and mental disorder into art. This model, and its particular abstraction of repetition, creates a new frame for reading these works together. But it is only when we begin to push out the frame's edges that we see how useful the model is for diagnosing deeper linguistic, stylistic, and thematic affinities.

REPETITION AS STYLE

Reading through a computational frame requires constant negotiation between the dimensionality reduction it affords and all the dimensions that come rushing back into view as we push out its edges to examine individual texts. Push too far and the frame falls apart, returning us to an interpretive mode in which every dimension potentially bears down on meaning. Push too little and our interpretation remains trapped by the frame's initial reduction. But expand the frame just enough to let in our initial dimensions of interest—orality, foreign grammar, substitution of plot for solipsistic focus, and mental disorder—and the works most like an I-novel appear to stretch expression to its extremes along one or more of these lines. Consider two of the works by Kasai Zenzō at the top of figure 3.3: "Shii no wakaba" (Young pasania leaves, 1924) and "Suikyōsha no dokuhaku" (A mad drunk's monologue, 1927). Edward Fowler notes that the former was dictated to a scribe over a twelve-hour period, lending the work an orality that "asserts itself emphatically and repeatedly" in part because Kasai refused to read over the dictation. This left him, like a

FIGURE 3.3 (OPPOSITE). Japanese works in each genre are ordered according to their predicted probability of being an I-novel (closest to 1) or a popular work (closest to 0). On the left are works labeled popular in the original corpus, and on the right are works labeled as I-novels.

meandering storyteller, to constantly hark back to his previous utterances through his selective memory of them, leading to "increasingly redundant summations . . . [and] frenzied yet almost formulaic musings about insanity."[63] The latter work, one of Kasai's last, was also dictated and "vigorously asserts its orality" as it strains "narrative continuity to the limit as the hero's obsession with the prospect of insanity intensifies."[64] Indeed, what little continuity there is revolves around the hero's struggle to resist a diagnosis as "insane" by the two women living with him. They treat him as a "simple neurasthenic," likening him to a deranged patient they had read about in the newspaper, and thus further eroding whatever sense of self he retained. The highly "disconnected" narrative style that was Kasai's hallmark can be found in both works. According to Fowler, his narrators shifted haphazardly from one episode to the next, calling attention to the disruption of narrative flow as they churned repeatedly over the same mental ground.[65]

Further down in figure 3.3 is *Giwaku* (Suspicion, 1913), dubbed by critic Hirano Ken to be Japan's first "true" I-novel. Offering a "narrative claustrophobia" akin to Kasai's works, its author, Chikamatsu Shūkō, is known for protagonists who exhibit a "myopic preoccupation with private life" and revel in "self-engendered doubts," producing an "isolated (as opposed to an individuated) consciousness" that is almost entirely cut off from political, social, or familial concerns and that dwells repeatedly on certain periods in the author's life.[66] The periods often involve abandonment by a former lover and the feelings of disgust, rage, and desperation that ensue as the protagonist combs his memory for evidence of deceit. In *Giwaku*, such feelings are all that the reader gets. The entirety of the novel's action takes place in the narrator's mind, as presaged in its opening lines: "Usually I hid under my quilt and, in my mind, imagined and redrew the scene of your murder and of my imprisonment; imagined and redrew it. While contemplating whose wife you'd become and how to find you, day after day I could think of nothing better but to imagine the same scenes over and over again, almost as if I were being suffocated."[67]

In the same year that *Giwaku* appeared, writer Funaki Shigeo remarked that, of the highest quality works currently being produced, "there were none that did not acknowledge the operation of the nerves (*shinkei*) to some degree."[68] Recall that this was a transitional period during which "mental illness was no longer understood as an unfortunate side effect of a heightened artistic sensibility, but almost a necessary condition for it, as the modern and the pathological became identified with each other."[69] The association of mental illness with literary genius became so fixed that by the early 1920s one could find a journal devoted to the topic of "abnormal psychology" (*hentai shinri*). Contributions included a series of pathographies that attempted to read individual author's literary style through known psychological disorders, but also a survey that had no qualms asking writers and critics of all persuasions (seventy of whom responded) to publicly divulge their own psychological abnormalities.[70] Within this wider frame, the stylistic features accentuated by Chikamatsu and Kasai seemed to be part of a broader strategy to conform to evolving aesthetic tastes. For them, these features became a solution to the problem of how to make mental disorder legible to readers and thus increase their chances of being read as artists of the highest caliber.

The earliest writer to land on this strategy was Mushanokōji, whose *Omedetaki hito* (A simple man, 1910) is judged the most like an I-novel of all the works analyzed. His "remarkable style," as Uno Kōji called it, constituted the very "origin of the I-novel," and this work in particular, as John Treat has asserted, "might be modern Japanese literature's most narcissistically invested work of fiction."[71] That this work—one that begins by openly declaring a belief in "the existence of a selfish literature, a literature for the self"—appears at the top of figure 3.3 is confirmation that this model is capturing something of what has made it so remarkable and extreme in the eyes of past and present critics alike. Similar to Kasai and Chikamatsu's works, the kind of mental disorder portrayed in *Omedetaki hito* is one of monomaniacal and narcissistic obsession, with repetition of internal thought and loose association driving much of the psychological description. Some critics attribute the repetition and lack of narrative structure to the fact that Mushanokōji relied heavily on a diary he was keeping at the time. Other critics have remarked on his innovative use of the first-person pronoun *jibun* (oneself, I) as part of his search for a new, more direct colloquial style. The most common pronouns used in speech (e.g., *watashi*, *boku*, *ore*) at the time implied a hierarchical relation with the listener, so the still uncommon jibun may have been his way of instantiating a neutral first-person identifier.[72] One of his earliest critics, fellow White-Birch Society member Arishima Takeo, was certainly taken aback by the work's directness. More than any other writer he knew, Mushanokōji eschewed the language of intellectuals and dilletantes. "The style is much like that of a plainly written essay, and it is almost uncanny to me how you so easily and directly record the complexity of your intertwined emotions." So direct, in fact, that Arishima felt as if his hand was being forcefully pulled into the author's "red, gelatinous" heart and commanded to "touch it, touch it."[73]

Hyperbole aside, *Omedetaki hito* was clearly doing something that struck readers, then and later, as a radical mode of literary address. Reading it through the four features highlighted by our model, one also viscerally feels its patterns of excess. Within the first page alone, the narrator tells us five times that "I am starved for women," each time repeating the phrase nearly word for word. Also apparent is the ever-presence of jibun, which is used as a subject marker in almost every other sentence and in ways grammatically unnecessary. It is as if the narrator is compelled to discursively reaffirm his self-presence at every instant lest the reader forget who is speaking. This compulsion becomes particularly acute in moments of prevarication that perpetually delay physical encounter with a young woman named Tsuru, with whom he is smitten. Indeed, the novella is essentially the story of his failed attempt to win her attention, replete with passages like this one.

> *I* hear that Westerners *think* Friday is taboo. *And* so for the past 2 or 3 years, when *I* want to go meet her, I make it a point not to go and meet her on Fridays. *But* there are times when *I think* this superstition is bad and go out. *But* that makes *me feel* a little odd. Since *she* moved, I have to travel a little further to meet her. *Thus* it bothers *me* to go out of my way and go on a Friday. *But* there are times when *I think* that's just superstition, superstition isn't good, and I go anyway. At those times *I've* even *thought* that it's probably better I don't meet her. *I* feel more upset about going on Friday than about the fact that I'm meeting Tsuru after not seeing her for nearly a year. *But I* want to meet her. *Then I think* that, after all, since I haven't seen her until now, it's better not to meet her, whether I've talked myself into it or not. *So* finally *I* give up on going to meet her.[74]

Highlighted in italics are the words that the computational model is most attuned to when it decides that *Omedetaki hito* is most I-novel-like: conjunctions at the beginning of sentences, first- and third-person pronouns that repeat in every sentence, verbs for thinking and feeling. When added to the low variability in lexical diversity, the result is a grammatical mentality that actively works to represent cognition as a constant mental back and forth. Almost every sentence gives us an externalized image of his momentary thoughts, each fastened to the next with the superficial glue that conjunctions provide.

Here and throughout the text, Tsuru serves merely as a screen on which to project these mental deliberations, which are not really intended for her anyway. The narrator's desire for her is motivated apropos of nothing and grows only more intense the longer he manages to avoid a physical encounter. She becomes an excuse for flights of fancy that have the narrator pondering the nature of lust, the nature of self, and the possible consequences for his own self-infatuation should he find a way to marry her. Nothing of the sort comes to pass. On the contrary, they physically meet only once, a chance encounter on a train during which the narrator fails again to turn thought into action. The following excerpt from this encounter also happens to belong to the lowest entropy passage (i.e., the most homogenous vocabulary) in all the works analyzed.

> I stood up just before the train got to Yotsuya. I looked at Tsuru. My eyes met with Tsuru's. Tsuru quickly turned her eyes away. I decided then to pass in front of her and stop. The train was coming to a stop, but Tsuru didn't stand. And her face was turned away from me. Finally the train stopped. I tried to pass in front of Tsuru. Then she suddenly stood. I put my hand on Tsuru's back. I decided to follow her off the train. Then, near the exit, a man with his child stood up. I didn't have the courage to rudely push past the man and follow right behind Tsuru. I let the two come between Tsuru and I.[75]

Repetition here suggests indecision, but it also slows down the action, linking each step to the next while preserving a sense of singular focus. When the narrator finally summons the courage to call out her name, she responds with a curt "Can I help you?" before walking off in another direction. Ignoring all indications to the contrary, he takes this as a sign of her love for him. But it is the last we see of her, which is as it must be. Were Tsuru to enter the story as a living, breathing character, she would derail jibun's one-track mind and force recognition of someone other than himself.

There is in Mushanokōji's "remarkable style" madness of a kind that is built around a self-centered narrative address with no precedent in Japanese letters. Writing just a few months after the publication of *Omedetaki hito*, Arishima was pained by his hunch that most people in Japan had not seen the work or else completely ignored it. "It is a bittersweet irony that at a time when critics heap praise on literary works just as long as they exhibit stylistic acumen, have mountains of *plot*, or depict degenerate lifestyles, that your work goes unrecognized and is buried in silence."[76] Why, he wondered, were Japanese readers unable to see through to the individuality (*kosei*) of the author? He chalked up the failure to a national tendency to find pleasure in frivolous deception and to see writers solely as entertainers. But if Mushanokōji had offered a cure to this national affliction, this fever for plot, no one but Arishima wished to be healed. Even he felt his friend had gone too far, urging him to widen his compassionate vision beyond himself so that he and others (including the lowly typesetter whose blood had somehow dripped onto Arishima's copy of *Omedetaki hito*) might have a place within this vision. As it was, Mushanokōji had shut himself away in a castle of his own design and seated himself before a mirror that mostly reflected his own form. All the natural and human elements visible from the window at his back appeared in the mirror "as merely a faint, ghostly light."[77]

Having opened the interpretative frame wide enough to see Arishima looking at Mushanokōji staring at himself, we find a useful convergence between the generic symptoms this computational model was designed to diagnose and the reactions of a contemporary reader to what was later deemed a prototypical I-novel. Such a fortuitous convergence does not happen in every case, of course, because this reductive model sees only a narrow portion of how the genre has historically been understood. Its perspective is not capacious enough to contain the genre in all its variation. Further down in figure 3.3, for instance, is Tōson's *Haru*, a work we know to be invested in the representation of mental breakdown. But on closer inspection we learn that the increasingly claustrophobic and disordered ramblings of Aoki only take over in the second half of the novel, thus dampening its impact on the work as a whole. Another work about which the model is uncertain is that other prototypical and certainly better known I-novel, Tayama Katai's *Futon* (The quilt, 1907). For some critics, this is the work that retroactively set the entire genre into motion, simultaneously shifting the course of modern Japanese literature away from Realist fiction modeled on the classical European novel and toward an autobiographical, confessional mode that saw value only in describing an author's personal life. However, if it gave the green light to turn the sordid details of one's private life into fiction—in this case the sexual desires aroused in the author by the young female student he agrees to mentor—*Futon* did not, as Fowler writes, "distinguish itself by its portrayal of individualistic consciousness."[78] It is precisely such intense portrayals, however, that the model seems to be good at capturing. In looking at points of nonconvergence between textual and social evidence, we learn something else about how this particular model *thinks* about the I-novel, and thus of the interpretive windows it both opens and closes as it brings texts into its equivalence space.

Another kind of clarity is gained when we look at popular works judged by the model to be more like an I-novel than many of the works initially labeled I-novel. Based on the texts singled out thus far, we know the model is good at identifying works enamored of vernacular style, intense psychological description, and mental breakdown. But this could describe any number of other I-novels in our corpus. It would be helpful to isolate the distinct stylistic key in which these works by Kasai, Chikamatsu, and Mushanokōji narrate the self. Some clues are offered when the generic divisions initially imposed on the corpora are loosened and we look at the varieties of "vernacular madness" that the model finds in works supposedly consumed by plot. What brings Kōga Saburō's "Ai no tame ni" (For love, 1926), Hamao Shirō's *Akuma no deshi* (The devil's disciple, 1929), Unno Jūza's "Fushū" (The possessed, 1934), and Kozakai Fuboku's "Ren'ai kyokusen" (Love graph, 1926) together at the top left of figure 3.3? A cursory glance suggests some possible shared patterns.

"Ai no tame ni" is comprised of five short memos (*shuki*) by a man, his wife, and a private investigator who each describe their role in a series of mishaps and miscommunications that leave the couple in possession of an infant whose mother they are desperately trying to find. *Akuma no deshi* takes the form of a paranoid, accusatory letter by a man who attempts, but fails, to murder his wife. It is addressed to the public prosecutor trying his case, who also happens to be his ex-boyfriend. He intends the letter to be a justification of his actions, but it devolves into a relentless, suffocating invective against his former lover as the man "struggles to push forth his own [heterosexual] identity through the appeal to an absent other."[79] "Fushū" is a woman's first-person oral account of her attempt to murder her mad scientist husband, only to fall victim to his obsession with dismembering and rearranging body parts to create more efficient humans—a surgical process she ends up narrating in great detail even as it is performed on her by her spurned husband. Finally, "Ren'ai kyokusen" is a long-winded letter from another mad surgeon addressed to the man about to marry his true love. In it he explains in gruesome detail his efforts to create a device that expresses graphically, like a seismograph, the magnitude of a person's love, and which he is in the process of attaching to a disembodied heart presently being reanimated by his own fast draining blood. As he reveals in his dying breaths, the heart is that of his former lover, the addressee's bride-to-be.

Epistolary or direct oral address, monomaniacal focus, crazed obsession—these qualities loosely bind the four popular works together, but they also bring them into the orbit of the I-novels already surveyed. Much of the social evidence introduced at the beginning of this chapter would dissuade us from reading these works through the I-novel genre, if only because the latter largely depends on a reading formation that welds literary content to authors' private lives. There is no world in which these narratives, mostly by writers of mystery and detective fiction, would be mistaken for autobiography. Textual evidence, however, hints at another history where works from both genres, regardless of the different purposes for which they were read, trafficked in a grammatical mentality and language of psychological description that relied on similar stylistic tendencies. Scholars have demonstrated how busy this traffic was in the mid-1920s for some detective novelists, in particular Edogawa Ranpō and Yumeno Kyūsaku. In Ranpō's case, it was just as the I-novel was coming into recognition that he embarked on an epistemological project to articulate "a method of detection based on human psychology," one that could, as one of his own characters puts it, "penetrate psychologically to the deepest part of a person's soul."[80] One of Ranpō's stories from 1928, *Injū* (Shadowy beast), even presented itself as a parody of the I-novel. If we already knew that certain authors were crossing the lanes that separated I-novels and popular fiction, figure 3.3 expands our view on this stylistic traffic, creating a pretext for reading *Omedetaki hito* alongside, for instance, Kōga's "Ai no tame ni." Social evidence might resist such a pairing, but it also misses the possibility of reading repetition as a style that circulated as a more general strategy for narrating abnormal psychology, whether plot driven or not.

How to think about stylistic circulation and influence with the evidence generated by computational models is the primary concern of chapter 4. Here my aim is to hint at the ways predictive models can hold a particular conception of a genre together even as they highlight where that conception diffuses into the linguistic space within which all literary expression is articulated. Kōga, who studied applied chemistry at Tokyo Imperial University and made his literary debut in 1923 with mysteries that invited readers to solve elaborate scientific puzzles, may not have been reading Kasai's last ramblings or Mushanokōji's adolescent flights of fancy, already a decade old by then. That Kōga's name is synonymous with debates in the 1930s dividing "serious" (*honkaku*) detective fiction from its "deviant" (*henkaku*) and more literary, less puzzle-driven varieties, is all the more reason not to associate him with the I-novel as cultural or reading formation.[81] And yet his "Ai no tame ni," published in the magazine *Tantei bungei* (Detective literature), begins with a first-person narrator who has spent the past several days in a feverish state trying to reconstruct the series of missteps that has left him in the possession of a stranger's infant child. A series of missteps that begins with him gazing on a woman and her child as they wait at a crowded bus stop; that has him offering to take the baby as they push onto the bus only to discover that she does not make it on; and which finds him desperately eyeing each new bus as it circles by, in hopes she'll be on it, and asking himself over and over again whether someone he knows will spot him, whether he should go to the police, whether the child will cry out and expose his crime. Here is a man so wracked by indecision and fear that he no longer seems in control of his mind because his mind is all we see. Somewhere in this madness begins a literary history that is attuned to how repetition, conscious or not, can be deployed in the service of common representational ends.

REPETITION WITH A DIFFERENCE: CHINA'S AGE OF CONFESSION

The loosening of generic divisions that the computational model affords can be extended to linguistic and cultural divisions as well. In fact, a primary motivation for the initial research behind this chapter was to develop a model for thinking about self-referential fiction in the wider context of East Asian literary modernity.[82] Where Japan has the I-novel, China has Romantic fiction, a genre seen as equally foundational to the formation of modern Chinese literature and similarly distinguished from other forms of fiction by its narrow autobiographical focus, extended psychonarration and vernacular style. Also, like the I-novel, it eludes easy definition and has been conventionally defined more by its social milieu than by a coherent set of generic qualities.[83] Some scholars have tended to focus on the distinct empirical features that set Romantic fiction stylistically apart from its contemporaries, including the consolidation of the modern written vernacular under the *baihua* movement and the adoption of Western grammatical elements and narrative modes.[84] Other scholarly and contemporary accounts insist that the works eschew narrative structure and plot in the service of representing mental disorder and madness.[85] As with the I-novel label, Romantic fiction is a classificatory container that holds a set of texts together while being as porous as a sieve.

Knowing that some of the same higher-order phenomena ascribed to the I-novel have been ascribed to works of Romantic fiction, and that many of the May Fourth generation of writers who penned these works studied in Japan during its "age of confession," it is tempting to consider whether repetitiveness similarly discriminates them from other kinds of fiction. Did these writers land on a similar stylistic strategy in creating their own brand of self-centered writing? To answer this question, and simultaneously test how well the model developed so far generalizes beyond its nation-centered frame, I apply an analogous model to a corpus of more than one hundred Romantic texts by May Fourth writers. Most are affiliated with the Creation Society (*Chuangzao she*), a literary collective formed in 1919 by students returning from Japan that is closely identified with a romanticist interest in examining and exploring personal subjectivity. The corpus includes works from the 1920s by Yu Dafu, Guo Moruo, and Zhang Ziping.[86] As a comparison corpus, one hundred works of contemporary popular literature were selected, including historical fiction and "Mandarin Duck and Butterfly" stories.[87] Chosen for their highly emplotted quality and lack of psychological focus, as in the Japanese case, most were written in an older vernacular style markedly different from that developed by Romantic writers. For this reason, the comparison is not directly parallel to the I-novel experiment in that the linguistic difference is sharper than that between I-novels and popular Japanese fiction.

The only reason this experiment can be performed at all is because the features used to model the I-novel are mostly language agnostic. This is true of all the measures of repetitiveness and lexical diversity as well as the diction-based measures relating to pronoun use and verbs of cognition and feeling, for which Chinese specific lists can be substituted.[88] Unfortunately, some of these features could not be measured as precisely in the Chinese case owing to less accurate optical character recognition (OCR), which in turn makes recognition of dialogue markers and part-of-speech tagging less reliable. Despite limitations in reproducing the model exactly, the result was a model that could distinguish Romantic from non-Romantic texts with near perfect accuracy. Moreover, it needed only average entropy and Yule's K to do so. Redundancy and uniformity of vocabulary alone are enough to separate the two corpora. That the model needs so little information to do this well is a clue that something more basic than style is at work here. Most likely, the model is picking up on the sharper linguistic difference separating these corpora. This is not to say, however, that the strong tendency toward repetitiveness found in Romantic works is entirely unrelated to psychonarration. For instance, as with the I-novels, we can find a similar association between heightened repetition and the use of words related to cognition and feeling (figure 3.4). Although the association is much weaker in the Romantic works than in the popular fiction, there

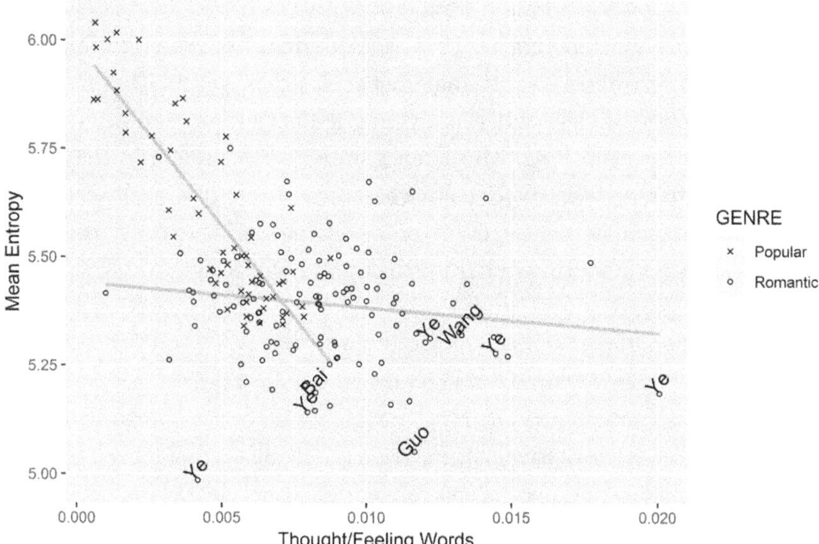

FIGURE 3.4. Scatterplot comparing values for mean entropy and proportion of thought/feeling words across all Chinese works classified as popular and Romantic. Linear regression lines are fit to each genre and show a strong negative correlation for popular works, but not for Romantic works. A few outlier texts by Romantic authors are labeled according to author surname: Ye Lingfeng, Bai Cai ("Weisheng"), Guo Moruo ("Tingzijian zhong"), and Wang Yiren ("Wo de gongzhuang").

are some authors who ply the extreme ends of both dimensions. Notable among them is Ye Lingfeng (1905–1975).

Ye occupies a shifting and uncertain position in the historiography of modern Chinese literature. A relative late comer to the scene of Romantic writing, Ye joined the Creation Society in 1925, a time when the group was already pivoting away from indulgent narratives of the self toward a politically inflected interest in national identity and class consciousness. Eager to capture a place in the burgeoning field of modern literature, he marketed himself as a dandy and an iconoclast, and he rapidly found success writing fiction that featured titillating love triangles, urban decadence, and Freudian-inflected depictions of sexual desire. This work also tended to focus on bodily and psychological "abnormalities" (from masturbation, castration, and homosexuality to bisexuality, suicide, and incest) in such a way as to, in his own words, "achieve mental confusion."[89] Such narratives would earn him a central place in the high modernist literature of the 1930s promoted by the so-called Neo-Perceptionist writers such as Mu Shiying, Liu Na'ou, and Shi Zhecun. But when he entered the literary scene in the mid-1920s, his work was aligned with Romanticism, earning him the status as a kind of second-generation Romantic writer.[90]

One of Ye's most repetitive texts is "Aidezhanshi" (Warrior for love, 1928), which features a love triangle between urban youth. The narrative alternates points of view between a young female author, Sophie, and her smooth-talking beau, Ping, who fancies himself a Napoleon in the realm of love. Displaying little dialogue or character interaction, each section is essentially an insular contemplation of the character's inner state. The story opens with Sophie writing in her journal, pining for Ping:

> I don't believe this is spring. Lower and lower, this bolt of grey canvas is already so low as to push down upon my head. I don't believe this sky has ever had a golden-red sun, I don't believe this sky has ever had a mirror-like moon. It's incapable of having them. These are all dreamed-of things, these are all lies told by fortunate people to unfortunate people. Do you believe? Do you believe this ground could have a strip of verdant-green grass, the blue-black stream at its side a pink-blossomed peach tree, under whose flowers a young man is just now embracing—What? I don't believe. I don't have the courage to write on.[91]

Close up it is easy to see how the recurrence of the words "lower," "I," and "believe" would culminate in a low entropy score. Such rhythm is sustained throughout the narrative and augments the excessively sentimental tone of the two narrators, thereby imparting the text with a strong dose of imaginative interiority. As the story progresses, Sophie becomes increasingly disillusioned by the affair, and Ping, conversely, grows ever-bolder in his lecherous pursuit of women. The story ends darkly when, to take revenge on Ping for his infidelity, Sophie gets him drunk and stabs him to death, triumphantly declaring herself a "warrior for love."[92] This violent reaction retroactively makes Sophie's repetitive writing style appear dangerously off-kilter and manic. Sophie is not a particularly sympathetic character, and the story should not be read as a feminist indictment of patriarchy. Instead, repetition stylistically augments Ye's penchant for the sensational, a flourish one scholar has characterized as "kitschy."[93] This kitsch can be read as an attempt to push the rhetoric of the modern self to excess, amplifying through excessive repetition the psychonarration characteristic of his Romantic predecessors.

Ye's stories are the most repetitive overall, but other important figures in the Romantic movement emerge when we look at the most redundant passages in the corpus. Yu Dafu's "Jiedeng" (Street lamps, 1926), for example, and Guo Moruo's novel *Luoye* (Fallen leaves, 1925) contain some extremely repetitive sections. On the whole, these works share with Ye's stories a number of characteristics, such as being written in the present tense and having a minimized plot. They also have the tendency to adopt a narrative mode emphasizing direct address, either in epistolary and diaristic framing devices or in the form of extended blocks of reported speech. Such vernacular style and ample reported speech likewise feature prominently in works with low entropy as determined by Kontoyiannis's measure, which captures repetition of longer sequences of words rather than just individual words. Here too are works by Ye Lingfeng as well as several Romantic short stories by Guo Moruo: "Shizijia" (Crucifix, 1924), "Ye Luoti zhi mu" (Ye Luoti's grave, 1924), and "Tingzijian zhong" (Within the pavilion, 1925). These latter texts feature repetition in ways even more obvious to the reader, whether in the frequent exclamatory or emphatic adverbial modifiers such as "extremely carefully, carefully . . . lightly, lightly" ("Tingzijian zhong") or the nearly verbatim duplication of sentences: "When the nurse reached out her hand to take his pulse, in a state of half-consciousness he instead said 'Ah, many thanks, auntie.' When the nurse again reached out her hand to place the thermometer under his right armpit, he again said 'Ah, many thanks, auntie'" ("Ye Luoti zhi mu").

Although Guo Moruo's stories all invoke a strongly maudlin atmosphere characteristic of the frustrated May Fourth individual (and, coincidentally, feature death), the Chinese texts with the highest rates of repetition are not limited to evocations of trauma or suffering. In fact, words evoking *kumen*, an influential sentiment connoting suffering or despair, do *not* correlate with lower entropy in any significant way. Instead, as in Ye's works, repetition plays out as a key source (or effect) of sexual titillation, sentiment, and free love, working counter to the Freudian death drive and toward something more like a pleasure principle.[94] The pleasure in these texts can be celebratory, guilty, narcissistic, libidinal, or manic, another reminder of how overdetermined a reading of repetition in and of itself can be, and how critical it is to constantly push against the edges of the computational frame.

AT THE MIRROR'S EDGE

Let me hold the frame a bit longer, however, and reflect on the equivalence spaces it projects and what they might offer histories of East Asian literary modernity centered (once more) on the narrativized self. What is gained by bringing Ye together with other Romantic writers in the way this frame does? What new diagnoses of the I-novel are possible when Ye is further paired with Mushanokōji and Kasai, or when they in turn are paired with other I-novel writers, or with genre authors Hamao and Kozakai? I have ventured some preliminary analyses in the latter cases, focusing on repetitiveness as the stylistic outcome of a common aesthetic investment in orality, epistolarity, and madness. In the former case, the pairing compels us to wonder why a writer on the trailing edge of self-referential Romantic writing is singled out as paradigmatic of a repetitive style, rather than a writer at its origins such as Mushanokōji and the I-novel. Is there a historical explanation for why this style is expressed most extremely only when Creationist Romanticism was at the cusp of dissolution?[95] In pulling together unique configurations of writers across generic and linguistic divisions, the computational frame opens sites of historical inquiry at once less tightly bound to established ways of dividing the past and less susceptible to the blind spots these divisions have etched into archival formations. At the same time, the sites are also more specific than something like a zeitgeist, wherein the genre of the I-novel becomes as diffuse as the "tenor of an age, dubbed Taishō by a feeble emperor, and therefore something that, like the air, we can hardly measure because we are so perfectly, comfortably, surrounded by it."[96] To see it every place is to see it no place at all, and potentially to see only ourselves as critics gazing into the text as mirror.

The computational frame falls somewhere between a kind of reading that hews closely to established categories of equivalence making (e.g., author, work, genre, period) and one that sees everything in everything else, such that no single category contains the meaning of a text. These are caricatures of hermeneutic extremes, to be sure—twin poles around which any reading of the literary past constantly triangulates itself. The frames afforded by computation are no different in having to perform this balancing act, contending with the historical categories they build upon and the individual interpretive choices that inform their construction. But they do so by being both more specific and reductive in how they represent texts as objects, and more naive in how they compare them, identifying commonalities across large textual surfaces that from other perspectives (other ways of holding texts together or keeping them apart) seem unreasonable or absurd. The key question is whether, through their unique triangulations, critics see the frames as opening windows onto facts of equivalence and patterns of difference that productively confirm or challenge facts and patterns arrived at by other means. More to the point, what new diagnoses do these frames offer once we turn each frame, like a mirror, back on ourselves?

Recall that I constructed the frame in this chapter by pairing social evidence (past ways of categorizing works) with textual evidence derived from a specific sample of works and a specific model of repetition. The aim was to find overlap between these two sets of evidence, which the model found in the space occupied by I-novels that harbored the greatest compulsion to repeat themselves—a compulsion that, by the judgment of the model, carried over to other generic, but also linguistic, contexts. That such convergences should happen around specific empirical traits is, as stated at the outset, hardly a new idea. Scholarship on the I-novel and Chinese Romantic writing describes many of the convergences arrived at by writers working to synthesize linguistic changes (e.g., vernacularization, adoption of Western grammar) with aesthetic pursuit of the psychologized self. In search of a grammatical mentality that reflected the anxieties of the modern individual, these convergences, as Karatani and others have argued, provided the textual conditions for the very "discovery" of this self. They were less a causal effect of newfound desires to express psychic interiors than a medium through which the expression of these interiors became possible.[97] My computational frame is a means to identify at greater scale the common stylistic elements that went into constructing this medium and to assess their degree of dispersion across the varied formal and stylistic convergences arrived at by writers. A means to single out authors who accentuated these elements, but also to scan the textual surfaces of East Asian literary modernity to see how these elements, as a kind of shared symptom of deeper cultural and linguistic shifts, radiated beyond the most acute instances.

Part of the motivation for identifying such shared structures, computationally or otherwise, is to counter the tendency to read back onto the literary "discovery" of the self an unmediated and transparent process of finding what was there—an autonomous self finding itself. These structures expose the artifice that, by the 1920s, was already being enshrouded in the mystifying *what* that opposed the I-novel to technique, to plot, to money. To insist that this *what* could not be measured by any extrinsic standard of value or utility was to build up the fiction that it was a literature of the self in all its irreducible particularity, ambiguity, and mad genius. In a word, its status as art. In the case of *Omedetaki hito*, this process began just as soon as it appeared. Upon first reading, Arishima immediately turned to his copy of Tolstoy's "What Is Art?," the 1897 essay that enshrined for a generation of writers the notion that art must resist imitation or professionalization to sincerely convey an artist's emotions. His choice foreshadows the model of value through which I-novels would later be read, one that located the truth of art in a rejection of the marketplace, in Romantic ideals of original genius, and in its inutility as entertainment or channel of information. This model, as Mary Poovey has demonstrated in the case of English fiction, was already a century in the making, and by the early 1900s it was entangled in practices of reading that maintained the division between "true" and merely "popular" art by rendering the former so difficult and multitudinous in meaning, but also so singular in stylistic unity and artistic vision, that only the expert critic, through intense struggle, could appreciate it. John Ruskin captured this orientation well when declaring that one should approach a "good book" as if one is an "Australian miner" searching for precious metal, "the metal you are in search of being the author's mind or meaning, his words are as the rock which you have to crush and smelt in order to get at it."[98]

Ruskin's "text mining" laid the foundation for the dominant strand of twentieth-century criticism against which computational forms of text mining now appear as a reaction. Namely, a brand of critical Formalism instantiated by Henry James and institutionalized as New Criticism, which rests on the core paradox that "invisible (but unmistakable) art produces truth [and that] the reader-critic makes this truth visible, partly by illuminating invisible artistry."[99] This brand is still with literary criticism, Poovey insists, even as it is adapted to new theoretical paradigms (e.g., New Historicism) that seek to connect individual texts to other texts and events through discourse analysis or seek to escape evaluative constraints imposed by fixed categories of aesthetic value (i.e., the canon). One consequence of its persistence is that textual interpretation, even when displacing the singularity or unity of a text by situating it in discourse or a wider field of production, which is to try to read it as historical evidence, often falls back on ahistorical assumptions and presentist biases. It falls back, that is, on "assumptions about organic unity and aesthetic value" unique to critical Formalism as a historical formation and to extrapolations of a "universal subject position" based on a critic's own reading experience.[100] A text comes to be seen as symptomatic of an age by being intensely mined for meaning and forced to divulge its deviance or departure from the invisible (but unmistakable) discursive norms of that age. These norms are in turn made visible by classificatory schema and evaluative criteria that the original authors and readers did not necessarily share. Poovey's point is not that such a practice of textual interpretation is in error, only that it mistakes what it is doing for actual historical *description*.

Just as the early reception of the I-novel reveals the legacy of a certain historical model of literary value, so does the genre's definitional ambivalence reveal the longer legacy of critical Formalism in deciding how to approach it. Should its texts be interpreted independently of the genre label, itself a retroactive reading formation that has little to do with the original contexts of production? Should they be interpreted through a posited discourse, one framed by the master concepts of narcissism, madness, or national character? Should they be read through formal and stylistic similarities to expose the artifice that underpinned the fiction of self-discovery? There will never be an easy synthesis of such approaches, beholden as they are to incommensurable ideological and epistemological perspectives on the relation of textual part to contextual whole. The I-novel, like fiction, is destined to be, as Fowler put it, an onion with an always elusive core. Critics will also never abandon the hard-won critical practice that sees every text as capable of being interpreted singularly and multidimensionally, and which necessarily sustains this sense of elusiveness, of the irreducibility of texts. But this is precisely why Poovey's insistence that we be aware of the categories and classificatory schemes latent within this practice is so valuable. For her, catalyzing this awareness means developing a mode of description that tries to recover "the functions that particular texts served . . . the ways in which various writers tried to differentiate among kinds of writing," where these functions are understood as a product of genre, discipline, and institutional position.[101] To do so is to briefly shake loose the moorings of the schemes and biases that present critics and readers invariably bring to past texts, including that which places value on a text's singular indeterminacy.

A principle aim of this chapter has been to illustrate how computational models can serve as mirrors for the social categories and classifications with which Poovey is concerned. These models helpfully frame this social evidence by juxtaposing it with textual evidence that has been deliberately compressed into unique kinds of equivalence spaces. Through these frames, they also reflect back to us our own predilections and predispositions as critics and readers. They are at once mirrors fashioned to hold social and textual evidence together in configurations of our own design, but also mirrors that bend and warp these configurations in ways that can seem alien to our existing ways of interpreting them. In Poovey's own proposals for new modes of historical description, she rejects counting and quantification as antithetical to interpretation, which for her remains the signature feature of literary studies as a discipline. But as I have insisted from the very start, the opposition of numbers to interpretation is itself a historical formation in need of questioning.

If computational models do not contribute to the exact mode of description Poovey has in mind, they are useful for probing the generic and classificatory schema that constantly shape acts of reading, writing, and evaluation. Useful because they can show us where schemata fall apart at the level of textual evidence; because they expose textual relations invisible to existing schema; and because they are themselves partial and biased, and thus open to critique and modification. A model focused on repetition as style is just one way of looking at things, and it is sure to behave differently when applied to other configurations of social and textual evidence. In fact, when the model is shown a corpus of "pure" or highbrow literature (*junbungaku*)—which includes titles by some of the same I-novel authors but which differ in their emphasis on plot, character, and realist description over personal confession—it can hardly tell them apart.[102] This is one more reason to keep pushing at this particular mirror's edges, but also a reason to investigate further how central was the compulsion to repeat in making the literary stand out from all that was not.

Chapter Four

INFLUENCE AND JUDGMENT

> The final thing I want to note is [*Ulysses*'s] difficulty. I, too, am not confident I've understood it. It should be compared to the ancient labyrinth designed by Daedalus—it is contemporary literature's maze.
>
> —DOI KŌICHI (1929)

Difficult as James Joyce's novel was for this reader in Japan, his fellow critics and writers eagerly followed him into the disorienting tunnels it cut through the human mind. If the previous chapter offered an image of the I-novel genre as a surface symptom of a deep rooted modern malaise, this chapter considers a more isolated phenomenon—the stream-of-consciousness technique, which feels more like a virus. It arrived with little warning, seemed to infect every young writer, and then just as quickly disappeared, leaving a few minor, embarrassing scars. Or so one story goes. The first victims were Japanese nationals traveling abroad in Chicago and Edinburgh, who read *Ulysses* in 1922, just after its publication in Paris and a few years after its serialization in *Little Review*, and who wrote or lectured about it for audiences back home.[1] In 1925, prolific translator of French poetry Horiguchi Daigaku wrote a pivotal essay linking *Ulysses* to "interior monologue" (*naishin dokuhaku*)—a term later critics would replace with stream of consciousness (*ishiki no nagare*)—and declaring Joyce's variation on the technique unprecedented in the novel's evolution as a world historical form.[2]

Doi Kōichi reiterated this sense of newness and innovation of stylistic form in his 1929 review and partial translation of *Ulysses*, at which point the virus really caught on.[3] The next few years saw two (!) full translations of *Ulysses* serialized in competing literary magazines. Translations of Paul Morand's *Open All Night* (1929), Woolf's *To the Lighthouse* (1931),

Proust's *Swann's Way* (1932), and Dorothy Richardson's *Pointed Roofs* (1932) appeared in various coterie magazines along with dozens of essays that attempted to define stream of consciousness and establish its literary significance.[4] More remarkable still, established and up-and-coming writers started to experiment with the method, producing nearly twenty works of short fiction indebted to this new mode of psychological expression. By 1931, one critic could quip that "it was hard to find works that didn't employ the so-called 'stream-of-consciousness' technique in just about every literary magazine one picked up."[5]

Pascale Casanova has argued that Joyce's *Ulysses* and *Finnegans Wake* "constitute one of the great indices . . . of distance from the Greenwich meridian [of literature]."[6] By this measure, the extent to which the stream-of-consciousness (SOC) technique caught on in Japan was simply a matter of writers and critics resetting their clocks. Horiguchi suggests as much in his essay. Borrowing a line from W. C. Williams's "The Great American Novel" (itself an imitation of Joyce's style already verging on parody), his sincere wish is to introduce the technique to prevent anyone from being able to say that Japanese writers, having learned of it a day too late, caused a great loss for world literature.[7] Looking beyond Joyce, Moretti has written that "it is no surprise that the stream of consciousness should be the most famous technique of the twentieth century: in view of what it has done, it fully deserves to be."[8] Volumes of criticism on SOC attest that it has indeed done many things, not the least of which is travel the world. Moretti counts "two basic 'strains,' and . . . a dozen variants" generated from the "morphological explosion of the twenties" that spread across Europe and America, but also Japan, and by the 1950s Latin America.

Alongside these stories of unimpeded diffusion across the globe, however, come stories of decline and failed transmission. Early critics and writers in Japan celebrated the radical newness of SOC and charted its circuitous routes through France, Italy, Germany, and America—or from Edouard Dujardin to Joyce, Richardson, Woolf, Valery, Waldo Frank, Conrad Aiken, and others—but later critics emphasized how few inroads it made in Japan. If writers at the time saw themselves as actively translating and adapting the technique as part of a generational break from staid literary conventions, later historians (including sometimes the writers infected by SOC fever) looked back on this moment, and on modernist writings in general, as part of a "passing phase" or a "Western rash" that came and went.[9] In retrospect, SOC appears to some as an object that never went anywhere in Japan because it was too different from existing literary conventions; because techniques of psychological representation were already established; because no one truly understood it; or because it was adopted in ignorance of the underlying symbolic apparatuses that necessitated its original use. SOC travels the world even as it is stopped in its tracks.

Such contradictory story lines may be endemic to histories of the circulation of cultural forms, but SOC stands out in how readily it has been accommodated by both narratives. These narratives crystallize a fundamental debate about the nature of literary influence across linguistic and cultural borders, one piece of a larger conversation about the terms of world literature and the judgments of equivalence or nonequivalence, similarity and dissimilarity, on which these terms are partly set. In this chapter, I enter this conversation at the point where it is concerned with what does and does not travel the world imagined as a shared space of literary exchange, albeit one both unevenly and asymmetrically structured. I use the case of SOC to argue for the potential of computational models to serve as interlocutors in this ongoing conversation. Specifically, I consider how the scaled-up judgments of equivalence and difference that these models afford, what I call "algorithmic competence," reframe the judgments that critics have routinely made about the (im)possibility of transnational and translingual influence.

The problem of literary influence across borders recapitulates the more general problem of intertextuality, a concept that designates a text's "participation in the discursive space of a culture." It calls attention "to the importance of prior texts" in determining a work's meaning and leads us to consider these texts as "contributions to a code which makes possible the various effects of signification."[10] As Jonathan Culler pointedly observes, however, this consideration is predicated on the assumption that this code is knowable, or intelligible. Whether one is trying to decipher this code from the perspective of the writer, reader, or critic, one must "mark out a manageable area of investigation" on which the grounds of the code's intelligibility is established. And this marking out, crucially, is never "an innocent strategy"; it always entails assumptions about the degree and manner by which texts can be related to one another at all.[11]

Broadly speaking, past strategies have relied on assumptions that lean toward structuralist or poststructuralist theoretical orientations. The former camp tends to posit a coherent system or structure against which the signification of a text can be read. From this end, intertextuality is conceived as a function of discursive regularities and recurrences in a delimited system, making it the task of the reader or critic to map the many ways a text fits into this system, even and especially when the intertextual relation is not explicit or intentional.[12] On the one hand, text becomes intelligible by virtue of its fluid, dynamic relation to a supraindividual assemblage of texts, an "architextural network," as Gerard Genette called it. Poststructuralist arguments, on the other hand, typically disrupt the notion of a stable chain of signification and imagine intertextuality as a mutable, transformative process whose locus of intelligibility is a reading/writing subject that is itself divided or fractured. Julia Kristeva, who originally developed the concept, saw it as an interaction between "symbolic" (socially signifying) and "semiotic" (unconscious drives, impulses, bodily rhythms) fields within both subject and text; Barthes saw intertextual codes as a "mirage of citations" dwelling within readers, themselves representatives of a general intertextuality.[13] Michael Riffaterre later proposed that "the only significant structure in a literary work is that which the reader can perceive," this perception being a function of the reader's "linguistic competence."[14] Competence denotes a "reader's familiarity with the descriptive systems, with themes, with his society's mythologies, and above all with other texts," such that greater competence leads to better readings of textual relation.[15] But if some competencies excel over others, then the presumed open-endedness and infinite variability of intertextual relation are in reality a back door to expertise situated in specific institutional and disciplinary structures (i.e., the position of the academic critic). Again, marking out an area of investigation is never an innocent strategy.

These two sides of the intertextuality coin parallel debates in theories of world literature, where the "cartographic impulse," as Nirvana Tanoukhi suggests, recasts influence as a problem of "portability": the degree to which texts circulate the globe (or not). This impulse, and the logic of portability that seeks to adjudicate the scope of foreign interference or carry-over, arguably resonates "both with structuralist theories of influence (literary interference, dependence, debt, etc.) and . . . with poststructuralist theories of reappropriation (literary resistance, subversion, cannibalization, etc.)."[16] On the structuralist end are Moretti and Casanova, who seek to model world literary space as an integrated system where "foreign form(s) and local materials" are, after the late nineteenth-century, combined according to the laws of a hierarchical market of literary exchange and local processes of formal compromise.[17] At the other end are scholars like Emily Apter, and Sandra Bermann and Michael Wood, who stress the "intrinsic alterity" of languages and the ways translation makes impossible the "complete or transparent transferral of semantic content." As a result, a universal system of textual exchange becomes unthinkable, or at least severely compromised by Eurocentric accounts that rely on inbuilt typologies derived from Western literary examples.[18] Somewhere in between is David Damrosch's model of world literature as the subset of literary works that "circulate beyond their culture of origin" but must be read through local transformations. One looks for common global patterns of circulation in this world literary space while attending to the interactions of particular languages with particular texts and audiences, thus allowing one to "see both the forest and the trees."[19]

Each of these models would have us tell a different story about SOC. It was a high-prestige international form that moved by virtue of its complicity with the conditions of global capitalist modernity—a narrative container filled with local content wherever it traveled. Alternatively, SOC circulated the world but only by being resolved into infinitely many worlds according to local conditions of reception. Then again, perhaps it is a story of immobility because every translation or adaptation of a SOC text shatters any pretense of an original or essential content unchanged by the interference of linguistic and cultural difference. Tanoukhi makes the point that all of these models are tethered to a logic of comparison underwritten by a notion of distance as a gap to be closed (or not) through formal compromise. This may be true, but my interest here is in how this shared logic generates competing strategies for marking out the areas of investigation through which the (im)possibility of circulation and formal compromise is deduced. In each case, boundaries are drawn by asserting specific aesthetic hierarchies and chronologies; by relying on the material evidence of reading and reception; or by foregrounding the variability and radical difference that translation introduces into the process. The boundaries of these models imply, in turn, different linguistic and cultural competencies on the part of reader, writer, and critic, even as they are themselves bounded by the presumption of centrality of "an object understood as literature, capable of both traversing national differences and uniting a variety of textual forms."[20] As Michael Allan persuasively argues, how literature becomes marked off as a category capable of having national and linguistic determination—whether by academics, prize committees, or other sites of institutionalization—is also "the story of how literature becomes, through forces of globalized literacy, the universalization of a mediated practice of reading in which rather particular conceptions of difference, experience, and subjectivity are made thinkable."[21]

Although I do not challenge this demarcation here, I am invested in the sociological thrust that calls attention to it. Specifically, I grant as much legitimacy to theoretical paradigms for evaluating textual influence as to the "social relationships, fields of powers, methods of working, and technologies of production associated with translation" that, for Isabel Hofmeyr, are "critical sites for understanding whether, and what kinds of, notions of equivalence might come into being."[22] How historical actors made decisions about the equivalence or nonequivalence of SOC texts are as much a focus of investigation as are the strategies adopted by theorists of world literature. If I do not question the category of literature in general, however, I adopt Allan's insistence that we question the kinds of competencies about literary judgment that are implied by any account of the world of world literature. When he asks, "What are the conditions for a text to be recognized as literature? In what ways does world literature define what literature is? How is a text included in the domain of world literature?," he is asking after the normative limits placed on the literary in these accounts. In an analogous way, by juxtaposing different models of world literature and different stories about SOC as a circulating form, I am asking about the competing normative limits surrounding evaluations of transnational literary influence. More specifically, I am asking what another form of competence, one we might dub "algorithmic," can tell us about these limits. What is the world of world literature as figured by computational models?

To be clear, such "algorithmic competence" does not provide a way out of the contested field wherein judgments about textual relations are made. It is no more neutral nor innocent in the ways it marks out an area of investigation or establishes relations of equivalence between texts. Indeed, whatever computational model is built to support this competence will invariably be implicated in the existing models we have of world literary relations, and it will gain viability only by being put in conversation with the stories we already tell of how literature does (and does not) travel the world.

What the model need not be, I insist, is firmly allied with or complicit in any one story simply because of its numerical foundations.[23] Expanding on some of the modeling techniques introduced in chapter 3, and shifting analytical focus from the document to the passage level, I develop a model of SOC as a set of linguistic and stylistic features with distinct distributional tendencies. I test the coherence of this model within and between two sites of circulation: SOC's rise to prominence in Anglophone literature and its subsequent moment of flourishing in Japanese literary circles. This repeated testing across multiple contexts exposes the algorithmic competencies afforded by the model, providing multiple opportunities to consider where they confirm or confound existing judgments about the circulation of SOC as literary form. This is as much an exploration of these competencies as it is an experiment in translating models from one linguistic context to another to see where they hold up and where they break down. And, finally, as in chapter 3, I consider how these new frames for interpretation alter the stories we are accustomed to telling about particular texts.

MODELING STREAM OF CONSCIOUSNESS IN ENGLISH

I will begin by building a computational model of SOC in English fiction in order to build a commensurate model for Japanese. Admittedly, proceeding in this order already feels like a commitment to a particular theory of literary circulation. It implies a geographical trajectory, where "foreign form(s)" radiate out from some agreed "Greenwich meridian" of world literature to meet "local materials." An alternative experimental design might first create a model of SOC rooted in Japan's local linguistic and literary contexts and then assess how well it predicts antecedent texts, both from Japan and elsewhere. If the design seems wedded to a particular theoretical vision, this is in part to test this vision according to a different method for judging equivalence. But it is also in part to test the stories we have of the success and failure of SOC in Japan. Japanese writers and critics saw this method/technique/form/style (there was little consensus on what to call it) as a foreign import that traveled by various routes to enter the field of Japanese literary production as a radically new and unfamiliar approach to the problem of representing human consciousness. Writers looked to the cultural authority of Dujardin, Joyce, and Woolf, among others, for clues on how to adapt this approach to existing modes of expression, but also in their own local quests for cultural authority.[24] Some of these same writers, followed by their postwar critics, would deny that these adaptive strategies had any lasting impact beyond the brief period when SOC held sway as an object of fascination and a source of cultural capital. To begin with a model of SOC in English is to recognize the structural asymmetries in which these writers worked. It is at once to search for shared patterns of preference in their adaptive strategies and to assess the legacy of these strategies once they began to seek authority elsewhere.

How can we model something that came by multiple routes and in varied shapes? SOC was a form that at once appeared concrete and real, but also diffuse and difficult to pin down. The extensive criticism on SOC in English paints a no less fuzzy and conflicted picture. Is it a novelistic genre? A mode of narration used selectively in a novel? A representation of specific levels of consciousness? A formal technique? An authorial style? Opinions have diverged from the start. Modernist critics and practitioners of SOC exploited its definitional ambiguity in their early attempts to describe it. Wyndam Lewis, for instance, famously complained that the stream-of-consciousness writer "robs works of all linear properties whatsoever, of all contour and definition . . . [resulting] in a jellyfish structure, without articulation of any sort."[25] Virginia Woolf, in contrast, saw these writers, especially Joyce, as concerned with the "myriad impressions [the mind receives]," with "the atoms as they fall upon the mind," "the flickerings of that innermost flame which flashes its messages through the brain."[26] Critic Erwin Steinberg, writing in the early 1970s, said of Woolf's description that "there has been no better operational definition of the stream-of-consciousness technique."[27]

That Steinberg could say this without irony hints at how much had changed in critical approaches to SOC since it first appeared, and how much had stayed the same. What had changed was the idea that SOC could be more formally described ("operationalized") by transforming a description like Woolf's into a set of identifiable (and even measurable) stylistic or linguistic features, as Steinberg proceeded to do. This impulse goes back to the first wave of interest in SOC, both in Japan and elsewhere. But by the 1970s, with the rise of structuralism and quantitative stylistics, and building on Formalist work done in the 1950s, some critics became increasingly invested in breaking SOC down into its constituent features or associative structures.[28] Dorrit Cohn captured this Formalist impulse well when she argued that "a linguistically based approach has the great advantage of supplying precise grammatical and lexical criteria, rather than relying on vague psychological and stylistic ones." Cohn's was a cautious optimism, however, as she warned that a linguistic approach oversimplifies the correspondence between spoken discourse and silent thought and can obscure the literary aspects of mental representation (e.g., irony, lyricism, sub- or superverbal functions).[29] Linguistic and structuralist approaches to SOC waned in the ensuing decades, although Moretti suggested again in the mid-1990s that "quantitative analysis might be an appropriate interpretive key for the 'mechanical form' of the stream of consciousness."[30] If this Formalist strain helped push beyond earlier, less precise formulations of SOC as a variation of "interior monologue" or a kind of "direct quotation of the mind," it did not achieve any firm consensus on what SOC was.[31] What it did leave behind is an extensive list of features attributed to SOC in general and to certain canonical works of SOC in particular. A record, in other words, of how scholars have tried to isolate parts of this amorphous jellyfish.

Included in this list are interior monologue, soliloquy, free indirect discourse, free association, the cross-referencing of imagery and symbols, leitmotifs, irregular punctuation, fragmented sentences, use of ellipses, paratactical paragraphs, truncated syntax, onomatopoeia, an emphasis on sensory perception, neologisms or agglutinations of words, polyglottism, lexical opaqueness or bombardment, castrated grammar, double negation, and the elision of articles, subject pronouns, or prepositions.[32] Each of these, the scholarly record suggests, has been used in varying degrees and combinations across the population of writers who experimented with SOC. As a group, they provide the basis for a capacious model of SOC that includes as many features as can be measured or approximated computationally. Here I include as many of them as possible to determine what narrower subset was consistent across many SOC passages and thus might have registered most powerfully for Japanese writers. Of course, in leaving out the more abstract and difficult to operationalize features, the model is admittedly not capacious enough. There is no straightforward way to turn subjective judgments about lexical opaqueness or the degree of free association in a passage into numbers. As a result, the model is constrained by the words and symbols that can be read from the page, or by what can be derived from their internal structure or by augmenting them with external information. It can include features that involve discrete symbols (ellipses), identifiable lexicons (neologism, onomatopoeia), and morphological elements (the relative presence of personal pronouns); it can also, as in chapter 3, approximate higher-order features (lexical bombardment, free indirect discourse, fragmented sentences) using lower-order elements.

This process of selection ultimately yields a model for SOC in English with thirteen features, each created in reference to the scholarly record and with the knowledge that corollary measures have to be developed for Japanese texts. The features include median sentence length (to capture rhythm of phrasing), proportion of nominalized sentences and proportion of verbless sentences (to capture sentence fragments), proportion of sentences beginning with a gerund phrase (an index of indirect interior monologue), total ratio of personal pronouns and proportion of sentences beginning with a personal pronoun (to capture their degree of elision), three measures of lexical diversity using the type-token ratio (TTR), the ratio of onomatopoeic words, the ratio of neologisms, the number of ellipses relative to passage length, and the proportion of sentences with elements of free indirect discourse.[33] This list draws attention to yet more lacunae in the model. It relies almost entirely on syntactical and narrative elements at the expense of features that measure the presence of sensory or perceptual elements (e.g., words related to color or specific imagery). Moreover, it privileges formal traits over content, in part because of the expectation that content varies too much across the novels where SOC appears. Should this combination of features be unable to consistently distinguish SOC from non-SOC passages, it will further convince us of its nebulous, intractable form. Should they prove a more reliable judge of SOC, however, then we learn something new about how this nebulousness was constrained.

To test this model, a corpus of SOC passages was created from a collection of sixty novels identified by scholars as either a canonical instance of SOC or as having some elements of SOC. As scholars have long noted, SOC typically appears in flashes, rarely establishing the overall form of the novel. Thus passages were identified within these sixty works that, by the judgment of myself and my collaborators, arguably embody the technique. On average, these passages were 1,200 characters long and five were taken from each novel, resulting in three hundred total. Included in the corpus are canonical examples from Dujardin, Joyce, Woolf, Richardson, Waldo Frank, and Proust, as well as lesser known or less well received experiments in SOC, such as those in Conrad Aiken's *Blue Voyage*, John Dos Passos's *Manhattan Transfer*, and Jean Toomer's *Cane*.[34]

The next step was to build a parallel corpus of passages against which to compare the SOC passages. This required collating a set of passages that were likely to contain few elements of SOC as defined by the model. In literary scholarship, SOC is sometimes viewed as a stylistic break with literary Realism in both the American and British traditions, suggesting that a set of formal features reliably differentiates them.[35] Even granting that certain forms of narrated consciousness are present in Realist works, SOC is often regarded as marking a new, if nevertheless related, stage in the evolution of these forms. Thus a parallel corpus of three hundred passages (all of them 1,500 characters long) was created by randomly sampling from sixty canonical Realist works that predate SOC and are not viewed as significant precursors to it. These include *Middlemarch*, *House of Mirth*, *Sister Carrie*, *Portrait of a Lady*, *Wuthering Heights*, and *Great Expectations*. These sampled passages were labeled "Realist" and became the initial basis on which to assess the validity of the model. To be viable, the model should at least be able to distinguish known instances of SOC from passages that have no direct relation to the technique.

Using a process similar to that described in chapter 3, the last step was to see how well a classifier based on the model could make this distinction. Utilizing all of the features and testing the classifier one hundred times (each time learning on 90 percent of the SOC and Realist passages selected at random), on average, the model was able to correctly predict the assigned category with 85 percent accuracy for individual passages.[36] Averaging these passage level predictions across all the passages in a given work, the accuracy rate climbed to 95 percent, indicating that most predictions fall above the 85 percent mark. Within the equivalence space generated by this model, SOC novels are not difficult to distinguish from decidedly non-SOC ones. Although biased toward formal features, the model has enough information to know what a SOC passage looks like roughly 85 percent of the time (as distinct from a Realist passage). In fact, it does not need all of the information it is given. Using the feature weights reported by the logistic regression classifier, it appears that features related to pronoun usage and gerund phrases are not useful in distinguishing SOC on the whole, even if, as scholars note, they are an essential element in *Ulysses*.[37] The results also indicate that some features are more discriminating than others. The more ellipses, onomatopoeia, and verbless sentences a passage has, the greater its chances of being a SOC passage. Conversely, the more neologisms it has, the less likely it is to be SOC. Of all the features, type-token ratio on all words is the most distinguishing: if TTR increases by one (i.e., as lexical diversity increases), the odds of a passage not being SOC increases by a factor of eighteen. In other words, SOC passages tend to use a much narrower range of vocabulary.[38] Scholars have long intuited the importance of TTR in differentiating SOC as a style, but these results illustrate the degree and scale at which the intuition holds.[39] Perhaps the most critical finding from these results, however, is that these features work in combination, and with relative consistency, across many diverse examples of SOC. At the core of this jellyfish, it would seem, is a certain degree of formal consolidation around a discrete set of linguistic features.

Having isolated this core, or at least the strain encoded in the model, we can return to the central question: What can the judgment of computational models add to existing models for evaluating literary influence at the world scale? Assuming the model has identified a reliable set of identifying characteristics that repeat across diverse examples of SOC in English, what do we learn by extending this model to other comparative contexts? Existing accounts tell us that it was a form that traveled well ("the most famous technique of the twentieth century"), touted as it often was as a truly distinct formal break with past and present convention. This perceived gap made it an object onto which stories of circulation and stylistic evolution could readily cohere, regardless of whether anyone could agree on what it actually was. Viewed collectively, one theory to which these stories point is of world literature as a "wave" that began in Paris and London ("the core") after the eighteenth century and radiated outward to Japan ("the periphery"), a wave increasingly defined by "sameness" as it moved. Under this theory, literatures of the periphery converge on the same forms that appear at the core within an increasingly unified system.[40] But one also finds in these stories a theory of world literature as adaptation or resistance in which objects like SOC do not really move at all. There is no material transfer of core forms into peripheral contexts because they are continually fragmented and transformed by linguistic or cultural divisions. A theory of constant differentiation rather than convergence.

Behind these competing theories, as suggested at the outset, are competing interpretative judgments about what does and does not constitute formal convergence. These judgments naturally vary with how formal equivalence is defined. A robust definition that includes every possible dimension along which two objects can vary will always find a difference between them. A sparse definition that compares objects along only a few dimensions will potentially see the same object everywhere. The size of the aperture through which formal equivalence is defined (i.e., how many dimensions one includes) has no small part in determining the theories of world literature that are visible through that aperture. The goal here is to consider what a computational aperture makes visible by virtue of its constrained, but also consistent, definitions of equivalence. What texts will it see as formally consistent with SOC as defined by this model, and do those texts have a place in the stories that critics have already told about how well SOC moved (or didn't) beyond its canonical modernist variants? To what theory of world literature will this model's judgments lend itself? To get at these questions, it is useful to look first at the circulation of SOC in English fiction—the Anglophone "semiperiphery"—before turning attention to Japan.

Determining how and how far this model of SOC spread in English requires creating a large corpus of Anglophone novels to search through. The one used here consists of 1,700 works published between 1923 and 1950, the majority by American writers but also including works by writers in England, Ireland, Scotland, Australia, Canada, and South Africa.[41] Using the same feature set and randomly sampling five equal-length passages from each novel, the resulting classifier is only slightly less accurate, averaging 83 percent at the passage level and 94 percent across all passages for a given novel. Yet because the object of comparison has changed, SOC looks slightly different than it did against older Realist novels. Nominalized sentences and neologisms are no longer a useful feature for distinguishing SOC, although the pronoun-based features are. In particular, higher proportions of pronouns at the beginning of a sentence now signal a higher likelihood of a passage being SOC. Other features, however, continue to signal in the same direction and with roughly the same strength. The core of the model holds together, in other words, even as there is movement at the edges. Such movement is not surprising. It is to be expected that what distinguishes SOC from a collection of mostly nineteenth-century novels is not going to be the same as what distinguishes it from works published during and after its modernist peak. The linguistic landscape against which its uniqueness is figured has shifted. That the originally specified model is accurate against both backgrounds, if for slightly different reasons, suggests something of its stability and structure, as well as its indeterminacy, as it is applied to different contexts. This variation within sameness becomes more pronounced as the model is carried over to the Japanese context.

Here, however, the flexibility of the model forces a decision about the version of SOC on which to focus when trying to trace its broader movement across the literary semiperiphery. Should it be SOC as it looks against the past, or SOC as it looks against the present and near future? In which direction would critics and readers at the time have mostly been looking when evaluating SOC as technique or form? An argument could be made for either version, and so too for a version that looked in both directions at once (i.e., by training and classifying against both Realist and contemporary fiction together). In this case, a choice was made to isolate a version of SOC that stood out against contemporary and later Anglophone works. As in chapter 3, the classifier built from this version can be used to predict the likelihood of a passage or novel being SOC or not. A probability score closer to 0 suggests a greater number of SOC elements, and a score closer to 1 suggests fewer such elements. Taking the average of the scores for all novels by year and plotting them over time shows the relative change in the number of SOC-like novels across the full span of the sample (figure 4.1).

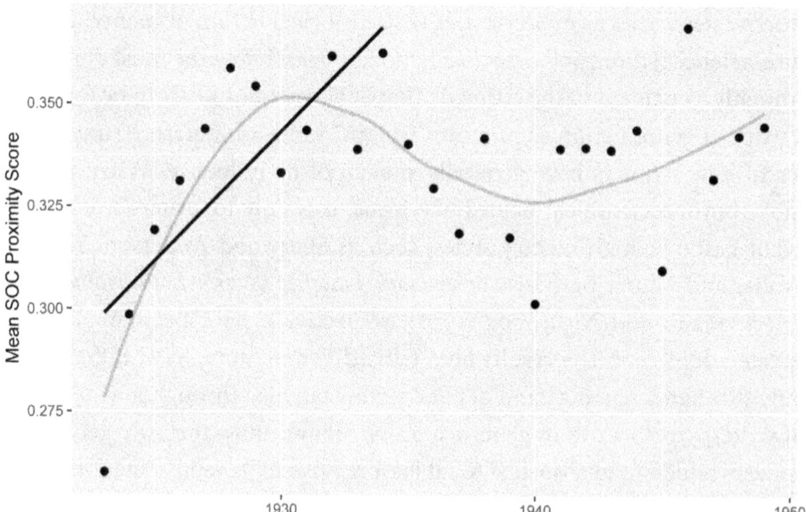

FIGURE 4.1. Inverted mean stream-of-consciousness (SOC) score for all works by year, 1923 to 1950. Scores are inverted so a higher score indicates proximity to SOC. A linear model (black) fit to the period 1923–1934 shows an increase in more SOC-like works. A loess curve fit to the entire data set (gray) shows a flattening out after 1935, when a structural break is observed.

For visual clarity, scores are inverted so that "1" indicates proximity to SOC. Between 1923 and 1934, the number of novels in this corpus that look more like SOC steadily rises, flattening out after 1935. A Chow test indicates that the rise is statistically significant ($p = .002$), with 1935 as a breakpoint in the overall trend. Within the equivalence space determined by this model, then, there is a potential story to be told of SOC's expanding influence after its recognition in the early 1920s, after which it entered a holding pattern of sorts, its constitutive elements now permanently folded into the part of the literary landscape visible with the Anglophone corpus.[42]

If the novels in this corpus look more like our SOC passages between 1923 and 1934, hinting at its increased use beyond the usual canonical suspects, it is worth asking whether the novels driving this trend share anything in common. Analysis of the nationality, gender, and race of the authors indicates no significant correlations with any category. Whether as independent variables or in combination, they do not explain the rising presence of SOC.[43] Turning to genre, another kind of social evidence, there is again little indication of correlation. After assigning genre labels to all the novels using Library of Congress metadata, it was determined that no single genre could be held responsible for the rise in SOC-like novels or their sustained presence in the corpus despite the collection containing works categorized as modernist, realist, historical fiction, romance, adventure, science fiction, and detective fiction, the last being the most dominant (roughly 33 percent of the corpus). That SOC is just as likely to be found in a work of genre fiction as in more "serious" kinds of literature runs counter to how scholars have generally spoken of its influence. When it does move beyond canonical figures like Joyce, it is only to writers working in avant-garde or high literary styles, such as Sherwood Anderson, Thomas Wolfe, and Djuna Barnes, whose *Dark Laugher* (1925), *Look Homeward, Angel* (1929), and *Nightwood* (1936), respectively, have been singled out as late adopters.[44] The results here tell a different story. SOC diffuses not only through a narrow band of elite writers but also through a wider band of writers irrespective of generic affinity. Significantly, the only genre that appears reluctant to absorb SOC, at least relative to its representation in the corpus, is detective fiction.

How should we contend with a model at once so good at distinguishing canonical moments of SOC and yet so awful at staying within the lines of established critical judgment when it looks at a wider swathe of fiction? Is this indication of a successful model, or a failed one? Here it is important to remember that the model's judgments are expressed on a continuum (from 0 to 1) and that they are made with respect to individual passages, not whole books. Deciding on whether to put its patterns of judgment into dialogue with our own thus requires digging into the SOC passages it finds and pressing again, as in chapter 3, on the edges of the computational frame. To take an extreme example, consider Jeffrey Farnol's *The Way Beyond* (1933), judged as one of the most SOC-like novels in our corpus. Farnol was a popular British author who wrote more than thirty genre novels, primarily romances. *The Way Beyond* is indeed a work of romantic fiction, a mid-century best seller of the genre. Unsurprisingly, no scholars have ever linked SOC to this work. Scholars of modernism and SOC tend to follow Joyce's contempt for the romance genre. In an oft-cited interview, Joyce starkly contrasts literary modernism against romance, denigrating the latter. If novels such as *Ulysses* realistically illuminate life as "jugs, and pots and plates, back-streets and blowsy living-rooms inhabited by blowsy women, and of a thousand daily sordid incidents," the romance novel merely provides "flimsy drop scenes."[45] At least since *Ulysses*, the ordinariness of high modernism has been pitted against the unreality of romances.

This passage from Farnol's novel contributes to the model's decision that it is more like SOC than not:

> Thus then they sat, Rosemary staring down at the bonnet strings her strong, shapely fingers were twisting and Richard gazing at her beautiful, down-bent face, whose loveliness was made even more alluring by its sudden, bewildering changes, or so thought Richard: This nose, for instance, though perfect in itself, yet because of its delicate, so sensitive nostrils, became positively adorable; this rose-red mouth, with its sweet, subtle curve of mobile lips, broke his heart when it dropped . . . and, by heaven, it was dropping now! He seized her hands to kiss and kiss them, he lifted her head that he might look down into her eyes, and gazing into these tender deeps, he questioned her in a voice anxious and a little uncertain.[46]

Within the strict confines of the model, this passage registers as more SOC-like because of the use of ellipsis to mark a state of reflection or contemplation; the exclamation mark outside of dialogue, signaling free indirect discourse; and a narrow vocabulary. These are enough to place the passage closer to something found in a Virginia Woolf novel than to all the other passages the model sees. Independent of these features, but still amenable to a broader definition of SOC, the passage also contains a quick shift from external description to interior monologue; long, meandering sentences; and an alliterative, aurally charged diction ("rose-red mouth," "sweet, subtle curve"). Not found in Woolf, of course, is such overwrought narrative content. This might be the line at which we decide the model's judgment has gone too far, allowing in as it does a variation on SOC that lacks the seriousness of its original modernist ambitions. It might also be the line where we admit a looser story of SOC's influence in the decade after *Ulysses*, wherein core features are selectively picked up and diluted as SOC radiates beyond a coterie of high modernist writers in England and America. How far to let the model's judgments influence our own (and those of past interpretive communities) is a decision that requires reading more such passages to understand what the model sees in them; for example, passages from novels by P. G. Wodehouse (*Heavy Weather*, 1933), Pearl Buck (*Sons*, 1932), and Peter Cheyney (*Dark Duet*, 1943).[47] Given the theoretical thrust of this chapter, I will momentarily delay this decision until I have moved the computational model to Japan. For it is in that context that I can best weigh the model's algorithmic competence against competing theories of world literature and the habits of literary judgment that sustain them.

MODELING STREAM OF CONSCIOUSNESS IN JAPANESE

Before moving the model into this new context, let me briefly revisit the stories told about SOC's rise and fall in Japan. Recall that the first narrative to emerge was a celebratory one that positioned Japan as a necessary stopping point in SOC's journey. SOC was a radical and liberating innovation in psychological description with which writers could strip away the decaying husks of their Naturalist forebears. Once the sheen of SOC had worn off, however, and the fever broke, a less optimistic narrative emerged, beginning with some of its most ardent early supporters. In 1935, Doi reissued his seminal essay on *Ulysses*; although acknowledging its continued value as a stylistic reference point, he added this assessment: "It is but an unfinished experiment. Not a masterpiece to be long cherished by readers, but a novel destined to be forgotten after shocking the world."[48] Itō Sei, a brash young poet who had spearheaded the first translation of *Ulysses* and who actively experimented with SOC, reflected after the war that his attempts to adapt the technique had failed because of the difficulty of reproducing it in Japanese, coupled with the expectation that fiction had to be short, thus limiting his ability to fully exploit it.[49] Future Nobel laureate Kawabata Yasunari, who was also an early adopter, prevaricated in his reflections too, at times acknowledging the transformative impact of Itō and others on the literary establishment and at times rejecting his own experiments in SOC as mere dabbling in a passing fad.[50]

Every fashion looks regrettable in hindsight, and these regrets have had a way of seeping into postwar critical accounts of how deeply SOC penetrated Japanese letters and the legacy of its impact. Ōta Saburō, one of the first postwar critics to extensively document the influence of Joyce in Japan, argued that the initial period of experimentation with SOC ended around 1932. Writers Itō and Kawabata had, by this point, "fully assimilated" the technique (*shuhō*) into their fiction after a brief, intense period in which they were "enamored only with the form" and the desire to replicate this newly acquired knowledge.[51] A later critic was more blunt: "The fiction [that used stream of consciousness] did little more than superficially imitate one aspect of Joyce's work. It contributed next to nothing to modern Japanese fiction."[52] Scholars offer several explanations for why SOC's flame burned out so quickly and completely. The technique was too different from established traditions of naturalist realism; writers like Itō were so focused on the form that they had missed the point of *Ulysses*, neglecting the content behind it and Joyce's unique understanding of human consciousness; the obsession with technique hindered writers' ability to position it within broader conceptions of the socially situated self, opening them up to critique from the left; or else this obsession caused them to chase after expressive modes untethered to internal motivations, thus producing overly contrived works.[53] Form had preceded function and left behind a collection of curious, but entirely forgettable, SOC knock-offs.

This narrative of failed influence forms a prominent strain in postwar criticism. All kinds of barriers are put in the way of meaningful intertextual relations, either to reinforce linguistic and aesthetic divisions or to quarantine experiments in SOC from the normal course of modern Japanese literature. Perhaps we should not be surprised that a technique so protean and difficult to grasp looks in retrospect like it made few significant inroads.

That the primary vectors for SOC, namely, Itō and Kawabata, also look back on it as a foreign technique briefly toyed with and then discarded only reinforces this perspective, especially as most criticism has concentrated on these canonical figures and Joyce's influence in particular. The perspective also recalls a key corollary to Moretti's theory that a "streamlining of formal solutions [is] imposed by the world market on the literary imagination." Despite his generous view on the possibilities of formal influence across borders, he acknowledges that some forms are less portable than others. If formal sameness readily incurs at the level of *plot*, the same does not hold for *style*, which is language dependent and finds "all sorts of obstacles" as it moves through the literary system. "In fact, the more complex a style is, the 'better' it is, the greater the chance that its most significant traits will be lost in translation."[54] If SOC is something more like style than plot, then surely it leans to the complex end of the spectrum. Yet how did the "most famous technique of the twentieth century" travel the world *and* get lost in translation? Ironically, while postwar criticism has emphasized the failure of SOC to travel far in Japan, it has had no trouble isolating elements that broke through to infect the prose of Itō and others. These include the use of montage, foreign or unfamiliar diction, incomplete sentences, nominalized endings, blending of subjective and objective description, repetition, the chaining of conceptual associations, short sentences, free indirect discourse, and parenthetical notation to mark interior monologue.[55] Not everything was lost along the way.

In contrast to this story of failed Formalist obsession, the picture we get from critics and writers in the years when SOC seemed to be everywhere is an inverse one. For most of them, there was little doubt that SOC was a technique that could and should be imported because it represented, primarily through *Ulysses*, such a radical innovation in psychological realism. SOC was a definite, concrete force to be reckoned with, variously labeled as a form (*yōshiki*, *keishiki*), technique (*tekuniku*), method (*metōdo*, *shuhō*), style (*buntai*, *sutairu*), and mode of expression (*hyōgen-hō*). Yet for all the attention it was paid as a new way to represent the complexities of the human mind, or as a thing worth assimilating, there was little discussion of technical specifics. Commentators pointed to examples from canonical sources, described in detail the idea of consciousness that SOC aimed to represent, debated the best ways to formally express this idea, and in one case, went so far as to rewrite a passage from *Ulysses* to reflect the critic's own ideas of how consciousness responded to reality.[56] Very rarely, however, did these commentators explicitly identify, at the linguistic or grammatical level, how SOC was actualized in its original languages or how best to reproduce its representational effects in Japanese. The general consensus was that it was simply worth emulating because it presented a more realistic, if no less linguistically mediated, account of how the human mind worked. As to the precise nature of its mediation, or how to domesticate it for Japanese readers, this was a debate that transpired only implicitly via translations and original experimentation.

Two general stories thus emerge. In the period when SOC went viral, we find a story of radical innovation and urgent borrowing but with few specifics on the mechanics of this process. In the period that followed, it is a story of failed transfer and superficial imitation but with many more specifics on where this process went awry. I do not juxtapose them here to reconcile them because each has validity within its own historical and evidentiary horizon. Limiting these horizons, however, are implicit judgments about where world literature happens, who gets to participate in it, and how that participation is organized. Judgments, for instance, that project a sense of simultaneity and synchronicity across the world but limit participation to those responsive to the aesthetic norms by which this world operates. Or else judgments that project a world in which writers at the periphery can only ever be derivative, reinforcing geographical hierarchies while shoring up the walls of national literature to make them impermeable to foreign substances. What do we miss when we assume the diffusion of something like SOC but lack a generalizable model that can follow its mutations across multiple actors regardless of whether we think they truly *got it* or not? Conversely, what is missed when we privilege narratives of untranslatability overfit to specific canonical instances and actors, or strict definitions of formal and stylistic equivalence? A computational model of SOC does not resolve these competing views, but it can, within its own narrow horizons of judgment about textual equivalence, cast a new light on their respective blind spots.

Generating this computational perspective to see where it does and does not align with the narratives presented thus far requires moving the model of SOC created for Anglophone fiction into a new linguistic and literary context. By design, the model relies on syntactic or lexical features that are independent of semantic content and for which approximate equivalents can be found in Japanese. This necessarily limits the kinds of SOC writing that can be identified in either linguistic context, but it has the virtue of focusing attention on formal and notational elements that were themselves easier to recognize on the physical page. For instance, it is fairly straightforward to measure sentence length, extract dialogue passages, and to count ellipses in Japanese, in part because writers had by the early 1900s fully incorporated Western punctuation practices. Parts of speech can also be identified with relatively high accuracy, making it possible to reproduce the pronoun-related features as well as the proportion of verbless and nominalized sentences. The latter two features similarly serve in Japanese as a proxy for incomplete or fragmented sentences. With respect to the word-based features in the model, these are relational in nature, relying on lexical categories (e.g., types, tokens, function words, proper nouns, neologisms, onomatopoeia) rather than on meaning.[57] Finally, although free indirect discourse is marked in Japanese by a different set of grammatical and lexical patterns, these are empirically detectable and provide an adequate proxy for instances of nonvocalized speech.[58]

That the model can be adapted to Japanese language texts is no guarantee that it will be able to differentiate SOC-influenced works and translations from other kinds of writing. Postwar criticism highlights a few of the same features, but much of this analysis is restricted to canonical figures such as Itō and Kawabata. There is every reason to believe that the model will not generalize to the Japanese context at all. To determine whether the broader group of writers who experimented with SOC did so by adopting some of the same formal features that differentiate it in English, and whether they did so consistently, means first building a corpus of SOC examples. For this I draw on nearly thirty titles that contain passages evocative of SOC. This includes translated passages from *Ulysses* (both translations), *To the Lighthouse*, *Swann's Way*, and Morand's *Open All Night*; passages from recognized or self-proclaimed SOC experiments, including works by Itō, Kawabata, Yokomitsu Ri'ichi, Hori Tatsuo, Nagamatsu Sadamu, and Kobayashi Hideo; and passages from works seen as early harbingers of a modernist turn in the representation of subjectivity, including Akutagawa's *Haguruma* (Cogwheels, 1927) and Kajii Motojirō's "Remon" (Lemon, 1925). The latter can offer clues to whether explicit experiments in SOC were drawing on already existing formal innovations, such as Akutagawa's noted use of montage in his late writings.

The next step was to create a corpus functionally equivalent to the Realism corpus; that is, a collection of passages that represented the narrative conventions from which SOC looked, to both practitioners and postwar critics, like a radical departure. Fortunately, the I-novel and "pure literature" corpora created for chapter 3 provide numerous examples of precisely the conventions against which SOC adopters believed they were rebelling. Itō Sei was arguably the most deliberate on this point, explicitly linking *Ulysses*, and the SOC style more generally, to his idea of a "new psychology literature" (*shin shinrishugi bungaku*) that did away with nineteenth-century novel forms (*yōtai*) no longer suited to representing the realities of human thought and perception.[59] New social realities, but also new models of the mind, required new forms that did not represent mental processes through a single unifying, objective lens, as if through "a microscope or high-speed movie camera."[60] Even one of Itō's most vocal critics at the time, Haruyama Yukio, who insisted that Itō disaggregate SOC as a technique from the novel form itself, granted that SOC greatly expanded the mental territory treated by the traditional "mental novel" (*shinri shōsetsu*).[61] Although neither said so explicitly, it was undoubtedly the preceding generation of Naturalist writers, only recently recognized as the progenitors of the I-novel, whom they had in mind when invoking past forms and traditions. Their "murderous realism," as Yokomitsu dubbed it in 1928, had become the explicit target of concurrent debates over literary Formalism by a new generation of modernist writers.[62] In this respect, I-novel writing is an appropriate analogue to nineteenth-century Realism for assessing whether, and how, Japanese experiments in SOC differentiated themselves.

Thirty titles were selected from the larger corpus of I-novels used in chapter 3, ranging in date from 1910 to 1928 and including at least one work from canonical authors Mushanokōji, Kasai, Chikamatsu, Katai, and Shiga, but also works from lesser known figures. Many of these titles were identified as most likely to be I-novels according to the model specified in that chapter. Using the same procedure as before, which involves taking repeated random samples of four passages from each of the titles and classifying them against the SOC passages, the classifier achieved about 95 percent accuracy at the individual passage level and over 98 percent accuracy when averaging these predictions across all passages in a work. The feature weights from the logistic regression model indicate that just five features were really needed to distinguish SOC from I-novel passages: lower TTR, fewer ellipses, more neologisms, more onomatopoeia, and more nominalized sentences. These features, viewed in combination, inscribe a decisive break from the I-novels, even though they were similarly concerned with narrating internal thoughts. The break is so decisive that no title (after averaging passage-level accuracy scores) falls below the 0.5 threshold that nominally separates SOC-classified passages from non-SOC ones (figure 4.2).[63] In fact, just one work falls anywhere close to the line: Mushanokōji's *Omedetaki hito*, that most narcissistic of Japanese novels. Significantly, when the same procedure is carried out on thirty titles from the "pure literature" (*junbungaku*) corpus, ranging in date from Kunikida Doppō's "Wasureenu hitobito" (Unforgettable people, 1898) to Tanizaki's infamous I-novel parody *Chijin no ai* (Naomi, 1924), the accuracy scores barely change. Moreover, the same five features signal in the same direction with near equal magnitude; only free indirect discourse becomes slightly more helpful in identifying SOC-like passages.

The degree of separation here lends force to the argument, made both by participants and later critics, that examples of SOC writing in Japan marked a significant formal break with the past. For the former group, many of whom were younger writers just getting their footing in the

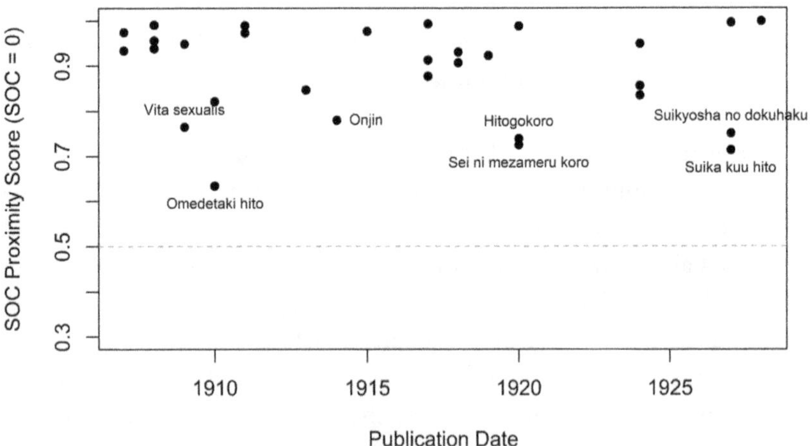

FIGURE 4.2. Classification results for works in the I-novel corpus, with works ordered by publication date on the x axis and by probability score on the y axis (0 = SOC). Lowest scoring works are labeled by title, and none fall below the 0.5 threshold.

literary establishment, the appearance of this internationally recognized and radically distinct style was an opportunity to expand, as Bourdieu puts it, the local space of literary possibilities at a moment when "revolution" still imposed itself as "the *model* of access to existence in the [literary] field."[64] Nagamatsu Sadamu, one of the young writers who both experimented with the technique and collaborated with Itō on translating *Ulysses*, said as much in 1931, emphasizing that the "method" of SOC signaled the "departure point of a new literature" that helped young writers to "quickly and eagerly catch up" with a new and necessary way of viewing contemporary reality.[65] This departure point would look to postwar critics like empty Formalism, and so radical that it put an end to SOC almost as soon as it had emerged. From the perspective of the computational model, both arguments hold up. SOC in Japanese really was something different. Yet the model provides this judgment without resorting to aesthetic evaluations that reduce formal influence and diffusion to matters of success or failure. It puts these judgments temporarily on hold to foreground the actual formal changes taking place.

That these formal changes can be captured with the same dozen features that were used for the Anglophone model of SOC is rather astonishing. That the significant features are not all the same, however, nor always signal in the same direction and with the same magnitude, also suggests that these formal changes were less a result of direct borrowing than of selective appropriation and recombination. Or, as Kirsten Gruesz has described it, a "complex selection process" that involved taking "what [was] useful from the model being copied, and leaving the rest."[66] Consistent across both contexts is that lower lexical diversity and increased use of onomatopoeia are indicative of SOC. The use of more sentence fragments also indicates a higher chance of being SOC in both cases, although this feature is best captured by nominalized sentences in the Japanese model and not verbless sentences, as in the Anglophone model. Neologism and ellipses remain important across contexts, although there values point in inverse directions. The results point to a degree of formal continuity in the process of diffusion, but also to divergence. And just as crucial, they suggest that the formal solution achieved by Japanese writers and translators was, on the whole, a collective one. That is to say, we find in the SOC passages a tendency to coalesce around the same narrow set of features, including the heightened repetition (i.e., lower lexical diversity) that certain key I-novel writers latched onto in developing their own strategies of psychonarration.

Naturally, the perception of coalescence is a function of the model itself and the tight frame it keeps on these texts to hold them in an equivalence space. There is certainly variation happening at the level of narrative content, and so too at the level of formal features, that this model does not represent. More of this variation will become apparent as I push on the frame to inspect individual passages. Even within the frame, however, there is internal variance with respect to how much the core features are accentuated. Just as in the previous chapter, the classifier returns a probability between 0 and 1, providing a continuum at each end of which lay the most SOC and non-SOC-like passages according to the model. The three texts that, on average, have the most SOC-like passages are two short stories by Nagamatsu and a translation of the "Proteus" chapter from *Ulysses*—a chapter Nagamatsu helped to translate with Itō that was famous for its stream-of-consciousness representation of Stephen Bloom's meandering thoughts as he lay atop the rocks at Sandymount Strand. That Nagamatsu's own SOC experiments, which he included in a list of SOC-inspired works in his 1931 essay, should align so closely with his cotranslation of Joyce seems, retroactively, to be a result readily explained by historical circumstance. A passage from one of Itō's own experiments, "Bunoa no hakken" (The discovery at the Café Bunoa, 1931), is ranked fourth most SOC-like, followed by the "Proteus" chapter from the second translation of *Ulysses*.[67] Biography could be made to stand in here for authorial style to tell a story about Nagamatsu and Itō as the writers most deeply influenced by *Ulysses* and the strain of SOC it represented. But it is important to keep in mind that the computational frame is at once making visible something very particular about the nature of that influence while also positioning it against a larger background to which biography alone does not provide access. Indeed, some of Nagamatsu's own statements reject the model's judgments.

On the first point, consider an excerpt from Nagamatsu's "Portrait of Mademoiselle Mako" (1931), which consists of several pages of extended interior monologue. The narration begins with the female narrator's musings about a recent love letter and quickly grows more fragmented and dispersed, slipping in and out of multiple recollected conversations before spiraling into a series of repetitive existential questions. Along the way she leaves scattered ruminations on geopolitics and the fate of Japanese women:

> Ecstasy of the movie theater. True *paradise*. Intoxication that smothers the breast. It's a fact that the ancients clasped their chests with iron rings so that their hearts wouldn't fracture on account of love. Figure of life. *American life*. How bright life is in America. "The Gloryfication of the American Girl!" [sic]. Pitiable Japanese girls. Who on earth will glorify Japanese girls? The *dingy* Japanese youth? Oh, American's *nonchalance*, American's boisterousness, American's recklessness, Americans with their hats off to the side, America's money, money, money—the Americans are all taking over the world. And then in order to compete with them, the red *Soviets*. *G.P.U.* 5 Year Plan. Countless translations of *Marxism*. And the laborers' light blue overalls. Wills of iron, *Marx's* iron laws.[68]

W. C. Williams wrote in his 1923 caricature of Joyce's style that "he has in some measure liberated words, freed them for their proper uses."[69] Moretti later took these "words words words words" seriously as a symbol of how "advertising and stream of consciousness pursue and implicate one another throughout" *Ulysses*.[70] This passage from Nagamatsu reveals his own fascination with the notion that interior thought might best be captured by a successive stream of words. In particular, words marked as foreign, words used repeatedly, and words given sentences of their own. These are the aspects of his prose (neologism, low TTR, nominalized sentences) that push his two works to the extreme end of the SOC continuum, along with passages from his own translation of *Ulysses*. Passages, for instance, like the following, from the opening lines of the "Proteus" chapter and translated here from the Japanese version as rendered by Nagamatsu and his collaborators. Of the 120 SOC passages in the corpus, this was judged the tenth most SOC-like:

> Visible things and their inescapable forms. If not more, then that at least I thought through my eyes. The signatures of things I read here, fruit of sea, ocean jetsam, encroaching tide, that rusty *boat*. Snotgreen, blue-silver, rust. Colored *signs*. Transparent things at their limit. But, he adds, in bodies. So, he knew of their bodies before they were colored. How? By knocking his head on them, surely. Move ahead in ease. Bald he was, and a millionaire, that teacher distinguishable by his face. The limit of transparency nears. Why

> does it come? Transparently transparent. If you can put five fingers through it, even if it is not a door, it is certainly a gate. Close your eyes and look. Stephen, in order to listen to the sounds of boots crunching the jetsam and shells, closed his eyes. You are, at any rate, myself walking through them, one step at a time. Passing through a sliver of space is a sliver of time. 5, 6. In sequence. Precisely. And the sound of those things is their inescapable form. Open your eyes. No. *Iesu*![71]

This passage, incidentally, is one Nagamatsu highlights in a 1934 essay on the style (bunshō) of Joyce, seeing it as paradigmatic of a narrative technique for weaving internal thought and external perception together until indistinguishable. The passage was highlighted again in 1934 by Hatano Kanji, who cites Nagamatsu's essay to help frame his own investigation into the psychological motivations driving stylistic differentiation (see chapter 1). Joyce and SOC, it turns out, helped to catalyze the revival of interest in style that set Hatano's quantitative imaginings about psychology and language into motion.[72] When Joyce's translated writing is compared with the SOC-inspired prose of Nagamatsu, as the model encourages, we see that this catalyzing effect owed much to formal methods that broke discrete words out from the natural flow of language and the narrative frame. One story the model has to tell about influence and SOC is of the undue pull these methods had on Nagamatsu's understanding and deployment of the technique, and so too on those peers whose works fall nearest the SOC end of the continuum: Itō, Kawabata, and Hori.[73] By this account, these writers too, if only for a moment, found something infectious in liberating words from their linguistic moorings.

Significantly, this was not the story that Nagamatsu himself would tell. In his own writings, he insists on his aesthetic autonomy, writing that "Mako" should not be read as a complete example of SOC, nor should Joyce's technique for psychological realism be treated as "an absolute ideal which we must all imitate. On the contrary, all technique is style, and to the extent that style belongs to each individual author, if our style should tend a little bit in one direction, that means nothing more than our worldview and sensibilities have also turned in that direction."[74] Influence, in other words, is a shifting frame of mind. That his story does not align with the restricted gaze of the model is not surprising. From the author's own situated perspective, there are many other dimensions, both formal and content-based, along which his deployment of SOC could be seen to diverge from Joyce. In terms of narrative ends, for example, the use of SOC in "Mako" arguably has more in common with Woolf or Proust because it functions as a style for depicting "exceptional circumstances" (e.g., a lover's panic and increasing delirium) and not for "absolute normality," as in *Ulysses*.[75] Yet by rendering a larger background through a narrower lens, the model points to a deeper layer at which influence operates, one in which stylistic affinity is expressed as a quantitative sensibility—a sense of how much or how little of a specific formal feature to include. At this layer, Nagamatsu's sensibility is more in sync with *Ulysses* than he admits. Itō's, Kawabata's, and Hori's own experiments are not far behind him in this larger background, reinforcing their role in helping to focus this underlying quantitative sensibility on the liberation of the word. Having isolated this sensibility, and tracked the degree to which it infected writers known to have experimented with SOC, I now turn to the question of how widely it spread.

INFLUENCE AHEAD OF ITS TIME

To be clear, what the Japanese model of SOC provides, as with the English model, is the ability to test whether a particular constellation of empirical features is expressed with any consistency in works written contemporaneous with, and after, the documented arrival of SOC as a formal technique. One reason to do this is to ensure that the radical formal break the model designates is not simply a product of general linguistic and stylistic drift. Literary language moved fast in this period, especially as each new generation sought to overturn the achievements of the previous one, and it is necessary to test whether experiments with SOC look equally distinctive to the model when compared with the other kinds of writing happening around it. The second reason is to generate an account of the afterlife of SOC to see where the model's judgments do or do not align with the stories that have been told about its lasting impact on Japanese letters. To generate such an account is simultaneously to return to the question of our willingness, as historians and critics, to put its judgments about textual equivalence in dialogue with those achieved by other means. What, ultimately, can this algorithmic competence offer once we allow it to roam beyond the texts that writers and critics have already diagnosed as the likeliest sites for the reception and mutation of SOC?

In order to address the first rationale, I repeat the procedure used for the I-novel and "pure literature" corpora with a corpus of thirty titles published between 1924 and 1937. It includes writing by several high-brow authors (e.g., Tōson, Akutagawa, Hayashi Fumiko), authors affiliated with the proletarian movement (e.g., Sata Ineko, Hayama Yoshiki, Hirabayashi Taiko), and popular authors of detective fiction in both its "mainstream" (*honkaku*) and "deviant" (*henkaku*) modes (e.g., Edogawa Ranpō, Hamao Shirō, Yumeno Kyūsaku). When SOC passages were compared to these more contemporary works, the full model classified at the passage level with 92 percent accuracy, averaging to about 97 percent accuracy at the work level. From the model's perspective, SOC is nearly as easy to distinguish from contemporary writing as from older works, suggesting that linguistic or stylistic drift is not a confounding variable. The only significant difference is that the presence of onomatopoeia is no longer a distinguishing feature, implying that these words were distributed across contemporary writing in such a way that any meaningful difference with SOC passages is leveled out. The other four discriminating features (TTR, nominalized sentences, neologism, and ellipses) continue to signal in the same direction with similar strength, with only the neologism feature weakening slightly in its predictive power. Also notable is that two works by Yokomitsu, "Kikai" (Machine, 1930) and "Muchi" (Whip, 1931), look more like SOC from this comparative viewpoint. Both are marked by a distinct turn toward representing radical interiority and away from the fragmented sentences and montage techniques of his earlier writing.[76]

That the model should, with slight variations, continue to discriminate SOC so well is both instructive and concerning. Instructive because it reinforces how tightly experiments in SOC coalesced around a core set of formal features. Concerning because it raises the possibility of having overfit the model to a too narrow set of traits and a too narrow set of texts. Keeping in mind that the model captures only a core piece of the SOC jellyfish as it manifested in Japanese fiction, leaving out all the ways this core was manipulated and added onto by individual writers, it is still worth investigating whether this core held together in any discernible measure. Did it travel beyond the original high-art environs where it was first cultivated, as in Anglophone fiction, or did it die a quick death after 1932, as critics suggest? Tracking its diffusion in the Japanese case, as in the English case, requires assembling a reasonably large sample of texts from the period when we expect to find signs of its life and afterlife. Here I draw on the Aozora corpus described in chapter 2 to create a sample of 718 titles (over 32,000 passages) published between 1925 and 1940.[77] As with the Anglophone corpus, this corpus should in no way be taken for the population of texts published during this period. Its representativeness suffers (and gains) from all the generic, gender, and other biases described previously. Nevertheless, it does provide a reasonably diverse body of writing through which to comb for passages that the model judges to be SOC and that have thus far escaped the judgment of critics.

The results of this search tell a different story than the one discovered in the Anglophone corpus (i.e., a quick rise followed by stagnation). Instead, and rather perplexingly, they suggest a story of influence in reverse (figure 4.3). Plotting the mean probability score across all titles, as was done with the Anglophone corpus, and inverting the direction so higher scores indicate closer proximity to SOC, we see that not only does SOC not travel anywhere after 1932 but that its presence spikes in 1929 before any major translations or experiments in SOC were published. There is also a slightly earlier blip in 1926. To make sure these results are not an artifact of the mean values, which are sensitive to extreme outliers and nonnormal

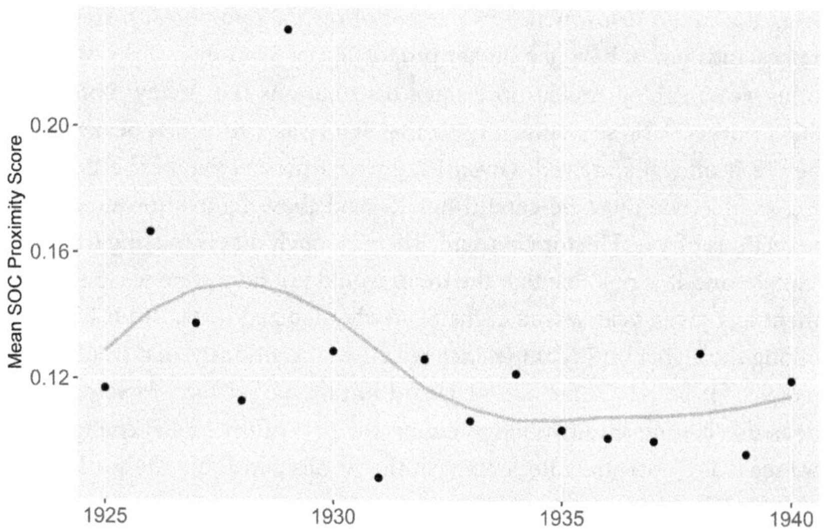

FIGURE 4.3. Inverted mean SOC score for all works by year, 1925 to 1940. Scores are inverted so a higher score indicates proximity to SOC. The year 1929 stands out as having the most SOC-like works.

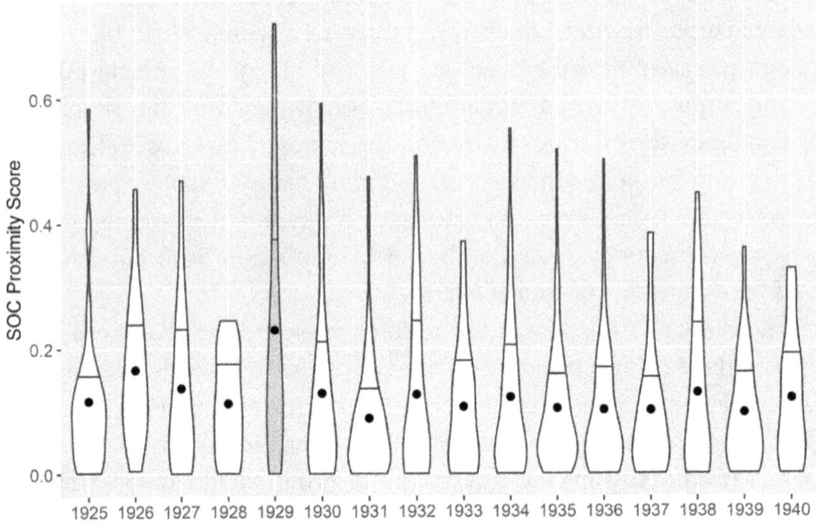

FIGURE 4.4. Violin plots showing the distribution of inverted SOC scores for all works by year, 1925 to 1940. A black dot shows the mean value of each distribution, and black lines show the 75th percentile.

distributions, I compare the yearly distributions with other measures. Figure 4.4 uses violin plots to show the distribution of inverted probability scores in each year, with lines in the plots indicating the 75th percentiles (e.g., the values below which 75 percent of the data points fall). Here, too, 1929 stands out as having a higher proportion of SOC-like works, whereas other years exhibit much more squat distributions (i.e., many more non-SOC works).[78] These results suggest that SOC was a virus that peaked even before it officially arrived. Given the limited perspective of the underlying sample, we must be careful not to read these figures too quickly as reflections of a real historical trend. There is much that is missing from the sample, and it is possible that the trend would not hold were we to supplement any given year with a cache of newly digitized texts. But it is worth taking the algorithmic competence seriously, if cautiously, that would have us look for literary influence backward in time rather than forward. How does this counterintuitive judgment on the part of the model change how we see it as a potential interlocutor in the stories told about the world travels of SOC?

Any year in literary history can look exceptional from the right vantage point. That 1929 turns out to be exceptional for a famous debate about literary form (*keishiki shugi bungaku ron*) makes it feel as though the model is truly on to something. Yokomitsu kicked off this debate in late 1928 in reaction to the surging strength of the proletarian literature movement, whose main proponents insisted that content was the determiner of form. He claimed that this stance was antimaterialist. To him, the object in literature was "the sequence of written characters" that constitute form, and the subject was the content that readers fantasize from this form, this content being "an energy that arises between the reader and the formal arrangement of written signs." To say, as leftist critics were doing, that content determines form was to suggest that it was a function of authorial intention, which was to have the subject-object relation exactly backward. Writing soon after Saussure's introduction to Japan, and seeing himself as extending Sōseki's earlier inquiries into the effect of form on reader response, Yokomitsu argued that the material of writing was never identical to the material that writing signifies. Its materiality disrupts the circuit between sign and thing, acting as a linguistic system and mechanism for the diverse significations generated by the literary text in the consciousness of readers, one ultimately cut off from the consciousness of the author. There is some debate about what Yokomitsu's theory implied for the status of the author because it could be argued that the author's consciousness similarly does not exist apart from the material form it takes in writing.[79] At the very least, it implied that the writer's task is to provoke awareness of writing's mediating function and to call attention to the normalized immediacy of a written vernacular that, although radical at its inception, looked to Yokomitsu and his modernist peers like a suffocating symbol of national standardization. Formalist experimentation was a way to break free from its stranglehold and the interiorities it represented, but also, as with Itō, a means to challenge these representations from the inside, as it were. A means to disrupt the circuit between sign and thing, between unconscious and conscious thought—a means to capture "the random fantasies, fragments of thought, entirely discontinuous stories and events, and the chaotic gradations these all collectively generate" in the human mind.[80]

The critic Nakamura Murao, writing in July 1929, saw these formalist rumblings as the result of a generational transition and increasing stasis in the literary field. On the one hand, the suicide of Akutagawa in 1927 and the death of Kasai Zenzō in 1928 signaled the passing of the field's former standard-bearers, a signal amplified by the low output of other members in this generation (e.g., Shiga, Tanizaki, Shimazaki, Tokuda Shūsei, Satō Haruo) who, as far as Nakamura could tell, were hardly being read anyway. On the other hand, ideological differences that were once a source of dynamism in the field, namely, between "bourgeois" and "proletarian" authors, felt less vital because of what Nakamura perceived as an increasing homogenization at the level of lifestyle and aesthetics. One bright spot in this moment of decline and stasis was the handful of young writers, Yokomitsu and Kawabata in particular, who had found a foothold in the literary establishment by intentionally shedding Naturalist techniques for new modes of expression. Another bright spot was the detective fiction that had been bubbling up over the past few years but "had just this year come into vogue with an explosive force." Nakamura reasoned that "detective novels were the literary form (*keishiki*) best suited to the conditions of the modern city; to the power of science and chemistry; to celebrating the highest mental abilities and strangest psychologies of machines and humans."[81]

In a roundtable discussion published in the same issue as Nakamura's essay, several high-profile contributors to the genre, including Edogawa Ranpō, Koga Saburō, and Hamao Shirō, were asked precisely this question—why was detective fiction so wildly popular of late? They were less sanguine about its use as a guide to the joys and depravities of modern urban life—it was just "make-believe," after all—but they agreed it offered an escape from the mundaneness of everyday life. A chance, for example, "to wonder what it might feel like to murder someone."[82] If detective fiction did have any truth to offer, it was probably in the realm of human psychology. Although on this point, too, the writers admitted to going out of their way to depict "abnormal people" whose character had to be artfully masked just enough to maintain suspense, but not so much as to seem inhumanlike.[83] In their own way, these writers were also experimenting with new psychologies of form.

From this admittedly small sample of voices, 1929 seems to have been experienced as a transitional moment for literary form, with various constituencies vying to inject new life into the tired expressions of their predecessors. It was in February of this year that Doi introduced bits and pieces of Joyce's mesmerizing labyrinth into the mix, although another year passed before it went viral. In the meantime, writers continued to search the space of expressive possibilities for ways of rendering human consciousness better suited to new theories of mind coming from psychology, linguistics, and criminology. My computational model picks up on those writers who, during this year of searching, landed on solutions that, through the model's narrow lens, look similar to the ways that SOC manifested in the early 1930s. It is interesting that amidst this group are writers representative of the different constituencies just described. Consider Inukai Takeru's "Arabia-jin Eruafi" (The arabian El Ouafi), for instance, which consists of eighteen 1,500 character passages, half of which are judged more SOC-like by the model. Inukai was arguably a member of the old guard, having made a name for himself in the late teens under the tutelage of Shirakaba writers Mushanokōji and Shiga. By 1929, however, he had endeared himself to the young modernists Yokomitsu, Kawabata, and Hori, contributing to the Formalism debate from their side and founding a new journal with them in October of that year. "Arabia-jin Eruafi" bears the clearest signs of their stylistic influence, opening with a scene of psychological description striking for its imagistic qualities and reliance on noun-ending sentence fragments. This passage in particular, which gets into the head of the Algerian-born Frenchman El Ouafi, who has just won the marathon at the 1928 Olympic games in Amsterdam, evokes the earlier SOC passages by Nagamatsu and Joyce and the ways they liberate words from narrative.

> Laying face up in the tub, *El Ouafi*'s chest was still panting like a fish. Just as is taught in ethnology textbooks, his hair was black, his copper forehead wide and his face long, but the pomade applied to his disheveled hair was pure *Paris*. It was *Coty*, a farewell gift from his neighbors in the old part of the city. His eyebrows furled, eyes shut, twisting the *shower* head, under the pouring warm rain he was possessed by hallucinations or memories, he could not tell which.—A canal-side windmill. White clouds. Summer grass. Trees. Girl. Dog. Butterfly. And then the runner always 10 meters behind him, now fast approaching, the Chilean *Plaza*. With protruding cheeks and like a character from a woodblock print, the Japanese *Yamada*. With hempen hair and well-matched blue running outfit, the majestic Finn *Marttelin*.—Announcing the arrival of the winner, the blare of the old-fashioned trumpet at the stadium gate. Roar of the crowd. And then finally, surrounding him in the long shadow of the evening sun, newspaper photographers. A record, 2 hours 32 minutes 57 seconds.—Voices noisily proclaimed. And then a moment later, just as he was now laying in the bath, he lay atop the grassy pitch, facing up to the sunset clouds, bathing in the flash of the cameras.[84]

The model also zeroes in on Hamao Shirō and Yumeno Kyūsaku, two writers who, like Edogawa, Kozakai, and others discussed in chapter 3, actively pushed at the generic boundaries of detective fiction by focusing on psychological deviance and aberration. Hamao and Yumeno have two or more works from 1929 with significant portions of SOC-like passages, although the most SOC-like among these are, upon inspection, experimenting with psychological description in ways different from passages seen so far. Instead of a verbal montage, there is an emphasis on repetition and mental churning as first-person narrators, whether via written letter or spoken word, assault readers with accounts of their inner machinations. One critic has noted Yumeno's penchant for using first-person narrators who construct elaborate realities from their partial (and usually) estranged perspectives in order "to thoroughly puncture our own arrogant fallacy that the world produced in our minds is the same as the world itself."[85] True to form, his "Shinamai no fukuro" (Bag of Chinese rice), a third of whose total twenty-seven passages fall closer to my model's version of SOC, is one long confession by a Russian hostess to a young Japanese patron about her desire to murder him. The opening lines establish a pattern of incessant monologue that is sustained throughout the work and which never give her patron, or anyone else, the chance to speak.

> Ah . . . I'm completely drunk . . . but please let me drink one more *cognac*, okay? . . .
>
> You drink too. Because tonight is special . . . Yes. I'm feeling special, tonight . . .
>
> I'll tell you why right now. I'm gonna tell you if you just drink one more cup . . . It's *truly* a frightening tale . . . No, no. I can't. No matter you're a Japanese military officer, if you hear this story to the end you'll almost certainly be *shocked* and high-tale it out of here . . .
>
> Ah, so tasty. I'm going to drink another. I'll get dead-drunk tonight . . . *Nichiewo*! . . . Don't you know of me, *Vanya* of the *Oblaako Restaurant*? . . . You see. Oh, I'm really gonna blather on tonight . . . *Ohohohohohoho* . . . But before you hear the story, there's a reason it's fine to let me drink as much as I want. Why? Because these days there have been many times, many times, when I've wanted to kill you . . . Oh, why that face? . . . *Hohohohohoho*. There's no need to look so scared. Go on, have a drink. The *champagne* is already open . . .[86]

The final writer singled out by the model in 1929 is Hori Tatsuo. Two of his works (from 1930 and 1933) were included in the SOC corpus because of their documented influence by the technique. According to the model, an earlier work, "Bukiyō na tenshi" (Awkward angel), also shares qualities of SOC texts in their actual viral moment.[87] Ten of the work's fifteen passages, in fact, are judged more SOC-like than not. What are we to do with the judgment of a model that reads Hori's future, and the future of SOC, in its past?

"Bukiyō na tenshi" was Hori's second-ever work of fiction, published in February in the literary magazine *Bungei shunjū*. Criticism at the time was of two minds about the kind of formal innovation it represented. Some critics lauded its formal freshness, praising how it turned mental description into rapid action. "With fiction like this, I might not need to go to the motion pictures I so love," quipped novelist Uno Chiyo in her review. The poet Murō Saisei declared that "Hori, more so than Yokomitsu even, belonged to a splendid new age."[88] These quotes were cited in a later review by Kawabata, who had heard the buzz only to find that the work lacked the power to hold his attention. For one, the immaturity of the content—basically the story of a young student infatuated with a café waitress—was hardly worth the extravagant expressions brought to bear on it. Second, despite the "intense formalist effort" the author expended in composing the work, all this effort thinned out when read in print. "How was the author himself not shocked by this miscalculation (*gosan*)? The work is of a form (*keishiki*) that raises this very question."[89] What follows is a snippet from Hori's "miscalculation," judged by the model as one of its most SOC-like passages.

> And then, once again, the previous silence returns. My complexion changes. I try to hide it with the smoke from my cigarette. But the silence that till now felt pleasurable suddenly makes it hard to breathe. The jazz strangles my throat. I grab the *glass*. I start to drink. But my crazed eyes visible at the bottom of the *glass* frighten me. I can't be here any longer.
>
> I escape to the *veranda*. The dimness cools my crazed eyes. And there, with no one looking at me, I can stare at the girl over there in front of the blowing fan. The breeze makes her grimace, but bestows on her an unexpected holiness. Suddenly the lines on her face quiver. She looks this way and smiles. For a moment I'm convinced she smiled because she caught me

> staring at her from the *veranda*. But I quickly realize my mistake. There's no way she can see my figure standing in the dim light from where she is. Was she giving a signal to someone to come over? It's probably Maki. She walks toward me, resolute.
>
> My hands feel heavy, like fruit. I place them on the rail of the *veranda*. The rail covers my hands in dust.[90]

Formal innovation, as with Mushanokōji in 1910, appears to happen again at the place where boy meets girl and can only stare anxiously, from a safe distance. Yet Hori himself expressed doubt about the innovativeness of the work, formal or otherwise. He conceded Kawabata's point in a brief essay the following year, admitting to his "miscalculation" and attributing it to the fact that he had mistakenly substituted "truth" (*shinjitsu*) for "poetry" (*shi*) and wrongly put equal faith in both. Citing the German phrase "Dichtung und Wahrheit" (Poetry and truth), which alludes to the subtitle of Goethe's autobiography, *Aus meinem Leben* (From my life, 1811–1833), Hori implies that he put too much faith in factual detail alone while neglecting the importance of its poetic and fictional fashioning.[91]

That Hori so readily acquiesced to Kawabata's critique, and that Kawabata himself would conduct his own formal experiments in representing the subconscious in 1930 (on the no less immature topic of female hysteria), hints at the rhetorical jousting happening here between two members of the new guard. Having blazed his own Formalist trail in the years prior, Kawabata had reason to keep the up-and-comer Hori in his place. Postwar critics, however, find in "Bukiyō na tenshi" the radical refashioning of the self that Kawabata and then Hori, likely in deference to him, denied. The refashioning is mediated largely through the strategic use of present-tense verb endings (*genzai shūshikei*). Hori's narrator alternates between this form of conjugation and the more conventional plain-past conjugation (*ta* ending) throughout the story, creating two distinct phenomenological realities. One defined by the indirect, temporal clarity of past-tense narration and the definitiveness it provides; the other by directness and temporal indifference in a way that generates ambiguity and uncertainty while shifting focus to the sensing self (as in the previously cited passage). The latter also has the effect of canceling out the authority of the narrating "I" by enveloping the reader in a present that is blind to what will happen next. By using this mode in moments when the "I" is dissembling or being reconstituted through interaction with others, such as under the waitress's gaze, and by threading these together with moments of narrative clarity, Hori dramatizes a self produced out of multiple interlacing points of view within consciousness. Such a dramatization, argues scholar Nakamura Shin'ichirō, allowed Hori to extend his powers of imagination to his protagonist's unconscious such that the complexity of human psychology was rendered not as a split subject but as overlapping cognitive layers. In the eyes of later critics, Hori's miscalculation looks like the inauguration of an unprecedented form of the psychological novel.[92]

These conflicting accounts of the text's formal significance perform in miniature the competing judgments leveled on the history of the stream-of-consciousness technique in Japan. True to this history, Hori has been described as "one of the first authors to be poisoned by foreign literature," and "Bukiyō na tenshi" was once deemed a "complete imitation" of Jean Cocteau's *Le Grand Écart* (1923), leaving its aesthetic fate to bounce between claims of innovativeness and imitativeness, success and failure, inspiration and contamination.[93] Reading these claims together, as with those made about SOC, exposes again how historical and institutional contexts prejudice the literary and linguistic competencies underpinning judgments of intertextual relation. When we add to these conflicting claims the algorithmic competency of my model, with all its attendant biases, another kind of blind spot is exposed. Nowhere in the reception history of "Bukiyō na tenshi" do we find mention of a possible connection to the SOC virus that would soon engulf Hori and many of his peers. Such a conjecture would have to reverse the temporal arrow of influence. Nor is the work ever situated in a historical moment that saw formal experiments in psychonarration happening across a diverse range of genres and generations. My model, however, provides reason to further investigate 1929 as a year when all of these experiments bubbled up simultaneously, pushing the boundaries of what it looked like to narrate the internal workings of the mind. Moreover, pushing them in ways that eventually came to resemble experiments in SOC from the early 1930s and, at least according to the model, resembled very little of what came after. Had the model singled out any other year so definitively, I might be more skeptical about pursuing such an investigation. It is precisely by situating its competency alongside others, however, that we learn whether or not the gaps between them can generate a new kind of story about SOC worth telling.[94]

Notably, the story that emerges here is patently different from that suggested in the case of Anglophone fiction. There it was a story of diffusion radiating out from elite modernist circles to a range of high and low cultural forms in ways that existing competencies have precluded scholars from seeing—a subtle variation on Moretti's and Casanova's wave model of circulation in which genre is the mediating dimension rather than geography. In the case of Japan, the story suggested is one of latent formal innovations that prepare the ground for foreign forms. When writers begin to actively domesticate the latter, they repeat and expand on earlier innovations in the process of recombining and reweighting the elements found in foreign forms. Rather than catch on, however, these efforts are confined to a small corner of the literary field, producing new forms that fail to take deep root or spread only after further dilution. This story challenges the wave model of world literature by drawing attention to local forms, rather than local content, as critical receptors for foreign ones. It also recognizes the portability of forms as a process of selection and recombination rather than of straightforward transference or imitation; less formal compromise, more formal reengineering.

The divergent stories relayed in each case support the idea that computational approaches to world literature are not inherently allied with either structuralist or poststructuralist theories. In truth, algorithmic competency cuts multiple ways. To be sure, these stories could be imagined without the computational model, if not at the same scale of evidence or with similar historical scope. But this gets to the heart of the other argument I seek to make in this chapter, which is that algorithmic competency can mark out areas of intertextual investigation in no way innocent, but also in no way more compromised, than other strategies deployed at other times and places. The way it forces hundreds of texts spanning multiple geographies and temporalities into a common equivalence space, breaking them into smaller units and comparing them along a select number of empirical dimensions, is obviously alien to strategies that allude to all the dimensions along which any two textual objects are nonequivalent. Yet this, too, is to project a different kind of universalized space, what Said once called "the labyrinth of 'textuality,' " which is then expertly navigated by the literary critic's deep linguistic and cultural competencies.[95] Both strategies are in turn alien to the historically and socially situated judgments of equivalence and difference that emerge from accounts of writers and critics, who had their own political investments in how best to tell the story of SOC.

These strategies for marking the space wherein the portability of literary form becomes (im)possible will figure difference (and relation) in their own, often incommensurable, ways. The question we must ultimately ask is whether the computationally mediated strategy is too alien to be of use in exposing and reflecting the normative limits of other competencies. In this instance, the strategy has drawn attention to the relative consistency and stability of a formal breakthrough spurred by the travel and translation of SOC's many variants into Japanese. Moreover, it allowed us to connect this breakthrough to a prior historical moment when writers with diverse generic leanings were searching for ways to remediate writing itself as a material expression of human consciousness. In light of these insights, I contend that how algorithmic competency has redrawn linguistic, generic, and temporal lines of difference is not so alien that we can outright ignore its judgments about textual influence and relation. But it is alien enough to make it worth adding to the many competencies that have previously trained our models of world literature.

Chapter Five

DISCOURSE AND CHARACTER

> Cocteau wrote that the only way to record poetry was to speak as if whispering. His actual recordings weren't "like whispering" at all. But when he says "like whispering," I think he's speaking to the very character of modern literature—a person subsumed by poetry, prayer, and confessions, writing them out in careful letters in a solitary room.
>
> —ITŌ SEI (1948)

Writing soon after the end of the Pacific War, and in the midst of a tumultuous few years in which the once expansive Japanese empire rapidly unraveled and collapsed in on itself, Itō projects in this epigraph a desire for a quieter time, when writers could willingly ignore the outside world in pursuit of solipsistic fictions. This, he claimed, had been the core tendency of modern Japanese fiction since Futabatei Shimei's *Ukigumo* (1887–1889), reaching its pinnacle around 1930.[1] In fixing the pinnacle at this year, Itō may have been recalling those heady times when he and others plumbed the depths of the unconscious in search of new psychological realities. If so, he was misremembering a period dominated as much by shouts as by whispers, with more and more writers finding it untenable to stay confined to their rooms. In 1929, in fact, the same pivotal year when much else in Japanese letters was in transition, Yokomitsu Ri'ichi serialized a novel that decidedly reversed fiction's dominant inward gaze and trained it on Japan's expanding, increasingly volatile empire.

Shanghai, known for its highly stylized depictions of life in the foreign settlements of the colonial metropole, traces the lives of several Japanese expatriates as they come to terms with their ethnic identity amid the city's diverse population (which included French, British, exiled Russians, native Chinese) and its heightening class and political tensions. The novel as a whole indexes a pivot, just one of many at the time, from a literature *for* the self to a literature *of* the other; from patterns of describing internal states to patterns of describing external surfaces. In the following scene, expat Sanki laments the futility of finding hope or ideals in present-day China.

> "I think you're right," said Takashige. "There's just no way to hold onto hopes or ideals in a place like this. For one thing, they don't understand such things here. The only thing they understand is *money* . . ."
>
> " . . . That's where the Chinese are *clever*. They've devised ways to make sure that all the money made here gets spent here. That they think of us as human at all is proof of the *kindness* of the Chinese."
>
> "Are you saying that the Chinese *aren't human*? That they're *gods*?," asked Koya.
>
> "They're avatars of men who *aren't human*. There's no place on earth where the people have mastered the art of *lying* as well as in China. But *lies* aren't just *lies* for the Chinese. They're a source of *righteousness* for them . . . if you don't understand the Chinese, then of course you won't understand the future course of the human race."[2]

Although Yokomitsu's now outward-facing gaze allows certain others to invade the frame of his Formalist experiments, they enter through a familiar mode of characterization, one reliant on a list of ready to hand adjectives and descriptors for "Chinese" (clever, inhuman, lies, lying) and confident in its assertions of the character of an entire people even as it couches them in the reliable trope of the inscrutability of the Other.[3] Here is a "discourse [that] 'commodifies' the native subject into a stereotyped object . . . a generic being that can be exchanged for any other native."[4] A discourse close kin to "the portrait of manners and customs" where "encounters with an Other can be textualized . . . as enumerations of traits."[5] It is Edward Said's Orientalist discourse: a representation or image of an Other not directly drawn (or not only drawn) from the author's experience but from a "huge library" of concepts, ideas, and experiences built up over time.[6] Sanki himself seems to recognize this borrowed aspect of the discourse later in the novel, when he gets the "sense that the ideas he held about himself [as Japanese] were not really his, but ideas he was made to think for the sake of Japan."[7]

This huge library and its connection to racial characterization in Japanese language fiction is the focus of this chapter. At the highest level,

I am interested in revisiting Said's original confrontation with this library in *Orientalism*, a confrontation as much about methodology as about the politics of literary criticism.

> One must repeatedly ask oneself whether what matters in Orientalism is the general group of ideas overriding the mass of material—about which who could deny that they were shot through with doctrines of European superiority, various kinds of racism, imperialism, and the like, dogmatic views of "the Oriental" as a kind of ideal and unchanging abstraction?—or the much more varied work produced by almost uncountable individual writers, whom one would take up as individual instances of authors dealing with the Orient.[8]

In deciding between the general or the particular, Said initially took a pragmatic approach. He insisted that these were really two perspectives on the same material. "Why would it not be possible to employ both perspectives together, or one after the other? Isn't there an obvious danger of distortion (of precisely the kind that academic Orientalism has always been prone to) if either too general or too specific a level of description is maintained systematically?"[9] Years later, fear of distortion morphed into resignation. Said had discovered in writing *Orientalism* that "you cannot grasp historical experience by lists or catalogues . . . some books, articles, authors, and ideas are going to be left out." This was less an epistemological problem for Said than a practical one. There was just too much to read. He gives the game away when he retreats to the logic of the case study and concedes that "selectivity and conscious choice" have had to rule his approach.[10]

In this chapter, I am concerned with how numbers might intercede in this long running tension between general context and individual utterance in the study of racial discourse, and how computation might ameliorate the distortions of a too systematic focus on either one.[11] Said's idea of a general library of Orientalist discourse has of course been expanded upon since its original formulation. We have come to recognize it as a dynamic, circulating body of texts and ideas accessed differently across time, space, and genres of writing (e.g., legal, sociological, economic, historical, and aesthetic). Etienne Balibar, Ann Stoler, Michael Hardt, and Antonio Negri, among others, have further shown the expansiveness of the racial thinking embedded in this library. It sustains social divisions and hierarchies through "race" understood not only as a set of biological and physical traits but as linguistic, psychological, somatic, and cultural markers that in turn intersect with gender and class-based markers as part of strategies of differential inclusion.[12] The rise of colonial empires in the nineteenth century was instrumental in this expansion, constituting what Balibar calls "neo-racism." Neo-racism was especially crucial to empires similar to Japan's, where the physical markers of race were less salient and where racial thinking thus needed to be buttressed by cultural, ethnic, linguistic, and more subtle markers of difference.[13] "Racial discourse" as I use it in the following pages is meant to imply this panoply of differential markers.

If theories about the constitution and circulation of racializing discourse under empire have grown in complexity and nuance since *Orientalism*, Said's methodological questions have largely remained unresolved. Whatever this discourse may consist of, and however it may move, it is understood to operate at scales beyond the individual utterance. Indeed, systematicity is part of what allows it to authorize violence at the scale of whole populations. The ease with which its categorizing logic is adopted and repeated, even as its contents forever mutate, is precisely what empires and their attendant racisms require to manage and mobilize vast groups of individuals—to put them, as it were, in their proper places. But how are we to address it at this scale? One of *Orientalism*'s core conceits, which was itself a methodological formulation, was that Orientalist discourse's effectiveness lay in its constricted vocabulary. Underlying all its different units (i.e., the vocabulary employed when the Orient is spoken or written about) is a "set of representative figures or tropes . . . [that] are to the actual Orient . . . as stylized costumes are to characters in a play."[14] Orientalist discourse sounds here like a vicious kind of information management—a way of abstracting out individual difference via the equivalence space of the theater wardrobe.

Yet it also sounds like John Frow's definition of novelistic character—"a mechanism for scaling up and down between orders of generality" to manage the ever-present tension between reading character as contingent particularity and as a stand-in for a larger class of persons.[15] In this instance, however, the mechanism remains stuck at the same high setting, subsuming Others under the stylized costumes of racially or ethnically marked types. To tease out the link between Said's theory of racial discourse and a theory of literary character, it is useful to dwell further on his choice of "vocabulary" as an analytic unit for thinking across the general and the particular. Stoler builds on this idea when she writes of "racial lexicons" derived from historically located "racial grammars" that tie "certain physical attributes to specific hidden dispositions." Thus, for example, the term "degenerate" could in the Dutch Indies become "an adjective that *invariably* preceded those labeled as poor and white."[16] The content of these lexicons will vary with the racisms within which they operate, but the sharing of specific vocabularies and codes and their repeated associations with constructed categories of people remains constant. Mary Louise Pratt alludes to a similar tension between the "lists of features" that consistently animate racializing discourse, reinforcing its enumerative and finite nature, and the multiplicity of ways that Others are codified.[17] In the extensive body of work on Japanese colonial and race relations, lexicons and lists make way for "tropes" and "markers" that demarcate the shifting boundaries of racial and ethnic inclusion and exclusion, or more recently the "semantic depth" of concrete identifiers such as place names and the less empirically tangible "moods and sentiments" that particularize preexisting images of difference.[18] This work too stresses the instability and amorphousness of these semantic units—these different vocabularies—as their underlying grammar transforms with evolving colonial policies and geographical context.

My interest here is in how this emphasis on variability, and the importance of reading for it in racializing discourse, is at root still predicated on the imagined coherence, temporary as it may be, of a semantics of race—a patterned system of signs and associations. This semantics is often treated as an invisible scaffolding against which the variable practices and experiences of racial Othering are understood to play out. What would it mean to bring this scaffolding (Said's stylized costumes) into sharper resolution? The sheer scale of this scaffolding has long made it easier for readers to fall back, as Said did, on "selectivity and conscious choice." A reluctance to address it at scale likely also stems from its presumed redundancy. Of what use is the general view if we already know intimately the racial ideas and desires organizing it? Yet to the degree it remains theoretically productive to read variability against coherence, or contingent particularity against larger regularities, I contend it remains methodologically valuable to find ways of giving more systematic attention to the general view, in this case via computational methods. Whatever view of a general semantics is acquired through these methods will naturally be inextricable from what the methods themselves are capable of seeing. This view will also be inextricable from the objects it is trained on. It may be that the scaffolding discerned in the academic and ethnographic texts Said was initially concerned with, and in which the lines of sight from representing subject to represented Other are presumably more direct, simply does not exist or is too haphazard and varying to discern in literature. Yet this intuition, too, stands to benefit from the kinds of larger-scale comparisons that computation affords.

For his part, Said insisted that literature, even when not overtly about empire, was just as valuable a resource for excavating the racist discourses subtending both imperial and colonial relations. "Nearly everywhere in nineteenth- and early-twentieth-century British and French culture we find allusions to the facts of empire, but perhaps nowhere with more regularity and frequency than in the British novel."[19] Decades of criticism on literature and empire have taught us that such allusions take a plethora of forms: literal references to the spaces of empire and its inhabitants; symbolic references indebted to ethnographic description and its embedded racial hierarchies; and formal narrative symptoms that occlude the factual content of empire while remaining conceptually beholden to it.[20] Characterization is the formal symptom that concerns me in this chapter. To investigate it as a manifestation of literature's allusive relation to empire, I take literally the metaphorical logic of Said's "stylized costumes," linking an analysis of the vocabulary of racial discourse to ways in which literary personhood is circumscribed in narrative fiction. If constricted vocabularies do become affixed to racialized Others under empire, it would be interesting to know how these same vocabularies might be distributed over what Alex Woloch defines as the "character-spaces" and "character-systems" of fiction written under empire.[21] Is there a correspondence between the costumes that racial stand-ins (e.g., "the Chinese") are made to wear and those used to dress up their individuated, narrativized incarnations? Characterization will serve here as a conceptual and methodological vehicle for exploring racial discourse as it is actualized and deformed across different scales and expressive mediums. As a way, that is, to reckon with how writers such as Yokomitsu borrowed from a library of racial concepts and ideas (and racialized character types), but also with how the shelves of that library might have been organized, if at all.

To do so, I propose a novel method for rendering the semantics of race at the scale of thousands of texts and across the decades when the Japanese state raced toward and retreated from empire: 1890 to 1960. The method is grounded in the intuition that this semantics is based on a constrained vocabulary affixed to racialized Others with cruel repetitiveness even as the elements of that vocabulary and the Others to which it is linked change with time and cultural context. I first use the method to determine how much repetition and structure there is in the vocabulary of racial Othering, comparing its shape in fiction with a large corpus of nonfiction essays taken from mainstream Japanese periodicals. Along the way, I carefully document the limitations of an approach focused on discrete lexical items with an eye to the complexities and ambiguities that a generation of scholars has shown to be integral to the representation of racial and ethnic identity under Japanese empire. Drastic reversals in official state policy and rhetoric; strict censorship of what can be said about colonizers and by the colonized; the culturally and linguistically hybrid subject formations arising from colonial relations—all add complexity to the practices of racial representation in this period, and thus indeterminacy to the interpretation of specific instances.[22]

Yet this indeterminacy, as Will Bridges has written, invites a kind of "madness" when it comes to reading fictions of race. For it "suggests the impossibility of finding *the* representative interpretation of fictions of race," or worse, opens the door to representative readings that, to fill the void of meaning, "run the risk of cross-applying some of our missteps from reading race in general to the reading of racialized texts." In these "micromoments of racial judgment," Bridges suggests, readers might be too quick to speak for the text through their own reductivist readings rather than letting it speak for itself.[23] As critics, however, we remain invested in the pursuit of representative readings because they elicit the structures or norms against which the individual writer can be positioned as agent of resistance, deviation, negotiation, or transgression. We read for these structures not because we believe them to be stable reflections of truth but because we know they were keenly felt and interiorized and acted upon by actual individuals. Here I wish to consider how a more general view of these structures might supplement micromoments of racial judgment, allowing texts to speak through *them*, in contrast to a reader's own internalized ideas of representativeness. By reading structures where they can be read, by teasing out their violent and oppressive repetitions, we obtain another means to trace their dissolution into the nexus of contingencies that define any particular interaction with them. "Character" will help to catalyze this dissolve, sliding us from the general patterns of racializing discourse found at scale down to the ways they are repeated and repurposed in literary texts, particularly in works concerned with the ambivalent status of colonial subjects. It is in this sliding between scales that we can start to read indeterminacy and contingency not as final explanation, but as situated effect of discourse and its suffocating repetitions.

MODELING THE SEMANTICS OF RACE UNDER EMPIRE

Identifying the repetitions that structure discourse requires, as in previous chapters, specifying a model of the kinds of repetition or regularity that are of interest. Here the units of interest are no longer the work or passage, but the word and sentence. Specifically, I want to determine whether certain words (e.g., lying, money, clever) tend to be associated, as in the *Shanghai* passage, with certain racial identifiers (e.g., Chinese). To put this in Said's terms, what is the vocabulary of racializing discourse and does it add up, at scale, to a consistent semantics of racial description and stereotyping? This question immediately leads to others: What do we mean by association? What counts as a racial identifier? How do we measure the consistency of association, where select words occur more often with select racial identifiers? More often than what? Any model we create must address each question in turn, invariably requiring assumptions and abstractions that make some verbal patterns more visible than others in the equivalence spaces it constructs. The model will be useful to the extent that its interpretive potential remains legible to the other models of reading it temporarily forecloses in order to proceed.

I first define association, as this goes to the heart of what is meant by a semantics of race and the theories of meaning underlying its computational extraction. Association is here to be understood as a measure of how frequently a word co-occurs with a racial identifier in a specified *window* of words before and after the identifier. I generally set this window size at twenty in the following analysis, although this parameter is adjustable. The more frequently a word occurs in the window, or "word context vector," the stronger its association with the racial identifier. This implies a *syntagmatic* relation between the word and identifier, although it is not a necessarily meaningful or interpretable relation. Some syntagmatic relations will be

TABLE 5.1
Context vectors for "Chinese" in passage from *Shanghai*

Left Context	Keyword	Right Context
handicap, since it's impossible to accumulate anything. That's where the	Chinese	are clever. They've devised ways to make sure that all
human at all is proof of the kindness of the	Chinese	Are you saying the Chinese aren't human? That they're gods?
of the kindness of the Chinese. Are you saying the	Chinese	aren't human? That they're gods?" asked Koya. They're avatars of
as in China. But lies aren't just lies for the	Chinese	They're a source of righteousness for them. If you don't
concept of righteousness, if you don't understand the	Chinese	then of course you won't understand the future course of
片輪 で なきあ 溜らん ね 。 そこ は	支那人	の 賢い 所 で 、 この 地 で とった 金
人間 だ と 思っ て い て くれる 所 が 、	支那人	の 優しい 所 さ 。 」 「 じゃ 、 支那人 は 人間 じゃ ない
くれる 所 が 、 支那人 の 優しい 所 さ 。 」 「 じゃ 、	支那人	は 人間 じゃ ない 神様 か 。 」 と 甲谷 は いっ
もう あれ は 人間 じゃ ない 人間 の 先生 だ 。	支那人	ほど 嘘つき の 名人 も 世界 の どこ に だって
の どこ に だって なかろ う が 、 しかし 、 嘘 は	支那人	に とっ ちゃ 、 嘘 じゃ ない ん だ 。 あれ は
に とっ ちゃ 、 嘘 じゃ ない ん だ 。 あれ は	支那人	の 正義 だ よ 。 この 正義 の 観念 の 転倒

syntactical, especially if the window size is small, and some will be semantic, as is the tendency with larger window sizes. Table 5.1 shows word context vectors for "Chinese" as derived from the translated *Shanghai* passage and the original Japanese using ten-word windows. At the scale of a single passage, the idea of "association" I am implementing here feels crude and narrow. Grammatical function words bearing no relation to "Chinese" are swept up in these windows; relevant words are captured even as grammatical relations are lost (e.g., negation); and repetition of the racial identifier leads to overlapping contexts and overrepresentation of some words. At the scale of hundreds or thousands of passages, however, and after filtering grammatical function words, the hope is that frequently colocated words will surface and provide an entry point for analysis.

In practice, they do not surface as readily as one would hope. We need to consider not only the frequency with which "lying," for instance, co-occurs with "Chinese," but also the chance of any words occurring in the same context window given their overall frequency in the corpus. Frequency of co-occurrence alone provides little evidence of the strength of association in general. Adding to this problem is the fact that word forms are also highly variable (e.g., lies, lying, lie), even when reduced to their lemmatized forms. This further lowers the odds of finding a statistically significant association, especially with smaller corpora and fewer opportunities to observe the words of interest. Analysis of syntagmatic relations is thus constrained by a problem of sparsity. There is another way, however, to extract higher-order associations between words from word context vectors. Rather than focusing only on co-occurrence, individual words can be related by their shared contexts. Looking at all the context vectors for "Chinese" in a corpus, for example, we can ask what other words tend to share similar vectors. This is to consider a word's *paradigmatic* relations or, to borrow linguist John Firth's more colloquial phrase, "to know [the] word by the company it keeps."[24]

Firth's formulation came on the heels of work by the linguist Zellig Harris, who laid the conceptual and statistical foundations for a "distributional hypothesis" of semantics in 1954. The hypothesis's core assumption is that two words are more similar in meaning the more similar are their contexts of usage (i.e., the more similar is the distribution of words appearing around them). This presumed correlation of distributional similarity with meaning similarity implies that the former can be used to estimate the latter. Harris's hypothesis relies on a deeply structuralist view of "meaning" as differential and rooted in distributional linguistic patterns. Where others insist that words acquire meaning by reference to objects and situations outside of language, or through concepts and ideas in the mind of the language user, Harris argues that there is a distributional correlate to any linguistic event.[25] Words hold meaning, in part, due to the lexical contexts they are consistently and repeatedly placed in by language users within a given linguistic community. Reductive as its underlying theory of meaning may be, the distributional hypothesis has proved useful in the decades since it was proposed for thinking about semantic spaces and the patterns of word usage that demarcate them. Its utility has only grown with the emergence of computational methods capable of capturing the contours of these spaces at ever-larger scales.

One such method is word embedding models. In simplest terms, these models extract word-context pairs from a corpus and then train a predictive model to identify the target words that best predict a set of context words, or vice versa.[26] Every word is then *embedded* in a lower set of several hundred artificial dimensions that attempt to represent the semantic or syntactic relation of every word to every other word in this reduced space. Within this space, words that are more proximate (i.e., have similar values along all the dimensions) will tend to share the same context words and thus tend to be either semantically or syntactically similar, as predicted by the distributional hypothesis. Results are highly corpus dependent, varying with the direction of prediction, the context window size, and the number of dimensions used. But, in general, word embedding models offer a way to explore semantic space in large text collections by clustering semantically related words.[27] Humanists have been drawn to these models as a means to read semantic clusters as proxies for historical concepts; to track changes in these clusters over time; to explore semantic ambiguity by relating words to the multiple, overlapping clusters in which the models situate them; and even to identify patterns of racial, gender, class, and other forms of bias to which these models seem especially well attuned.[28] Indeed, their ability to detect bias is of value to scholars who wish to interrogate normative structures of discourse and the language of stereotype, even as it warrants critical suspicion of their deployment in social media platforms and search engines under the pretense of algorithmic objectivity.[29]

Previous applications of word embedding models to literary or historical study tend to use the semantic spaces they generate as the endpoint of analysis; here I leverage the space in a novel way to analyze paradigmatic and syntagmatic relations together. Specifically, as described in more detail in the next section, I use this space to expand focus from discrete words associated with racial identifiers to larger semantic clusters of words. This addresses the sparsity problem by allowing words like "lies" and "lying" to be combined into a single semantic unit using the information contained in the word embedding space. These clusters of semantically related words amplify the weaker signals of individual words. Moreover, they allow me to identify higher-order semantic associations specific to the corpus under analysis. This is important because one should expect the semantic relations derived from literary language to be different from those in nonliterary writing. Partly to test this expectation, and partly to demonstrate how context dependent word embeddings are, I analyze two distinct, but temporally aligned corpora. One contains nearly two thousand works of fiction from the Aozora collection described in chapter 2, published between 1890 and 1960. To this corpus have been added more than thirty hand-picked works of colonial fiction by Japanese, Korean, and Taiwanese writers. The other corpus contains roughly nine thousand articles and essays evenly sampled from popular general interest magazines published between 1887 and 1957.

To complete the model we need to specify the "racial identifiers" of interest and outline a procedure for measuring the strength of association between these identifiers and the semantic clusters derived from the corpora. The first step requires deciding how to account for the many terms that circulated under empire to mark racial and ethnic categories. Yokomitsu, for instance, used the now derogatory term *shinajin* for "Chinese," the most common term used in the fiction corpus overall, occurring 648 times; other terms are used as well: *chūgokujin* (253), *chūgoku no hito* (18), *shina no hito* (11), *chūgoku no hitobito* (6), and *chūgoku minzoku* (2). Although each has different connotations, focusing on them separately would lessen the chance of discovering a significant semantic association. For this reason, I provisionally group all of them under the label "Chinese" in order to identify semantic clusters that collectively adhere to this one set of racial identifiers. The same kind of grouping is done for "Japanese," "Korean," "Westerner," "Native," and "Burakumin," an internal minority group long treated as pariahs owing to their associations with animal slaughter and leather manufacture. For each group, I use secondary sources and the corpora themselves to identify the widest possible range of explicit racial identifiers while also excluding terms I deem too ambiguous or too specific (table 5.2).[30] Collating them under one category label elides their differing valences, but these valences can be recovered by going back to the original texts once a set of associated semantic clusters is identified. What I cannot recover with this model, however, let alone capture, are moments in which racial and ethnic Otherness go under a different name, or remain unsaid, either to avoid censorship or to evade the sedimented meanings of racial markers.[31] How to reconcile the patterns of representation we do see with how racializing discourse perpetually hides or is contested in the shadows of these patterns is a question that must continually be posed as the analysis proceeds.

TABLE 5.2
Unified labels and the Japanese racial identifiers that comprise them

Unified Label	Identifiers Included in Unified Label
日本人 (Japanese)	日本の人々、日本の人、大和民族、日本民族、日本の民族、日本民衆、日本国民、日本の国民、ジャップ、和人、内地人
韓国人 (Korean)	朝鮮人、朝鮮民族、朝鮮の人、朝鮮の人々、鮮人、半島人
中国人 (Chinese)	中国人、中国民族、中国民衆、中国の民衆、中国の人、中国の人々、 支那人、支那の人、支那の民族、支那の民衆
西洋人 (Westerner)	西洋の人、白人、毛唐、欧州人
土人 (Native)	蕃人、蛮族、蕃族、生蕃、熟蕃、高砂族、本島人、蛮人、野蛮人
部落民 (Burakumin)	穢多、非人、新平民

After isolating the racial identifiers of interest and finding the semantic clusters appearing around each through a procedure detailed in the next section, I can then measure the strength of association. Here I compare every pair of racial categories (e.g., "Japanese" and "Chinese") and determine whether a cluster appears next to one or the other more often than would be expected if we naively assumed these frequencies to be unrelated, or independent from each other. Each category is thus paired against every other category, all the semantic clusters appearing around each are counted, and a statistical test is performed to identify significant clusters based on a set threshold (e.g., $p < .05$).[32] If words in the semantic cluster for "lying," for instance, show up around identifiers for "Chinese" more often than identifiers for "Japanese," all else being equal, "lying" is marked as significant. If it appears with relatively equal frequency, or too infrequently to produce a significant difference, it is ignored. Built into the procedure is a binary framework that assumes certain vocabularies will be consistently applied to one category of people over another. Once again, the desire to read at scale narrows the kind and complexity of racializing discourse it is possible to observe.

Reductive though this model is, its binary logic is not unfamiliar to the operation of such discourse in imperial Japan. As scholars of the period have long pointed out, this discourse, even when filtered through assimilationist ideologies of racial equality and fraternity, asserted various categorical and hierarchical differences between self ("Japanese") and other ("not-Japanese").[33] Countless case studies document the manifold ways in which the identities of imperial subjects were coconstituted in the course of imagining what it meant to be "Japanese," with differences often aligned on a spectrum of familiar dichotomies (e.g., masculine/feminine, human/animal, modern/unmodern, civilized/primitive, white/black). The machinery of colonial modernity, and its subsequent unwinding in the postwar period, drove the play of difference in racial and ethnic discourse and its real-world effects. Scholars have also shown, however, the variability of the output of this machinery across the multiple places, times, and scales of experience over which colonial modernity unfolded. It was neither stable nor under total authoritative control. Between the colonization of Taiwan in 1895 and the unraveling of empire under the U.S. Occupation (1945–1952), there were marked shifts in the predominant orientation of racializing discourse. What was early on a "civilizational" mode that placed Japan, in imitation of the West, atop a teleological hierarchy of cultural and socioeconomic progress subsequently transitioned to an "ethnographic" mode that embraced cultural pluralism and a multiethnic imaginary before finally succumbing to an always latent hyper-ethnonationalist mode after the war.[34] These transitions roughly paralleled changes in government policy, which progressed from a strict period of overt military coercion (*budan seiji*) to a more liberal period of limited political and cultural freedoms (*bunka seiji*), and finally to a period of forced assimilation after 1937 wherein imperial subjects were no longer encouraged to simply mimic Japanese cultural practices and behaviors, but were compelled to *be* Japanese.[35]

These are just some of the higher-level dynamics that shaped racializing discourse under Japanese empire. At the level of the individual text or event, these dynamics are further atomized by institutional, cultural, discursive, technological, personal, and other local contexts. Decades of scholarship on the colonial period have taught us to read for these micro-level interactions that destabilize any coherency or consistency we might attribute to colonial and imperial discourses on race and ethnicity. Rare is the concern expressed by Said about the distortions introduced by focusing too systematically on the particular perspective. Indeed, the general, or the normative, is more likely to be figured as an illusory or nonexistent second-order derivative of an infinitely expanding set of particularized views.[36] Using this reasoning, we should expect a naive model of racial discourse let loose on thousands of texts across six decades of imperial ascendancy and collapse to find no patterns at all. Yet, as much as previous scholars have emphasized the need to read individual instances or marginal cases, this has not stopped them from imagining invisible structures that make marginality legible in the first place. These structures continually haunt the case study method as "tropes" and "figures of speech," a "philosophically incoherent generalized field," a "malleable and fluid construct," "psychogeograpical terrain," or "protean affect," to cite a few of the ways that scholars have recognized structure in their readings of particulars.[37] Even acknowledging that no single general perspective exists in which to locate the particular, there is still a tendency to posit lower orders of generality whenever the particular is read as a function of discourse, even a nonresponsive one. Computational methods and digitized corpora put pressure on these suppositions by challenging us to find evidence for the patterns and repetitions that lend to discursive structures their cultural and political force, however amorphous and indeterminate it might be. They are an opportunity to reason explicitly about what the particular view stands to gain from a more systematic pursuit of the general.

RACIAL DISCOURSE AS SEMANTIC GRID

I begin this pursuit with a corpus of nearly nine thousand nonfiction articles randomly sampled from six general interest periodicals published between 1887 and 1957. These include the mainstream magazines *Kokumin no tomo* (The nation's friend: 1887, 1888), *Taiyō* (Sun: 1895, 1901, 1909, 1917, 1925, 1928), and *Chūō kōron* (Central review: 1933, 1941, 1949, 1957), as well as magazines geared to female audiences: *Jogaku zasshi* (Women's education magazine: 1894, 1895), *Jogaku sekai* (Women's education world: 1909), and *Fujin kurabu* (Ladies' club: 1925). Dates indicate the years from which samples have been obtained for each periodical. The mainstream magazines were especially important venues for debates about Japan's evolving cultural and political relationships with its neighbors, but all were critical sites for discourse on Japanese identity as it adapted to tumultuous shifts in the wider geopolitical landscape. Notably, these samples were not drawn with the intent of capturing racial discourse. The collection was assembled by the National Institute for Japanese Language and Linguistics for the purpose of performing diachronic analysis on Japanese written language. The main concern in building the collection was to ensure it represented a diverse array of content spread out evenly over time.[38] Figure 5.1 shows the chronological distribution of the twenty-two million lexical items in the collection, which is relatively constant over time aside from a brief dip in 1928.

Naturally, it would be preferable to strategically sample documents that directly pertain to discussions of colonial relations or racial and ethnic categories. Unfortunately, no digital archive yet exists that can be sampled so directly and at sufficient scale. What this corpus does offer is a comparative baseline for the analysis of fiction that follows. Specifically, it helps to understand how the previously described model works on language that is less allusive in its representation of reality, more intently descriptive of real-world events, and presumably more transparent in its citation of ideological discourse. What it is able to say about the semantics of racial discourse, in particular, is constrained by its unique composition, but here too it offers a comparative baseline for what we will find in the fiction. In fact, the number of amalgamated racial identifiers present in the corpus suggests that

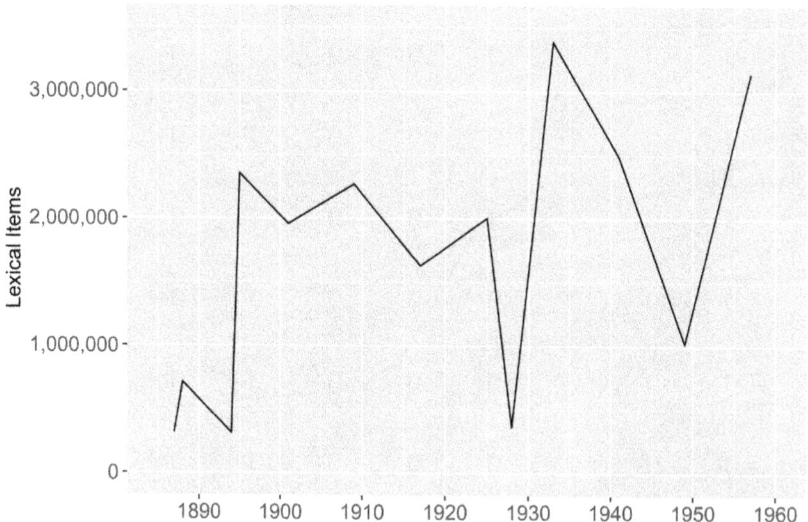

FIGURE 5.1. Number of lexical items per year in the nonfiction magazine corpus from 1887 to 1957. There are nearly nine thousand articles in the corpus containing roughly twenty-two million lexical items.

its ties to discourse on racial and ethnic Others is not trivial. Terms for "Korean" occur 482 times in 2 percent of articles; 1,229 for "Chinese" (5 percent); 573 for "Westerner" (3 percent); 800 for "Native" (3 percent); and just 98 for "Burakumin" (1 percent). In contrast, terms for "Japanese" occur 5,273 times across 16 percent of all articles in the corpus.

Taiyō and *Chūō kōron* account for the bulk of these instances since they constitute the bulk of the corpus. When we normalize the counts by the total words in each periodical sample, however, we learn that *Taiyō* and *Jogaku zasshi*, which were published in the years of imperial expansion into Taiwan and Korea, devoted twice the amount of attention to racial Others. The attention they give to "Japanese," in contrast, is roughly equal to that of *Kokumin no tomo* and *Chūō kōron*. Relative to time, the use of terms for marked Others peaks precisely in the early period of expansion, whereas references to "Japanese" peak in 1909 (just prior to the annexation of Korea) and in 1949, just as the discourse of a homogeneous, mono-ethnic Japanese race was undergoing quick consolidation (figures 5.2 and 5.3). These initial figures already point to ways that the corpus delimits what our model can tell us. Racial identifiers with higher occurrences provide a more robust signal, and thus more confidence that any distinctive semantic associations

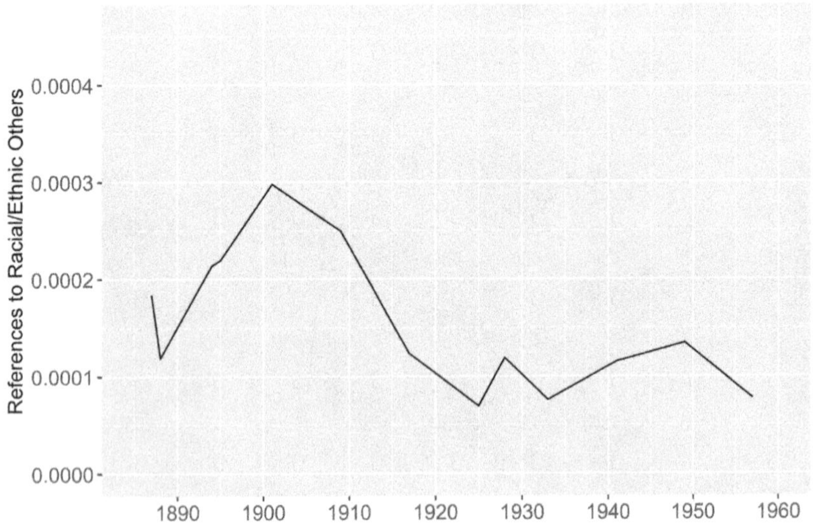

FIGURE 5.2. References to racial/ethnic Others in the nonfiction corpus as a proportion of total lexical items.

FIGURE 5.3. References to Japanese in the nonfiction corpus as a proportion of total lexical items.

(as compared with Japanese) are not random. Conversely, semantic associations for less frequent identifiers will be biased by a narrower sample of texts. The figures also suggest that the period from 1894 to 1909 is more likely to influence the results than other periods, although the extent to which this is true must be verified by inspecting each semantic association found in the corpus and the passages on which they are based.

The first step in isolating these associations is to derive the overall semantic space of the nonfiction corpus by training a word embedding model.[39] This space will be used to generate the semantic clusters whose association with specific identifiers is then measured. Recall that the closest neighbors of a given word in this space will be words that tend to share the same contexts (i.e., they are surrounded by similar words) within this particular corpus. Table 5.3 shows the ten closest words to the seed terms "Japanese," "Westerner," "Korean," "Chinese," "Native," and "beautiful" according to a single fitted model. For the first four, the closest words are generally other markers of ethnicity and nationality, with some exceptions. The word "we" (*wareware*), for instance, is semantically close to "Japanese" because of the common phrase "we Japanese," and thus the words are more likely to share similar contexts. Closer to "Native" are words associated with specific

TABLE 5.3

Ten most semantically similar words for seed terms in nonfiction corpus

Similarity Rank	日本人 **(Japanese)**	西洋人 **(Westerner)**	韓国人 **(Korean)**	中国人 **(Chinese)**	土人 **(Native)**	美しい **(Beautiful)**
1	西洋人 (Westerner) 0.84	日本人 (Japanese) 0.84	中国人 (Chinese) 0.73	日本人 (Japanese) 0.82	西洋人 (Westerner) 0.68	優しい (elegant) 0.76
2	中国人 (Chinese) 0.82	東洋人 (Easterner) 0.77	外国人 (foreigner) 0.70	西洋人 (Westerner) 0.76	アイヌ (Ainu) 0.67	艶やか (bewitching) 0.74
3	東洋人 (Easterner) 0.78	中国人 (Chinese) 0.76	日本人 (Japanese) 0.68	朝鮮人 (Korean) 0.73	住民 (inhabitants) 0.66	瑞々しい (vibrant) 0.73
4	外国人 (foreigner) 0.76	外国人 (foreigner) 0.72	露人 (Russian) 0.68	外国人 (foreigner) 0.73	酋長 (chieftain) 0.66	金髪 (blonde) 0.73
5	朝鮮人 (Korean) 0.68	人種 (race) 0.7	チュウゴク (China) 0.65	支那 (China) 0.70	未開 (uncivilized) 0.65	清純 (pure) 0.73
6	国人 (Japanese) 0.68	黒人 (Black) 0.68	帰化 (naturalize) 0.64	チュウゴク (China) 0.69	エスキモー (Eskimo) 0.65	ベール (veil) 0.72
7	我々 (we) 0.67	土人 (Native) 0.68	西洋人 (Westerner) 0.63	サクソン (Saxon) 0.66	中国人 (Chinese) 0.64	中肉 (medium build) 0.72
8	米人 (American) 0.66	サクソン (Saxon) 0.65	国人 (Japanese) 0.63	アンナン (Annam) 0.66	ツングース (Tungus) 0.64	豊頬 (plump cheeks) 0.73
9	ジュヌヴィエヴ (Genevieve) 0.66	米人 (American) 0.65	夷狄 (barbarians) 0.63	アングロ (Anglo) 0.66	先住 (indigenous) 0.62	慎ましやか (reserved) 0.72
10	ガイド (foreign land) 0.65	欧人 (European) 0.64	韓民 (Korean) 0.62	在留 (resident) 0.66	チュクチ (Chukchi) 0.62	おっとり (calm) 0.72

indigenous groups or that connote indigeneity. That "uncivilized" is also in the list hints at some of the prejudicial associations latent in the corpus. Closest to "beautiful" are a few adjectives connoting a refined feminine beauty and several physical traits presumably associated with this ideal.

Reasonable as the results from this single word embedding model seem, they raise two concerns about how to generate interpretable semantic clusters from this semantic space. The first is apparent in the fact that words further down in these lists do not exhibit obvious semantic similarity with their seed terms. That is, it becomes harder to imagine them substituting for the seed term below a certain similarity score. The process of generating clusters relies on these scores by gathering up the most proximate terms in succession for a subset of all words in the corpus, so we have to choose a reasonable cutoff point at which to stop adding words. For the nonfiction corpus, I set this threshold at 0.65 after observing results for multiple seed terms across different runs of the model. The second concern, less apparent from the table alone, is that word embedding models are inherently stochastic. This means that the semantic spaces they generate will vary slightly each time they are fit to a corpus. To control for this variation, which becomes more pronounced the smaller the corpus, it is best to measure the semantic similarity of words across multiple fitted models, thus ensuring that the semantic clusters generated are not overly biased toward certain texts or authors. I employ such a "bootstrap sampling" procedure here to generate clusters using the five thousand most frequent words in the nonfiction corpus.[40]

With these clusters generated, we can now test which disproportionately co-occur with specific racial identifiers relative to "Japanese," and vice versa. The output of this process is a list of significant clusters for every pairwise comparison (e.g., "Japanese" versus "Westerner") and a value indicating how frequently the words in a cluster appear within twenty words of the first racial identifier (i.e., as a proportion of all occurrences of that identifier). Upon merging these clusters into broader semantic categories, the results can be displayed as a grid with darker cells indicating the strength of association between the identifiers and categories (figure 5.4).[41] Strength here is simply the sum of the proportional values of all words in a category that occur with the specific identifier, lists of which are provided in the appendix in table A5.1 and A5.2. With this grid comes a powerful lens with which to explore the contours of racializing discourse as it gathers around or avoids different racial identifiers. The grid is as interesting for

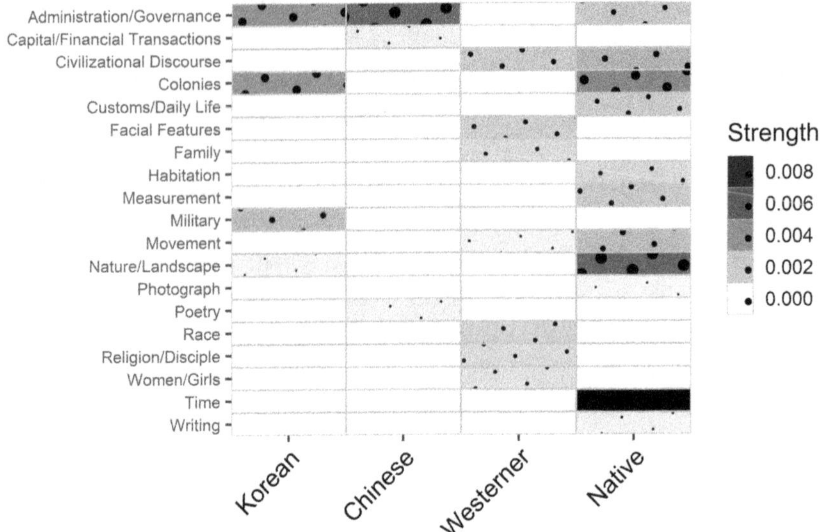

FIGURE 5.4. This grid shows the semantic clusters significantly associated with references to racial Others when compared with references to Japanese in the nonfiction corpus. The darkness of the cells reflects the "strength" of each cluster, which is measured as the sum of proportional values of all words in the cluster that occur with the specific identifier. The size and density of dots are scaled to the cell shading and simply help to distinguish shaded cells from blank ones.

its darker peaks and the ridge lines they occasionally form across identifiers as for the blank valleys that hint at the relative absence of association. Thus it is notable, if not surprising, that the clusters related to "Administration/Governance"—which consist of words such as rule (*tōchi*), subject (*shujin*), cabinet (*naikaku*), governor (*chiji*), and the names of various ministries—coalesce around potential or actual subjects of colonial rule and not "Westerner." Or that "Civilizational Discourse," consisting of words like civilization (*bunmei*), history (*shi*), evolution (*shinka*), and species (*jinrui*), adheres more to "Westerner" and "Native" than to "Chinese" and "Korean," against whom civilizational lines of distinction were less easily drawn owing to centuries of cultural and social exchange. Harder to reconcile at this low resolution is the apparent monopoly "Native" has on "Customs/Daily Life" (habits, customs, meals, sleep) and "Time" (yesterday, tomorrow, morning, afternoon, night).

If some cells in the grid appear more legible than others, however, none are a transparent window into the particularities of the data. Any interpretation offered at this level will be prone to the subjective biases of the analyst. An empty cell, for instance, could mean several things: that the semantic cluster does not co-occur at all with the racial identifier; that it co-occurs in relatively the same proportion as compared with "Japanese"; or, more subtly, that it occurs just infrequently enough to seem probable given the relative frequency of that identifier compared to "Japanese." Moreover, the lightest cells may reflect just a handful of textual instances dispersed across a few texts, making broad generalizations about discursive tendencies spurious at best. "Photograph" (*shashin*), for example, appears just four times in the same context window as identifiers grouped under "Native."[42] Finally, even where there is a stronger signal, it is driven by specific words whose syntactic relation to the identifier in question is highly variable given the twenty-word window (on either side) used by the model. Low as the resolution of this grid may be, it still points in intriguing directions as long as we are willing to sharpen the image by returning to the texts. Consider "Facial Features," for example, a cluster strongly associated with terms for "Westerner" and comprised of these words: eye, face, laugh, countenance, stare, lips, expression, eyelids, smile, and complexion. Between 1895 and 1957, these words appear with "Westerner" in thirty-one passages. Six of them are false positives with no obvious syntactic or semantic relation. The rest, however, expose distinct discursive threads, one that treats smiling and laughter as markers of racial difference and another that singles out ethnically Japanese individuals whose faces have an uncanny affinity with those of "Westerners."

Digging down in this way allows us to validate the magnitude and direction of particular semantic associations and potentially channel this analysis toward further digging or else outward to other texts and contexts, as I do in the following section. Even at this low resolution, however, there is plenty of productive speculation yet to be done. For one, we can reverse the direction of comparison and identify semantic clusters that coalesce around words for "Japanese" relative to the other identifiers. That is, which discourses are disproportionately activated when "Japanese" are the topic of conversation? And for which racial Others are they conversely diminished or not given equal emphasis? The semantic clusters that emerge from such a comparison (figure 5.5) hint at how different the conversation can be and some of the lines along which this difference cuts. Words grouped under "Spirituality/Ethics," for instance, including spirit (*seishin*), morality (*dōtoku*), ethics (*rinri*), and religion (*shūkyō*), are overrepresented with

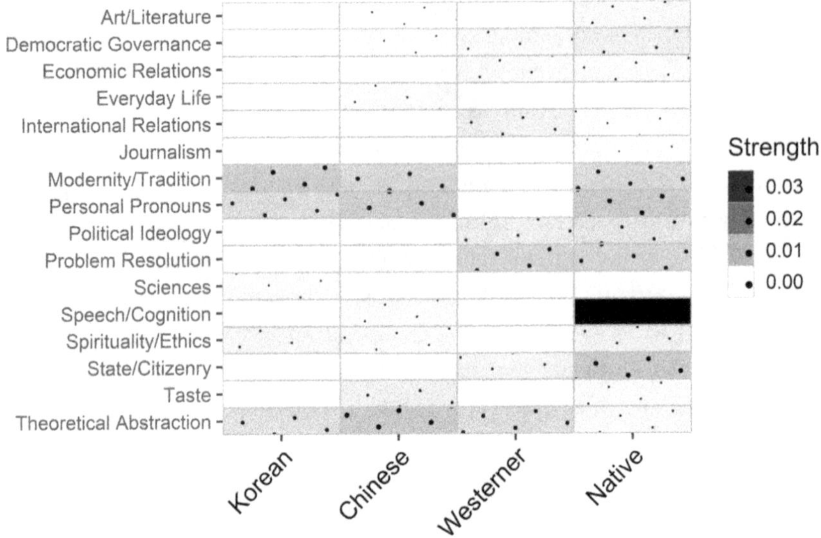

FIGURE 5.5. Semantic clusters associated with references to Japanese compared with references to racial Others in the nonfiction corpus.

"Japanese" compared to all other identifiers except "Westerner." The same holds for words indicating contemporaneity, including the modern age (*kindai*) and the present (*gendai*).

This result lends support to the idea that racial Others positioned lower in civilizational hierarchies were not regularly deemed relevant subjects when discussing matters of spirituality and modernity. Or that when they were, a different vocabulary was used. Also striking are the many semantic clusters that appear more frequently with "Japanese" as compared to "Native." Of these, the most unequally apportioned is the "Speech/Cognition" cluster, which includes the verbs say (*iu*), think (*omou*), know (*shiru*), contemplate (*kangaeru*), and understand (*wakaru*). These words collectively co-occur with "Native" at a ratio less than the null hypothesis of the statistical test would predict. This hypothesis assumes they will co-occur at fairly equal rates relative to the overall frequency of "Native" and "Japanese," an assumption met for "Westerner" and "Korean."[43] That it is not met for "Native" (nor "Chinese," if to a lesser degree) invites us to speculate about why this cluster of words, in particular, is more likely to be held back when natives or indigenous others are the topic of conversation.

To gain additional perspective on these results and how specific they are to the magazine corpus, we can repeat the same analysis on the fiction corpus. Focusing on the magazines first establishes a proof-of-concept on which we can build grids of semantic intelligibility for fiction, which we might imagine to be more tenuous and blurry owing to the rhetorical techniques and indirectness of literary language. I will build these grids from the refined Aozora fiction corpus described in chapter 2, to which I add prewar texts missing exact dates of first publication and the corpus of I-novels described in chapter 3. In addition, I purposely sample thirty-three works from the three volume series *"Gaichi" no Nihongo bungaku sen* (Selected works of "colonial" Japanese language literature).[44] Although a mere fraction of the material produced in or about the colonies by both Japanese and non-Japanese writers, these works encompass a wide range of geographical, ethnic, and ideological positionalities spanning Korea, Taiwan, Manchuria, and the South Seas. The complete fiction corpus thus contains 1,905 works, published between 1889 and 1960 and containing nearly fifty million lexical items.[45]

Figure 5.6 shows the distribution of lexical items by year (for texts with verified dates of publication) and reinforces that the bulk of the corpus lies

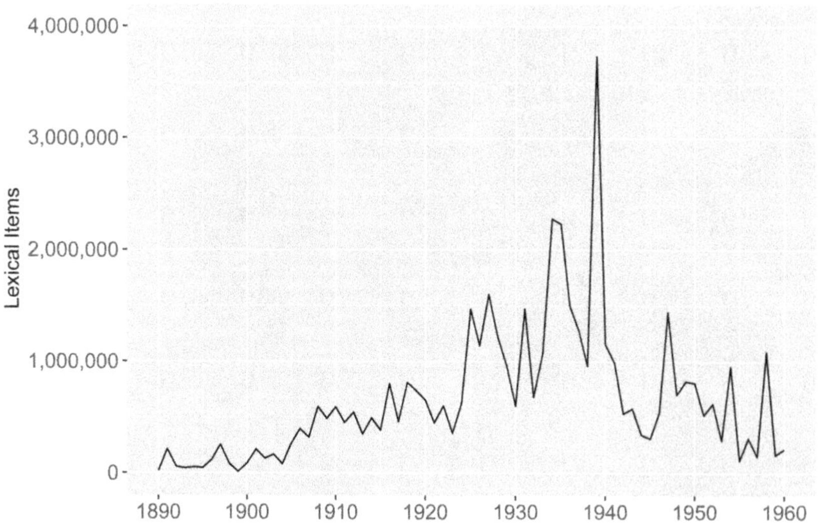

FIGURE 5.6. Number of lexical items per year in the fiction corpus from 1889 to 1960. There are 1,905 works in the corpus containing nearly fifty million total lexical items.

between 1925 and 1940. References to racial Others, grouped again under overarching labels, break down by frequency and percentage as follows: "Westerner" occurs 966 times across 12 percent of titles, "Chinese" 921 times (9 percent), "Native" 837 times (8 percent), "Burakumin" 468 times (7 percent), and "Korean" 372 times (3.5 percent). Relative to the size of the corpus in any given year, these identifiers are most frequent in the period 1922 to 1942, which saw Japanese imperial expansion accelerate through increased political, economic, military, and civilian involvement overseas (figure 5.7).[46] With this came a heightened popular awareness of the colonies as places inextricably bound up with domestic affairs, even if only as an escape, but also of the increased circulation of bodies, both by desire and force, throughout the empire.

The number of Koreans residing in the mainland, for instance, was more than 120,000 by 1924, up from several thousand two decades earlier. If we assume that their increased physical presence led to increased representation, then the fact that "Korean" is again the least frequent racial identifier indicates a blind spot in the corpus. It may also be that physical proximity leads to less overt forms of racial Othering, or forms of self-censoring, to which our model of racial discourse is not attuned. Still, the steep tapering off of references to racial Others after the Pacific War, as the political and

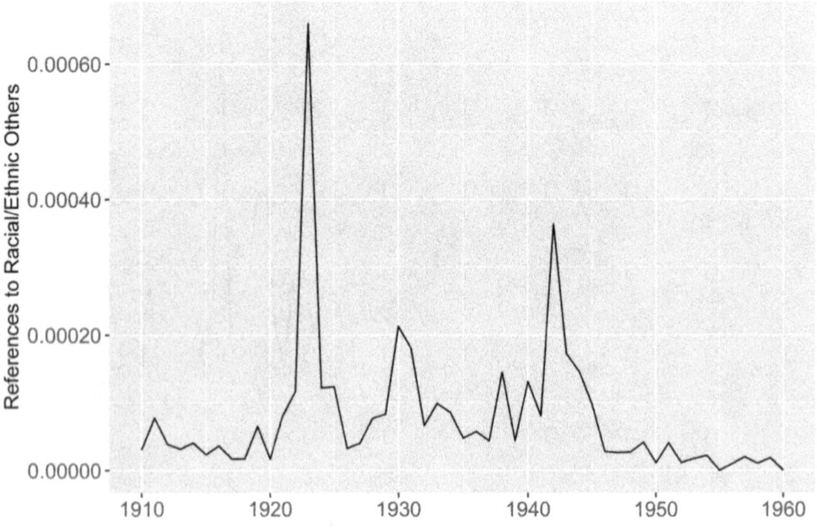

FIGURE 5.7. References to racial/ethnic Others in the fiction corpus as a proportion of total lexical items.

discursive machinery of decolonization kicked into high gear, suggests that the corpus is tracking real shifts in the geo-political landscape. Similarly, the references to "Japanese," which occur 2,274 times across 21 percent of titles, are most pronounced in the years 1940 to 1950, just as the talk of Others disappeared and as public opinion converged around a theory of Japanese people as belonging to a single homogeneous race (figure 5.8).[47]

These distributional patterns are important to keep in mind as we evaluate the semantic grids produced from this corpus. Table 5.4 shows the ten words semantically closest to each of the racial identifiers in a single word embedding model.[48] There are some striking continuities with the results from the magazine corpus. The closest terms to "Japanese," "Westerner," and "Chinese," for instance, are nearly the same, suggesting a robust and consistent set of context words that all three share in the respective corpora. Disparities grow the further down we look in each column, but most of the words still point to other nations or nationalities, even if not the same ones. In contrast, "Korean," "Native," and "Burakumin" are positioned in semantic space such that words related to countries and nationality are diluted by the force of semantic vectors related to class, status, and animality. "Korean" appears in similar contexts as words connoting manual labor and lower socioeconomic status, notably "coolie" and "construction worker" (*dokata*);

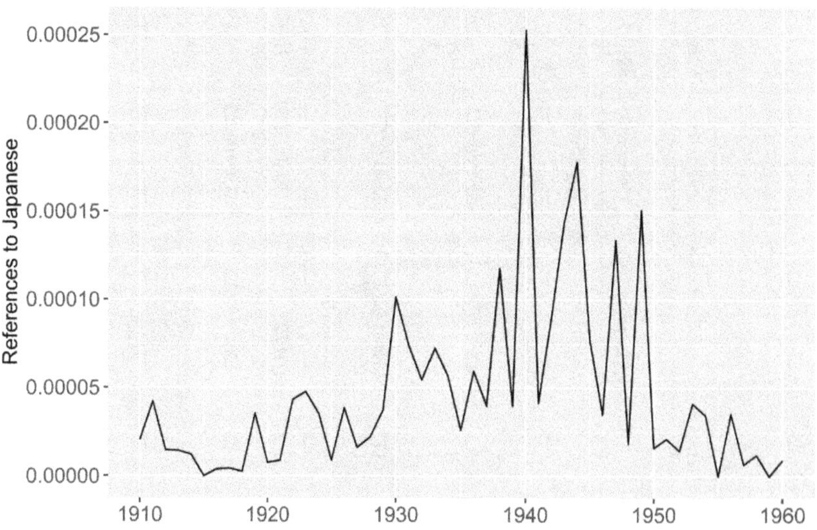

FIGURE 5.8. References to Japanese in the fiction corpus as a proportion of total lexical items.

TABLE 5.4
Ten most semantically similar words for seed terms in fiction corpus

Similarity Rank	日本人 (**Japanese**)	西洋人 (**Westerner**)	韓国人 (**Korean**)	中国人 (**Chinese**)	土人 (**Native**)	部落民 (**Burakumin**) 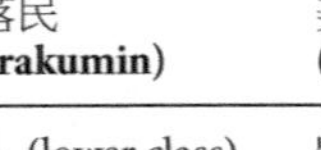	美しい (**Beautiful**) 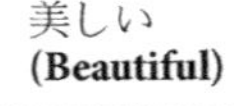
1	西洋人 (Westerner) 0.82	日本人 (Japanese) 0.82	中国人 (Chinese) 0.73	西洋人 (Westerner) 0.79	人猿 (primate) 0.79	下人 (lower class) 0.79	艶やか (bewitching) 0.79
2	中国人 (Chinese) 0.79	中国人 (Chinese) 0.79	日本人 (Japanese) 0.7	日本人 (Japanese) 0.79	酋長 (chieftain) 0.79	下郎 (servant) 0.79	清らか (pure) 0.79
3	東洋人 (Easterner) 0.77	外国人 (foreigner) 0.76	クーリー (coolie) 0.65	東洋人 (Easterner) 0.73	遊牧 (nomad) 0.73	乞食 (beggar) 0.73	妖艶 (enchanting) 0.73
4	ヨーロッパ (Europe) 0.74	東洋人 (Easterner) 0.75	這人 (enter) 0.63	朝鮮人 (Korean) 0.73	中国人 (Chinese) 0.73	浪人 (unemployed) 0.73	気高い (noble) 0.73
5	ロシア (Russia) 0.74	黒人 (Black) 0.73	農民 (farmer) 0.63	外国人 (foreigner) 0.72	狼 (wolf) 0.72	世迷い言 (grumble) 0.72	可愛らしい (cute) 0.72
6	ドイツ (Germany) 0.73	イギリス (England) 0.69	土方 (construction worker) 0.62	チェコ (Czech) 0.71	東洋人 (Easterner) 0.71	売僧 (liar, grifter) 0.71	臈たける (fine) 0.71
7	人種 (race) 0.72	インド (India) 0.69	下級 (lower class) 0.62	ハジン (**) 0.7	野牛 (bison) 0.7	町人 (merchant) 0.7	初々しい (young, fresh) 0.7
8	アメリカ (America) 0.72	ドイツ (Germany) 0.68	兵卒 (soldier) 0.62	インド (India) 0.69	猛獣 (wild beast) 0.69	分際 (status) 0.69	豊麗 (voluptuous) 0.69
9	国籍 (nationality) 0.71	フランス (France) 0.67	不逞 (lawless) 0.62	支那 (China) 0.69	バール (bar) 0.69	鼠賊 (petty thief) 0.69	あどけない (innocent) 0.69
10	民族 (race, people) 0.71	アメリカ (America) 0.67	ロシア (Russia) 0.62	ロシア (Russia) 0.69	黒人 (Black) 0.69	主持ち (apprentice) 0.69	愛らしい (cute) 0.69

"Burakumin" exhibits similar tendencies, albeit with a different assortment of words; and "Native" appears to be substitutable for modes of indigenous life (e.g., chieftain, nomad) as well as certain types of animals (e.g., primates, wolves, and wild beasts). In some cases, a rare word registers as semantically similar because it appears frequently enough in the same narrative context as the racial identifier. Thus we have to be careful about generalizing from any single semantic association. But the table does evince the higher degree of polysemy to which these latter three identifiers are subject. For "Korean" and "Burakumin," it is a polysemy similarly distributed across socioeconomic lines, reflecting perhaps the documented tendency, especially after annexation of the country in 1910, of Koreans to be conflated with burakumin as equally "inferior," but also the fact that Koreans in the metropole often lived alongside burakumin in the same ghettos, working the same menial jobs.[49]

Although we might expect these known biases to be accentuated in the semantic grids generated from the fiction corpus, the biases turn out to be both harder and easier to read. Harder in some cases because the lines of difference are less starkly drawn than with the magazine corpus. Consider the clusters that co-occur with "Japanese" in significantly frequent proportions relative to the other racial identifiers (figure 5.9), and for which

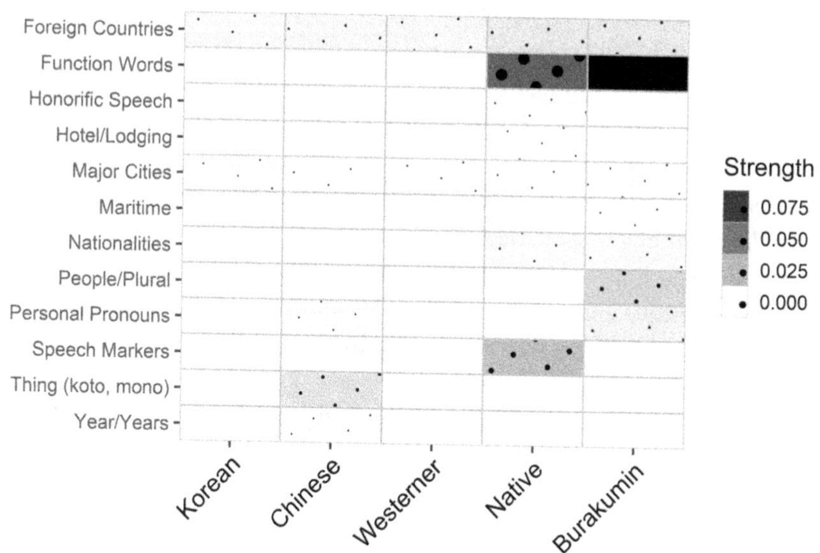

FIGURE 5.9. Semantic clusters associated with references to Japanese compared with references to racial Others in the fiction corpus.

details are again provided in the appendix in tables A5.3 and A5.4.[50] They are at once more generic and mundane but also more opaque than those in the magazines. Is there any significance to the apparent tendency of foreign countries and capitals (e.g., London and Paris) to co-occur with "Japanese"? Is it because talk of Japanese nationals excites talk of their cosmopolitanism? Where are the readily legible signs of racial and ethnic hierarchy seen earlier?

One semantic association that does carry over from the nonfiction results is that between "Native" and words signifying speech. Here, however, it is not verbs of speech and cognition that are disproportionately held back from "Natives" relative to "Japanese," but words specific to quoted speech and dialogue, including simple vocal expressions (e.g., yes, no, huh) and sentence final markers used to indicate a question, exclamation, or to invite agreement (e.g., *ka*, *yo*, *ne*). It appears that in fiction too the "Native" is disproportionately silenced relative to other groups. Yet aside from this one instance, the rest of this semantic grid feels comparatively flat and opaque. It may be that the semantic clusters we would expect to be exaggerated in discussions of Japanese uniqueness or superiority are more equally distributed in fiction or articulated less overtly. If, as Robert Tierney asserts, official colonial discourse was inherently duplicitous to begin with, and oscillated between rhetorics of racial sameness and otherness with little conceptual coherence, we should expect its manifestation in fiction to be that much more malleable and ambiguous.[51] Which is not to say that hierarchies of racial difference were not encoded in other, subtler ways, as countless close readings of colonial era works attest. Only that they do not obviously coalesce around references to "Japanese" or "mainlanders" (*naichijin*) in any systematic way. The model is too coarse to be able to delineate clear lines of semantic difference at this scale either because they are not repetitive enough at the lexical level or because lumping all references to "Japanese" together means that the potentially varied underlying signals cancel each other out.[52]

When we reverse the direction of the model's gaze, however, and consider the semantic clusters disproportionately affixed to racial Others relative to "Japanese," we find patterns that more easily lend themselves to readings of racializing discourse (figure 5.10). For one, certain cells in the grid recall associations found in the magazine corpus, hinting at possible "structures of attitude and reference" or "consistencies of concern" shared by works with no

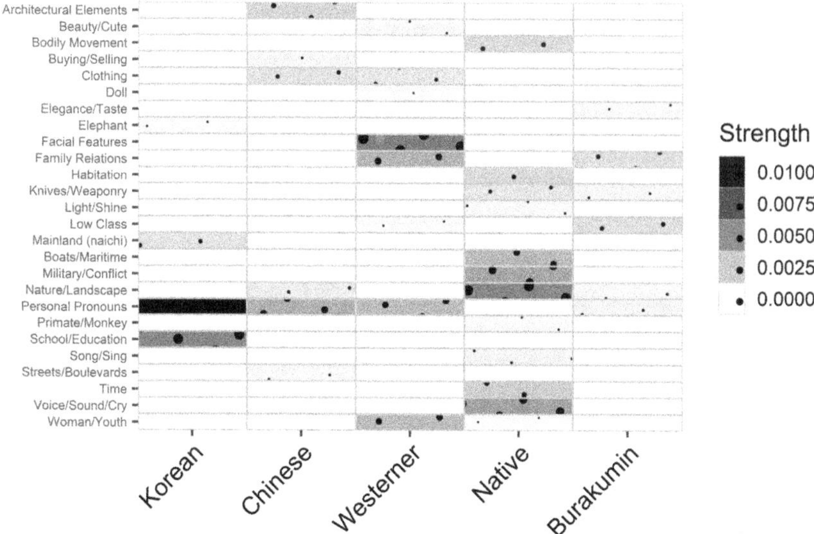

FIGURE 5.10. Semantic clusters associated with references to racial Others compared with references to Japanese in the fiction corpus.

other obvious relation than being composed under conditions of empire.[53] "Chinese," for example, is paired with the semantic clusters "Buying/Selling" (the verbs "to buy" and "to sell") and "Architectural Elements" (consisting of the words glass, window, wall, pillar, paint, building, brick, street, and boulevard). What previously showed up as an association with the language of high finance and economic relations reappears as an association with the vernacular of monetary exchange and of commercial storefronts. "Westerner," to cite another example, retains its association with faces, eyes, and facial expression, although noses, eyebrows, and beards have now been added to the mix. Significantly, it also retains its association with woman (*onna*) and youth (*wakai*), both as their own category and as embedded within "Family Relations," a cluster which includes wife (*nyobō*), daughter (*musume*), father (*chichioya*), and son (*musuko*). Finally, "Native" once again exhibits semantic associations with words related to nature and landscape (e.g., forests, groves, undergrowth, leaves, birds, islands) as well as time (e.g., morning, evening, night). Such points of coincidence must be confirmed by closer analysis of the passages in which these clusters are activated, but that there is significant overlap at this scale of abstraction is itself remarkable.

Equally significant are the cells in the grid that indicate a semantic divergence from the nonfiction corpus. Each leaves a trail of lexical bread crumbs for later researchers to follow.[54] Is there, for instance, a racist logic to the shared association of "Chinese" and "Westerner" with a cluster of words for clothing and dress? What explanation might we give for the relative absence of associations with "Korean," aside from an overriding fixation on words related to education (e.g., students, teachers, school)? More prosaically, why is the latter more often accompanied by neutral personal pronouns (he, her, myself) and the former racial groups more often boxed in by the vulgar variants of these pronouns (*ore*, *yatsu*, *aitsu*, *kisama*)? These questions require us to stretch out the clean lines of the grid and disaggregate the passages provisionally fused together to create them.[55]

Here I will do this with the cluster "Voice/Sound/Cry," which is significantly associated with references to "Native." It is a compelling cluster for its obvious contrast with the observed tendency to dissociate the "Native" from verbs for speech and cognition in the magazine corpus. As a kind of compensation for this tendency, the fictional "Native" is offered speech and thought in their embodied, visceral form—in verbs such as cry (*naru*), scream (*himei*), and yell (*wameku*) but also in words signifying the auditory manifestation of these actions: voice (*koe*), noise (*oto*), shout (*sakebigoe*), reverberate (*hibiku*), waah (*waa*), and wa! (*wattsu*). The final two represent onomatopoetic expressions for crying and surprise, respectively. What explains this cacophony of screams and shouts?

Scanning the corpus for moments when these words co-occur with "Native" (i.e., within twenty words) produces seventy-eight passages ranging in date from 1901 to 1951. Forty-six of these are from two novels by popular genre author Kunieda Shirō (1887–1943): *Sabaku no koto* (Ancient desert capital, 1923) and *Kariforunia no takarajima* (California's treasure island, 1925). Published in mass market journals aimed at adolescent boys, both revel in the standard stuff of pulp adventure fiction: far-flung locales, heroic male figures, spies and detectives, guns and arrows, and marauding enemy bandits.[56] Here the enemies are bands of natives (*dojin*) whose encroaching "war cries" (*toki no koe*) strike fear in the hearts of protagonists; who emit collective shouts (*kansei*) as they listen intently to their chieftain; who gather to drink in large crowds and create a noisy din (*gayagaya wameki*); who scream and cry out (*himei*) as they flee or are struck dead.

In rare instances, the voices are mildly more pleasant, as when the "rustic singing voices" (*hinabita utagoe*) of young maidens collecting rubber sap echo through the woods or when voices old and young harmonize in pure, worshipful song (*kiyoraka na utagoe*). Even in these cases, however, it is not discrete voices or words that are heard but speech reduced to sound reduced to synchronized collectivity, leaving no room for individuated communication or reflective thought. Together, the passages recall the excessively "lively" or "agitated" ethnic subjects found in abundance in American literature—what Sianne Ngai calls "the exaggeratedly emotional, hyperexpressive, and even 'overscrutable' image of most racially or ethnically marked subjects in American culture."[57] Kunieda, for his part, projected a homegrown version of this image synchronized with what Kawamura Minato calls "popular (*taishū*) orientalism," a phenomenon of the early 1920s that saw South Seas islanders increasingly marked as racial and ethnic Others in popular literature (especially for boys).[58]

That Kunieda's vocally animated image of the "Native" drowns out other signals in the data reveals as much about his relation to trends in popular literature as it does about the model used to capture these signals. Kunieda is clearly doubling down on these trends, using vocal "animatedness" to project "the image of the overemotional racialized subject, abetting his or her construction as unusually receptive to external control."[59] But this raises a methodological and interpretative question: whether to down sample his repeated invocations of "Native" or let them dominate, as I do here. As a corrective, one could sample a single racial identifier per document when identifying significant semantic clusters.[60] But this sampling strategy risks overlooking the compound effects that make racializing discourse so effective for information control and management—a discourse that compresses the "Native" voice into a narrow range of expression by having it speak the same way over and over again. In Kunieda's repetitions is the opportunity to see a racist trope pushed to its extremes for exaggerated effect.

Although including all of Kunieda's references to "Native" intensifies the "Voice/Sound" cluster in the semantic grid, it does not mean the trope is unique to him. The other passages show that Kunieda is pounding on a note played elsewhere in the corpus, if more softly. A note that is sounded in Sōseki's *Kokoro* (1914) when the protagonist, pining for his beloved and fearing that his traveling companion K might be harboring the same affections, loses emotional control. "I grew restless and ceased to enjoy the book I was reading; I stood up all of a sudden and started shouting in a loud voice. I couldn't console myself with lukewarm remedies like reciting a poem or singing some song. All I could do was scream like a savage (*yabanjin no gotoku wameku*)."[61] The same note is sounded in scenes of encounter with incomprehensible native others, such as in the final part of Tani Jōji's world travelogue *Odoru chiheisen* (Dancing horizons, 1934). Upon landing at Port Said, north of the Suez Canal, the narrator describes a chaotic scene of merchants, tradesmen, and people of all colors and ethnicities who crowd the arriving passengers, and from which is heard the cry, "Galla! Galla! Galla! Galla! Galla! Galla! Galla! Brrrrr! (*sic*) It was a local (*dojin*), of course. A magician. The young Black man sat cross-legged on the deck of the boat, arranging and flipping over what appeared to be two brass cups, all the while yelling in a loud voice."[62] It is a note that rings even into the early postwar in Sakaguchi Angō's classic whodunit, *Furenzoku satsujin jiken* (Intermittent murder cases, 1947). There, a main character, upon equating Javanese and Balinese dancers with the erotic sensibilities of Japan's ancient past, "stands up and begins the hip-swaying dance of the South Seas native. He'd even mastered their songs. His hand and hip movements, his singing, were vivid and lively; his raucous voice (*domagoe*) sounded as if it were straight from the South Seas."[63]

The association of an animated voice with the overemotional "Native" subject thus rings out across a diverse range of time periods and genres, immediately recognizable even in these snippets of extracted text. Said once called for English novels written under empire to be read *contrapuntally*, seeing their various themes as playing off one another to create a polyphony in which can be heard "concert and order, an organized interplay that derives from the themes, not from a rigorous melodic or formal principle outside the work."[64] Out of this order emerge the cultural essentializations and condensations seen here—structures of attitude and reference that "do not arise from some pre-existing (semi-conspiratorial) design," but are bound up with the development of Japan's cultural identity as imagined in a geographically conceived world.[65] One does not need computation's "general" perspective to recognize these structures as they are encapsulated in discrete moments. As in the previous examples, the themes that convey these structures are written to resonate with minimal context. They are effective precisely because, as Ngai argues, they have reduced the difference between types and stereotypes—“between social roles and ‘individualities that [project] particular ways of inhabiting a social role’ ”—by limiting the social roles of certain groups in ways that others are not.[66] The “native” voice as it appears in Japanese fiction is so easy to hear because it is heard in so few ways. If we already know this intuitively, the general perspective allows us to grapple concretely with the scope and magnitude of these limitations and their unequal dispersion across different racialized bodies. It also makes visible the discrete elements that hold these dominant themes together, sharpening our ability to hear those moments when the elements are recombined, warped, or otherwise interspersed with other notes to generate more complex, less predictable themes. As before, an equivalence space built from deliberate abstractions invites further loosening of its reductive frame through the very patterns of difference it exposes.

RACIAL CHARACTER(S)

Character offers a conceptual and methodological hinge by which to perform this loosening. As much as Kunieda’s racialized caricatures symbolize narrowing social roles at the level of general discourse, they also reflect the formal constraints of novelistic character operating at its highest order of generality. They are characters of the flattest kind, where “flatness” is understood as both a textual effect and a function of the narrative’s distributed attention. A textual effect because the list of traits and attributes used to describe them are overtly restricted, rendering them at once typical and socially legible, but also highly allegorical. A function of distributed attention because, as Alex Woloch argues persuasively, novelistic narration, especially of the Realist kind, cannot help but attend to its “too many people” in unequal measure. The result is an inherent tension in the Realist novel between its few round protagonists and its many flat minor characters that stems precisely from its two contradictory generic achievements: “depicting the interior life of a singular consciousness and casting a wide narrative gaze over a complex social universe.”[67] Kunieda’s novels are not strictly allied with the protocols of Realism as Woloch delimits them, but they nevertheless rely on an economy of character that subordinates, through descriptive flattening, their too many native characters in order to make room for the singular voices, actions, and thoughts of their male, mostly Caucasian and Japanese, protagonist heroes.

The flatness of these natives is partly an effect of the generic racial identifiers used to name them. At the same time, the frequent repetition of the identifier means that Kunieda's natives morph into structurally essential minor characters. They are much less than individuated people but more than one-time stage props. Still the voice cluster sticks to them. It is the very semantic window, in fact, through which they became visible in my model. Here we return to the questions with which we began: Do the semantic clusters associated with racial Others adhere to named characters standing in for those Others? Are patterns of association at the highest order of generality (e.g., noisy, screaming, inarticulate natives) repurposed in order to animate characters richly individuated under the aesthetic dictates of realism? If so, how are the words that comprise these associations distributed across the character-spaces and systems engineered by writers to depict the contact and confrontation of racial and ethnic difference under empire?

That a discursive conduit exists between the character-spaces and systems of the novel and the real-world social relations that writers aim to depict is supported by existing theories of characterization. Woloch, for instance, argues that the many flat, minor characters who are "incompletely pulled into a narrative" subtend the empirical precision of Realist aesthetics and its twin imperatives of narrow psychological description and wide social gaze. Minor characters perform an essential structuring function—and increasingly so in the nineteenth-century Realist novel—that sets the richly described minds of principal protagonists against peripheral figures who are flattened out by allegorical description in order to bring more of them into a novel's social universe. The price paid for this skewed distribution is the novel's own awareness that it must elide the "human particularity" of the many to benefit the few, in turn generating a tension between "reference and structure [that] is itself so socially significant [because it is] grounded in the problematic elimination or functionalized compression of real persons in the actual world." The unequal structure of the character-system is, for Woloch, exactly where novels often "touch history."[68]

Where Woloch focuses on contact with the history of capitalism and the abstraction of social relations to economic utility, others focus on contact with the history of race relations. Phillip Brian Harper is particularly incisive on this point. He argues that the promise that Realist novels give to readers of a fictive world as socially complex as the real, objective one is always broken by the pressure to accurately delineate subjective experience and pull back from the "depictive comprehensiveness" otherwise promised. When this pulling back leads to the absence of certain kinds of individuals (e.g., virtuous Black men), or worse, their reduction to stereotypes that diminish complexity by "characterizing through a minimal number of distinguishing attributes," we get a representational domain whose reality is predicated on its extensiveness with the real world but that in fact is restricted by obviously biased decisions. Most insidiously, readers acquainted with the proffered stereotypes can mistake this artificially limited domain—often synchronous with that mapped out in a protagonist's consciousness—for reality as they know it.[69]

For Harper and Woloch, the Realist injunction to account for everyone and the self all at once invariably means privileging the narrative actualization of some human beings over others in ways that reflect real divisions in society. For me, the theory of such a relation is motivation to investigate the interaction of racial discourse at a general level with specific characterizations of racialized Others in colonial-era fiction. To wit, it leads me to ask whether the price of flattening these Others was paid in the semantic currencies exposed by my model of racializing discourse. Or to come at the problem from a different angle, when colonized writers were given the chance to write themselves out of the margins and into rounded characters, however circumscribed and censored, did they use the same currency?

Although the Realist injunction carried different valences in Japan, writers and critics throughout the modern era wrestled with the problem of characterization and realist aesthetics in ways that echo debates in Europe, and from which came the normative idea that "novels, to be good novels, had to be *about* character."[70] In the case of English novels, as Deidre Lynch has argued, they had to be about characters who were valued for their "indescribability, their exceptionality, and their polyvalence"—characters whose truth lay buried in "an inside story of secrets, hidden motivations, and unplumbed depths."[71] An emphasis on interiority, and on the particularized details that add up to what is taken for roundedness, constituted a novel reading formation in eighteenth-century England.

This formation put pressure on an older one in which the distinctiveness of character mattered more as a sum of surface traits read through established systems of social categorization and valuation. These earlier systems developed in response to a rapidly commercializing and territorially expanding society for which it became useful to sort and typologize the many circulating faces and bodies via, as Lynch puts it, "impersonal mechanisms of coherence and comprehensibility."[72] In the late 1700s, when some began questioning the capacity of these mechanisms to discern whether a particular attribute was truly characteristic of someone or merely an accessory, there arose a call to read and write character in deeper, more personal, less *typical* ways. This shift set the stage for the rounded central characters of nineteenth-century Realism who pushed their more "superficial" predecessors to the margins and made them seem all the shallower, and less human, for it. Typological thinking did not go away, as Woloch and Harper remind us, but became the devalued background against which "real" individuals could be recognized, and so too "good" novels.

In Japanese letters, rounded characters came to stand for the mark of "good" (and also modern) fiction at the mythologized moment of modern literature's inception. In *Shōsetsu shinzui* (Essence of the novel, 1885–1886), young upstart critic Tsubouchi Shōyō famously made psychological characterization a cornerstone of his vision for a literature befitting the new age. Rendering in miniature the epochal shifts in reading formations documented by Lynch, Shōyō insisted that fiction writers should be like psychologists who "plumb the depths of human feeling (*ninjō*)" and "depict in meticulous detail, omitting nothing, the inner workings of the mind so as to illuminate this feeling." Writers and dramatists were not to rely on external behavior or actions to intuit the interior thoughts of humans, as they had in the past. Shōyō considered interior thought and exterior behavior as distinct phenomena whose causal relation was highly variable and thus hard to measure or determine. When writers failed to give attention to the complexities and particularities of a character's inner thoughts, settling instead on an idealized representation that made thought and action wholly consistent, they ended up with "marionettes" rather than human beings.[73] For Shōyō, it was a focus on the most superficial, exaggerated qualities of humans that made theatrical characters tiring to watch and the thinnest, predictable versions of their written selves.[74]

Two decades later, and with the ground prepared for a sharp turn to psychological realism and the rise of the I-novel, Natsume Sōseki offered his own opinion while maintaining a similar implicit distinction between complex and simple characters. In his 1908 lecture on "The Attitude of a Creative Artist," he saw characterization as a problem of managing the distribution of characteristics (*tokusei*) used to render characters as real people and, similar to Shōyō, criticized the long-held assumption that "successful" characters were ones whose activities (*katsudō*) in a novel, however varied, were entirely without contradiction. By this he meant that their movements were unified under just a few signs (*kigō*)—"a courageous person, a kind person, a selfish person"—reducing them to one thing. Sōseki dubbed this "novelistic character," which he opposed to the "natural character" of real-life people rife with contradictions, "appearing very cool and indifferent about others' health, for example, but extremely anxious about their own; rude and unsociable toward their family, but the politest of men toward friends." Novelists and playwrights were starting to try to represent these contradictions, but the result was characters that looked poorly written. "I suppose that the more objective and particular the depiction, the easier it is to produce characters that don't cohere. You tend to get a character that can't be summed up in one word, or a character who is hard to remember." If such characters struck readers as "scattered, easily deformed, even mysterious," however, it's because they saw them with "eyes trained by existing novels." Sōseki speculated that, with time, the more writers took an interest in "objective description" (*kyakkan-teki byōsha*), which to him meant a focus on particularity, the less that readers would notice such deviations from the typological thinking of old.[75]

Another two decades on, this prediction looked like a self-fulfilling prophecy for writers (and readers) at the center of the literary establishment. In the intervening years, as described in chapter 3, the orthodox marker of true, or "pure," literature (*junbungaku*) became the degree to which an author focused in excruciating particulars on the inner workings of the protagonist's mind no matter how contradictory or scattered. In his 1935 essay "Junsui shōsetsuron" (Treatise on the pure novel), Yokomitsu lamented just how narrow the path of junbungaku had become because it made readers feel as if just one character in a work, usually the author, was capable of thinking things. "The novels are as good as blind to the societal fact that lots of people are each thinking things on their own. . . . Noticing this, we realize that Japanese-style descriptive realism, itself an extension of diary literature . . . has come to have no need for the majority of people."[76] As Woloch might say, junbungaku had cut off Realism's other foot, refusing to cast its narrative gaze over a complex social universe.[77]

To suture this foot back on, Yokomitsu proposed the pure novel (*junsui shōsetsu*) as a synthesis of pure literature and popular fiction oriented through a "fourth-person perspective" (*yoninshō*). This perspective, a "self seeing the self," would catalyze techniques for expressing the "thought" (*shisō*) that organized character relations in the author's mind—relations that were constituted not by each character's every thought but by the "convergence of their surfaces of revolution (*kaitenmen*)."[78] Attaining such a perspective still left him to solve the fundamental technical problem of deciding where the rendering of a real person into a "novelistic character" should begin and end, especially as these characters multiplied in the space of the novel. For this Yokomitsu offered no concrete solutions, nor did he consider what consequences there might be for an unequal distribution of narrative attention. Instead, echoing Shōyō and Sōseki, he argued that the successful pure novel will concentrate not only on the role of chance (*gūzen*), as that which mediates between the exterior actions and inner thoughts of characters, but also on the "grand chance" (*dai gūzen*) that results when these smaller, individual accidents assemble and "collide together everywhere in the everyday."[79]

These glimpses into the long debate over novelistic character in Japan are a reminder of the specific roads down which Realism traveled in Japanese letters—roads so narrow that critic Masao Miyoshi could hyperbolically claim, echoing all those before him, that "the characters in the Japanese novel are almost always types, and not living individuals."[80] This he attributed to the obsession with self-narrative, making an explicit contrast with the richly drawn characters of Western novels. In truth, proletarian, modernist, and popular writers routinely questioned the value of psychologically well-rounded characters made to inhabit social universes that were in truth artificially depopulated islands. Looking beyond the I-novel, one finds that "the Japanese novel" is made up of more complex character-systems and spaces than Miyoshi was willing to admit. Even limiting our view to the I-novel, however, it is still worth asking about the Others who did and did not flicker into conscious view of I-novel protagonists and about their links to the shifting economies of racial character under Japanese empire. A representational domain not intended to be extensive with the real social world still has ideological consequences if it remains consistent across the minds of so many. It can compound the underrepresentation of the interiors of certain Others, but also raise the stakes for these neglected Others when they (or those who claim to speak for them) are called upon to put their *selves* at the center of such domains. When Yokomitsu's call for a fourth-person realism morphs by essay's end into an insistence that "the time has come to think about ethnicity (*minzoku*)" by seeing Japan from without as much as from within, the inverse corollary is that other ethnicities warrant the same balance of focus.[81] He is reluctant to say as much, but later critics would take up his mandate for realistic characterization and insist that colonized Others also be drawn from the inside.

This insistence came with a catch for those Others writing in Japanese, however, as they faced the inexorable and perennial double bind of being expected to write the individualized self while also representing a racial or ethnic collectivity. They had to be unique and predictable all at once. Consider the reception of Kim Saryang's Akutagawa-prize-winning novel *Into the Light* (1940), praised by contemporary Japanese critics for its "sharp interiority" compared to works by other Korean authors, but also described as an "ethnic psychology of the Korean people" and an "I-novel which has the tragic fate of an entire people [*minzoku*] squeezed into it."[82] Or consider what two critics had to say in 1939 when advocating for the realistic portrayal of Manchurians to counter the exotic and idealistic rendering of Manchuria as fairy-tale land. One urged writers to "discover the selves inside of [Manchurian people]," which for him meant "depicting the truth of their lifestyle."[83] The other called upon writers to investigate what the Manchurian people were "eating, wearing, and *thinking*," again treating inner thought as synonymous with the surface features of customs and lifestyle.[84]

Although this double bind is familiar as a manifestation of the inherently uneven politics of representation under Japanese empire, and of representing subaltern voices more generally, my point here is to highlight a structural parallel with the formal challenges of characterization addressed by Shōyō, Sōseki, and Yokomitsu in turn. They struggled with how to relate interior to exterior elements in ways that neither wholly unified them, because this led toward predictable stereotypes, nor in ways that relied on pure chance, because this created unintelligible characters. This mirrors the double bind of having to strike a balance between expression of the individuated self and the imagined collectivity for which non-Japanese subjects were expected (or forced) to speak. Too much interiority and the racial or ethnic character assumed by the racializing gaze is unrecognizable; too many external characteristics and one falls back into pure exoticism. In this sense, the struggle and debate over the representation of colonized

Others was both a negotiation with racial discourse *and* a negotiation with character-systems. A negotiation, more precisely, with the constraints these systems put on how fixed or loose the interior/exterior relation could be for characters, especially the minor ones drawn into these systems. If we imagine this relation as a dilation between relative fixity and looseness, to what degree is this dilation informed by the vocabularies affixed to racialized Others at the point of their total reduction to costume (i.e., as they appear in the semantic grids)? Do such vocabularies persist when Others become more than flattened stage props? Do they play a part in how their character's costumes are either filled out or ripped apart at their suffocating seams?

That fictional characters can be understood as partly a function of discrete vocabularies distributed unequally across them has led to important developments in the computational study of character.[85] Andrew Piper uses the term "character-text" to denote the "words that stand in a dependent relationship to a character," not including words used in dialogue.[86] He extracts this character-text from English novels using a computational procedure that resolves the multiple pronouns and aliases used for any one character and identifies the actions taken by, but also the modifiers applied to, each character (i.e., verbs and adjectives).[87] No such method exists for Japanese, but character-text can be searched in less complex ways. Here I use the notion of the context-window again with character names as the anchor word. That is, I search for passages in which words from the voice cluster appear in the same context window as a character name. Moreover, I search only the subset of texts in which terms for "Native" appear more than ten times. This exploratory procedure allows me to determine whether the voice cluster is activated as a facet of characterization in this small sample of texts.[88] It also returns us to the complete text as the unit of analysis; it is only through close reading that we can decide whether the voice cluster is doing meaningful work vis-à-vis characterization. Yet we return through a vocabulary whose unequal distribution across racial lines has been attested to at a more general level and, thus, whose influence on character-texts can be newly interpreted against this background.

The ad hoc search procedure generates a list of 478 context windows from thirteen of the fifteen texts searched.[89] In the two Kunieda texts discussed earlier, *Kariforunia no takarajima* and *Sabaku no koto*, words from the voice cluster are found in 17 percent and 14 percent of all character-context windows, respectively. Passages from more literary meditations on South Seas islanders are also included in this list, in particular Nakajima Atsushi's *Hikari to kaze to yume* (Light, wind, and dreams, 1942) and Satō Haruo's "Machō" (Demon bird, 1923), where voice words are found in roughly 2 percent of all context windows. Any of these texts are potentially a portal for peering deeper into how "voice" is activated around major or minor characters. Here I focus first on a short story, "Shunkan" (1921), by popular author Kikuchi Kan. It bears all the trappings of the "popular Orientalism" that was then dressing South Seas islanders in predictable colonialist tropes. Unlike Kunieda's adventure fiction, however, it put the present at a distance by retelling a thirteenth-century tale of a Buddhist monk of noble blood, Shunkan, exiled for treason to an island south of Kyūshū. This distancing allowed him to smuggle "Western colonial island narratives" into this tale of exile and turn it into a tale of settler colonialism.[90]

Abandoned on a remote southern island with two of his accomplices, Shunkan is initially figured as a castaway. Bathed in sunlight, he sits atop a hill of sand under clear blue skies staring vacantly at the sea and sky and the rippling clouds, all metonymic references to distant tropical locales that were coming under Japanese imperial control at the time of the story's publication. Only when his pardoned accomplices are allowed to return home a year later, leaving Shunkan to suffer alone, do we learn that the island is inhabited. The rest of the story tells of his escape from this purgatory by taking a "native" girl as his wife, teaching her the "graceful language of the capital," and eventually raising a family together on a small plot of land.[91] Many years later, his former valet Ario returns to bring him home after Shunkan too is pardoned, but he refuses to go and tells Ario to convey to others back at the capital, including his former wife, that they should think of him as being as good as dead. A tale of exile from civilization becomes, by the end, a tale of domesticating racialized Others through language education and interracial marriage. Of the three retellings of the tale of Shunkan to appear in as many years—Kurata Hyakuzō did a dramatic rendering in 1920 and Akutagawa Ryūnosuke wrote his own "Shunkan" in 1922—Kikuchi's is the most complicit in colonial ideology, in particular an emergent assimilationist strain known as *dōka*.

Dōka emerged in the 1920s as a vague ideological configuration and marked a shift in colonial policy from "recognizing the particularity of colonial society" to one of extending Japan's imperial system by renewing "emphasis on education and harmony between the races." As Leo Ching argues, its vagueness as policy resulted from uncertainty about how the elements of the Japanese nation as essence should be extended to different peoples, but also about what these elements should be. The legitimacy of Japanese rule was asserted through a presumed cultural hierarchy that, predicated on a degree of racial and ethnic sameness, left room for its contestation and rearticulation by the colonized Other.[92]

"Shunkan" is easily read through this ideology because it offers a version of its ideal outcome: a relatively conflict-free transition wherein colonizer and colonized each relinquish something of their former cultural identity in order to live in mixed-racial harmony. For Shunkan it is the exterior veneer of "modern" civilization—living in nature transforms his body into a deeply browned, disheveled, and muscular form unparalleled even by the "devil-like natives" (392).[93] For the girl it is something more essential—her mother tongue and familial ties—which seem to fall away effortlessly because we learn little of them at the beginning. This asymmetrical erasure of difference is another way to read "Shunkan" through dōka: as a representation of the "contradictory act of assimilating while discriminating" that the fantasy of an undifferentiated self/other made possible, particularly in relation to those who could be seen as culturally and racially contiguous (e.g., Okinawans, Koreans, Taiwanese).[94] This ambivalent attitude toward difference is captured well in the final lines of the story, as Ario looks back from his departing ship to see father and mother walking home with their five children frolicking joyfully about them. "At first he was thinking how pitiful they looked, like a herd of animals or something, but before long he noticed warm tears inexplicably running down his cheeks" (401).

That Ario has the last word on Shunkan's character returns us to the frame through which this text came to our interpretive attention. Namely, that it speaks to colonial ideology in part by thematizing "voice" as a medium of characterization. Significantly, it is not the "native" girl whose character is shaped by this theme, for she remains throughout a minor figure almost entirely rendered at the level of exterior features. Instead, the voice cluster is most active around Shunkan and, upon closer reading, emerges as the very hinge by which his character is flipped *inside out*. When we read the story with an attention to how voice and sound intercede in the shifting dynamics of interior and exterior description, Shunkan's characterization appears as a gradual slide from contemplative subject to voiceless object that has him playing the part of a screaming "native" and, by the end, a nearly incomprehensible one. His flattening into stereotype is largely achieved by shuffling his character-text from a language of internalized mental angst to one of action and visceral affect, amounting to a dismantling of his psychological self. In the opening pages, the latter is carefully established by dwelling on Shunkan's feelings of guilt and longing for home as he is increasingly ostracized by his frustrated and desperate compatriots. These feelings come to a head at a pivotal moment just before they leave the island: "With every corner of his chest filled by sadness and pent-up anger, he [sat there] with folded arms, stewing in thought" (380). As his mind wanders off to memories of family and home, he is suddenly brought back to the present by the shouts of the two men who spot a sail on the horizon. This is the ship that will take them home, but not before anchoring offshore for a night, leaving the abandoned Shunkan to scream, shout, and curse at the ship until dawn. "Shunkan's voice grew hoarse, until finally his wailing became as feeble as the cries of an injured seagull. But no matter how hoarse his voice got, he continued to shout relentlessly" (383).

This scene is the first moment in which the voice cluster is excessively activated around Shunkan, and it signals an important transition in the process of his being turned inside out. The scene ends with his voice entirely gone and the narrator pulling back to describe him as circling madly atop a shoreline cliff like an animal (*kemono*). He teeters between basic survival and thoughts of suicide until another moment of deep contemplation leads to an epiphany: life on this remote island is exactly what can liberate him from his earthly desires and obsessions, freeing his mind to experience the reality before him. His mind is now "as free as a child's," and his yells begin to sound "childish" too. At this point Shunkan sheds "customs" (*shūkan*) associated with his former life in order to do as the "natives" do, a decision that, at the level of characterization, sparks a narrowing of the divide between thought and action (388). Days that were once filled by anguished rumination turn into days of planning, activity, and routine. It is only in this transition that we learn there are "natives" (*dojin*) present on the island at all, reinforcing their status as a mere plot device. They appear only when Shunkan needs a model to imitate, which he does almost entirely through observation at a distance. The first direct encounter we hear about is with the unnamed young girl who approaches him one day and initiates an extended exchange of rapt gazes and facial expressions. Everything happens on the surface. When the girl finally breaks the silence the next day, the representation of her voice conforms almost perfectly to the patterns of racial discourse exposed in our semantic grid. Through Shunkan's ears, we hear it first as a sudden, incomprehensible yell (*sakebi*); then he notices it has a certain rhythm (*inritsu*), which makes the yelling recognizable as song (*uta*), albeit one with an "unfamiliar tune" and "entirely unintelligible words." The voice communicates nothing about her, serving instead as a vehicle of pure feeling (*kanjō*) by which Shunkan cannot help but be moved (396).

Instead of prompting an audible reply, however, the girl's vocal gesture marks a closing off of Shunkan's thoughts, and so too his voice, from the reader. It is not that he stops speaking. On the contrary, he wields his voice in ways true to assimilationist ideology, teaching his now wife to converse and write in the "language of the Yamato people" (i.e., the language of "pure" Japanese). She speaks too, for we are told that Shunkan feels no greater joy than when he hears her use the "elegant language of the capital" (397–98). And yet none of this is represented in dialogue, nor do we get access to their internal thoughts. They are simply a happy couple going through the motions—another child, another good harvest, a newly built hut—stock figures in a play about mixed-ethnic harmony and domestic bliss.

Shunkan's transformation from speaking imperial subject to voiceless "native" type is made permanent in the story's final section, which is focalized through his former retainer Ario. Upon reaching the island, Ario spends days fruitlessly looking for Shunkan before stumbling upon "a male and female native" whose "human voices" (*hitogoe*) unexpectedly sound like *Yamato kotoba*. A mole above the man's eyebrow confirms for Ario that this is his former master, and they have a brief, tearful reunion. Yet try as Ario might to persuade Shunkan to return home, he refuses. Throughout this back and forth it is only Ario we hear, aside from the final parting words when Shunkan says that he should be considered "as good as dead" by all back home. Yet not even this is represented as verbatim transcription: "Since his *Yamato kotoba* had such a heavy accent, Ario couldn't remember the words exactly as he had spoken them" (399–401). From the view of this not yet assimilated colonizer, then, what others might see as the ideal endpoint of dōka ideology is instead a terrifying flattening of the self that obscures the relation of interior to exterior by dressing it in "native" garb. That "voice" was used to perform this flattening in 1921 makes "Shunkan" an early stitch in a costume that a coming wave of popular Orientalism would make fashionable.

"Shunkan" shows us how the voice as racializing trope could deflate the psychologically rounded subject. A second work that turns up in the search of character-text shows how the trope itself could be expanded and burst open. Oh Shō-yū's (Wang Changxiong) "Honryū" (A torrent), published in 1943 in the journal *Taiwan bungaku* under strict government censorship, stands in near diametric opposition to the location of "Shunkan" in the literary field. Written by a colonial writer raised in Taiwan and educated in Japan, it is narrated in the first person by an imperial subject who has returned to his native island after ten years of living in Tokyo and must confront his dual linguistic and ethnic identity at a time when assimilationist policy no longer left any room for recognizing the particularity of the colonized Other. As Ching argues in the case of Taiwan, the heightening of colonial tensions and political resistance in the 1920s steered the more ambiguous ideology of dōka toward the stricter principles of *kōminka* (imperialization), which enforced submission to, rather than harmony with, the Japanese imperial system. Whereas "Japanization" under dōka "was largely articulated as a problematic of the colonizer—as a failed, or yet to be realized, colonial ideal," under kōminka it was internalized as "exclusively a problematic of the colonized, viewed as an incomplete 'imperial subject.' "[95] Oh's story self-consciously positions itself at the heart of this problematic. For all the ways it is antithetical to "Shunkan," however, it shares an attention to voice as a dimension along which to sketch and perturb the outlines of "native" character.

Oh had reason to confront this character because of Taiwan's ambiguous position in the Japanese colonial imagination. As home to a diverse array of aboriginal peoples as well as ethnic Chinese, it "encompassed both extremes of colonial experience: illiterate, primitive 'savages' and cultivated, highly literate ethnic Chinese."[96] But it was the former to whom literary figures and early ethnographers gave the bulk of their attention. Journalists were also complicit in this imbalance, responding eagerly whenever violence erupted between indigenous groups and settler Japanese communities, the most dramatic incident being the Musha uprising of 1930. As a result of this skewed focus, Taiwan's inhabitants were circumscribed by the same set of discourses that were active in producing popular images of South Seas "natives." Literature set in these locales tended to generate diametrically opposed images of the "native," with the "violent, irrational headhunter" more often associated with Taiwan and the "innocent, happy primitive" more often associated with the South Seas, but the regions were effectively conjoined by this same mark of civilizational difference.[97] The term used to designate people of Taiwan in the colonial period—"islander" (*hontōjin*)—itself reflects a tendency to imagine them as "natives" first and ethnically Chinese second, if at all. It was the latter group, however, who constituted the first generation of writers and intellectuals to come of age under colonial rule and who pushed back on this skewed vision while projecting an autonomous Taiwanese identity imagined simultaneously for itself and for the needs of Japanese empire.[98]

Signs of this resistance show up in works like "Honryū" that dramatize the psychological plight of Taiwanese intellectuals educated on the mainland. In a story by Chin Kyokoku (Chen Xu-gu) from 1930, a student just back from Tokyo responds to the staring eyes of Japanese on the train by declaring to himself: "I successfully passed the higher school exam; I'm someone who represents Taiwan; I'm a brilliant Japanese; I'm absolutely not the ordinary native (*dojin*) or ethnic inferior (*rettō minzoku*) that you all think I am."[99] Oh's first-person narrator expresses a similar sentiment at one point, berating himself for all the times he feared that his accent might give too much of his Taiwanese origins away:

> What a despicable man you are. Aren't [your actions] clear proof that you're belittling Taiwan itself? Taiwanese people are not Chinese, nor are they Eskimos. On the contrary, is there any difference between them and those born on the mainland (*naichi*)? Be proud! Proud that you too are a Japanese imperial subject (*Nihon shinmin*).[100]

Although "Eskimo" is here used in place of "native," the association is clear and reinforces the extent to which Taiwanese were aware of being seen through this category of racial and ethnic Other. This reality makes the appearance of the "voice" cluster in the character-text of "Honryū" all the more salient because it invites us to read its activation in this story through the semantic grids of racial discourse generated earlier.

Part of the reason Oh's story is in the fiction corpus is because of the critical reception it has received from scholars of Taiwan's colonial period literature, which has ensured its repeated anthologization. It has been recognized as emblematic of the *kōminka* ideology under which it was written and censored, but also a nuanced reflection on the impossibility of conforming to the identity politics this ideology demanded.[101] Critics argue that "Honryū" achieves this delicate balance between ideological conformity and critique through a tripartite character structure that simultaneously maps out the limited range of subject positions available to young Taiwanese men under kōminka ideology. At the center of this structure is the first-person narrator who, three years prior, returned to his rural hometown to take over his father's medical practice after spending ten years studying on the mainland (*naichi*). As the story opens, he thinks back to the night he left Tokyo and pines for the city's vibrant, stimulating atmosphere. His current life, in contrast, is defined by feelings of boredom, ennui, and persistent melancholy. He longs to escape from this state of affairs, but concern for his aging mother prevents him from doing so. It is around this time that Itō Haruo, an instructor of Japanese language (*kokubun*) at a nearby middle school, visits his office with a terrible cold and fever. In the course of examining his chest and throat, the narrator becomes mesmerized by Itō, mostly because he cannot determine if he is Japanese (*naichijin*) or Taiwanese (*hontōjin*). Before he can work up the nerve to ask him, he must attend to his next patient, Lin Bonian, who happens to be a fifth-year student at Itō's school. He has been treating Lin for several months for pleurisy, an inflammation of the membrane covering the lungs that hinders breathing. The rest of the plot unfolds around these three figures, brought together for a brief instant in the physician's office for symptoms that directly affect the voice.

The plot tracks the evolving relationship of these three through the lens of the narrator's own budding identity crisis. As Chen Wanyi notes, past critics have tended to slot them into three distinct roles: Itō, whose wife is Japanese, represents a fully assimilated imperial subject; Lin, who is more critical of full assimilation, retains affection for his native home and family as he contemplates moving to the mainland to enter university; and the narrating "I" is a neutral observer, who contrasts Itō with Lin to come to terms with his own relation to kōminka. Later critics, like Chen, read this tripartite structure as a staged debate over the kind of "Taiwanese mentality" (*Taiwanjin seishin*) that this generation of elite intellectuals will build and pass along to the next.[102] Others, like Tarumi Chie, read it through the split-subject of the narrator himself, who wavers between idolization of Itō and fond respect for the younger Lin. This indecision is seen to parallel the split-subject of modern Japanese literature, with Japan standing in for "the West" and "modernity" standing in for the real and symbolic object around which interiority is fashioned.[103] The work's earliest Japanese critic, writing in 1944, expressed an analogous recognition of the particularity of the narrator's account as well as its generalizability. For him, the work's "I-novel form" allowed for the figures of Itō and Lin to be understood just "as they are" (*aru ga mama*) through their personal interactions with the narrator (and author). This, in turn, made it possible for the critic "to imagine the Taiwanese intellectual as a single, remarkable type (*taipu*)."[104] Rounded psychological characterization of a man's struggle with identity paradoxically allows for his flattening back into a general type, recalling the double bind into which colonized writers were squeezed just as they started to tear at the seams of their stylized costumes.

If more recent critics avoid replicating this double bind, they tend to offer allegorical readings of the story's characters that orient them toward assimilation as the end goal of identity formation. By attending to the dispersion of the voice cluster across the story's entire character-system, however, we see a wider semantic backdrop against which all the characters struggle to figure themselves as assimilated. As the opening scene in the narrator's office foreshadows, the struggle is rooted as much in the body as in the mind, with the problem of the voice surfacing first as a kind of affliction or ailment. In Lin's case, the ailment is more protracted and serious, the result of overexerting himself in *kendō* and other physical exercise. Itō's ailment, however, seems at first more superficial, a simple cold that he has ignored for too long. But as he laughs at his own stubborn pride, the narrator hears in his nonchalance something more ominous. "For all the magnanimity shown in his face, there were complex shadows and lines hidden in his laugh" (221).[105] A sense that Itō's voice is masking a deeper reality continues to trouble the narrator. "I presumed Itō was Japanese (*naichijin*) and yet while I couldn't have guessed from his accent, based on the outline of his face, his build, his eyes and nose, somehow or other I saw him as Taiwanese (*hontōjin*). Call it the acute and neurotic sixth sense of a person born in the colonies, but when I was on the mainland I could guess in one glance, and without exception, if someone was Korean, Chinese, or whatever" (222). In this instance his eyes deceive him, however. What he sees on the outside does not match what he hears coming from the inside.

Reticent to ask Itō directly, he probes Lin after his checkup and learns that Itō is indeed Taiwanese by birth.

Joyful and elated to hear this news, the narrator is genuinely surprised that a Taiwanese man with a level of sophistication indistinguishable from a Japanese is living in his hometown. When Itō stops by the narrator's home a few days later, his words and actions make him only more of an enigma. The narrator is struck, for instance, by Itō's insistence on speaking only Japanese (*kokugo*) even when he is addressed in Chinese (*hontōgo*) by the narrator's mother.[106] He finds this odd but is nevertheless mesmerized by Itō's speaking. Listening to him carry on about the Japanese spirit as rooted in knowledge of the *Kojiki*—an eighth-century historical chronicle legitimating Yamato rule—the narrator fixates on the light that seems to emanate from Itō's face. At this early point in the story, Itō's impeccable Japanese, heard and felt as a splendid radiance, becomes for the narrator the defining characteristic of his perfect and total assimilation. Itō specifically praises the *Kojiki* for lacking any distortion between word (*kotoba*) and sense (*kokoro*), which only reinforces for the narrator the notion that his enigmatic aura derives from his unification of speech and mind through mastery of a "Japanese" voice (224). In contrast, the characterization of Lin veers to the opposite extreme. The narrator derides him as "childish" and of "slight build"; as being "unapproachable" and "evasive"; a "strange one" who lacks a "bright disposition" and is "always silent with a lonely air about him" (226–27). Just as Lin's medical condition is represented as more chronic and deep-rooted than Itō's, so too are the faults in his character, embodied specifically in his reticence to speak.

The stark lines of the story's character-spaces begin to blur at a New Year's gathering at Itō's home. Upon arrival, the narrator is greeted by Itō's "raised, nearly screeching voice" and enters to find Lin sitting on the floor, despondent and silent. Both are invited to stay for dinner, although not before the sight of Itō's wife and mother-in-law prompt an interior monologue in which the narrator regrets not having the conviction to bring his own former Japanese beloved back to Taiwan. Soon after, the radiant veneer of Itō's character (and voice) is stripped away as Lin's voice comes haltingly, but ardently, into focus. The catalyst for this inversion is the sudden appearance of Itō's real mother, who implores him to visit his ailing father. Minor as her position in the character-system is, she is the fulcrum on which its balance is destabilized. Significantly, her characterization is almost entirely focalized through her voice. When she arrives at the door, the narrator overhears her faltering Japanese and deduces right away that she is both an elderly woman and Taiwanese. As she begs her son to come home, now in her native tongue, her voice becomes tear-filled, and the narrator is unable to understand her clearly (229). Her voice is pure signifier, communicating nothing but her ethnic and gender identity. Itō bruskly sends her away, but the brief encounter has upset his internal equilibrium. His voice is filled with frustration now, and he returns to his guests "agitated and out of breath." Their mood has changed too. "The room had already fallen into empty silence, and it felt as if the only thing intermingling was the sound of our breathing. Actually, I too felt my throat warming and constricting, as if I'd lost my voice" (230). Itō tries to recover the mood by hurriedly breaking into a popular folk song from Japan's Nagano region (*ina bushi*), but there is no going back in the narrator's mind nor in the character-spaces of the text.

Lin's voice emerges soon after this incident. After leaving the party early, he waits in the dark for the narrator and calls out to him as he steps outside. "The sound of his voice was low and jittery in the dark but spurting forth intensely" (231). Highly agitated and stuttering, Lin reports that the elderly woman was indeed Itō's biological mother, and that he had abandoned her. He knows this because she is also his aunt. Lin breaks into tears, and the narrator takes note. "It was in this single moment that the intense emotion usually buried deep in his heart finally struck me. That such passion was coming from the taciturn Lin, whose timidity was so at odds with his physical body, was almost uncanny" (232). Just as Lin's inner character begins filling out in the narrator's mind, the smooth veil of Itō's voice is pulled back. His father's funeral, for instance, brings news that croup, an infection of the upper airways that impedes breathing, had left him blurting out strange curses and maledictions at the end of his life. At the funeral itself, out of a cacophony of wailing elderly women, emerges the familiar voice of Itō's mother. The narrator remarks that "it was as if the emotional pressure born of a long period of endurance had suddenly exploded. A desperate cry, cursing everything while seeming to call on the deceased, carried on with no self-restraint" (234). Through the voices of these minor figures, Itō's own character becomes tightly anchored to images of the exaggerated, inscrutable "native" voice from which he had originally appeared to float free. Rejection of his familial roots in order to dawn the robes of an assimilated "Japanese" ironically leaves Itō's "real" native costume more exposed than ever. Lin, meanwhile, comes to the aid of his grieving aunt after the funeral, raising his voice in such a way that the narrator hears in it a "tone of resistance" to Itō's unfilial actions (235).

From this point forward Lin's voice grows ever more confident—a confidence reflected both at the level of his increasing physical vitality and his willingness to stand up to Itō and refuse an approach to assimilation that requires severing one's filial roots. He is no less ardent in his desire to assimilate, using martial arts and his physical body (blood, muscle, and gut) as the medium by which he will "connect to the Yamato spirit." Nor is the narrator any less admiring of what he has now come to recognize as "the flowers of ancient *bushidō* starting to consciously sprout in the hearts of Taiwanese youth" (240). At this late stage of Japanese empire, all roads lead to assimilation no matter the route taken. The difference for Lin, as he expresses to the narrator in a letter after entering the Martial Arts Academy in Kyoto, is that he vows to be "an outstanding Japanese" and "an outstanding Taiwanese" simultaneously. This means not feeling ashamed by his "southern origins," but also continuing to adore his mother regardless of what an "unseemly native" she may be (247).

Here again it is the figure of the mother on which the character's identity hangs in the balance. And like Itō's mother, we come to know her first through the quality of her voice. When the narrator visits her at home after Lin has left for the mainland, he notes a resemblance to Itō's mother. Yet her "softly quivering voice" affects him differently as she relays news of her son's departure. "Touched by the deep parental affection that flowed from this old woman's mouth on account of her unrefined, artless Chinese, I suddenly became choked up with warm tears" (243). Through this woman he will learn the entirety of Itō's back story—his parents' resistance to letting him study on the mainland unless he promised to study medicine; his betrayal of that desire by choosing national literature studies instead; his offer to pay Lin's own educational expenses no matter the course of study. Readers in turn learn all this from the narrator, who is inclined to offer his own account because the old woman was "prone to repeating herself, her story-telling extremely tangled and lacking in coherence" (244). Even when the female "native" voice speaks it is never really heard.

The narrator is left to grapple with this new information in the text's final pages. His simple reversal of affective polarity with regard to Itō and Lin—positive associations flipping to negative and vice versa—is short-circuited by the knowledge of Itō's heavy personal sacrifices to preserve his intellectual freedom, but also of the financial sacrifices made to preserve Lin's. Their freedom is constrained by the narrow range of subject positions available to educated Taiwanese under kōminka, yet in the immediate context of the narrative it represents the possibility that chance still has a role to play under these constraints. As the narrator says to Lin's mother at the end of their meeting, "Future Taiwanese can become honorable soldiers, even civil servants; it would also be okay, I think, for them to cultivate new directions in the arts. My point is that it's awfully wasteful to kill the individuality (*kosei*) a person is born with" (246–47).

Wasteful (*mottainai*) because it kills one's innate abilities and desires (like the author's former desire to be a writer), but also because it reduces the number of possible paths to self-actualization and personhood. What the narrator comes to realize through the background information provided by Lin's mother is that his surface characterizations of Itō and Lin, whether positive or negative, elided the dynamic processes underlying how they presented themselves. It seemed to him as if interior mentalities and exterior manifestations were working in lockstep, their very coordination audible in the quality of the two men's voices, when in fact interior and exterior were not in sync at all. For all that their voices, and those of their mothers, signaled to the narrator about the "type" of person they were—a type still indelibly tied to the "native" voice as costume—by the end he sees Itō and Lin as characters in process. He reads their appearances and actions, especially those of Itō, as the indirect and complex effect of a deep mental anguish precipitated by the "double lives" that all the island's youth had to navigate (249).

The clearest indication of this transformation—from a more allegorical mode of reading character to one that loosens the relationship of surface and depth—is the state of indecision and indeterminacy in which Oh leaves the narrator by story's end. There is no obvious path forward that will cleanly resolve the gap between interior and exterior and leave him feeling whole. In the minds of readers, the narrator also ultimately appears as a character in process. The final image we get of him only reinforces the gap between inner thought and external voice. As the narrator wanders the outskirts of his hometown, he cannot shake loose the memory of the funeral scene and Itō's rejection of his wailing mother. It "endlessly flickers" in his mind and encapsulates the hidden struggle over identity that might explain Itō's confounding outward behavior. It is the key, it seems, to reading Itō's character, which by extension makes it the key to reading the narrator's own, struggling as he is with how to relate to his natal home. At the surface, however, the final image is of him muttering repeatedly, "just let it go, just let it go." A narrator so wracked with emotion that, unable to bear it any longer, he "raced down from the top of the hill yelling 'Shit!, Shit!' I ran like a child. Stumbling, sliding, buffeted by the wind, I just kept on running" (250). He is himself draped in a version of the "native" voice as costume—overscrutable, emotional, hyperexpressive. It is a costume we can now read between the lines of the general and particular perspective, although its return at the story's end only reinforces how tightly its threads did bind.

THE LIMITS OF CHARACTER

The discriminative operations performed by the voice in all these fictions of empire, indeed its flexibility and legibility as a marker of racial and ethnic difference, have everything to do with its phenomenological status. Voice is an active site for encoding (and deconstructing) difference because it so easily maintains, but also blurs, the boundaries that humans draw between speech and sound, language and noise, thought and action. Those who do not speak one's tongue readily become those who speak only in tongues. In the Japanese imperial context, one need only recall how readily voice was used—in the form of on the spot dialect tests—to single out and murder Koreans in the immediate aftermath of the Great Kantō earthquake in 1923.[107] I selected the voice cluster as a wedge for prying open the semantic grids based on an intuition that it would offer an interpretively rich site to read closely the character (and characters) of racial discourse. Skeptics will ask why this intuition was not applied directly to "Shunkan" or "Honryū," thereby bypassing the computational model altogether. But to suggest that these interpretative processes are one and the same ignores the epistemological work carried out by the model. It ignores how my reading of the voice cluster was produced in dialogue with the model's general perspective, and is thus inseparable from it. And it falsely implies that a more direct reading would be less prone to a critic's internalized models of judgment, which can fill the void of indeterminacy in ways more opaque and no less reductive of what a text has actually said.

The skeptic's voice returns us full circle to Said's original methodological dilemma. Is it the general group of ideas that matters in Orientalist and racial discourse, or the varied work of uncountable individual writers? What is knowledge of one without knowledge of the other? Ian Baucom adds a further twist to this dilemma in his comments on the underlying epistemology of historicist method. In conversation with James Chandler's study of English romantic historicism, Baucom writes that "to 'historicize' any given event, text, or phenomenon is . . . to 'situate' it . . . within the 'peculiar historical' confines of its 'age,' and then to read the character of that thing as . . . determined by its situation, to read it thus as both a type for and typical of its situation." This, however, requires inventing in advance "the very *concept* of the situation or period of time as an abstract category of analysis." Absent the invention of such categories, the historicist method could not exist. The critical rub is that historicism tends "to mask this second (in fact, preliminary) operation, to treat situations not as artificial forms of time which it has invented but as natural entities which it has discovered."[108] The same can be said of the discursive situations that we invent to historicize texts. Where a computational approach productively disrupts this tendency is by making explicit the act of invention as a series of discrete, but debatable, interpretive choices. Rather than mask the preliminary operation of category invention, it places that operation front and center, opening it up to negotiation. To the extent it creates a general perspective (a "*concept* of the situation") to which scholars have equal access, and on which a tentative collective consensus can be reached, it provides a shared situation (i.e., the semantic grids) in which to "historicize" all the variation we seek to read into particular texts. The general perspective comes into view as an artificial, contestable object of knowledge on its own, not as the naturalized, and thus obscured, outcome of an attempt to situate the character of a single thing.

I interrogated this object by focusing on a single cell in the semantic grid for fiction. The greater interpretive potential of these grids, however, lies in what they suggest of how racializing discourse under empire split along specific lines of semantic association, marking certain bodies in some ways and certain bodies in others. Or in some cases marking them not at all, at least not in ways to which the model is attuned. Where the grids do expose lines of differentiation, they are an opportunity to focus on the specific vocabularies that adhered to racialized subjects and reflect on their comparative distribution in the library of racial discourse. They are an opening to investigate other semantic clusters in the grid to see what discriminatory work they are doing and how that work is apportioned across the discursive spaces represented in the underlying corpora. The grids could also be pushed open wider by multiplying the cells and exposing how racial vocabularies are distributed when "Japanese" is not the locus of comparison. In the case of the "Native" voice, we would find that it is similarly distinctive when compared to references to "Westerner," but not when compared with "Korean" or "Chinese," reinforcing an alignment of "Japanese" with "Westerner" at the top of a racial hierarchy underneath which colonized subjects sounded equally noisy and loud.[109] Furthermore, the grids invite us to search for instances in which a cluster associated with one racial identifier (e.g., facial features and "Westerner") is used in conjunction with a different one. These moments will stand out as all the more significant and consequential knowing that they are cutting against the grain of general discursive trends. A third opening is found in the empty cells, which point to all the ways that racializing discourse evades empirical approaches and how our corpora may be biased by inequalities and erasures intrinsic to the print archive itself. These cells compel us to find better ways of reading for implicit bias at scale and to augment the digital record such that minor voices can better stand out. Finally, these semantic grids potentially open dialogues on comparative racisms so that we might, for example, read them alongside vocabularies of discrimination pulled from other conditions of empire and investigate borrowings from libraries of racial discourse that circulated elsewhere.

Much remains to be read from these semantic grids. Here I have tried to direct our gaze to the interpretive horizons made visible in the movement from particular to general and back. The concept of character was the hinge for this movement, allowing me to trace a specific vocabulary of racial Othering from its patterns of explicit use to its patterns of dissolution. To trace, that is, how this vocabulary loosened its grip on characters as their stereotyped, stylized costumes were rounded out. Especially by writers seeking to overturn entrenched character-systems that respond to and reinforce real social inequalities and systematically leave whole groups of people to play minor, flattened parts. Baucom reads this interaction of characterization and inequality deeper—into the very origins of speculative capital and the logic of commodification that underwrote its extension to the eighteenth-century trans-Atlantic slave trade. He finds written into the insurance contracts of merchant slave ships a kind of "novelization" of a collective imaginary that, through allegorical abstraction, "inflicted on millions of human beings the violence of becoming a 'type': a type of person, or, terribly, not even that, a type of nonperson, a type of property, a type of commodity, a type of money." Allegory is not merely the literary counterpart of commodity capitalism but an "epistemological condition of possibility: a mode of representation which enables and clears the ground for a form of capital which is an intensification and a wider practice of it."[110]

To observe character at its allegorical limits is to traverse the most visible contours of this epistemological condition at a time when speculative capital and its dreams of empire turned so many millions of individual bodies into types. Knowledge of these limits is valuable. By building a model to expose them at scale, moreover, a path is opened to explore where the model, and the mode of stereotypical representation it is meant to capture, breaks down. Or even to explore the inverse of this mode, in which "rounded" characters are created not by the dissolution of biased vocabularies into noise but the substitution of vocabularies that appear unbiased only to those privileged enough to see and be seen through them. In this way, character, perhaps more so than popular critical terms such as "identity," has a lot yet to say about racial discourse as it circulated between the formal constraints of fiction and the real-world situations and institutions where it served to sow and maintain racial and ethnic divisions.

Character can reveal how the privileging of individuated voices for some is predicated on the subordination of one kind of character to another, and the universalization of such voices in a way that effaces character altogether. Some voices have the privilege of sounding human because they are portrayed as sounding like nothing before heard. The hushed, solitary voice that Itō Sei posits as the essence of modern literature in this chapter's epigraph performs this same sleight of hand. He presents it as the authentic voice aspired to by fiction, its impact and directness made all the more real by its conflation with the material voice of the author. Everything extrinsic to the voice, every context through which it might be construed as typical or representative, is here stripped away. For Itō, it was a voice best heard not from Cocteau, it turns out, but Joyce. On the same record he found Joyce's "hushed, gloomy tenor," reading "in his confusing English" from a part of *Finnegan's Wake*. "Now this," he wrote, "was truly 'like whispering.' "

> This was an inner voice that seeped into the heart—the voice of a novelist who tried to pursue in English the deepest interior voice of humanity, from its ugly and ignorant lows to its sublime heights. When I heard this voice of his, I felt like I understood Joyce the writer. It made me feel how essential was the task of one who composed works that dissected humanity through techniques that thoroughly chased down the inner voice's thoughts (*uchinaru koe no hassō*).[111]

Read against the terrain traversed by this book, it should be obvious how historically constructed is Itō's feeling here and how unevenly distributed was the kind of voice that provoked it. Coming as it does in 1948, just as the memory of Japan's empire is quickly and strategically being erased, there is something yet more ominous in his insistence that the voice of humanity, and that of the universalized inner self, be delivered in a soft whisper. Now we can hear that whisper against the screams and shouts of those who could not be heard otherwise in fiction, whose characters were denied even the fantasy of speaking as if whispering.

Epilogue

DIFFERENCE IN NUMBERS

The mind of [Tokyo's] cake eaters cannot be determined by asking one man or another; but if the actions of the citizens as a whole are charted statistically, there will emerge a definite pattern governing the consumption of steamed mochi cakes.

—FUKUZAWA YUKICHI (1875)

In the early 1870s, with the French medical debates a distant memory and its victors awash in a flood of numbers, the statistical revolution spurred by Poisson and Quetelet spilled into Japanese intellectual circles. In 1875, as the new Meiji government continued to find its footing, educator and political philosopher Fukuzawa Yukichi published *Bunmeiron no gairyaku* (An outline of a theory of civilization), one of the many texts of the era to engage with statistical ideas. One idea that particularly fascinated him was the average. Applied to the national rather than the physical body, he saw it as a tool to understand "the spirit of an entire nation and the general tenor of its knowledge and virtue," which were impossible to see or hear at the level of individual citizens. "If by chance one did see or hear it, one's visual and auditory impressions would always be contradictory and a fair judgement would be impossible." Analyzed at the individual level, the workings of the mind were too variable and complex. Yet take "all the human sentiments in the land *en masse* [and] compare them over a long period of time," and one can "detect certain patterns of human conduct about which we can no more err than if we were looking at an object's physical shape or reading letters cut into a block of wood." The average renders the whole of a country's knowledge and virtue "as tangible as a physical object," its current and future course as predictable as the weather.[1]

I return to the history of the average, seen now from Japan, to again draw parallels with the present. Its early reception is similarly a site for thinking about the average before it became recognized fact and before there was agreement on its application to real-world phenomena. In contrast with the French medical debates, this moment lay at the intersection of not just inter- and intradisciplinary divisions but also at the intersection of linguistic and cultural ones. At first glance, Fukuzawa's grasp of statistical ideas feels both rudimentary and susceptible to the worst ways that civilizational discourse and historical determinism interacted in the mid-nineteenth century. A simple aggregate measure standing in for a theoretical fiction that, like the "average patient," cannot be experienced directly but is treated as if it is a solid object. Worse still, this fiction is easily converted into the racist and culturally essentializing "facts" of such statistical popularizers as Henry Thomas Buckle, whose *History of Civilization in England* (1857) won him fame (and condemnation) across Europe for the ways it transformed statistical regularities into natural laws such that "climates and land masses determine the course of history more than the apparent free choices of political actors."[2] Buckle generated these laws from regularities made visible in the torrent of numbers and tables churned out by state-run statistics bureaus, finding in the regularities of crime and suicide rates, in particular, the moral index of a society.

Fukuzawa alludes to Buckle's discovery of such "definite patterns," but he was equally struck by how these regularities made the free, independent actions of individuals appear as a preordained arrangement, whether in the case of suicide or, in his own quotidian example, the case of Tokyo sweets shops, which always seemed to prepare just the right amount of steamed rice cakes to be sold on any given day.[3] Here we see him translating statistical ideas into a local idiom, testing its application to the actual economy rather than to the political one. But he would go further, using these ideas to reason across theories of social morality and political agency. In truth, his interest in the idea of an average national spirit was less an affirmation of Buckle than a reaction against the moral passivity of his statistical fatalism and its environmental determinism, with which he reinforced the trope of Asian governments as inherently despotic. For Fukuzawa, numbers were a way to level the playing field by making visible, and thus mutable, the people's "intellectual powers," granting them political agency where entrenched moral hierarchies and value systems, whether foreign or homegrown, had judged them politically inept.[4] In all of this we are reminded that the average and its attendant epistemologies were not there for Fukuzawa's taking. He was constructing them on the fly, refracting them against his own convictions about individual difference while navigating the new spaces of comparison, as well as epistemological uncertainty, they produced. *The Values in Numbers* has itself been an argument for reading this uncertainty back into numbers while performing for the present, and in the specific context of Japanese literary studies, a similar balancing act of construction on the fly.

This performance is guided by a conviction that quantitative methods can productively refigure the relations of things, including texts, by projecting them into equivalence spaces that expand the possibilities of comparison via a deliberate reduction of dimensionality. These spaces are able to generate new theoretical fictions that, like the average in its day, contend with existing forms of knowledge. The fictions offered in this book naturally feel tenuous when compared with past fictions that are now so well recognized as to be commonsensical. This tenuousness is also a function of my own disciplinary location. We know that the average became a "recognized fact" only via long chains of institutional, infrastructural, and community investment; that it was both informed by and also expressed assumptions and values that turned its projected fictions toward various uses and abuses. Even so, it is easier to admit the beneficiary uses of these projections in medicine and politics, where holding physical and national bodies in relations of equivalence and difference can aid in the planning of treatment and policy at greater scales. In literary studies, it can still be hard to imagine numbers as doing anything but erasing the absolute particularity and variability of aesthetic meaning. Critics remain leery of the supposed fictions they offer because the disciplinary habit has been to privilege the fictions (and values) that come from reading each and every work, of knowing firsthand the particular surfaces and symptoms of each textual body. This is the kind of knowledge our disciplinary art values most.

There are many historical and theoretical reasons for a heightened suspicion of numbers. One is that our disciplinary art, as Karatani Kōjin has argued via Kant, relies at its root on the ability to recognize and judge objects by taste (pleasant or unpleasant), which typically means also "bracketing" out nonaesthetic modes of recognition, namely, the scientific (true or false) and the ethical (good or bad). Numbers, often seen to be aligned with the scientific outlook, are also bracketed out for this reason. The result is that just as "it is not recommended that a surgeon see his patient aesthetically or ethically while diagnosing or operating," as Karatani puts it, it is not recommended that a critic see texts scientifically, which has meant numerically.[5] As the French medical debates show, however, the recommendation has not always held for surgeons. Neither has it always held for literary critics, as illustrated by the intellectual genealogy traced in chapter 1. The disciplinary habits of mind that decide what to bracket, and how, are deeply historical and subject to ongoing perturbation. Nevertheless, they have consistently fallen into distinct ruts that make it easy to forget that no one bracket need be mistaken for reality itself, or that "bracketing other domains is not the same as eradicating them." Kant insisted that "we bracket and unbracket flexibly, whenever required."[6]

I have sought such flexibility in this book by chipping away at a view of numbers as the exclusive property of the scientific domain. I have tried decoupling numbers from an association with objective certainty or positivist truth by showing how open they have been to interpretation, contestation, and competing value systems; and how open they are, in their application, to users' subjective choices and judgments. Such decoupling makes it easier to appreciate their portability across scientific, aesthetic, and ethical domains, capable of fixing *and* loosening habits of mind that bracket one from another. This capacity stems in part from the way they pull many disparate objects into relations of equivalence and difference that can then be juxtaposed with relations established by other means. This need not be done in the name of a singular scientific certainty, or in a singular way, but with the intent of playing different, even incommensurable, forms of certainty and judgment off each other.

Even allowing for this flexibility and playfulness, there is still no avoiding the fact that the equivalence spaces numbers construct are heavily constrained. They are constrained by what it is possible to represent and model of literary and linguistic phenomena quantitatively; and by technical asymmetries that limit what objects can be brought into these spaces, thus reinforcing cultural hierarchies by reproducing asymmetries of knowledge that leave large swathes of the historical record invisible. They are constrained by cultural, historical, and linguistic differences that resist any reduction to equivalence, however approximate or provisional. Finally, the spaces are constrained by the disciplinary and institutional settings that produce and consecrate methods for creating them. When these methods are borrowed and adapted to literary or cultural objects, we cannot ignore the "recognized facts" built around them by existing communities of scholars (e.g., statisticians). Knowing that communities sustain these facts, however, and that their terms are perpetually renegotiated (see recent debates over p-values in the social sciences), leaves the door open to others to participate in these negotiations or even to reconstruct the facts for their own communities of practice. Johanna Drucker, for instance, has argued for the reinvention of scientific visualization practices in ways that align with the emphasis on individual variation and irreducibility in humanities disciplines.[7] Yet complete reinvention comes with its own costs if it cuts off the possibility of shared knowledge systems. The more modest proposal of *The Values in Numbers* is that we take established and emergent practices in computer science, linguistics, and sociology and put them in dialogue with practices of knowledge making in literary study, both to qualify their "facts" about literary language and textual meaning and to modify their practices for our own disciplinary ends.

Owing to this dialogic intent, the equivalence spaces I have erected and torn apart in this book are hybrid in nature. They straddle and mediate between different disciplinary practices of knowledge construction, but are also works in progress that have to be adjusted and tuned to the factors that constrain their application to literary study. The chapters have progressed in a way that foregrounds the provisional and flexible quality of these spaces, using them to slide across different scales of analysis (corpus, genre, paragraph, passage) while making clear at each step the assumptions and interpretive choices informing their construction. Each shift in scale brought a corresponding shift in the literary phenomena the spaces address: from the representativeness of individual works in national canons to stylistic repetition in dozens of works; from intertextual influence across international borders to the global circulation of racial discourse. Each space, like the average, supports theoretical fictions necessarily grounded in existing theories, models, and histories of the phenomena they address. Grounded, that is, in disciplinarily familiar ways of relating individual objects to one another and to their contexts. Each space has been useful to the extent it offered an alternate vantage point from which to reflect on other fictions and the values informing them. They suggest alternate lines of differentiation and distinction by holding objects together in spaces of equivalence that numbers alone have the capacity to construct. Not as a replacement for fictions arrived at by other means, but as supplementary evidence that, true to its hybrid and ad hoc nature, can be openly interrogated, dismantled, or invested in as communities of interpretation see fit. Facts, as it were, in the making.

As facts so obviously in process, they are subject to intensified claims and counterclaims about their utility. They have also had less time to benefit from intellectual and infrastructural investment by the literary studies community, especially within the specific subfield of modern Japanese literature.[8] Nonetheless, I have argued throughout the book that these "facts" can add to our understanding of topics of longstanding concern to scholars in this field. Much ink has already been spilled on modern canon formation and the I-novel, on the translation of modernist form and the representation of racial difference under empire. I chose these subjects in part for their familiarity; it is easier to make the case for numbers when they offer new perspectives on what we already thought we knew. Even when they only validate prior knowledge, they do so in ways that potentially expand our capacity to generalize this knowledge to noncanonical or less obvious cases. Naturally, the value of numbers for reading Japanese literature will become easier to argue for the more they are able to contribute to the topics and texts that presently animate research in the field. That said, we should not too hastily move past the problems and questions to which scholars have repeatedly returned, and whose surfaces have only been scratched by the case studies in this book. For one, these studies explore problems and methods that have gained currency with scholars of other literatures who are using computational methods. Spending more time with them can expand the range of perspectives on these problems and thus help restore to "distant reading" some of its original comparative thrust. Second, the case studies add up to a larger story that not only gains from such comparative study but is enfolded in anxieties about individual difference and representation, and in defenses of aesthetic value, that the use of numbers has long provoked.

This story, put simply, is about practices of writing the self and other(s) under shifting conditions of imperial and colonial power. A story about how such practices evolve and interact across time and space, and about their uneven distribution across lines of racial, ethnic, gender, class, and aesthetic difference. It is an old story, to be sure, but one not yet told through the kinds of frames computation affords. It is also a global story to the extent that how subjects narrate the self and others can coalesce into patterns that circulate across networks of economic, social, and cultural power. Patterns of psychological and mental representation, for instance, as with the I-novel and stream-of-consciousness writing I analyzed in chapters 3 and 4. These were patterns formed in the crucible of Japanese writers' confrontation with foreign models and practices of self-expression—a confrontation that was as much about adapting the models to local constraints as securing access to a cosmopolitan republic of letters wherein self-contemplation and self-disintegration were valued as indexes of aesthetic achievement. Chapter 5 turned to patterns of an inverse sort, namely, patterns of racially and ethnically biased language. There I analyzed practices of racial Othering homegrown in the soils of Japanese empire yet also seeded by tropes as natural to readers of pulp adventure fiction in the United States as in Japan. On the one hand, then, patterns of individuation and subtle differentiation; on the other, patterns of classification and gross generalization.

Literary and cultural historians have written about these patterns as both dialectically intertwined and simultaneously shaped by material conditions. They are coconstituted even as the character of their relation fluctuates with shifts in the structures of power. From the side of empire, Jed Esty's study of late English modernism speaks to the complex historical dynamics that can be read into representations of colonizing subjects. Following Adorno, Esty considers modernist representations of the subject as always "shaped by (not detached from) specific and objective social conditions," tracing how the expansion and contraction of British empire in the prewar period left its mark on these representations "as visible and narrative data but [also] as unexpected formal encryptments and thematic outcroppings in ostensibly domestic texts."[9] For him, representations of consciousness under high modernism are best understood as embedded in the centers of metropolitan power that underwrote them, not a mere "cosmopolitan indulgence," as Lukacs once put it. If the writers behind these representations felt their tortured consciences to be an effect of the "universal" modern condition, this sense of universality necessarily depended on "the silence of the non-Western world." They were "modern" subjects whose experiences of mental anguish and fragmentation were predicated on the denial of such experiences to their non-Western and nonmodern counterparts. Indeed, they often looked to these counterparts as salve for their modern condition, offered up to them as the "expropriated shards of those putatively more complete, more tribal, or more traditional societies overseas."[10]

This sense of completeness depended on the patterns of classification and caricature that allowed societies and peoples to be summed up as such, or what Franz Fanon described as the "unreflected imposition of a culture." Writing from the position of the colonized, Fanon's work crystallizes the degree to which this imposition could be felt as a suffocating blanket of words. It was "a constellation of postulates, a series of propositions that slowly and subtly—with the help of books, newspapers, schools and their texts, advertisements, films, radio—work their way into one's mind and shape one's view of the world of the group to which one belongs."[11] Try as he might to fashion a sense of his own self as a corporeal, experiencing subject, he confronts an image of his own body already woven "by the other, the white man . . . out of a thousand details, anecdotes, stories."[12] These stories add up to a collective unconscious that imposes on his black body an imagined reality not felt as his own—one that resists and refuses any empirical evidence to the contrary. Here Fanon uses the example of the representation of Black men as sexually potent beings, phallic stand-ins, who incite horror or lust in White women. "Now, what is the truth? The average length of the penis among the black men of Africa, Dr. Palès says, rarely exceeds 120 millimeters (4.6244 inches). Testut, in his *Traité d'anatomie humaine*, offers the same figure for the European. But these are facts that persuade no one."[13] This appeal to numerical precision, and specifically the theoretical fiction of the average, as a counter to the fictions that prop up racial hierarchies holds echoes of Fukuzawa. Fanon's larger point, however, is that the weight of cultural impositions by those in power deny his own body access, at least in their eyes, to the representations of consciousness that depend on his body *being* a certain way.

Esty and Fanon's arguments epitomize how patterns of individuation and generalization can be read as dialogically intertwined, their interaction determined by broader historical and social dynamics with stark implications for individual psyches. These readings may feel like common knowledge, but I invoke them to consider the theoretical implications of rereading at the scales afforded by computational methods. Fanon himself wonders what it would mean to tackle these patterns at scale, musing at one point that "it would be astonishing, if the trouble were taken to bring them all together, to see the vast number of expressions that make the black man the equivalent of sin."[14] Would it not be astonishing if we also bothered to assemble all the expressions that make certain representations of consciousness the equivalent of subjectivity for a given time and place, or for a specific group of people? What can we gain by confronting their sheer empirical weight? Is it worth the trouble?

The Values in Numbers has proposed several ways to model expressions of individuation and generalization, although they are only a first step toward capturing all the variation we know to exist in them. Insufficient too are the samples on which this modeling relies. Yet if we allow that, over time, these models will come to represent literary phenomena in increasingly complex and nuanced ways, and that digital collections will capture ever-greater cross sections of the print archive, then one path down which these facts in the making lead is further comparative study of the distribution of these patterns over time, place, genre, and communities of writers. This could help in theorizing their rise and fall with imperial expansion and contraction; their circulation in and between the regions deterritorialized and reterritorialized in this process; even their further differentiation within local contexts. Such explorations could help identify variations in who and how these patterns subjugate, and in who is and isn't granted the privilege of becoming subjects through them. Computation, by making it easier to hold the overwhelming evidence of cultural impositions together, can help refine or generate theories of how they operate across disparate contexts. In making these impositions visible at scale, it can also expose the imaginations they underwrite to enhanced scrutiny, potentially helping to loosen their grip on the realities of those subjected to them.

In the case of Japan, the global comparative dimension of computational approaches has added significance because the country's modern writers oscillated between the subject positions of colonized and colonizer. While writing through cultural impositions woven from thousands of details told by the White man, they also wove their own suffocating tapestries. At once the focus of a racializing, "aestheticentrist" gaze, they also turned it on others, silencing the voices of non-Japanese and internal peripheral communities to create idealized screens on which their fractured modern selves could be projected. Karatani describes this gaze as applied to Japanese culture by Western intellectuals as showing passionate love and respect while bracketing out "the concerns of pedestrian Japanese who live their real lives and struggle with intellectual and ethical problems inherent in modernity." The gaze designates its objects as "intellectually and ethically inferior" while aesthetically worshiping this inferior other, deceiving the viewing subject into a false conceit that they treat these others more than equally.[15] It is the same gaze that Japanese writers turned on their colonial subjects, or increasingly on themselves as the politics of fascism made it expedient to seek cultural completeness and unity internally, much as the English turned inward with the contraction of empire in the 1930s and then reinscribed "universal status into the particularist language of home anthropology."[16] If the interplay of these dual subject positions is well known for individual writers, or even at the scale of groups of writers organized by social location, the case studies in this book suggest the possibility of following this interplay at the scale of hundreds of writers across decades of literary output. The possibility, that is, of reading large-scale patterns of literary individuation and generalization against the rise and fall of these patterns elsewhere, but also the possibility of reading them doubly—as a response to cultural impositions that ignored the pedestrian mental and psychological concerns of Japanese and yet also built over the silence of others to make these concerns feel sufficiently universal, modern, and cosmopolitan.

The ability to identify and read these patterns will only ever be as good as the models and corpora through which they become legible. Their resolution will always seem too low, too lossy, as compared with that produced by practices of reading that do not obviously sacrifice individual difference and variation for the equivalence spaces of computation. The aim of these models and their constructed spaces, however, is not to project a complete, singular picture of the phenomena under analysis. Their explanatory power comes from iterative adjustment of their parameters and assumptions, through their application to different samples, a dismantling of their frames, and by juxtaposition with other forms of judgment and scales of explanation. But also, and here is where the possibilities of comparative work become all the more critical, through their translation and movement between historical and cultural contexts. To the extent that literary studies becomes increasingly open to reading with numbers, it is imperative that the facts in the making proposed in one cultural context (e.g., nineteenth-century English literature) not be allowed to harden too quickly into facts generalizable to all.

If distant reading's original comparative thrust intended to secure a more comprehensive, totalizing view, this thrust can be productively redirected toward identifying how models developed in one context can and cannot be translated into others. Searching for patterns of individuation and generalization as they manifest under colonial power structures should be as much about identifying points of overlap and repetition as about finding gaps and differences revealed through the failure to move models from one context to another, or through the different interpretations required by their projected equivalence spaces. These spaces are meaningful only in relation to other spaces and only when resituated in the particulars they necessarily abstract away. Indeed, the case studies in this book have been an argument for the importance of working *in-between* cultural contexts as a way to develop critical literacy of computational methods. No matter how simplistic or obvious the choices and calculations behind the methods, we can more easily recognize the values invested in them when we see what does and does not move with them as they travel. The average, to return to where we began, is as much a story about its shared use by French physicians in the 1830s, Buckle in the 1850s, and Fukuzawa in the 1870s as it is a story about the divergent values they all derived from the very same calculation.

Similarly, the latest revolutions in quantitative method are receptacles into which today's literary "numerists" pour divergent values while also sharing a sense of promise, circumspect as it may be, in the power of these methods to generate new knowledge. This book is no exception. The techno-utopian undertone found in the experiments of these numerists surely feeds off of the widespread exuberance surrounding statistical tools (e.g., machine learning) that, much like the average in its heyday, have seized the imagination of so many sectors of society. Then as now, we live in a moment when established forms of knowledge and judgment are rendered uncertain by newer information ecologies and an onslaught of facts in the making promising to bring these ecologies into sharper focus. To participate in the exuberance of this moment, even at a critical distance, may seem terribly misguided with the benefit of historical hindsight. Just as the average and its statistical kin ultimately served to justify violent, racist projects (e.g., eugenics), scholars have amassed an overwhelming body of evidence to show how the tools and technical systems being built in the name of "artificial intelligence" reinforce and amplify existing social inequities and biases at massive scales, creating what Ruha Benjamin has called the "New Jim Code."[17] To engage with these newest engines of difference making can seem a patently heretical venture for literary critics trained to expose and dismantle knowledge structures that reinforce political, economic, and social hierarchy through essentialization and reduction of individuals.

While preserving this necessary skepticism, in *The Values in Numbers* I have sought to redirect its critical force by relativizing the worldview that makes it seem only too obvious. A worldview in which numbers are internal to the scientific and social abuses to which they are put, and thus external to how difference is understood and figured in aesthetic or humanistic terms (i.e., not quantitatively). This view is sustained by an epistemological bracketing that, on the one hand, makes it hard to decouple numerical methods from the values invested in them, closing off the possibility of altering these values by recognizing the hardened "facts" they support as facts in the making. On the other hand, this bracketing reinforces the exceptional nature of the aesthetic view as wholly distinct from, and incapable of engaging, the scientific outlook. It is an exceptionalism amplified in no small part by the legacy of poststructuralism, or what Hayden White called the Absurdist school of criticism, which takes "delight in revealing that the science of the human . . . is actually impossible, because of the nature of the preferred object of that science, i.e., language, and the nature of the technique alone capable of analyzing that object, *bricolage*, which is less interested in coherency and logical consistency (the attributes of any science known to history) than improvisation and attention to the function of the phenomenon in its specific spatio-temporal-cultural locale."[18] In this impossible science, the meaning of linguistic utterances derives from systems of signs that vary with locale, no single meaning having any more objective truth content than any other. All expression is equally figurative in the sense that it can never be precisely literal and is thus forever subject to the "freeplay" of signifying differences that can be read into it.[19] From this vantage, numerically figured differences, relying on the projected equivalence of things and their locales, can only freeze such play in its tracks.

If literary criticism has long since descended from its poststructuralist heights, White's characterization captures the extreme edges of an "aestheticentrist" bracketing that still informs the field's habits of mind. This book is born of such habits even as it asks readers to consider the costs of clinging to them at the exclusion of others or treating them as the sole monopoly of the aesthetic domain. What is sacrificed when we refuse to unbracket and bracket more flexibly, or fail to recognize that the antinumerical attitudes that seem so obvious to an aestheticentrist gaze are created in its own negative self-image? What avenues of interpretation and aesthetic thought are left unexplored when we relegate numbers to pedestrian concerns that supposedly lie outside the elevated domain of art and literature, or the sophisticated and nuanced ways that we interpret these objects? We have seen how writers and critics over the last century have tried to open up such avenues when revolutions in numerical method and information promised alternatives to established habits of mind in the aesthetic domain. As literary scholars face our own present-day revolutions, it is imperative that we do not respond by doubling down on one kind of intellectual bracketing over another. This not only forecloses on opportunities for cross-pollination between communities of knowledge formation, as if conceptual traffic between them were impossible, it also limits the possibilities for each to relativize the bracketed perspectives of others. Even more troubling, it unnecessarily excludes us from the negotiations that are currently constructing and defining the theoretical fictions (and soon to be "facts") of our global information age. Only by inserting ourselves into these negotiations can we have a hand in reimagining these fictions from the ground up and rewriting, as Benjamin puts it, their "default settings."[20]

As these fictions come to further organize our access to the literary past through digital archives and search engines, or mediate the production and reception of cultural material through algorithmic recommendations; as they become the academy's reigning scientific lingua franca through newly consolidated data science programs and I-schools, it is in our interest to engage these fictions rather than bracket them out. Not to blindly adopt them, or substitute them for our own established theoretical fictions, but to imagine for ourselves a more proactive role in their construction. In a moment when there is still indeterminacy around them, and they have yet to harden into cold fact, we should strive to inhabit multiple fictions so that contrasting figurations of difference and variation might flow between them. But also so that we might be in a position to critically evaluate the assumptions baked into numerical figuration and inject or counter with assumptions shaped by the compulsion to read and evaluate difference across each and every textual body. What would it mean, to recall earlier moments of indeterminacy, to inhabit both sides of the French medical debates? Or, like Fukuzawa, to internalize them, just as he imagined the average as tool for reading the collective national spirit while insisting that individual minds and lives were, "like a phantom or a demon," too changeable to be "subject to conceptualization or quantification."[21] Would we find in this dual frame of mind an openness to thinking about difference and variation across knowledge domains at a time when their boundaries seem newly permeable? A two-way mirror, perhaps, reflecting back our own epistemological phantoms even as it allows us to peer in and haunt those on the other side.

APPENDIX

TABLE A2.1

The complete list of 139 representative works of modern Japanese literature compiled by the National Japanese Language Research Institute in 1980. Rank corresponds to the number of members on the selection committee who voted for that work. Works are ordered by rank and then publication date. Members of the ten-person committee were told to select one hundred works from a larger list of 1,506. For details, see "Yōrei saishū no tame no shuyō bungaku sakuhin mokuroku," ed. Kokugo Jiten Henshū Junbishitsu (Kokuritsu Kokugo Kenkyūjo, 1980).

Title	Author	Publication Date	Rank
或る女	有島武郎	1911–1913	10
無限抱擁	滝井孝作	1921–1924	10
暗夜行路	志賀直哉	1921–1939	10
墨東綺譚	永井荷風	1937	10
浮雲	二葉亭四迷	1887–1889	9
五重塔	幸田露伴	1891–1892	9
たけくらべ	樋口一葉	1895–1896	9
あらくれ	徳田秋声	1915	9
腕くらべ	永井荷風	1916	9
田園の憂鬱	佐藤春夫	1918	9

(*continued*)

Title	Author	Publication Date	Rank
檸檬	梶井基次郎	1925	9
蟹工船	小林多喜二	1929	9
舞姫	森鷗外	1890	8
武蔵野	国木田独歩	1898	8
城の崎にて	志賀直哉	1917	8
蔵の中	宇野浩二	1919	8
雪国	川端康成	1935–1947	8
野火	大岡昇平	1951	8
山の音	川端康成	1954	8
金閣寺	三島由起夫	1956	8
今戸心中	広津柳浪	1896	7
思出の記	徳冨蘆花	1900–1901	7
吾輩は猫である	夏目漱石	1905–1906	7
何処へ	正宗白鳥	1908	7
黒髪	近松秋江	1922	7
伸子	宮本百合子	1924–1926	7
伊豆の踊り子	川端康成	1926	7
海に生くる人々	葉山嘉樹	1926	7
善心悪心	里見淳	1926	7
放浪記	林芙美子	1928–1948	7
縮図	徳田秋声	1939	7
李陵	中島敦	1943	7
聖ヨハネ病院にて	上林暁	1946	7
桜島	梅崎春生	1946	7
俘虜記	大岡昇平	1948	7
虫のいろいろ	尾崎一雄	1948	7
死者の奢り	大江健三郎	1957	7
当世書生気質	坪内逍遙	1885–1886	6
にごりえ	樋口一葉	1895	6
金色夜叉	尾崎紅葉	1897–1899	6
高野聖	泉鏡花	1900	6
野菊の墓	伊藤左千夫	1906	6
破壊	島崎藤村	1906	6
蒲団	田山花袋	1907	6
田舎教師	田山花袋	1909	6
阿部一族	森鷗外	1913	6
鱧の皮	上司小剣	1914	6
明暗	夏目漱石	1916	6
性に眼覚める頃	室生犀星	1919	6
友情	武者小路実篤	1919	6
波	山本有三	1928	6
蓼喰ふ虫	谷崎潤一郎	1928–1929	6
機械	横光利一	1930	6

Title	Author	Publication Date	Rank
春琴抄	谷崎潤一郎	1933	6
蒼氓	石川達三	1935	6
故旧忘れ得べき	高見順	1935–1936	6
普賢	石川淳	1936	6
老妓抄	岡本かの子	1937	6
歌のわかれ	中野重治	1939	6
細雪	谷崎潤一郎	1943–1948	6
白痴	坂口安吾	1946	6
暗い絵	野間宏	1946	6
牡丹燈籠	三遊亭円朝	1884	5
あひびき	二葉亭四迷	1888	5
かくれんぼ	斎藤緑雨	1891	5
火の柱	木下尚江	1904	5
坊ちゃん	夏目漱石	1906	5
婦系図	泉鏡花	1907	5
三四郎	夏目漱石	1908	5
新世帯	徳田秋声	1908	5
それから	夏目漱石	1909	5
すみだ川	永井荷風	1909	5
家	島崎藤村	1910–1911	5
こゝろ	夏目漱石	1914	5
道草	夏目漱石	1915	5
和解	志賀直哉	1917	5
子をつれて	葛西善蔵	1918	5
山椒魚	井伏鱒二	1923	5
河童	芥川龍之介	1927	5
太陽のない街	徳永直	1929	5
夜明け前	島崎藤村	1929–1935	5
粘	丹羽文雄	1932	5
人生劇場	尾崎士郎	1933	5
晩年	太宰治	1933–1936	5
若い人	石坂洋次郎	1933–1937	5
くれなゐ	佐多稲子	1936	5
風立ちぬ	堀辰雄	1936–1938	5
山月記	中島敦	1942	5
焼跡のイエス	石川淳	1946	5
夏の花	原民喜	1947	5
人間失格	太宰治	1948	5
猟銃	井上靖	1949	5
朝霧	永井龍男	1949	5
真空地帯	野間宏	1952	5
楢山節考	深沢七郎	1956	5
佳人之奇遇	東海散士	1885–1897	4

(*continued*)

Title	Author	Publication Date	Rank
風流仏	幸田露伴	1889	4
多情多恨	尾崎紅葉	1896	4
牛肉と馬鈴薯	国木田独歩	1901	4
千鳥	鈴木三重吉	1906	4
俳諧師	高浜虚子	1908	4
耽溺	岩野泡鳴	1909	4
微光	正宗白鳥	1910	4
歌行燈	泉鏡花	1910	4
土	長塚節	1910	4
お目出たき人	武者小路実篤	1911	4
雁	森鷗外	1911–1913	4
銀の匙	中勘助	1913–1915	4
毒薬を飲む女	岩野泡鳴	1914	4
羅生門	芥川龍之介	1915	4
末枯	久保田万太郎	1917	4
カインの末裔	有島武郎	1917	4
多情仏心	里見淳	1922-1923	4
痴人の愛	谷崎潤一郎	1924	4
竹沢先生と云ふ人	長与善郎	1925	4
嵐	島崎藤村	1926	4
春は馬車に乗って	横光利一	1926	4
玄鶴山房	芥川龍之介	1927	4
渦巻ける烏の群	黒島伝治	1927	4
業苦	嘉村礒多	1928	4
聖家族	堀辰雄	1930	4
途上	嘉村礒多	1932	4
美しい村	堀辰雄	1933	4
暢気眼鏡	尾崎一雄	1933	4
紋章	横光利一	1934	4
仮装人物	徳田秋声	1935	4
厚物咲	中山義秀	1938	4
麦と兵隊	火野葦平	1938	4
死者の書	折口信夫	1939	4
連環記	幸田露伴	1940	4
夫婦善哉	織田作之助	1940	4
悉皆屋康吉	舟橋聖一	1945	4
かういふ女	平林たい子	1946	4
晩菊	林芙美子	1948	4
少将滋幹の母	谷崎潤一郎	1949–1950	4
遙拝隊長	井伏鱒二	1950	4
武蔵野夫人	大岡昇平	1950	4
異形の者	武田泰淳	1950	4
驟雨	吉行淳之介	1954	4

TABLE A5.1

This table provides a list of the individual words that compose each semantic cluster in figure 5.4 (representation of racial others versus Japanese in nonfiction corpus). Words correspond to their lemmatized, Unidic tokenized representation, which may be different from their representation in the original texts and will sometimes include a translation of the word (e.g., アメリカ-America). Note that lists may be a combination of several smaller clusters, and that each word contributes differently to the "strength" of a cluster's association with a racial identifier. For details, see the summary files in the "results_kindai_bootstrap" folder, which can be found in the chapter 5 folder in the code and data repository. The cluster labels are intended to capture the majority of semantically similar words in the cluster.

Cluster Label	Cluster Words
Administration/Governance	公, 主人, 内閣, 大臣, 辞職, 次官, 県, 府, 内務, 知事, 支那, マンシュウ, 事変, トウア, 日支, 勃発, 省, 文部, 外務, 大蔵, 統治, 主権, 委任, 地方
Capital/Financial Transactions	銀行, 金融, 資金, 公債, 預金, 投資, 証券, 利子, 支払い, 金額, 総額, 貸し付け, 手形, 債務, 償還, 現金
Civilizational Discourse	文明, 史, 近世, ギリシャ, 古代, 中世, 人類, 動物, 進化, 生物, ダーウィン
Colonies	朝鮮, タイワン, 地, 植民
Customs/Daily Life	習慣, 風俗, 食事, 馳走, 荷物, 寝る, 眠る, 床, 起きる, 寝
Facial Features	目, 顔, 笑う, 様子, じっと, 見詰める, 表情, 唇, 微笑, 顔色, 眉, 瞳, 顔付き
Family	彼女, 父, 子供, 母, 妻, 娘, 兄, 伯父, 姉, 妹, 母親, 伯母, 嫁, 息子, 両親, 父親
Habitation	住む, 村, 部落, 小屋
Measurement	尺, 幅, 面積, 町歩, 耕地, 図, 巻, ページ, 版, 参照, 判
Military	軍, 兵, 軍隊, 兵力, 将校, 部隊, 武装, 撤退, 軍事, 防衛, 基地, 戦略, 空軍
Movement	歩く, 遊ぶ, 散歩, 行, 上る, 下る, 東, 西, 北, 南
Nature/Landscape	火, 江, 山, 丘, 島, 付近, 海岸, 川, 湖, 谷, 海, 港, 沿岸, 湾, 雨, 降る, 雪, 森, 石, 水, 森林
Photograph	写真
Poetry	詩, 句
Race	人種
Religion/Disciple	教, 徒
Women/Girls	女, 少年, 少女
Time	明日, 昨日, 今夜, 午後, 午前, 年, 日, 月, 翌, 夜, 時, 頃, 際
Writing	文字

TABLE A5.2

Lists of words composing the semantic clusters in figure 5.5 (representation of Japanese versus racial others in nonfiction corpus).

Cluster Label	Cluster Words
Art/Literature	芸術, 美術, 絵画, 彫刻, 展覧, 思想, 文学, 小説, 現代, 作品, 批評, 作家, 哲学, 文芸, 文壇
Democratic Governance	政治, 政党, 議会, 民主, 憲法, 憲政, 立憲, 共和, 君主, 議院, 政体, 党, 派, 保守, 反動, 官僚, 権力, 藩閥, 会, 会議, 委員, 決議, 大会, 総会, 理事, 加盟, 開催, 権利, 原則, 基本, 保障, 人権
Economic Relations	経済, 政策, 国際, 貿易, 財政, 国内, 金融, 為替, 通貨, 対外, 対支, 対米, 資本, 銀行, 産業, 統制, 市場, 金融, 為替, 資金, 企業, 恐慌, 信用, 財界, 投資, 対外, インフレ, 正貨
Everyday Life	生活, 日常
International Relations	経済, 国家, 建設, 体制, 軍事, 戦時, 国防, 強化, 高度, 要請, 平和, 条約, 協定, 保障, 両国, 日米, 講和, 締結, 通商, 安保, 協約, 国交, 条項, 協商, 調印, 貿易, 締結, 通商
Journalism	新聞, 記者, 時事, 読み売り
Modernity/Tradition	的, 化, 現代, 近代, 伝統, 高度, 中世, 社会, 思想, 文学, 古典
Personal Pronouns	私, です, さん, ね, 僕, 貴方, わ, 御前, 為さる, 本当, 下さる, いらっしゃる, 急度, 仰る, 我が, 我, 自分, 彼女, 自身, 俺, 御, って, 父, 母, まあ, 奥, 兄, いらっしゃる, 伯父, 姉, 仰る, 旦那, ええ, あんな, 伯母, 婆, 爺
Political Ideology	ソ連, 共産, 民主, ソビエト, スターリン, レーニン, 主義, 党, ソ連, 共産, 批判, 中国, ハンガリー, 党員, ハンガリアン, 中共, 左翼, ファシズム, 右翼, 対立, 陣営, 自由, 民主, 権利, 言論, 平等
Problem Resolution	問題, 提起, 解決, 重大, 関連, 課題, 当面, 論議, 指導, 努力, 協力, 援助, 参加, 支持, 強化, 協同, 要請, 共存, 考え, 意見, 主張, 立場, 理論, 批判, 解釈, 本質, 見解, 結論, 的, 政策, 行動, 具体, 積極, 合理, 基本, 徹底, 消極, 自主, 全面, 自発
Sciences	研究, 学, 科学, 化学, 応用, 生物, 数学, 生理
Speech/Cognition	精神, 意識, 認識, 自覚, 反省, 言う, 思う, 考える, 見る, 考え, 理解, 判断, 了解, 信頼, 把握, 納得, どう, 知る, 分かる, 知れる, はっきり
Spirituality/Ethics	思想, 宗教, 道徳, 観念, 哲学, 倫理, 道義, 精神, 倫理, 確信, 信念, 決意
State/Citizenry	国民, 国家, 人民, 民衆, 大衆, 国, 我が, 我
Taste	そう, 良い, 悪い, 宜しい, 旨い, 憎い, 不味い
Theoretical Abstraction	的, 段階, 過程, 本質, 形態, 必然, 理念, 普遍, 意味, 現実, 理論, 根本, 内容, 性質, 性格, 意義, 具体, 形式, 表現, 基本, 過程, 見解, 自体, 客観, 論理, 本来, 特徴, 原理, 抽象, 概念, 把握, 限界, 主体, イデオロギー, 独自, 特質, 史的, 観点, 内面, 近代, 積極, 要素, 単なる, 基礎, 徹底, 根底, 価値, 認識, 課題

TABLE A5.3

Lists of words composing the semantic clusters in figure 5.9 (representation of Japanese versus racial Others in fiction corpus).

Cluster Label	Cluster Words
Foreign Countries	日本, アメリカ-America, ドイツ-Duits, インド-India, 英国, イギリス-Inglez, 支那, フランス-France, 外国, ロシア-Rossiya
Function Words	だ, が, です, よ, ね, ます, 居る
Honorific Speech	貴方, 為さる, 申す, 存ずる, 仰る, 申し上げる, いいえ
Hotel/Lodging	ホテル-hotel, パリ-Paris, 旅館, アパート-apartment
Major Cities	ホテル-hotel, パリ-Paris, フランス-France, ロンドン-London, トウキョウ, ヨコハマ
Maritime	船, 海, 港, 沖, 小船, 隻, 汽船
Nationalities	日本人, 外国人, 西洋人, 中国人
People/Plural	達, 皆, 人, 男
Personal Pronouns	我, 我が, 私, 僕, 貴方, 君
Speech Markers	か, よ, ね, な, い, ええ, ぜ, えっ, へえ, いいえ, え, かしら
Thing (*koto*, *mono*)	事, 物
Year/Years	年, 箇月, 年間

TABLE A5.4

Lists of words composing the semantic clusters in figure 5.10 (representation of racial Others versus Japanese in fiction corpus). For details, see the summary files in the "results_fic_bootstrap" folder, which can be found in the chapter 5 folder in the code and data repository.

Cluster Label	Cluster Words
Architectural Elements	窓, 壁, ガラス-glass, 塗る, 塗り, 壁, 天井, 柱, 板, 建物, 煉瓦
Beauty/Cute	美しい, 可愛い, 可愛らしい
Bodily Movement	逃げる, 逃げ出す, 追い掛ける, 倒れる, 転がる, よろよろ, 飛び出す, 逃げ込む
Buying/Selling	買う, 売る, 買い
Clothing	着る, 服, 靴, 履く, 帽子, 袴, 洋服, 外套, 帽, シャツ-shirt, 上着, ズボン-jupon, 着物, 脱ぐ, 羽織, 寝巻き, 上着, 背広
Doll	人形
Elegance/Taste	風情
Elephant	象
Facial Features	顔, 瞳, 横顔, 表情, 顔付き, 鼻, 眉, 髭
Family Relations	女, 娘, 女房, 父親, 息子, 子, 親, 弟
Habitation	小屋, 部落
Knives/Weaponry	刀, 剣, 槍, 太刀, 刃, 武器, 矢, 弓, 射る
Light/Shine	光, 光る, 輝く, ちらちら, きらきら
Low Class	下種, 乞食, 卑しい
Mainland (*naichi*)	内地
Maritime	船, 沖, 小船, 艘, 隻, 港, 汽船
Military/Conflict	兵, 軍, 隊, 軍, 敵, 戦, 戦う, 戦い
Nature/Landscape	島, 根, 根元, 木, 栗, 川, 川原, 堤, 森, 林, 木立ち, 茂み, 葉, 枝, 梢, 幹, 鳥, 烏, 羽, 小鳥, 雀, 道, 麓, 海岸, 岬
Personal Pronouns	彼, 自分, 彼女, 己, 汝, 俺, 奴, ぜ, 彼奴, やがる, 此奴, 貴様, 其奴, 旦那, わっし, てまえ
Primate	猿
School/Education	生徒, 教師, 教員, 青年, 学生, 生, 学校, 大学, 高等
Song/Sing	歌, 歌う
Streets/Boulevards	街, ギンザ, 大通り
Time	日, 夜, 朝, 晩, 昨夜, 今夜, 夕方, 翌日
Voice/Sound/Cry	声, 悲鳴, わっ, 叫び声, 音, 聞こえる, 響く, 鳴る, 悲鳴, 喚く, わあ, どっと
Woman/Youth	女, 若い, 乙女

ACKNOWLEDGMENTS

I began writing this book in a time of national political upheaval, when many of the values and institutions central to democratic civil society were coming unraveled. I finished it during an even more unsettling time, as the very fabric of society was coming unglued in the face of a global pandemic. Needless to say, it has been an interesting few years in which to think about facts, truth, and the values invested in them by different communities. I am incredibly grateful to all those who have supported me in these efforts as collaborators, teachers, critics, and friends. I know this book would not have survived this tumultuous period without them.

Every book takes a village, but this one had me knocking on more doors and enlisting the aid of more neighbors than I could have imagined at the outset. Close to home at the University of Chicago, I was lucky to begin my journey with long-time collaborator Richard Jean So, whose endless energy kept me going in the early days of learning how to program and to think with numbers. I also learned a lot about writing and argument from our collaborative projects, and the ideas in this book owe much to the long hours spent discussing those projects. James Evans and his Knowledge Lab kept the fires of this conversation burning in these years, and I am thankful to him and other lab affiliates—especially Eamon Duede, Jacob Foster, Aaron Gerow, Elizabeth Pontikes, and Misha Teplitskiy—for their ongoing institutional and intellectual support. Another important early guide and collaborator was Yuancheng Zhu, who taught me much of what I know about statistics and whose generosity is endless. His expertise and ideas are woven indelibly into the case studies in this book and the code that underlies them, and I consider him a coauthor on much of the quantitative thinking that went into the project. I'm also grateful to Peter Leonard for his early support of my computational work and for introducing me to the ins and outs of the digital humanities field as I was first finding my way through it.

Less directly involved, but no less essential to the maturation of this book, were my faculty and student colleagues at the University of Chicago. Their abiding curiosity about the work, foreign as it must have felt at times, provided invaluable moral support, and I benefited immensely from their healthy skepticism along the way. I'm especially thankful in this regard to Michael Bourdaghs, Seth Brodsky, Susan Burns, Kyeong-hee Choi, Chelsea Foxwell, Clovis Gladstone, Tim Harrison, Paola Iovene, Reginald Jackson, Patrick Jagoda, Robert Morrissey, John Muse, Haun Saussy, David Schloen, and Ayako Yoshimura. I've also been blessed with the chance to collaborate with amazing graduate and undergraduate students who have contributed to the work in ways direct and indirect, both as a sounding board for ideas and by assisting with the mundane but essential labor that determines the success of any data-driven project. Aliz Horvath, Athena Kern, David Krolikoski, Nicholas Lambrecht, Jae-Yon Lee, Helina Mazza-Hilway, Alex Murphy, Nicholas Ogonek, Simone Oliver, Sabine Schulz, and Brian White deserve special mention in this regard.

As this book led me into new fields of knowledge, it has also led me to new friends and colleagues whose paths I otherwise might not have crossed. Experimental methods, for all their fragility and uncertainty, are wonderful for lowering disciplinary fences. This project would have been impossible without the enthusiastic support of these colleagues and their informed critique. Within Japanese studies, I've had the pleasure of working with a growing network of scholars and librarians who, like myself, have been thinking about the impact of the digital on our field, including Jonathan Abel, Raja Adal, Amy Catalinac, Paula Curtis, Molly Des Jardin, Sarah Frederick, Toshie Marra, Kyoko Omori, Mark Ravina, Catherine Ryu, Keiko Yokota-Carter, and Jonathan Zwicker. I'm also grateful to Michael Emmerich, Ken Ito, Ted Mack, Ann Sherif, and Keith Vincent for their constant encouragement and support of the work over the years.

In Japan, I'm indebted to Nagasaki Kiyonori, Akikusa Shun'ichirō, and especially Ogiso Toshinobu for their ongoing intellectual support. Professor Ogiso graciously hosted me as a visiting scholar at the National Institute for Japanese Language and Linguistics (NINJAL), where he leads a project, "Construction of Diachronic Corpora and New Developments in Research on the History of Japanese," that was essential to the analysis in chapter 5. Within the broader field of East Asian studies, I've been fortunate to collaborate with a group of younger scholars who've had transformative impacts in their own fields when it comes to using computational methods. I've learned a tremendous amount from Javier Cha, Thomas Mullaney, Donald Sturgeon, Jeffrey Tharsen, and Paul Vierthaler, among many others. Anatoly Detwyler has been an especially valuable interlocutor and was instrumental in helping lay the conceptual ground for the analysis that eventually became chapter 3.

Looking even further afield, this project has grown up alongside and in dialogue with scholars at the forefront of research in cultural analytics. They have been a constant source of inspiration and a perpetual reminder of how methodologies can bring together new kinds of intellectual communities even as they sow division elsewhere. I've been lucky to be involved with the Novel TM initiative, supported by Canada's Social Sciences and Humanities Research Council, which has served as an intellectual home away from home. There are too many in this group to acknowledge individually, but all should know they are a large part of what's kept me going. I'm especially grateful to Mark Algee-Hewitt, Sarah Allison, Maria Antoniak, David Bamman, Matt Erlin, Andrew Goldstone, Ryan Heuser, Natalie Houston, Matthew Jockers, Laura McGrath, David Mimno, Laura Nelson, Andrew Piper, Teddy Roland, Tim Tangherlini, Ted Underwood, Scott Weingart, and Matt Wilkens for being such inspiring role models in the marriage of computational methods with literary and cultural analysis. I've also been fortunate to work with and learn from Katherine Bode, Jo Guldi, and Tom McEnaney, who gave invaluable feedback on the book in the manuscript stage. Finally, thank you to teachers at the University of Chicago, University of Washington, and the University of Michigan's ICPSR program, who were willing to play along with the idea of a literary scholar wanting to learn statistics, computational linguistics, and data visualization. Much of this learning would not have been possible without the support of a Mellon Foundation New Directions Fellowship and the Neubauer Collegium of Culture and Society.

Early versions of this work were presented in a variety of forums, and I benefited greatly from audience feedback I received at the University of California Berkeley, Indiana University Bloomington, University of Michigan, University of Pennsylvania's Word Lab, Bard College, Boston University, Stanford University, Columbia University, University of Pittsburgh, and Michigan State University. At the manuscript review stage, I was lucky to receive detailed and generous comments from three content reviewers and two data reviewers. I appreciate deeply the time they gave to this thankless task, and the manuscript is certainly better for their efforts. Thank you to Christine Dunbar, my editor at Columbia University Press, for taking a risk on such an unusual project and for gracefully shepherding it through the publication process. I'm also grateful to Susan Pensak, Christian Winting, and all the staff at the press and at KnowledgeWorks Global Ltd., including Ben Kolstad.

Some material in chapter 3 previously appeared in the *Journal of Cultural Analytics* (May 2018) as "Self-Repetition and East Asian Literary Modernity, 1900–1930," coauthored with Anatoly Detwyler and Yuancheng Zhu. Some material in chapter 4 appeared in the *Modern Language Quarterly* (September 2016) as "Turbulent Flow: A Computational Model of World Literature," coauthored with Richard Jean So.

It goes without saying that those closest to home are ultimately the ones without whom a village remains lifeless. To the friends and family in the United States and Japan who sustained me throughout, I can't thank you enough, especially Allison Alexy, Beth Holt, Jason Frydman, Bob and Maho Laplante, Tina Post, Mark Temelko, Saiki Kenji, Itai Hiroaki, the Tomizawas, the Nasu family, and my parents. And thank you finally to my wife Mea and my children, Kai and Iris, for keeping me grounded even when the ground felt like it was being pulled from under us. This book is dedicated to them.

NOTES

The code and data repository for this book is available at https://github.com/hoytlong/Values_In_Numbers. All materials are organized by chapter. For details about the code and data associated with each chapter, see the "ReadMe" file included in each chapter folder.

INTRODUCTION

1. Cited in Peter Cryle and Elizabeth Stephens, *Normality: A Critical Genealogy* (Chicago: University of Chicago Press, 2017), 80. For a full account of this debate and its immediate historical context, see chap. 2.
2. Ian Hacking provides a historical overview of the reception of Poisson and Quetelet's ideas in medicine and other disciplines in the nineteenth century in Ian Hacking, *The Taming of Chance* (Cambridge: Cambridge University Press, 1990), 95–114. These ideas facilitated a broader epistemological shift from classical, subjective notions of probability to frequentist interpretations of statistical data that treat observed regularities of social phenomena as objective empirical fact.
3. Cryle and Stephens, *Normality*, 82. This resistance to numbers as somehow usurping the role of subjective expertise and judgment played out in a similar fashion across scientific fields in the nineteenth and twentieth centuries. For succinct histories of how this dynamic unfolded in biology, physics, and psychology, see Gerd Gigerenzer et al., *The Empire of Chance: How Probability Changed Science and Everyday Life* (Cambridge: Cambridge University Press, 1989).
4. Cryle and Stephens, *Normality*, 83.
5. Cryle and Stephens, *Normality*, 81–87.
6. Timothy Brennan, "The Digital-Humanities Bust," *Chronicle Review*, October 15, 2017, https://www.chronicle.com/article/the-digital-humanities-bust/.

7. John Whittier Treat, "Japan Is Interesting: Modern Japanese Literary Studies Today," *Japan Forum* 30, no. 3 (2018), https://www.tandfonline.com/doi/full/10.1080/09555803.2018.1441171.
8. Nan Z. Da, "The Computational Case Against Computational Literary Studies," *Critical Inquiry* 45, no. 3 (Spring 2019): 638–39. Emphasis in original.
9. "Bad readers," writes Merve Emre in her fascinating study of midcentury reading practices in the United States, are those "individuals socialized into the practices of readerly identification, emotion, action, and interaction." Although she is interested in a specific kind of "bad" reading, she also makes clear that it was a social category partly constituted by those intent on defending practices of reading tied to elite academic institutions and serious literature. I use the phrase here to remind us that the critique of numbers is at once a defense of certain kinds of institutionalized reading practices. See Merve Emre, *Paraliterary: The Making of Bad Readers in Postwar America* (Chicago: University of Chicago Press, 2017), 3.
10. Cryle and Stephens, *Normality*, 62. A recent example of this is described in Richard Harris, "As Artificial Intelligence Moves Into Medicine, the Human Touch Could Be a Casualty," *All Tech Considered*, April 30, 2019, https://www.npr.org/sections/health-shots/2019/04/30/718413798/as-artificial-intelligence-moves-into-medicine-the-human-touch-could-be-a-casual.
11. See Nicholas Dames, *The Physiology of the Novel: Reading, Neural Science, and the Form of Victorian Fiction* (Oxford: Oxford University Press, 2007); Chad Wellmon, *Organizing Enlightenment: Information Overload and the Invention of the Modern Research University* (Baltimore, MD: Johns Hopkins University Press, 2015); Yohei Igarashi, "Statistical Analysis at the Birth of Close Reading," *New Literary History* 46, no. 3 (Summer 2015): 485–504; Rachel Sagner Buurma and Laura Heffernan, *The Teaching Archive: A New History of Literary Study* (Chicago: University of Chicago Press, 2020); Sean Michael DiLeonardi, "Cryptographic Reading: Machine Translation, the New Criticism, and Nabokov's *Pnin*," *Post45*, January 17, 2019, http://post45.research.yale.edu/2019/01/cryptographic-reading-machine-translation-the-new-criticism-and-nabokovs-pnin/; and Janice Radway, *Reading the Romance: Women, Patriarchy, and Popular Literature* (Chapel Hill: University of North Carolina Press, 1991).
12. Cited in Cryle and Stephens, *Normality*, 8–9. They draw here on the account of normalization given by Foucault in *The History of Sexuality* and *Discipline and Punish*, noting how much subsequent scholarship on normality has ignored the productive and individuating functions that Foucault highlights.
13. Cryle and Stephens, *Normality*, 93–94.
14. My discussion of disciplinary "facts" draws a great deal on Alain Desrosières's discussion of the history of statistics, of which more will be said in chap. 1. See, especially, Alain Desrosières, *The Politics of Large Numbers: A History of Statistical Reasoning*, trans. Camille Naish (Cambridge, MA: Harvard University Press, 1998), 335–37.
15. These monographs, which have provided influence and inspiration to my own work, include Sarah Allison, *Reductive Reading: A Syntax of Victorian Moralizing* (Baltimore, MD: Johns Hopkins University Press, 2018); Katherine Bode, *A World of Fiction: Digital Collections and the Future of Literary History* (Ann Arbor: University of Michigan Press, 2018); Andrew Piper, *Enumerations: Data and Literary Study* (Chicago: University of Chicago Press, 2018); Daniel Shore, *Cyberformalism: Histories of Linguistic Forms in the Digital Archive* (Baltimore, MD: Johns Hopkins

University Press, 2018); and Ted Underwood, *Distant Horizons: Digital Evidence and Literary Change* (Chicago: University of Chicago Press, 2019).

16. Franco Moretti, "Conjectures on World Literature," *New Left Review* 121, no. 1 (January-February 2000): 58–60. Emphasis in original. As Moretti notes, the original insight for thinking about these foreign forms and local materials is from Masao Miyoshi, who Jameson contrasts with Karatani.
17. Andrew Goldstone, "The *Doxa* of Reading," *PMLA* 132, no. 3 (May 2017): 639. Emphasis in original.
18. An excellent overview of the issues encountered when performing computational analysis on non-English texts is provided in Quinn Dombrowski, "Preparing Non-English Texts for Computational Analysis," *Modern Languages Open* 1, no. 45 (2020), https://doi.org/10.3828/mlo.v0i0.294.
19. Karatani Kōjin, *Origins of Modern Japanese Literature* (Durham, NC: Duke University Press, 1993), 186.
20. See the headnote at the start of this section for a link to the book's code and data repository. All text data has been made available to the extent allowed under current copyright law.
21. Arguments abound for what distinguishes the current numerical turn in literary studies. A few examples are Ted Underwood, "A Genealogy of Distant Reading," *Digital Humanities Quarterly* 11, no. 2 (2017), http://www.digitalhumanities.org/dhq/vol/11/2/000317/000317.html; Matthew Jockers, *Macroanalysis: Digital Methods and Literary History* (Urbana: University of Illinois Press, 2013); Alan Liu, "The Meaning of the Digital Humanities," *PMLA* 128, no. 2 (March 2013): 409–23; and Daniel Allington, Sarah Brouillette, and David Golumbia, "Neoliberal Tools (and Archives): A Political History of Digital Humanities," *Los Angeles Review of Books*, May 1, 2016, https://lareviewofbooks.org/article/neoliberal-tools-archives-political-history-digital-humanities/.
22. Cryle and Stephens, *Normality*, 90, 86–87.
23. On the relation of inferential statistics to eugenic thought, see chaps. 4 and 8 of Desrosières, *The Politics of Large Numbers*; and Tukufu Zuberi, *Thicker Than Blood: How Racial Statistics Lie* (Minneapolis: University of Minnesota Press, 2001). On the erasure of labor and bodies, see Lauren F. Klein, "Dimensions of Scale: Invisible Labor, Editorial Work, and the Future of Quantitative Literary Studies," *PMLA* 135, no. 1 (January 2020): 23–39. Recent work on how algorithms reinforce racial, economic, and other social inequalities include Safiya Noble, *Algorithms of Oppression: How Search Engines Reinforce Racism* (New York: New York University Press, 2018); Cathy O'Neil, *Weapons of Math Destruction: How Big Data Increases Inequality and Threatens Democracy* (New York: Crown, 2016); and Virginia Eubanks, *Automating Inequality: How High-Tech Tools Profile, Police, and Punish the Poor* (New York: St. Martin's, 2018).
24. Fredric Jameson, "Foreword: The Mirror of Alternate Modernities," in Karatani, *Origins of Modern Japanese Literature*, x.

1. FACTS AND DIFFERENCE

1. Ian Hacking, *The Taming of Chance* (Cambridge: Cambridge University Press, 1990), 35.

2. Desrosières borrows the phrase from economic historian Jean-Claude Perrot. Alain Desrosières, *The Politics of Large Numbers: A History of Statistical Reasoning*, trans. Camille Naish (Cambridge, MA: Harvard University Press, 1998), 323.
3. Desrosières, *The Politics of Large Numbers*, 12.
4. Natsume Sōseki, "Excerpts from *Theory of Literature*," in Natsume Sōseki, *Theory of Literature and Other Critical Writings*, trans. Michael Bourdaghs, Atsuko Ueda, and Joseph Murphy (New York: Columbia University Press, 2009), 42.
5. Sōseki, "Preface to *Literary Criticism*," in Natsume Sōseki, *Theory of Literature and Other Critical Writings*, trans. Michael Bourdaghs, Atsuko Ueda, and Joseph Murphy (New York: Columbia University Press, 2009), 215. These prefatory comments were given as part of a seminar in 1905.
6. In Sōseki, "Preface to *Literary Criticism*," 218–19, Sōseki uses this phrase and takes it to mean an object about which certain empirical facts can be agreed upon and compared (e.g., the types of rhymes that a verse contains, the number of lines it has) similar to the way natural phenomena are studied by scientists.
7. Karatani Kōjin, *Origins of Modern Japanese Literature*, ed. Brett de Bary (Durham, NC: Duke University Press, 1993), 11.
8. Michael K. Bourdaghs, Atsuko Ueda, and Joseph A. Murphy, trans., introduction to *Theory of Literature and Other Critical Writings*, by Natsume Sōseki (New York: Columbia University Press, 2009), 13–25.
9. Sōseki's dissatisfaction with these structures can be dated to his time in London. Natsume Sōseki, *Theory of Literature and Other Critical Writings*, trans. Michael Bourdaghs, Atsuko Ueda, and Joseph Murphy (New York: Columbia University Press, 2009), 29.
10. Michael Gordin, *Scientific Babel: How Science Was Done Before and After Global English* (Chicago: University of Chicago Press, 2015), 29.
11. Sōseki, "Preface to *Literary Criticism*," 235.
12. Karatani makes this point about the motivations for Sōseki's turn to scientific language in Karatani Kōjin, *Marukusu sono kanōsei no chūshin* (Kōdansha, 1978), 186–95.
13. Sōseki, "Preface to *Literary Criticism*," 230–31.
14. Bourdaghs, Ueda, and Murphy, introduction to *Theory of Literature and Other Critical Writings*, 12.
15. Nakayama Shigeru observes that Japan's early scientific community, whether in the natural or human sciences, had a "planned" character because state sponsorship preceded specialization and privatization. Nakayama Shigeru, *The Orientation of Science and Technology: A Japanese View* (Folkestone: Global Oriental, 2009), 102.
16. Komori Yōichi, *Sōseki o yominaosu* (Chikuma Shobō, 1995), chap. 4.
17. On the importance of the tabular form to the foundations of statistics in the early nineteenth century, see Desrosières, *The Politics of Large Numbers*, 21. Tables facilitated a shift, although not without controversy, from the "literary" description of diverse data points to a tabular description that permitted simultaneous comparison of these points across multiple values.
18. See Ōkubo Takeharu, *The Quest for Civilization: Encounters with Dutch Jurisprudence, Political Economy, and Statistics at the Dawn of Modern Japan*, trans. David Noble (Leiden: Global Oriental, 2014), chap. 2.
19. Ōkubo, *The Quest for Civilization*, 88. On Fukuzawa's engagement with statistics at this time, and his later turn to double bookkeeping as a frame through which

to figure gender equality, see Hansun Hsiung, "Woman, Man, Abacus: A Tale of Enlightenment," *Harvard Journal of Asiatic Studies* 72, no. 1 (June 2012): 1–42.

20. On Fukuzawa's *Outline of a Theory of Civilization* and its role in the construction of national history as civilizational discourse, see Christopher Hill, *National History and the World of Nations* (Durham, NC: Duke University Press, 2008), 68–81.
21. Haga Yaichi, *Haga Yaichi icho* (Fuzanbō, 1929), 133. All translations are my own unless otherwise noted.
22. Haga, *Haga Yaichi icho*, 129.
23. Atsuko Ueda, "*Bungakuron* and 'Literature' in the Making," *Japan Forum* 20, no. 1 (February 2008): 28–30.
24. As cited in Lee Yeounsuk, *The Ideology of Kokugo: Nationalizing Language in Modern Japan*, trans. Maki Hirano Hubbard (Honolulu: University of Hawai'i Press, 2010), 130–32. Lee provides a detailed overview of these debates and their role in shaping the institutional structure of linguistics as a field of study.
25. Gerd Gigerenzer et al., *The Empire of Chance: How Probability Changed Science and Everyday Life* (Cambridge: Cambridge University Press, 1989), 44.
26. Desrosières is especially instructive on this topic, but also see Gigerenzer et al., *The Empire of Chance*; and Theodore M. Porter, *The Rise of Statistical Thinking, 1820–1900* (Princeton, NJ: Princeton University Press, 1986).
27. Mark Anderson provides an excellent overview of where Haga's writings intersect with the ideology of national essentialism and civilizational discourse in Mark Anderson, *Japan and the Specter of Imperialism* (New York: Palgrave Macmillan, 2009), 153–72.
28. Sōseki, "Excerpts from *Theory of Literature*," 52.
29. Sōseki, "Excerpts from *Theory of Literature*," 68, 65.
30. Sōseki, "Excerpts from *Theory of Literature*," 59. Sōseki attempted to represent this idea graphically as an inverted pyramid overlaid with a grid. Squares in the grid correspond to different values of F, which vary with spans of time (e.g., minutes, hours, days, centuries) as measured backwards from the focal point of conscious attention. This visualization is reproduced on the cover page for this book.
31. Ueda makes a similar point that none of the registers of Sōseki's formula are privileged over any other. See Ueda, "*Bungakuron* and 'Literature' in the Making," 31.
32. Nicholas Dames, *The Physiology of the Novel: Reading, Neural Science, and the Form of Victorian Fiction*, (Oxford: Oxford University Press, 2007), 37. Emphasis in original.
33. Dames, *The Physiology of the Novel*, 47, 29.
34. Dames, *The Physiology of the Novel*, 28.
35. Bourdaghs, Ueda, and Murphy, introduction to *Theory of Literature and Other Writings*, 25–26.
36. Natsume Sōseki, *Sōseki shiryō: Bungakuron nōto*, ed. Muraoka Isamu (Iwanami Shoten, 1976), 412. Bain's work is not referenced in these notes.
37. Dames, *The Physiology of the Novel*, 38.
38. Dames, *The Physiology of the Novel*, 76–77.
39. Sōseki, "Preface to *Literary Criticism*," 220–21.
40. Sōseki, "Excerpts from *Theory of Literature*," 118–19.
41. Sōseki, "Excerpts from *Theory of Literature*," 118.
42. Natsume Sōseki, "Sōsakuka no taidō," in *Sōseki zenshū* (Iwanami Shoten, 1995): 16:234–35.

43. Vernon Lee, *The Handling of Words and Other Studies in Literary Psychology* (London: John Lane, 1927), 189.
44. Lee, *The Handling of Words*, 189–90.
45. Dames, *The Physiology of the Novel*, 186–87.
46. Sōseki makes this point most forcefully in Sōseki, "Sōsakuka no taidō," 174–76.
47. Sōseki, "Excerpts from *Theory of Literature*," 119.
48. On Richards and the end of the physiological novel theory, see Dames, *The Physiology of the Novel*, 247–55. It is also critical to note that Richards used word frequency lists and statistical analysis as technical supports for the interpretative methods now recognized as close reading. Namely, he saw lists of commonly used words (epitomized in the Basic English system developed with C. K. Ogden) as a tool for teaching students how to better paraphrase, and thus interpret, poetry. See Igarashi Yohei, "Statistical Analysis at the Birth of Close Reading," *New Literary History* 46, no. 3 (Summer 2015): 485–504.
49. As Massimiliano Tomasi discusses, this surge of interest was crucial to linking rhetoric as a field of study to debates happening in literary circles around the rise of vernacular style. See Massimiliano Tomasi, *Rhetoric in Modern Japan: Western Influences on the Development of Narrative and Oratorical Style* (Honolulu: University of Hawai'i Press, 2004), 89. Hatano recalls being shocked by the abundance of books on English rhetoric that he found in Tokyo's used bookstores when he first began his research, certainly a legacy of this Meiji period interest. Hatano Kanji, "Watashi no ayunda michi—shūjigaku to shinrigaku," *Nihongo-gaku* 3, no. 12 (December 1984), 112.
50. Hatano Kanji, *Bunshō shinrigaku*, in *Hatano Kanji zenshū* (Shōgakkan, 1990–1991), 1:8. Hatano fails to mention an eight-volume series on the topic of *bunshō* published this same year, to which he and dozens of writers and critics contributed. See Sakimoto Kazuo, ed., *Nihon gendai bunshō kōza* (Hōseikaku, 1934). In 1937, other writers capitalized on Tanizaki's success, most notably Kume Masao with *Bunshō no tsukurikata* (How to Create Style) and Kikuchi Kan with *Bunshō tokuhon* (A Primer on Style).
51. Hatano, *Bunshō shinrigaku* (1990-1991), 23.
52. Hatano, *Bunshō shinrigaku* (1990-1991), 60. According to Hatano, associationist theory explains language production through the lens of individual mental experience, ignoring the social effects of stylistic choices in favor of coupling them to internal sensations. In this model, the flow of consciousness is transformed into fixed units in the mind that are then associated with one another, via language and specific rhetorical techniques, to reconstitute experience and to communicate it to others.
53. On this transition to a more dynamic conception of form and a focus on art as determined by its relation to forms existing before it, see Victor Erlich, *Russian Formalism: History-Doctrine* (New Haven, CT: Yale University Press, 1955), 251–71.
54. Bally is often remembered as the coeditor of Saussure's *Course in General Linguistics* (1916), compiled from students' notes of lectures given in 1907, but he was an accomplished linguist in his own right. He published his treatises on stylistics, *Precis on Stylistics* (1905) and *Treatise on French Stylistics* (1909), coincident with Saussure's lectures and formulated a number of the systemic notions present there. See Anthony Pym, *Translation Solutions for Many Languages: Histories of a Flawed*

Dream (London: Bloomsbury Academic, 2016), 2. Kobayashi translated Bally's *Language and Life* (*Seikatsu hyōgen no gengogaku*, 1929), originally published in 1913, just a year after translating *Course in General Linguistics* (*Gengogaku genron*, 1928).

55. Pym, *Translation Solutions for Many Languages*, 2–3. Emphasis in original.
56. Hatano, *Bunshō shinrigaku* (1990-1991), 63.
57. Hatano, *Bunshō shinrigaku* (1990-1991), 79.
58. Hatano, *Bunshō shinrigaku* (1990-1991), 84. Notably, Lewin gave a series of lectures at Tokyo Imperial University in 1933.
59. For more on Lewin's theory of a "life-space," see Alfred J. Marrow, *The Practical Theorist: The Life and Work of Kurt Lewin* (New York: Basic Books, 1969), chap. 4.
60. Hatano, *Bunshō shinrigaku* (1990-1991), 89.
61. Hatano, *Bunshō shinrigaku* (1990-1991), 105. Hatano admitted that the latter tasks would be difficult, involving clinical assessment of the authors and reader response experiments. These would have to wait for further study.
62. Hatano, "Watashi no ayunda michi," 111–12. This volume was part of a twelve-volume series on the science of language, commissioned by the publisher Meiji Shoin.
63. Hatano Kanji, *Bunshō shinrigaku <shinkō>* (Dai Nihon Tosho, 1965), 201. Hatano acknowledged the influence of Lee's work only in the 1950s, after a colleague pointed out the parallels. He originally found her work while reading a special issue from 1926 on "Art and Thought" in the *Journal de Psychologie*. When he asked Matatarō about her, he referred him to her book.
64. Brian McVeigh provides an intellectual and institutional history of psychology in Japan in Brian McVeigh, *The History of Japanese Psychology: Global Perspectives, 1875–1950* (London: Bloomsbury Academic, 2017). Incidentally, Matsumoto was trained by Motora Yūjirō, who is recognized as the founder of modern psychology and as the one who originally introduced Sōseki to the field when he was a student. Motora worked on psychological studies of poetic rhythm in the 1890s, an interest that Matsumoto continued in his studies on the psychology of painting.
65. Hatano gives no indication of where he acquired statistical literacy. The primer by Tanaka Kan'ichi is *Kyōiku-teki tōkeiho* (Shōwa Shuppansha, 1928). On the development of intelligence testing and other statistical measures in Japan, see McVeigh, *The History of Japanese Psychology*, 132–36.
66. Gigerenzer et al., *The Empire of Chance*, chap. 3.
67. Another point of possible contact with statistics is the statistical studies of E. L. Thorndike, as described in Igarashi, "Statistical Analysis at the Birth of Close Reading." I have not found direct mention of them by Hatano, but their impact on the field of educational psychology was significant from the early 1920s onward. The studies created ranked lists of words based on frequency in children's reading material and were meant to guide the acquisition of vocabulary.
68. Hatano Kanji, "Ichi shinrigakusha no ayumi," in *Hatano Kanji zenshū* (Shōgakkan, 1990–1991), 2:2, 2:13.
69. Hatano, *Bunshō shinrigaku* (1990-1991), 103–4. Specifically, Hatano wondered if empirical differences corresponded to two "ideal types" of style that, like prime numbers, were irreducible to one another.
70. Hatano, *Bunshō shinrigaku* (1990-1991), 112.
71. Hatano, *Bunshō shinrigaku* (1990-1991), 112–13.

72. George Udny Yule, "On Sentence-Length as a Statistical Characteristic of Style in Prose," *Biometrika* 30, no. 3–4 (1939).
73. Kawabata Yasunari, "Gendai sakka no bunshō," in *Kawabata Yasunari zenshū* (Shinchōsha, 1999), 32:58–59. The essay, which originally appeared in *Bungei kōza* in October 1925, was seen by Hatano as a forerunner to the new wave of interest in rhetoric and style.
74. Hatano, *Bunshō shinrigaku* (1990-1991), 114–15. Specifically, Hatano sampled thirty sentences from the beginning of each work and twenty sentences from the end. He chose to exclude dialogue from his samples because these required a different kind of stylistic analysis.
75. Hatano justified his decision by arguing that writers thought in terms of *ji* because most used standardized manuscript sheets (*genkō yōshi*) consisting of a 20 × 20 matrix of squares (*masu*) with one character per square. Incidentally, these were also the units in which most authors were paid. He later found that measures of sentence length by *ji* and by words were highly correlated, but the former was still superior because it was more objective. See Hatano, *Bunshō shinrigaku <shinkō>* (1965), 203–4. Yule similarly wrestled with problems of how best to define what counted as a sentence and a word.
76. On the construction of the idea of the average by Adolphe Quetelet and ensuing debates about its validity as a valid measure of social tendencies, see Desrosières, *The Politics of Large Numbers*, chap. 3; Porter, *The Rise of Statistical Thinking*, chap. 2; and Hacking, *The Taming of Chance*, 112-14.
77. Hatano, *Bunshō shinrigaku* (1990-1991), 119–20.
78. Hatano, *Bunshō shinrigaku* (1990-1991), 144.
79. Desrosières, *The Politics of Large Numbers*, 73–77.
80. Hatano later recounted that when researching *Bunshō shinrigaku* he felt an acute need to establish a representative baseline for length derived from a large survey of fiction and nonfiction texts, including essays and newspaper articles. He was overwhelmed by the sheer scope of such an endeavor, however, which led him to focus on author-to-author comparison. Hatano, "Watashi no ayunda michi," 113.
81. Gigerenzer et al., *The Empire of Chance*, 45–48.
82. Desrosières, *The Politics of Large Numbers*, 82.
83. Hatano, "Ichi shinrigakusha no ayumi," in *Hatano Kanji zenshū* (Shōgakkan, 1990–1991), 4:13.
84. For a summary of Kikuchi's and Nakamura's arguments, see Edward Mack, *Manufacturing Modern Japanese Literature: Publishing, Prizes, and the Ascription of Literary Value* (Durham, NC: Duke University Press, 2010), 143–54.
85. Hirabayashi Hatsunosuke, "Iwayuru kagaku-teki hihyō no genkai," in *Hirabayashi Hatsnosuke ikōshū* (Heibonsha, 1932), 75–86.
86. Tsuchiya Noboru, "Bungeigaku ni okeru hōhō-teki jikaku," in *Nihon bungakuron kō*, ed. Tsubouchi Sensei Kanreki Kinen Kai (Bungakusha, 1938), 28–29.
87. Kobayashi Hideo, "*Bunshō shinrigaku* o yomu," in *Gengo to buntai* (Sanseidō, 1937), 120–27.
88. Ichikawa Takashi, "Buntai to buntairon," *Kokubungaku: kaishaku to kanshō* 21, no. 4 (April 1956): 107–11.

89. See, for example, Tokieda Motoki, *Bunshō kenkyū jōsetsu* (Yamada Shoin, 1960), 26–41; and Hino Sukezumi, "Buntai kenkyū no ichi hōkō," *Kokugo kenkyū*, no. 12 (June 1961): 24–25.
90. Yasumoto Biten, "Bunshō shinrigaku," in *Bunshō to buntai*, ed. Morioka Kenji et al. (Meiji Shoin, 1963), 191.
91. George Miller, *Language and Communication* (New York: McGraw-Hill, 1951), 81.
92. Cybernetics and information theory also influenced several structuralist thinkers in the 1950s, including Claude Lévi-Strauss, Roman Jakobson, and Jacques Lacan. They formed collaborative networks with the likes of Claude Shannon and Warren Weaver and similarly became enamored of the notion that communication could be modeled probabilistically. A history of this period is given in Bernard Dionysius Geoghegan, "From Information Theory to French Theory: Jakobson, Lévi-Strauss, and the Cybernetic Apparatus," *Critical Inquiry* 38, no. 1 (2011): 96–126.
93. The roster of members was published in *Keiryō kokugogaku*, no. 14 (1960): 71–77.
94. Matsuyama Yō and Miyajima Yoshiko, "Hyōgen kenkyū to suryōka no mondai," *Keiryō kokugogaku* 3 (1957): 28.
95. Matsuyama and Miyajima, "Hyōgen kenkyū to suryōka no mondai," 29.
96. Nakamura Akira, "Kotoba no bi to chikara," in *Kotoba no kagaku*, ed. Endō Yoshimoto et al. (Nakayama Shoten, 1958), 5:2.
97. To his credit, Nakamura compares his results with those obtained by Hatano in a larger study from 1950 and recognizes that his own results are sensitive to the population of texts from which he sampled. Nakamura, "Kotoba no bi to chikara," 10.
98. Nakamura decided to take four hundred prose phrases (*ku*) from the beginning of each work, where a phrase is a continuous sequence of characters between punctuation marks. This choice raised several other interpretive issues: How much should one sample? From what part of a work? Should it be done randomly? If the narrative focus at the start of a work is limited to just mental description, or just action, would this skew the sample given the tendency of the latter toward shorter phrases? If so, would it be better to randomly sample from the works instead? By sampling the same number of phrases, is there a risk of observing a smaller number of sentences if a writer uses lots of phrases per sentence? Nakamura, "Kotoba no bi to chikara," 4–9.
99. Nakamura, "Kotoba no bi to chikara," 12–14.
100. The period 1940 to 1955 marked a radical transition in the discipline of psychology with the institutionalization of statistical methods for inference. The acceptance of these methods marked a transition in the conceptualization of the human mind itself, from something seen as behaving according to deterministic laws to behaving more probabilistically, much like a statistician. For a detailed history of this transition, see Gigerenzer et al., *The Empire of Chance*, chap. 6.
101. Unlike Nakamura, Yasumoto based his decisions about what made a representative work on several literary dictionaries. He describes how he created his sample corpus in Yasumoto Biten, "Bun no nagasa to kuten no kazu," *Keiryō kokugogaku*, no. 8 (1959): 15.
102. Yasumoto Biten, *Bunshō shinrigaku no shinryōiki* (Seishin Shobō, 1960), 26.
103. Yasumoto, *Bunshō shinrigaku no shinryōiki*, chap. 1.

104. The lesson prefigures some of the ways thinking through models, particularly those that inform machine learning methods, have become a nexus of interpretive energy for computational literary criticism. Particularly noteworthy is Andrew Piper, "Think Small: On Literary Modeling," *PMLA* 132, no. 3 (May 2017): 651–58; and Richard Jean So, " 'All Models Are Wrong,'" *PMLA* 132, no. 3 (May 2017): 668–73.
105. Yasumoto's 1959 thesis, titled "Foundational Research Toward Building a Characterology of Style: A Classification of 100 Contemporary Writers with Factor Analysis," applied the method of factor analysis to a study of style. Factor analysis was a popular method of dimensionality reduction originally developed by the psychologist Charles Spearman in the early twentieth century. It came to be widely utilized in intelligence research and psychometrics for identifying underlying, hidden factors that explain variation in a larger set of observed, interrelated variables. Yasumoto was one of the first anywhere to apply such an advanced technique to literature. A year later, one of the first attempts to apply factor analysis to English literary style was carried out by American psycholinguist John Carroll. See John Carroll, "Vectors of Prose Style," in *Style in Language*, ed. Thomas A. Sebeok (Cambridge, MA: MIT Press, 1960), 283–92.
106. It is important to highlight here the symbiotic relationship between the desire for more data points and the intertwined histories of labor, technology, and gender that underwrite it. Kabashima pays thanks to the human "computers" who contributed to the project in the book's preface, all of whom were women. For an eloquent account of how labor gets erased from histories of data, see Lauren F. Klein, "Dimensions of Scale: Invisible Labor, Editorial Work, and the Future of Quantitative Literary Studies."
107. Kabashima Tadao and Jugaku Akiko, *Buntai no kagaku* (Kyoto: Sōgeisha, 1965), 1–15.
108. For a more detailed account of the theories of expression and communication that underlie his quantitative experiments, see Kabashima Tadao, *Hyōgenron* (Kyoto: Bunkōsha, 1964).
109. Kabashima, *Hyōgenron*, 17–18. The distinction is akin to Seymour Chatman's typology of "narrative" versus "descriptive" text types. In an earlier essay, Kabashima used "summary" (*samarii*) and "scene" (*shiin*) to label each type. Kabashima Tadao, "Buntai no heni ni tsuite," *Kokugo kokubun* 30, no. 11 (November 1961): 23–38.
110. Kabashima and Jugaku, *Buntai no kagaku*, 26–30.
111. Referring to Hatano, the authors use this as evidence to argue that Tanizaki's stylistic antipode is not Shiga but rather Ibuse. Kabashima and Jugaku, *Buntai no kagaku*, 122–23.
112. See Kabashima Tadao, "Buntai no gogaku-teki kenkyū," in *Bunshō to buntai*, ed. Morioka Kenji et al. (Meiji Shoin, 1963), 235.
113. After the 1960s, these scholars continued to produce work on style and expression, in the form of both popular style guides and more academic studies. Yasumoto turned his attention to historical linguistics and the origins of the Japanese language; Nakamura wrote on the history of rhetorical theory in Japan and produced comprehensive taxonomies of emotional and affective expression.
114. See Rachel Sagner Buurma and Laura Heffernan, "Search and Replace: Josephine Miles and the Origins of Distant Reading," *Modernism/Modernity Print +*, April 11, 2018, https://modernismmodernity.org/forums/posts/search-and-replace; and

Thomas Nelson Winter, "Roberto Busa, S. J., and the Invention of the Machine-Generated Concordance," *Classical Bulletin* 75, no. 1 (1999): 3–20. Josephine Miles, incidentally, had begun arguing for the value of counting in literary criticism in the late 1930s when she was working on a doctoral thesis about the use of metaphor in Wordsworth's poetry. The foundational work of Miles and Busa took off in the following decades as computing resources became more accessible. By the 1970s, there was enough interest in digital texts and concordancing to support several journals and conferences intent on bringing the study of linguistics, humanities, and computing together. See Susan Hockey, "The History of Humanities Computing," in *A Companion to Digital Humanities*, ed. Susan Schreibman, et al. (Malden, MA: Blackwell Publishing Ltd, 2004), 7-8.

115. In one example from 1988, Miyajima Tatsuo tried to verify and extend Yasumoto's study of Chinese character usage. See Miyajima Tatsuo, "'Kanji no shōrai' sono ato," *Gengo seikatsu* 436 (1988): 50–58. Miyajima used recipients of the prestigious Akutagawa literary prize (1935–1985) to build a comparison corpus.
116. Joseph A. Murphy, *Metaphorical Circuit: Negotiations Between Literature and Science in 20th Century Japan* (Ithaca, NY: Cornell University East Asia Program, 2004), chaps. 4 and 5.
117. See, for example, the October 1954 and October 1955 issues of *Gengo seikatsu*; the April 1956 issue of *Kokubungaku: Kaishaku to kanshō*; the August 1956 issue of *Bungakukai*; and the October 1959 issue of *Kokubungaku: Kaishaku to kyōzai no kenkyū*.
118. The trial was initiated by the state against Itō and the publisher of his recent translation of D. H. Lawrence's *Lady Chatterley's Lover*. Hatano explains the nature of his role in the case in Hatano, *Bunshō shinrigaku* (1990-1991), 383. On the trial itself, and the use of social scientific evidence as a means to critique the subjective morality of the state's representatives, see Ann Sherif, *Japan's Cold War: Media, Literature, and the Law* (New York: Columbia University Press, 2009), chap. 2.
119. Itō Sei, "Sutairu no hassei," in *Shōsetsu no hōhō* (Iwanami Bunkō, 2006), 207. The essay was originally published in the November 1947 issue of *Gunzō* under the title "Sutairu ron" (Theory of Style).
120. Itō, "Sutairu no hassei," 203.
121. Etō Jun, *Sakka wa kōdō suru* (Kōdansha, 1959), 105–9.
122. Stanley Fish, "What Is Stylistics and Why Are They Saying Such Terrible Things About It?," in *Is There a Text in This Class?: The Authority of Interpretive Communities* (Cambridge, MA: Harvard University Press, 1980), 72.
123. Roland Barthes, "Style and Its Image," in *Literary Style: A Symposium*, ed. Seymour Chatman (London: Oxford University Press, 1971), 8.
124. Barthes, "Style and Its Image," 9–10.
125. See Fredric Jameson, *The Prison-House of Language: A Critical Account of Structuralism and Russian Formalism* (Princeton, NJ: Princeton University Press, 1972), chap. 1; and Jonathan Culler, *Structuralist Poetics: Structuralism, Linguistics, and the Study of Literature* (Ithaca, NY: Cornell University Press, 1975), 131–40.
126. See, for instance, the groundbreaking sociological work of Janice Radway, *Reading the Romance: Women, Patriarchy, and Popular Literature* (Chapel Hill: University of North Carolina Press, 1991).
127. Maeda Ai and Katō Shūichi, *Buntai* (Iwanami Shoten, 1989).
128. Morioka Kenji, *Buntai to hyōgen* (Meiji Shoin, 1988), 110–11.

129. Morioka, *Buntai to hyōgen*, 112–15. For example, when authors compose dialogue, the stylistic choices they make have less to do with authorial uniqueness than with the social and cultural locations in which they wish to situate the voices of their characters.
130. Morioka, *Buntai to hyōgen*, 111–12.
131. Michael Bourdaghs, "Introduction: Overthrowing the Emperor in Japanese Literary Studies," in *The Linguistic Turn in Contemporary Japanese Literary Studies: Politics, Language, Textuality*, ed. Michael Bourdaghs (Ann Arbor, MI: Center for Japanese Studies, 2010), 4.
132. Bourdaghs, "Introduction," 3.
133. Bourdaghs, "Introduction," 5.
134. Komori Yōichi, *Buntai toshite no monogatari* (Chikuma Shobō, 1988), 3.
135. Komori, *Buntai toshite no monogatari*, 6–8.
136. Komori, *Buntai toshite no monogatari*, 9.
137. Komori, *Buntai toshite no monogatari*, 10.
138. Komori, *Buntai toshite no monogatari*, 347–49. Komori draws here on a Japanese translation of Neumann's "Art and Time" published in 1979. It originally appeared in German in 1954.
139. Komori, *Buntai toshite no monogatari*, 18.
140. Franco Moretti, *Signs Taken for Wonders: Essays in the Sociology of Literary Forms* (London: Verso, 1988), 13.
141. Consider Victor Shklovsky's remark in 1923 that "art is not created by the individual will, by the genius. The creator is simply the geometrical point of intersection of forces operative outside of him." Cited in Erlich, *Russian Formalism*, 253.
142. Moretti, *Signs Taken for Wonders*, 24–25.
143. Moretti, *Signs Taken for Wonders*, 26. At the time, Moretti argued that formal conflict was motivated by what he believed was literature's basic function: securing consent. By this he meant that it reconciled individuals in a pleasant and imperceptible way to society's prevailing cultural norms (27). Through Freud, he read modern literary forms as attempts by writers to achieve a formal compromise between conflicting psychical forces.
144. Moretti, *Signs Taken for Wonders*, 27.
145. Andrew Goldstone, "The *Doxa* of Reading," *PMLA* 132, no. 3 (May 2017): 636.
146. Franco Moretti, *Distant Reading* (London: Verso, 2013), 179. A brief history of his Stanford Literary Lab and the groundbreaking work of its members is provided by Ted Underwood, "The Stanford Literary Lab's Narrative," *Public Books*, November 2, 2017, http://www.publicbooks.org/the-stanford-literary-labs-narrative/.
147. The most significant contributions to corpus construction (both literary and otherwise) have come from the National Institute for Japanese Language and Linguistics, which is the successor to the National Japanese Language Research Institute formed in 1948. Assisting these efforts are historical linguists who have pioneered the application of quantitative method to classical literary texts, including scholars Kondō Yasuhiro, Yamamoto Hirofumi, and Kondō Miyuki.
148. See, for instance, Nagamine Shigetoshi, *<Dokusho kokumin> no tanjō* (Nihon Editā Sukuru Shuppanbu, 2004). Following this methodological thread, Jonathan Zwicker writes eloquently on the value of quantitative method for book history in Jonathan Zwicker, *Practices of the Sentimental Imagination: Melodrama, the Novel,*

and the Social Imaginary in Nineteenth-Century Japan (Cambridge, MA: Harvard University Asia Center, 2006).

149. See Franco Moretti, *Endoku: <Sekai bungaku shisutemu> e no chosen*, trans. Akikusa Shun'ichirō et al. (Misuzu Shobō, 2016).
150. Thomas Mullaney offers valuable reflections on the consequences of these asymmetries for how we narrate global histories of technology in Thomas Mullaney, introduction to *The Chinese Typewriter: A History* (Cambridge, MA: MIT Press, 2017).
151. Desrosières, *The Politics of Large Numbers*, 323.
152. Jameson, *Prison-House of Language*, viii.
153. Chad Wellmon, *Organizing Enlightenment: Information Overload and the Invention of the Modern Research University* (Baltimore, MD: Johns Hopkins University Press, 2015), 4–5, 10.
154. Wellmon, *Organizing Enlightenment*, 10–11. Emphasis in original.

2. ARCHIVE AND SAMPLE

1. An emerging body of scholarship tackles the range and complexity of these constraints from the perspectives of materiality and the politics of archival creation and curation. On the construction of literary archives, see especially Katherine Bode, *A World of Fiction: Digital Collections and the Future of Literary History* (Ann Arbor: University of Michigan Press, 2018); and Michael Gavin, "How to Think About EEBO," *Textual Cultures* 11, no. 1–2 (2019): 70–105. Roopika Risam writes on how these constraints intersect with the politics of postcolonialism in Roopika Risam, *New Digital Worlds: Postcolonial Digital Humanities in Theory, Praxis, and Pedagogy* (Evanston, IL: Northwestern University Press, 2019); and Catherine D'Ignazio and Lauren Klein argue persuasively for thinking about data via intersectional feminism in Catherine D'Ignazio and Lauren Klein, *Data Feminism* (Boston: MIT Press, 2020). For a recent discussion of the issues surrounding the creation and collection of cultural data, see Amilia Acker and Tanya Clement, "Data Cultures, Culture as Data—Special Issue of Cultural Analytics," *Journal of Cultural Analytics* (April 2019).
2. Cited in Siva Vaidhyanathan, *The Googlization of Everything (And Why We Should Worry)* (Berkeley: University of California Press, 2011), 150. The quote is from a 2006 *New York Times Magazine* article by Kevin Kelly.
3. Vaidhyanathan, *The Googlization of Everything*, chap. 5.
4. John Guillory, *Cultural Capital: The Problem of Literary Canon Formation* (Chicago: University of Chicago Press, 1993), 30.
5. Jacques Derrida, *Archive Fever: A Freudian Impression*, trans. Eric Prenowitz (Chicago: University of Chicago Press, 1998), 17. Emphasis in original.
6. Bode defines biography as "attempts to identify the ideas, values, definitions and meanings, the theories and biases, that underpin and produce the collection, so as to enable a more critical and astute reading of the information it contains." See Katherine Bode, *Reading by Numbers: Recalibrating the Literary Field* (London: Anthem Press, 2012), 19.
7. The choice of these three perspectives has to do with both limitations of space and the availability of certain data sets at the time of writing. In the future, I can

imagine gaining equally valuable perspectives through information about literary prizes, critical reviews, or lists of bestsellers.

8. Noguchi Eiji and Miyakawa Teruko, "Aozora bunko no monogatari," in *Aozora Bunko* (2005), accessed November 9, 2016, http://www.aozora.gr.jp/cards/001739/files/55745_58656.html.
9. Tomita Michio, *Hon no mirai, Aozora Bunko* (1997), accessed April 19, 2018, https://www.aozora.gr.jp/cards/000055/files/56499_51225.html.
10. Tomita Michio and Yamada Shōji, "Intabyū·Aozora Bunko ni tsuite," in *Komonzu to bunka: bunka wa dare no mono ka* (Tokyodō Shuppan, 2010), 197–99.
11. For astute analysis of how the reading of single texts came to be linked to literary criticism's institutional identity from the late nineteenth century, see Mary Poovey, *Genres of the Credit Economy: Mediating Value in Eighteenth- and Nineteenth-Century Britain* (Chicago: University of Chicago Press, 2008), chap. 5; and John Guillory, "Close Reading: Prologue and Epilogue," *ADE Bulletin* 149 (2010): 8–14.
12. Bode nicely summarizes critiques of quantitative methods in this vein. The quotes are from critiques of Moretti by Katie Trumpener and Robert Tally, respectively. Bode, *Reading by Numbers*, 10.
13. Andrew Piper, "There Will Be Numbers," *Journal of Cultural Analytics* (May 2016), https://culturalanalytics.org/article/11062. Piper extends this argument in *Enumerations*, arguing that literary criticism lacks "a science of generalization." That science, for him, comes in the form of *models* that make explicit the "representativeness of our own evidence" as we move from textual detail to large social contexts. Andrew Piper, *Enumerations: Data and Literary Study* (Chicago: University of Chicago Press, 2018), 6–12.
14. Jonathan Culler, *The Pursuit of Signs: Semiotics, Literature, Deconstruction* (Ithaca, NY: Cornell University Press, 1981), 47.
15. An extreme version of this defense of scaling up, and a critique of anecdotal evidence, is found in Matthew Jockers, *Macroanalysis: Digital Methods and Literary History* (Urbana: University of Illinois Press, 2013), 6–8.
16. Lauren Berlant, "On the Case," *Critical Inquiry* 33, no. 4 (June 2007): 663.
17. Berlant, "On the Case," fn1.
18. Berlant, "On the Case," 665.
19. Rob Kitchin, "Big Data, New Epistemologies and Paradigm Shifts," *Big Data and Society* 1, no. 1 (April-June 2014): 2.
20. See Craig M. Dalton et al., "Critical Data Studies: A Dialog on Data and Space," *Big Data and Society* 3, no. 1 (January-June 2016): 1–9; and Daniel A. McFarland and H. Richard McFarland, "Big Data and the Danger of Being Precisely Inaccurate," *Big Data and Society* 2, no. 2 (July-December 2015): 1–4.
21. Andrew Iliadis and Federica Russo, "Critical Data Studies: An Introduction," *Big Data and Society* 3, no. 2 (July-December 2016): 3.
22. Kitchin, "Big Data," 4.
23. Bode makes this point most forcefully in Katherine Bode, "The Equivalence of 'Close' and 'Distant' Reading; Or, Toward a New Object for Data-Rich Literary History," *Modern Language Quarterly* 78, no. 1 (2017): 77–106.
24. Most prominent among these are Stephen Best and Sharon Marcus's proposed "surface reading," Rita Felski's call for "postcritical reading," and Caroline Levine's argument for a "new formalism."

25. On the history of ideas about "representativeness" and "exhaustiveness" in the field of statistics, particularly how they relate to evolving methodologies of statistical sampling, see Alain Derosières, *The Politics of Large Numbers: A History of Statistical Reasoning*, trans. Camille Naish (Cambridge, MA: Harvard University Press, 1998), chap. 7. On the nonantagonism of case and non–case study approaches in the social sciences, see John Gerring, "What Is a Case Study and What Is It Good For?," *The American Political Science Review* 98, no. 2 (2004): 341–54.
26. Klaus Krippendorf, *Content Analysis: An Introduction to Its Methodology* (Thousand Oaks, CA: Sage, 2004), 19. Krippendorf notes that unconscious selective bias was one of the major justifications for content analysis in its original formulations.
27. Krippendorf, *Content Analysis*, 20.
28. Cited in Krippendorf, *Content Analysis*, 28. The quote is from Bernard Berelson and Paul Felix Lazarsfeld, *The Analysis of Communication Content* (1948), which provided an overview of the field at that time and outlined some of its principle units of analysis and technical problems (e.g., sampling, reliability).
29. On inductive and abductive inference, see Krippendorf, *Content Analysis*, 36–38.
30. Krippendorf, *Content Analysis*, 113, 24, 33.
31. Krippendorf, *Content Analysis*, 112–13.
32. Each of these techniques is described in more detail in Krippendorf, *Content Analysis*, 113, 116–20.
33. A full account of the sampling procedure and resulting list is provided in "Yōrei saishū no tame no shuyō bungaku sakuhin mokuroku," ed. Kokugo Jiten Henshū Junbishitsu (Kokuritsu Kokugo Kenkyūjo, 1980).
34. Krippendorf, *Content Analysis*, 121.
35. Most of the duplicates in Aozora are the result of titles that have been transcribed in both their original and modernized orthographic formats. The full collection was scraped from the Aozora website (https://www.aozora.gr.jp/) using the database index provided on the site. Code for scraping Aozora can be found in the chapter 2 folder of the code and data repository. I have created an easily searchable version of the collection with the Textual Optics Lab at the University of Chicago, available here: https://artflsrv03.uchicago.edu/philologic4/aozora/
36. In both cases, I use the Chikuma Shōbo editions to ensure relative comparability.
37. Nakamura Mitsuo famously made these claims in *Nihon no kindai shōsetsu* (1961), citing writer Nagai Kafū's own assertions along these lines. Jonathan Zwicker discusses the implications of this idea in Jonathan Zwicker, *Practices of the Sentimental Imagination: Melodrama, the Novel, and the Social Imaginary in Nineteenth-Century Japan* (Cambridge, MA: Harvard University Asia Center, 2006), 29–30.
38. See Zwicker, *Practices of the Sentimental Imagination*, chap. 3; Indra Levy, *Sirens of the Western Shore: The Westernesque Femme Fatale, Translation, and Vernacular Style in Modern Japanese Literature* (New York: Columbia University Press, 2006); and Karen Thornber, *Empire of Texts in Motion: Chinese, Korean, and Taiwanese Transculturations of Japanese Literature* (Cambridge, MA: Harvard University Asia Center, 2009).
39. Akikusa Shun'ichirō, "Jutsugo toshite no 'sekai bungaku': 1895–2016," *Bungaku* 17, no. 5 (September 2016): 10.
40. On these moments of selection, see Brian Dowdle, "Why Saikaku Was Memorable but Bakin Was Unforgettable," *Journal of Japanese Studies* 42, no. 1 (Winter 2016):

106–9; Ishii Jun, "1910 nendai ni okeru toshokan sentei jigyō—*Toshokan hyōjun mokuroku* o chūshin ni," in *Toshokan to shuppan bunka* (Yayoshi Mitsunaga Sensei Kiju Kinenkai, 1977), 55–68; and Akikusa, "Jutsugo toshite no 'sekai bungaku': 1895–2016," 7–9.

41. Mary Hammond, *Reading, Publishing, and the Formation of Literary Taste in England, 1880–1914* (Aldershot, UK: Ashgate, 2006), 94.
42. Hammond, *Reading, Publishing, and the Formation of Literary Taste*, 91–92.
43. A reproduction of the advertisement can be found in Obi Toshito, *Shuppan to shakai* (Genki Shobō, 2007), 198–99.
44. For a list of books published in the Everyman's series, see A. J. Hoppé, *The Reader's Guide to Everyman's Library* (London: Dent, 1960).
45. Cited in Obi, *Shuppan to shakai*, 198–99, 195.
46. Cited in Hammond, *Reading, Publishing, and the Formation of Literary Taste*, 106–7.
47. This percentage was generated by cross-referencing titles with a comprehensive index of Taishō and Shōwa-era literary translations described in the following paragraphs.
48. Cited in Obi, *Shuppan to shakai*, 201–2.
49. See, for example, David Damrosch, *What Is World Literature?* (Princeton, NJ: Princeton University Press, 2003); Giselè Sapiro, "Globalization and Cultural Diversity in the Book Market: The Case of Literary Translations in the US and in France," *Poetics* 38 (January 2010): 419–39; Priya Joshi, *In Another Country: Colonialism, Culture, and the English Novel in India* (New York: Columbia University Press, 2002); and B. Venkat Mani, *Recoding World Literature: Libraries, Print Culture, and Germany's Pact with Books* (New York: Fordham University Press, 2017).
50. *Meiji-ki hon'yaku bungaku sōgō nenpyō*, vol. 51 of *Meiji hon'yaku bungaku zenshū*, ed. Kawato Michiaki et al. (Ōzorasha, 2001). Due to the challenges of performing OCR on this volume, only publication year and original language were captured for each entry.
51. *Meiji·Taishō·Shōwa hon'yaku bungaku mokuroku*, ed. Kokuritsu Kokkai Toshokan (Kazama Shobō, 1959).
52. For an analysis of foreign literary trade as mediated by modernist poetry magazines, see Hoyt Long, "Fog and Steel: Mapping Communities of Translation in an Information Age," *Journal of Japanese Studies* 41, no. 2 (Summer 2015): 281–316.
53. Publication figures are taken from *Shuppan nenkan*, an annual trade journal that republished government statistics on publishing trends. The truncated time frame is due to these statistics not beginning until 1881 and going unrecorded from 1943 to 1949. Ideally, one should calculate these percentages based on discrete volumes, and not on individual translations, but the Taishō/Shōwa metadata does not allow for aggregation to the volume level. For an analysis of the Meiji period translation data particularly focused on literary translation as a profession, see James Hadley, "The Beginnings of Literary Translation in Japan: An Overview," *Perspectives: Studies in Translation Theory and Practice* 26, no. 4 (2018): 560–75.
54. In one of the earliest data-supported studies of literary translation, Ōta Saburō finds a similar decline in a data set compiled from card catalog records at the Ueno Library and Japan PEN Club. He finds no corresponding decline in rates of publication for original works. Along with the "High Treason Incident," he posits that

the Russo-Japanese War and the onset of World War I may have had a role in the drop-off. See Ōta Saburō, "Hon'yaku bungaku," vol. 14 of *Iwanami kōza Nihon bungaku-shi* (Iwanami Shoten, 1959), 21.

55. Jay Rubin notes that translations by Molière and Maupassant came under particular scrutiny. When the Ministry of Education formed a Committee on Literature in 1911 to ostensibly reform literature toward the state's moralistic aims, it set as one of its goals the commissioning of "great" foreign literature containing "great ideas." Skeptical observers found the whole idea both paradoxical and ludicrous given the state's past attitude toward foreign works, and indeed very little came of the venture. Jay Rubin, *Injurious to Public Morals: Writers and the Meiji State* (Seattle: University of Washington Press, 1984), 199–212.
56. John Galsworthy, *Shūto sono hoka*, trans. Ōtani Gyōseki (Dai Nihon Tosho, 1914). Ōtani, incidentally, had been sent to study in London by the Ministry of Education from 1909 to 1911 and was a student of Lafcadio Hearn's, whose work he would translate in the 1920s.
57. In more technical terms, a significant p-value means that there is evidence to reject the null hypothesis: that the coefficients in the linear models fit to each subsample are equal, and thus a model fit to the entire sample would perform just as well. To determine the p-value, the sum of squared residuals of each of the fitted models (on the whole sample and the two subsamples) are combined to produce the Chow statistic, which is then compared to a test statistic from the F distribution based on number of parameters and sample size.
58. It is important to note that the change to copyright law in 2018 did not reinstate copyright for authors who died prior to 1968. It only extended copyright to seventy years for those who died in 1968 or later.
59. Edward Mack, *Manufacturing Modern Japanese Literature: Publishing, Prizes, and the Ascription of Literary Value* (Durham, NC: Duke University Press, 2010), 112.
60. On the history of this anthology, see Wada Yoshie, *Chikuma Shobō no sanjūnen 1940–1970* (Chikuma Shobō, 2011), 237–43; and Onoue Yukio, *Shuppan gyōkai* (Kyōikusha Shinsho, 1991), 180–82.
61. Nakamura Mitsuo, "Literature Under the Occupation," trans. Atsuko Ueda, in *The Politics and Literature Debate in Postwar Japanese Criticism 1945–1952*, ed. Atsuko Ueda et al. (Lanham, MD: Lexington Books, 2017), 258.
62. Guillory, *Cultural Capital*, 30.
63. Cited in Mack, *Manufacturing Modern Japanese Literature*, 97–98.
64. Saitō Mineko notes that the "Library Law" (Toshokan Hō) of 1950, which spurred the building of new public libraries, and the "School Library Law" (Gakkō Toshokan Hō) of 1954, which mandated that every primary and secondary school have its own library, drastically increased demand for reference volumes and anthologies. Saitō Mineko, "Nihon bungaku zenshū to sono jidai (jō): Zenshū ga shuppan bunka o riido shita koro," *Bungei* 54, no. 1 (2015): 44.
65. Mack, *Manufacturing Modern Japanese Literature*, 94–95.
66. The full list can be found in Hashimoto Motome, *Nihon shuppan hanbai-shi* (Kōdansha, 1964), 366–76.
67. The Nichigai index is less comprehensive when it comes to author anthologies, including just four of the twenty-four listed by Hashimoto. However, the index also includes several author anthologies he does not list.

68. Takashima Ken'ichirō, "Kadokawa Shoten *Shōwa bungaku zenshū* no hanbai senryaku—sengo zenshūbon būmu to bungaku jōkyō o megutte (1)," *Kindai bungaku kenkyū* 21 (2004): 1. He argues that changes in paper production, which became easier and cheaper to produce after government restrictions were lifted, was the main causal driver for the rapid rise in *zenshū* publication.
69. Saitō Mineko, "Nihon bungaku zenshū to sono jidai (ge): Kongon no rokujū nendai kara zenshū baburu no hōkai made," *Bungei* 54, no. 2 (2015): 350–53.
70. Author labels were taken from a digital version of Shinchōsha's *Nihon bungaku jiten* and applied to every author in the Nichigai index. Authors not in the dictionary, and who had ten or more entries in the index, were labeled manually using other reference sources, such as Wikipedia. For prodigious authors who worked in multiple genres (e.g., Iwano Hōmei, Miyazawa Kenji, Nagatsuka Takashi, Satō Haruo), works of fiction were labeled manually.
71. As this problem is potentially further compounded for authors who were prolific poets, I have filtered out omnibus anthologies strictly dedicated to poetry.
72. Takashima, "Kadokawa shoten *Shōwa bungaku zenshū* no hanbai senryaku," 4. Length was certainly not a limiting factor for *Nobi*, which is tied for the most anthologized title even by absolute count. Shiga Naoya's epic *An'ya kōro* (A Dark Night's Passing) is tied for fifth most anthologized.
73. One place to begin this inquiry is the Japan PEN Club, a national literary association with which most writers and poets were affiliated in the postwar period. An official roster published in 1979 lists 1,101 members, 13.6 percent of whom I verified as female. The roster is from Iwaya Daishi, *Nihon Bungeika Kyōkai gojūnenshi* (Nihon Bungei Kyōkai, 1979). For a recent quantitative study of demographic shifts in female authorship across more than two centuries of English fiction, see Ted Underwood, David Bamman, and Sabrina Lee, "The Transformation of Gender in English-Language Fiction," *Journal of Cultural Analytics* (February 2018), https://culturalanalytics.org/article/11035.
74. Richard So, Yuancheng Zhu, and I address these issues as they impinge on the problem of race in Richard So, Hoyt Long, and Yuancheng Zhu, "Race, Writing, and Computation: Racial Difference and the US Novel, 1880–2000," *Journal of Cultural Analytics* (January 11, 2019), https://culturalanalytics.org/article/11057.
75. In a list of 1,014 out-of-copyright authors assembled by Aozora (as of 2018), just over 5 percent are female.
76. Anno Izumi and Nichigai Asoshiētsu, *Kyōkasho keisai sakuhin 13000: yonde okitai meichō annai* (Nichigai Asoshiētsu, 2008).
77. On the history of literature as it has intersected with secondary language education and textbooks, see Ken K. Ito, "Reading *Kokoro* in the High School Textbook" (paper presented at Sōseki's Diversity: A Workshop, University of California, Berkeley, CA, May 2015); Ishihara Chiaki, *Kokugo kyōkasho no shisō* (Chikuma Shobō, 2005); and Sano Miki, *"Sangetsuki" wa naze kokumin kyōzai to natta no ka* (Taishūkan Shoten, 2013).
78. "Maihime" peaks at 25 percent in 1985 before trending downward. It is important to keep in mind that textbooks are divided into grade levels, with specific *teiban* texts assigned to each level. The percentages in this figure reflect the totals for all levels. On the postwar canonization of "Sangetsuki," see Sano, *"Sangetsuki"*.

79. For purposes of comparison, I exclude foreign and premodern authors from these lists. But it is worth noting that Murasaki Shikibu, the Brothers Grimm, Edgar Allan Poe, and Arthur Conan Doyle are in the list of the top twenty most accessed authors.
80. In choosing the appropriate statistic to measure correlation of ranked lists, one first has to decide if there is an objectively true ranking or if the lists are generated by observers in the absence of a true ranking. Here it is the latter case, and I want to measure how well the observations agree. A second consideration is whether the ranked lists have ties. Mine do, and thus require a modified Kendall's tau statistic, as explained in Julián Urbano and Mónica Marrero, "The Treatment of Ties in AP Correlation," *ICTIR '17 Proceedings of the ACM SIGIR International Conference on Theory of Information Retrieval* (October 2017): 321–24. A third consideration is whether one wants to give more weight to how well rankings match at the top of the lists as opposed to treating all rank levels the same. For this, one can use AP correlation. Here I do not give preference to rankings at the top.
81. My use of the mean as a cutoff point is somewhat arbitrary and was necessary to limit the size of the corpus so dates of first publication could be identified for every work. It is critical to note that the date of first publication does not always correspond to the edition of the work included in Aozora. Volunteers generally use anthologized versions of texts rather than the text as originally published or serialized. Further study is needed to assess the range and scale of changes and elisions introduced by this reliance on anthologies.
82. The figures for this data are provided in the file "Shuppan_Nenkan_Data.xlsx," which can be found in this book's code and data repository in the chapter 2 folder.
83. On the idea of "outer limits" and a "relational mode of reasoning" about large samples, see Ted Underwood, *Distant Horizons: Digital Evidence and Literary Change* (Chicago: University of Chicago Press, 2019), 176–78.
84. All texts in this book have been tokenized and part-of-speech tagged using the MeCab tokenizer and UNIDIC dictionary for morphological analysis. The latter represents the current state of the art in automatic parsing of Japanese language texts and was developed by linguists at the National Institute for Japanese Language and Linguistics.
85. The phrase is taken from Desrosières, who describes how these political and cognitive processes helped define "a pertinent whole," and indeed the idea of "representativeness," as sampling methods evolved in various schools of statistics. Alain Desrosières, *The Politics of Large Numbers: A History of Statistical Reasoning*, trans. Camille Naish (Cambridge, MA: Harvard University Press, 1998), 234. The whole became a "fact" as much through conceptual processes as through collective agreement.
86. Josephine Miles, *Major Adjectives in English Poetry: From Wyatt to Auden* (Berkeley: University of California Press, 1946), 306–8.
87. For a critique of comparison on epistemological and ethical grounds, see Natalie Melas, "Merely Comparative," *PMLA* 128, no. 3 (May 2013): 652–59.
88. Stanley Fish, "What Is Stylistics and Why Are They Saying Such Terrible Things About It?" In *Is There a Text in This Class?: The Authority of Interpretive Communities* (Cambridge, MA: Harvard University Press, 1980), 134.

89. Alan Liu, *Local Transcendence: Essays on Postmodern Historicism and the Database* (Chicago: University of Chicago Press, 2008), 259–60.
90. The previously cited works of Bode, Piper, and Underwood are exemplary of the kinds of debate happening around sampling as methodological and epistemological practice.

3. GENRE AND REPETITION

1. See, for example, Karatani Kōjin, *The Origins of Modern Japanese Literature*, ed. Brett de Bary (Durham, NC: Duke University Press, 1993; James Fujii, *Complicit Fictions: The Subject in the Modern Japanese Prose Narrative* (Berkeley: University of California Press, 1993); and Janet Walker, *The Japanese Novel of the Meiji Period and the Ideal of Individualism* (Princeton, NJ: Princeton University Press, 1979).
2. See Robert Hegel and Richard Hessney, eds., *Expressions of Self in Chinese Literature* (New York: Columbia University Press, 1985), in particular Leo Ou-fan Lee, "The Solitary Traveler: Images of the Self in Modern Chinese Literature": 282–307; Jaroslav Průšek, *The Lyrical and the Epic: Studies of Modern Chinese Literature* (Bloomington: Indiana University Press, 1980); Lydia Liu, *Translingual Practice: Literature, National Culture, and Translated Modernity—China, 1900–1937* (Stanford, CA: Stanford University Press, 1995); and Yoon Sun Yang, *From Domestic Women to Sensitive Young Men: Translating the Individual in Early Colonial Korea* (Cambridge, MA: Harvard University Press, 2017), which challenges the male-centered frame that so often dominates histories of modern self-narrative in East Asia.
3. Edward Fowler, *The Rhetoric of Confession: Shishōsetsu in Early Twentieth-Century Japanese Fiction* (Berkeley: University of California Press, 1988), 3.
4. Tomi Suzuki, *Narrating the Self: Fictions of Japanese Modernity* (Stanford, CA: Stanford University Press, 1996), 5–6. The other quotes are by Mark Bould and Sherryl Vint as cited in Ted Underwood, *Distant Horizons: Digital Evidence and Literary Change* (Chicago: University of Chicago Press, 2019), 334; and by Jacques Derrida as cited in Andrew Piper, *Enumerations: Data and Literary Study* (Chicago: University of Chicago Press, 2018), 97.
5. See Underwood, *Distant Horizons*, chap. 2; and Piper, *Enumerations*, chap. 4. I also explore these ideas in Hoyt Long and Richard Jean So, "Literary Pattern Recognition: Modernism Between Close Reading and Machine Learning," *Critical Inquiry* 42, no. 2 (Winter 2016): 235–66.
6. This summary of Hirabayashi's views is given in Edward Mack, *Manufacturing Modern Japanese Literature: Publishing, Prizes, and the Ascription of Literary Value* (Durham, NC: Duke University Press, 2010), 164. For an overview of Nakamura's position, as well as those who joined him in criticizing the I-novel, see Mack, 151–66; and Edward Fowler, *The Rhetoric of Confession*, 44–51.
7. From Kume Masao, "The I-Novel and the Mental State Novel," described in detail in Mack, *Manufacturing Modern Japanese Literature*, 157–60.
8. From Uno Kōji, "My Views on the 'I-Novel.'" Cited in Mack, *Manufacturing Modern Japanese Literature*, 160–61; and Seiji Lippit, *Topographies of Japanese Modernism* (New York: Columbia University Press, 2002), 29.

9. On what has come to be known as the "plotless novel" debate, see Lippit, *Topographies of Japanese Modernism*, 44–50.
10. Jonathan Zwicker, *Practices of the Sentimental Imagination: Melodrama, the Novel, and the Social Imaginary in Nineteenth-Century Japan* (Cambridge, MA: Harvard University Asia Center, 2006), 168.
11. Robert Darnton, *The Forbidden Bestsellers of Pre-Revolutionary France* (New York: Norton, 1995), 169.
12. Franco Moretti, *The Bourgeois: Between History and Literature* (London: Verso, 2013), 19.
13. Piper, *Enumerations*, 3–4.
14. J. Hillis Miller, *Fiction and Repetition: Seven English Novels* (Cambridge, MA: Harvard University Press, 1982), 1–2.
15. These ideas are described in James Williams, *Gilles Deleuze's Difference and Repetition: A Critical Introduction and Guide* (Edinburgh: Edinburgh University Press, 2013), 11–12.
16. For the full list, see Gabriel Altmann and Reinhard Köhler, *Forms and Degrees of Repetition in Texts* (Berlin: Walter de Gruyter, 2015), 5–6.
17. Deborah Tannen refers to these multiple contexts of repetition as "dimensions of fixity," noting that although "all expressions are relatively fixed in form, one cannot help but notice that some instances of language are more fixed than others. . . . There is, first, a continuum of relative fixity in form, another of relative fixity with respect to context, and a third with respect to time." Deborah Tannen, *Talking Voices: Repetition, Dialogue, and Imagery in Conversational Discourse* (Cambridge: Cambridge University Press, 2007), 55.
18. Its use can even be unconscious, such as when a speaker repeats what someone has said with a split-second delay or otherwise imitates her speech. When this imitation becomes obsessive, or automatic in the sense of not being motivated by external stimuli, then repetition can be read as a symptom of mental or neurological maladies. For an extensive list of possible interpretations of repetition, see Altmann and Köhler, *Forms and Degrees of Repetition in Text*, 2–3; and Tannen, *Talking Voices*, chap. 3.
19. Selections were based on Fowler, *The Rhetoric of Confession*; Hasegawa Izumi, "Meiji·Taishō·Shōwa shishōsetsu sanjūgo sen," *Kokubungaku: kaishaku to kanshō* 27, no. 14 (1962): 77–90; and Akiyama Shun and Katsumata Hiroshi, eds., *Watakushi shōsetsu handobukku* (Bensei Shuppan, 2014). Additional texts were identified by author entries in the *Nihon kindai bungaku daijiten* and selected based on their degree of autobiographical content. Finally, I included several texts that are hallmarks of Naturalist style (e.g., Tokuda Shūsei's *Arakure*, Arishima Takeo's *Aru onna*) but are not recognized as I-novels. Texts are from Aozora or were digitized manually from print editions. Thirty-five unique authors are represented in the corpus. The full list of texts can be found in the file "Ch3CorpusMetadata.xlsx," included in the chapter 3 folder of the code and data repository.
20. The popular corpus draws on the Aozora archive and contains titles by eighteen unique authors.
21. This approach has the benefit of returning a statistic for determining significance but still has the downside of not being able to account for the "burstiness" of language (i.e., when a word is high in frequency because it is the subject of particular

discourse, as with character names). Code for both approaches is provided in "jp_feature_extraction.ipynb." For a comparison of the many statistical approaches to distinctive word analysis and the relative merits and weaknesses of each, see Burt L. Monroe, Michael P. Colaresi, and Kevin M. Quinn, "Fightin' Words: Lexical Feature Selection and Evaluation for Identifying the Content of Political Conflict," *Political Analysis* 16 (2008): 372–403.

22. Shimamura Hōgetsu, "Jo ni kaete jinseikanjō no shizenshugi o ronzu." Cited in Fowler, *The Rhetoric of Confession*, 100.
23. See Fowler, *The Rhetoric of Confession*; Irmela Hijiya-Kerschnereit, *Rituals of Self-Revelation: Shishōsetsu as Literary Genre and Socio-Cultural Phenomenon* (Cambridge, MA: Harvard University Council on East Asian Studies, 1996); and Barbara Mito Reed, "Language, Narrative Structure, and the *Shōsetsu*" (PhD diss., Princeton University, 1988).
24. See Kisaka Motoi, *Kindai bunshō seiritsu no shosō* (Osaka: Wazumi shoin, 1988), chaps. 4–5; and Seko Katashi, *Kindai Nihon bunshō-shi* (Hakuteisha, 1968), chap. 3. On the distinction between vernacular style and shifts in conceptual and grammatical structure, see also Karatani, *The Origins of Modern Japanese Literature*, 49–51; and Suzuki, *Narrating the Self*, 44. Kisaka singles out Naturalist writers specifically for their heavy adoption of Western syntax and expressive forms. Kisaka, *Kindai bunshō seiritsu no shosō*, 382–83. As Suzuki notes, Tanizaki Jun'ichirō made this connection as early as 1929, insisting that Naturalist writers were largely responsible for the westernization of the modern vernacular style. Suzuki, *Narrating the Self*, 176.
25. This flexibility, some argue, is what allowed for the slippages between narratorial authority and character viewpoint that blurred the I-novel's status as realist fiction. See Reed, "Language, Narrative Structure, and the *Shōsetsu*," 144–69; and Fowler, *The Rhetoric of Confession*, chap. 2.
26. For a thorough review of this criticism, particularly the contributions of Itō Sei, Hirano Ken, and Kobayashi Hideo, see Fowler, *The Rhetoric of Confession*, chap. 3; and Hijiya-Kirschnereit, *Rituals of Self-Revelation*, chap. 9.
27. These are descriptions given, respectively, by Yasuoka Shōtarō (25), Yokomitsu Ri'ichi (52), Kume Masao (47), Itō Sei (63), and Uno Kōji (7) as cited in Fowler, *The Rhetoric of Confession*.
28. Cited in Walker, *The Japanese Novel of the Meiji Period*, 197fn2.
29. Christopher Hill, "Exhausted by Their Battles with the World: Neurasthenia and Civilization Critique in Early Twentieth-Century Japan," in *Perversion and Modern Japan*, ed. Nina Cornyetz and Keith Vincent (London: Routledge, 2009), 243.
30. On the "neurasthenia novel," see Hibi Yoshitaka, *'Jiko hyōsho' no bungaku-shi* (Kanrin Shobō, 2002), 228–34. For a detailed account of how modern authorship came to be equated with mental aberration, see Pau Pitarch-Fernandez, "Cultivated Madness: Aesthetics, Psychology and the Value of the Author in Early 20th-Century Japan" (PhD diss., Columbia University, 2015).
31. David Baguley, *Naturalist Fiction: The Entropic Vision* (Cambridge: Cambridge University Press, 1990), 207.
32. Cited in Pitarch-Fernandez, "Cultivated Madness," 26.
33. Cited in Hill, "Exhausted by Their Battles with the World," 252.
34. The level of redundancy may even be stable across languages. See Marcelo A. Montemurro and Damián H. Zanette, "Universal Entropy of Word Ordering

Across Linguistic Families," *PLoS ONE* 6(5): e19875, https://doi.org/10.1371/journal.pone.0019875.

35. Walter Ong, *Orality and Literacy: The Technologizing of the Word* (London: Routledge, 1991), 39–40.
36. Tannen, *Talking Voices*, 49.
37. For a recent survey of work on repetition and colloquial style in literature, as well as a superb attempt to scale up this work quantitatively, see Marissa Gemma, Frédéric Glorieuz, and Jean-Gabriel Ganascia, "Operationalizing the Colloquial Style: Repetition in 19th-Century American Fiction," *Digital Scholarship in the Humanities* 32, no. 2 (June 2017): 312–35.
38. Lippit, *Topographies of Japanese Modernism*, 28–29.
39. Tanizaki Jun'ichirō, *Bunshō tokuhon* [1934] (Chukō Bunko, 2013), 70–72.
40. In the limited scholarship on the influence of *oubunmyaku* on Japanese, it is Naturalist writers such as Shimazaki, and members of the Shirakaba group (White Birch Society), including Mushanokōji and Arishima Takeo, who are singled out as perfecting the adoption of foreign elements. Kisaka makes the case that the representation of interiority itself demanded the kinds of clear delineation of subjects and subject-predicate relations that Western grammatical forms afforded. Kisaka, *Kindai bunshō seiritsu no shosō*, 378–83.
41. Tanizaki, *Bunshō tokuhon*, 63–68, 78–80.
42. Sigmund Freud, "Remembering, Repeating, and Working-Through" [1914], in *Standard Edition* 12 (London: The Hogarth Press and the Institute of Psycho-Analysis, 1953–1974): 145–57.
43. George Zipf, *Human Behavior and the Principle of Least Effort* (Cambridge, MA: Addison-Wesley Press, 1949), 21. The thesis was originally formulated in George Zipf, *The Psycho-Biology of Language: An Introduction to Dynamic Philology* (Boston: Houghton Mifflin Company, 1935). His theories are summarized in William Levelt, *A History of Psycholinguistics: The Pre-Chomskyan Era* (Oxford: Oxford University Press, 2013), 453.
44. Zipf, *Human Behavior and the Principle of Least Effort*, 285–87.
45. John B. Carroll, "Analysis of Verbal Behavior," *Psychological Review* 51 (March 1944): 102–19.
46. Wendell Johnson, *Language and Speech Hygiene: An Application of General Semantics, Outline of a Course* (Chicago: Chicago Institute of General Semantics, 1939), 11.
47. Levelt, *A History of Psycholinguistics*, 456.
48. Roman Jakobson, "Langue and Parole: Code and Message," in *On Language*, ed. Linda R. Waugh and Monique Monville-Burston (Cambridge, MA: Harvard University Press, 1990), 97–98; and Anthony Wilden, *System and Structure: Essays in Communication and Exchange* (London: Tavistock, 1972), 35–37.
49. See, for example, Wilhem Fucks, "On the Mathematical Analysis of Style," *Biometrika* 39, no. 9 (1952): 122–29. Fucks applied information theory to stylistics by comparing the entropy of syllables in prose versus poetry.
50. Gustav Herdan, *Language as Choice and Chance* (Groningen: P. Noordhoff, 1956), 167.
51. For critiques of entropy as a measure of lexical richness, see Philippe Thoiron, "Diversity Index and Entropy as Measures of Lexical Richness," *Computers and the Humanities* 20, no. 3 (1986): 197–202; and David Hoover, "Another Perspective on Vocabulary Richness," *Computers and the Humanities*, 37, no. 2 (2003): 151–78.

52. A "word" is defined as any single morphological unit, including grammatical particles, as determined by the MeCab-Unidic tokenizer. Across 1,200 of these 1,000 word segments, there are on average about 1,500 individual phonetic and Chinese characters.
53. Ioannis Kontoyiannis, "The Complexity and Entropy of Literary Styles," *NSF Technical Report* 97 (June 1996–October 1997): 1–15. This is a nonparametric entropy measure in the sense that it is not bound to the smaller contexts (unigrams, bigrams, etc.) of Markov-based entropy measures. For each position *i* in a text's sequence of units (here individual characters), it looks for the longest sequence starting at *i* that does not occur prior to *i*. For example, at *i* = 100, it will scan for the longest sequence of characters that does not occur in the previous 100 characters. It uses these lengths at various *i* to estimate an entropy value for the text as a whole. The size of the window across which we can look for matching sequences depends on the length of the shortest texts in the corpus, but the entropy score itself is not correlated with text length.
54. See George Yule, *The Statistical Study of Literary Vocabulary* [1944] (Hamden, CT: Archon Books, 1968). The measure is calculated as follows: $10{,}000 \times (M_2 - M_1)/(M_1 \times M_1)$. M_1 is the number of word tokens. M_2 is calculated by multiplying the number of words at a given rank frequency by the square of that rank (e.g., all words occurring 2 times multiplied by 2^2) and then summing over these values. Yule's K assumes that word frequency in a sample of text follows a Poisson distribution, treating words as fixed events that occur with a known average rate for any interval (i.e., the length of the sample). Herdan later corrected for this assumption, developing a modified K that was widely adopted in the 1960s as a stylistic measure for the concentration of vocabulary, including attempts to analyze schizophrenic language. Juhan Tuldava provides an overview of these measures in Juhan Tuldava, "Stylistics, Author Identification," in *Quantitative Linguistics: An International Handbook*, ed. Reinhard Köhler et al. (Berlin: Walter de Gruyter, 2005), 374. See also Arthur Holstein, "A Statistical Analysis of Schizophrenic Language," *Statistical Methods in Linguistics* 4 (1965): 10–14.
55. Tuldava, "Stylistics, Author Identification," 375. Guiraud's C is the sum of frequencies of the fifty most frequent "content" words divided by two times the total number of content words.
56. On the relation of Yule's K to entropy measures, see Kumiko Tanaka-Ishii and Shunsuke Aihara, "Computational Constancy Measures of Texts," *Association for Computational Linguistics* 41, no. 3 (2015): 481–502.
57. The test is a pairwise t-test with Bonferroni correction. Significance simply means that the null hypothesis (that the mean values in each sample are equal) is rejected at the $p <= .05$ level. Tests and results are documented in the "Analysis.R" file associated with this chapter in the data and code repository.
58. For an explanation of the logistic regression classifier, see Underwood, *Distant Horizons*, appendix B. A regression algorithm simply infers a relation between two variables based on the degree to which a change in one variable correlates with a change in the other. With multiple independent variables (our features), this inference is extended to as many dimensions as there are variables.
59. Best subset selection is a process for testing every possible combination of features (up to fifteen) to determine the combination that produces the highest classification

accuracy. Variables that do not contribute to strengthening the accuracy are left out. In chapter 4, I demonstrate a more hands-on approach to selecting features and interpreting their explanatory contribution. All code and results for classification are contained in the "Classifier.R" file associated with this chapter.

60. These words were extracted using the chi-square test on more than six hundred segments in the lowest quartile for mean entropy and the same number of segments in the topmost quartile. "GetChunks.R" contains code for extracting these segments.
61. I focus on the sentence level for pronouns to account for their repeated presence from sentence to sentence, rather than just their overall ratio. These pronouns include two dozen honorific and orthographic variants for "I," "he," and "she." For conjunctions and connective words, I use a list of more than eighty identified by Kisaka in a study on their introduction and changing use from the Meiji to Taishō periods. See Kisaka, *Kindai bunshō seiritsu no shosō*, chap. 5. The full lists are provided in "jp_feature_extraction.ipynb."
62. Grammatical function words are also known as "stop words." I manually constructed a list of these words based on the I-novel and popular fiction texts. Examining the 1,000 most frequent items in these texts, I selected 202 items that have little semantic meaning on their own. Because of the corpus specific nature of these lists and the definitional ambiguity that surrounds stop words, one must be careful when applying them across different historical and generic contexts. That said, they have long been recognized as valuable aids in stylistic analysis and authorship-attribution research.
63. Kasai was frequently bedridden during his last years of life due to excessive drinking, and it was only through dictation that publishers could extract material from him. See Fowler, *Rhetoric of Confession*, 272–74.
64. Fowler, *Rhetoric of Confession*, 284–85.
65. This holds true of the two other Kasai titles at the top of figure 3.3, "Shiji o umu" (A Stillbirth, 1925) and "Nakama" (In the Same Boat, 1921).
66. Fowler, *Rhetoric of Confession*, 151–52.
67. Chikamatsu Shūkō, *Giwaku*, in *Gendai Nihon bungaku taikei* (Chikuma Shobō, 2010), 21:326.
68. Cited in Hibi, *'Jiko hyōsho' no bungaku-shi*, 228. The statement was made in a review of recent works by Shiga Naoya.
69. Pitarch-Fernandez, "Cultivated Madness," 33.
70. Pitarch-Fernandez provides a detailed description of these pathographies by critic Itō Ken and the general survey, which was conducted in 1923. Pitarch-Fernandez, "Cultivated Madness," 53–75.
71. Uno is cited in Lippit, *Topographies of Japanese Modernism*, 29. See also John Whittier Treat, *The Rise and Fall of Modern Japanese Literature* (Chicago: University of Chicago Press, 2018), 110.
72. See Kōno Toshirō, "*Omedetaki hito* no 'jibun,'" *Kokubungaku: Kaishaku to kyōzai no kenkyū* 4, no. 6 (May 1959): 78–83; and Ikeuchi Teruo, "Mushanokōji Saneatsu to 'Shirakaba'—'jibun' no seisei katei," *Kokubungaku: Kaishaku to kanshō* 64, no. 2 (February 1999): 44–49.
73. Arishima Takeo, "*Omedetaki hito* o yomite," *Shirakaba* 2 (April 1911): 102–3.
74. Mushanokōji Saneatsu, *Omedetaki hito*, in *Gendai Nihon bungaku zenshū* (Chikuma Shobō, 1973), 40:7–8.

75. Mushanokōji, *Omedetaki hito*, 25.
76. Arishima, "*Omedetaki hito* o yomite," 105. Emphasis mine. Arishima uses the English "plot" in this passage.
77. Arishima, "*Omedetaki hito* o yomite," 103.
78. Fowler, *Rhetoric of Confession*, 122.
79. Keith Vincent, "Hamaosociality: Narrative and Fascism in Hamao Shirō's *The Devil's Disciple*," in *The Culture of Japanese Fascism*, ed. Alan Tansman (Durham, NC: Duke University Press, 2009), 397. Vincent's essay offers a provocative reading of the work's sexual politics while confirming the presence of stylistic features to which the model is most sensitive.
80. As cited in Satoru Saito, *Detective Fiction and the Rise of the Japanese Novel, 1880–1930* (Cambridge, MA: Harvard University Asia Center, 2012), chap. 6. On the intersection of psychological theory and detective fiction in this period, especially as centered on the figure of the doppelgänger, see Miri Nakamura, *Monstrous Bodies: The Rise of the Uncanny in Modern Japan* (Cambridge, MA: Harvard University Asia Center, 2015); and Baryon Tensor Posadas, *Double Visions, Double Fictions: The Doppelgänger in Japanese Film and Literature* (Minneapolis: University of Minnesota Press, 2018).
81. On Kōga's role in these debates, which also involved Ranpō and critic Hirabayashi Hatsunosuke, who wrote a preface to one of Kōga's early works, see Yoshida Morio, *Tantei shōsetsu to Nihon kindai* (Seikyūsha, 2004), 15–22.
82. This initial research was conducted in collaboration with Anatoly Detwyler and Yuancheng Zhu. See Hoyt Long, Anatoly Detwyler, and Yuancheng Zhu, "Self-Repetition and East Asian Literary Modernity, 1900–1930," *Journal of Cultural Analytics* (May 2018), https://culturalanalytics.org/article/11040. This section leans heavily on the corpus building and analysis performed by Detwyler for this earlier essay. All code and data for this analysis can be accessed at the article URL. Much of the analysis of Japanese texts has been refined and expanded for this chapter, but the central findings remain the same.
83. See, for example, introduction to "Creation Society Literature," in *Zhongguo Xinwenxue daxi* 5, ed. Zheng Boqi (Shanghai: Liangyou tushu yinshua gongsi, 1981). Chih-tsing Hsia suggests in his classic study that, beyond the writings of a handful of representative individuals, Romanticism's single distinguishing quality was a "maudlin sentimentality . . . completely deficient in restraint and objectivity." See Chih-tsing Hsia, *A History of Modern Chinese Fiction*, 2nd ed. (New Haven, CT: Yale University Press, 1971), 95. Leo Ou-fan Lee argued a few years later that Romanticism was best defined sociologically, by way of its group libraries and clashes of personalities. Leo Ou-fan Lee, *The Romantic Generation of Modern Chinese Writers* (Cambridge, MA: Harvard University Press, 1973), 22.
84. See Edward Gunn, *Rewriting Chinese: Style and Innovation in Twentieth-Century Chinese Prose* (Stanford, CA: Stanford University Press, 1991); Liu, *Translingual Practice*; Haiyan Lee, *Revolution of the Heart: A Genealogy of Love in China, 1900–1950* (Stanford, CA: Stanford University Press, 2007); and Raymond Hsu, *The Style of Lu Hsun: Vocabulary and Usage* (Hong Kong: Centre of Asian Studies, University of Hong Kong Press, 1979).
85. Yu Dafu's works, for example, have been singled out for emphasizing journeys that are "incomplete, aimless, and marked with uncertainties." Cited in Liu, *Translingual*

Practice, 149. And Guo Moruo famously responded to early criticism of one of his works by saying "that it was a mistake to read his story as a straightforward narrative with a beginning, a climax, and an ending—he was trying to present the unconscious in the form of dream symbolism." Also cited in Liu, *Translingual Practice*, 131.

86. This corpus takes as its core the texts and authors named by Zheng in *Zhongguo Xinwenxue daxi*, vol. 5. It draws primarily on the pre-1925 works he lists to avoid mixing in the more political, mass-inflected works that Guo Moruo promoted after the May Thirtieth Incident.
87. The core of this collection draws on titles listed in the seminal "Mandarin Ducks and Butterfly Literature," Wei Shaochang, ed., *Yuanyang Hudie pai yanjiu ziliao* 2 (Shanghai: Shanghai wenyi chubanshe, 1962). However, many of the texts may not be strictly "Mandarin Ducks and Butterfly" works but popular (and commercially successful) works of "historical fiction" in the vein of *Romance of the Three Kingdoms*.
88. Included in the list of verbs for cognition and feeling were the following: 想, 觉得, 想起, 觉, and 感觉. This list also included a few nouns that potentially reflect scenes of internal thought or emotion: 心理, 知道, 感到, 思想, and 感情. One diction-based measure that was not reproduced from the Japanese case is the measure that tracks conjunction use; this was not part of the original experiment.
89. Cited in Yingjin Zhang, *The City in Modern Chinese Literature and Film: Configurations of Space, Time, and Gender* (Stanford, CA: Stanford University Press, 1996), 211.
90. Ye's liminal position made him difficult to classify in his own time but has also left him an understudied figure in scholarship today. This marginalization is partly due to his attacks on Lu Xun in the late 1920s, and his politics during the 1930s. Zhang, *The City in Modern Chinese Literature and Film*, 208.
91. Ye Lingfeng, *Ye Lingfeng xiaoshuo quanbian* (Shanghai: Xuelin chubanshe, 1997), 1:168.
92. This ending foregrounds Ye's debt to Oscar Wilde's *Salome* and its depiction of a femme fatale who kills in the name of love. See Xiaoyi Zhou, "Salome in China: The Aesthetic Art of Dying," in *Wilde Writings: Contextual Conditions*, ed. Joseph Bristow (Toronto: University of Toronto Press, 2003), 295–316.
93. "Although Ye Lingfeng's fiction contains 'newness' and experimentation, he is clearly committed to kitsch, which suggests repetition, banality, triteness. . . . [his stories are] at once avant-garde and receptive to mass culture." See Jianmei Liu, "Shanghai Variations on 'Revolution Plus Love,'" *Modern Chinese Literature and Culture* 14, no. 1 (Spring 2002): 82, 84.
94. Freud is especially warranted here as many of the Romantic writers featured his ideas, and Ye Lingfeng was a particular devotee of Freudian psychology. Jingyuan Zhang, *Psychoanalysis in China: Literary Transformations 1919–1949* (Ithaca, NY: Cornell University Press, 1992), 105.
95. Shu-mei Shih describes Ye's emergent literary group in the late 1920s as taking "Guo Moruo's 'explosion of the self' and Yu Dafu's self-indulgence to an extreme, aggrandizing the self in defiance of all constrictive norms and celebrating sexuality without the kind of anxiety that had troubled their May Fourth predecessors." See Shu-mei Shih, *Lure of the Modern: Writing Modernism in Semicolonial China, 1917–1937* (Berkeley: University of California Press, 2001), 255.

96. Treat, *Rise and Fall of Modern Japanese Literature*, 121.
97. Karatani, *Origins of Modern Japanese Literature*, 61.
98. Cited in Mary Poovey, *Genres of the Credit Economy: Mediating Value in Eighteenth- and Nineteenth-Century Britain* (Chicago: University of Chicago Press, 2008), 312–13. The quote is from a lecture Ruskin delivered in 1864, and in which Poovey finds the precursors to a reading formation that transferred the value of a literary work to the act of interpretation. It was because words were not referential or transparent that readers had to work, thus conferring value on literary texts that were not simply informative.
99. Poovey, *Genres of the Credit Economy*, 332.
100. Poovey, *Genres of the Credit Economy*, 344.
101. Poovey, *Genres of the Credit Economy*, 345.
102. This *junbungaku* corpus is composed of seventy titles with first publication dates ranging from 1898 to 1931. It includes canonical realist works by Sōseki, Tōson, Arishima, Ōgai, Akutagawa, and Tanizaki, but also works by Shiga, Chikamatsu, Uno Kōji, and Tokuda Shūsei, to whom I-novels have been attributed. Preliminary investigation shows that these titles diverge significantly from I-novels only with respect to the proportion of pronouns, with I-novels being slightly higher. Further investigation is needed to find out which "pure" literature titles are contributing to lower model accuracy.

4. INFLUENCE AND JUDGMENT

1. Kawaguchi Kyōichi, *Shōwa shonen no* Ulysses (Misuzu Shobō, 2005), 53–61. First to get a copy was Takagaki Matsuo, who read it in issues of *Little Review* procured at the Walden Bookstore in Chicago. Doi Kōichi acquired the Paris edition while traveling in Scotland. Both went on to become important translators and scholars of American and English literature.
2. See Horiguchi Daigaku, "Shōsetsu no shinkeishiki toshite no 'naishin dokuhaku,'" *Shinchō* (August 1925): 6–9.
3. Doi Kōichi, "Joisu no *Ulysses*," *Kaizō* 11, no. 2 (February 1929): 24–47.
4. Scholar Ōta Saburō compiled a bibliography of essays and translations related to James Joyce, and more generally to the stream-of-consciousness style. It lists more than two hundred items for the years 1918 to 1941, the majority published between 1929 and 1933. See Ōta Saburō, "Jeimuzu Joisu no shōkai to eikyō," *Gakuen* 175, no. 4 (April 1955): 14–38.
5. Cited in Hojō Fumio, "Jeimuzu Joisu to Nihon kindai shōsetsu (I)," *Publications of the Institute for Comparative Studies of Culture Affiliated to Tokyo Woman's Christian College* 41 (1980): 35.
6. Pascale Casanova, *The World Republic of Letters*, trans. M. B. Devevoise (Cambridge, MA: Harvard University Press, 2004), 103.
7. Horiguchi, "Shōsetsu no shinkeishiki toshite no 'naishin dokuhaku,'" 9. Williams's novel was originally published in Paris in 1923.
8. Franco Moretti, *Modern Epic: The World-System from Goethe to García Márquez*, trans. Quintin Hoare (London: Verso, 1996), 124.

9. These phrases were used by Donald Keene in his framing of Japanese modernist writings as a kind of brief deviation or sidetrack from an implied normal, because domestically rooted, track. Cited in William J. Tyler, introduction to *Modanizumu: Modernist Fiction from Japan, 1913–1938* (Honolulu: University of Hawai'i Press, 2008), 8. Tyler and others have since offered powerful critiques of this earlier framing.
10. Jonathan Culler, "Presupposition and Intertextuality," in *The Pursuit of Signs: Semiotics, Literature, Deconstruction* (Ithaca, NY: Cornell University Press, 1981), 103.
11. Culler, "Presupposition and Intertextuality," 105.
12. On structuralist approaches to intertextuality, especially as articulated by Genette, see Graham Allen, *Intertextuality* (London: Routledge, 2000), 96–111. Andrew Piper has connected Genette's ideas to the topological spaces created by computational models in Andrew Piper, "The Wertherian Exotext: Models of Transnational Circulation" (paper presented at the Modern Language Association Annual Meeting, Chicago, January 2014).
13. Kristeva's original formulation of the concept was in fact intended as a critique of a semiotics that maintained its objectivity by avoiding the human subject who performs the utterance under consideration. See Allen, *Intertextuality*, 32–50. Similarly, Barthes wrote that "*I* is not an innocent subject that is anterior to texts. . . . The *I* that approaches the text is itself already a plurality of other texts, of infinite or, more precisely, lost codes (whose origins are lost)." Cited in Culler, "Presupposition and Intertextuality," 102. Emphasis in original.
14. A summary and critique of Riffaterre's argument is given in Jay Clayton and Eric Rothstein, *Influence and Intertextuality in Literary History* (Madison: University of Wisconsin Press, 1991), 23–26.
15. Michael Riffaterre, *Semiotics of Poetry* (Bloomington: Indiana University Press, 1978), 5.
16. Nirvana Tanoukhi, "The Scale of World Literature," in *Immanuel Wallerstein and the Problem of the World: System, Scale, Culture*, ed. David Palumbo-Liu, Bruce Robbins, and Nirvana Tanoukhi (Durham, NC: Duke University Press, 2011), 87.
17. Franco Moretti, "Conjectures on World Literature," *New Left Review*, 121, no. 1 (January–February 2000): 60. Also Casanova, *The World Republic of Letters*.
18. See Sandra Bermann and Michael Wood, *Nation, Language, and the Ethics of Translation* (Princeton, NJ: Princeton University Press, 2005), 4–7; Emily Apter, *Against World Literature: On the Politics of Untranslatability* (London: Verso, 2013), 8–16.
19. David Damrosch, *What Is World Literature?* (Princeton, NJ: Princeton University Press, 2003), 4–5, 26.
20. Michael Allan, *In the Shadow of World Literature: Sites of Reading in Colonial Egypt* (Princeton, NJ: Princeton University Press, 2016), 18.
21. Allan, *In the Shadow of World Literature*, 29.
22. Isabel Hofmeyr, *The Portable Bunyan: A Transnational History of* The Pilgrim's Progress (Princeton, NJ: Princeton University Press, 2004), 14.
23. For a critique of Moretti's quantitative analysis as inimical to nonstructuralist models of world literature, and to interpretation more generally, see, especially, Apter, *Against World Literature*, 50–56.
24. As Kirsten Silva Gruesz argues, to focus only on innovation and originality in disenfranchised writers (i.e., those on the periphery of literary hegemonies) is to deny

them one of the things they seek in imitating others: "the kind of cultural authority that arises from similitude, from having effectively (or even ineffectively) identified oneself with language forms that signify power." It, too, she reminds us, is an act with inherent political interest. See Kirsten Silva Gruesz, *Ambassadors of Culture: The Transamerican Origins of Latino Writing* (Princeton, NJ: Princeton University Press, 2002), 29.

25. Cited in Leon Edel, *The Modern Psychological Novel* (New York: Dunlap, 1964), 91.
26. Cited in Erwin Steinberg, *The Stream of Consciousness and Beyond in "Ulysses"* (Pittsburgh, PA: University of Pittsburgh Press, 1973), 5–6.
27. Steinberg, *The Stream of Consciousness*, 6.
28. In addition to Steinberg, see Liisa Dahl, *Linguistic Features of the Stream-of-Consciousness Techniques of James Joyce, Virginia Woolf, and Eugene O'Neill* (Turku: Turun Yliopisto, 1970); Seymour Chatman, *Story and Discourse: Narrative Structure in Fiction and Film* (Ithaca, NY: Cornell University Press, 1978).
29. Dorrit Cohn, *Transparent Minds: Narrative Modes for Presenting Consciousness in Fiction* (Princeton, NJ: Princeton University Press, 1978), 10–11.
30. Moretti, *Modern Epic*, 155.
31. On SOC as a form of interior monologue, see Robert Humphrey, *Stream of Consciousness in the Modern Novel* (Berkeley: University of Berkeley Press, 1954); and Lawrence Bowling, "What Is the Stream of Consciousness Technique?," *PMLA* 65, no. 4 (1950): 333–45.
32. In addition to already cited works, see Melvin Friedman, *Stream of Consciousness: A Study in Literary Method* (New Haven, CT: Yale University Press, 1955); and Robert Scholes and Robert Kellogg, *The Nature of Narrative* (Oxford: Oxford University Press, 1966).
33. For English, the elements of free indirect discourse are simply the presence of "!" or "?" at the end of nondialogue sentences. To capture onomatopoeia and neologisms in English, a dictionary-based approach was used. In the first case we relied on a curated list of onomatopoeia. In the second, an English dictionary published in 1913. Type-token ratio (TTR) was measured on all words, all words except stop words, and all words except stop words and proper nouns, providing three separate measures. Each is a slightly different index of lexical diversity.
34. Metadata and code associated with the analysis of Anglophone texts can be found in the github repository at https://github.com/hoytlong/TurbulentFlow. This analysis was originally carried out with Richard Jean So. See Hoyt Long and Richard Jean So, "Turbulent Flow: A Computational Model of World Literature," *Modern Language Quarterly* 77, no. 3 (September 2016): 345–68. This chapter is a complete revision of the article, including revised code and analysis for the Japanese texts. The code and analysis for the Anglophone texts, however, remains largely the same.
35. Scholes and Kellogg, *The Nature of Narrative*, 193–206.
36. Prior to this procedure, known as randomized k-fold cross validation, the realist passages were also randomly sampled to create balanced classes. As there are only 120 SOC passages in total, compared with 2,010 realist passages, 4 from each of the 30 realist novels were selected for each test. These 120 passages are then, like the SOC passages, split into training and test sets (90 percent training, 10 percent test). A development set was not held out owing to the restricted size of the SOC sample.

37. Dahl, *Linguistic Features of the Stream-of-Consciousness Techniques*, 16, 34; Cohn, *Transparent Minds*, 94.
38. Other features deemed statistically significant, if less discriminative, were median sentence length, free indirect discourse, and TTR minus stop words (which lean toward SOC), as well as nominalized sentences (which lean away from SOC). The relative importance of features varies slightly with the sample of realist passages trained on, but the direction they lean is consistent across multiple samples.
39. On repetition and TTR as distinguishing features, see Dahl, *Linguistic Features of the Stream-of-Consciousness Techniques*, 49–50; and Steinberg, *The Stream of Consciousness*, 155–58.
40. Franco Moretti, "World-Systems Analysis, Evolutionary Theory, *Weltliteratur*," in *Immanuel Wallerstein and the Problem of the World: System, Scale, Culture*, ed. David Palumbo-Liu, Bruce Robbins, and Nirvana Tanoukhi (Durham, NC: Duke University Press, 2011), 70–71.
41. These 1,700 works are drawn from the much larger Chicago Novel Corpus, constructed at the Chicago Text Lab from a list of the most frequently held novels by American authors published between 1880 and 2000 as cataloged by WorldCat. The corpus comprises ten thousand volumes, with peak holdings around 1900 and the 1980s, and represents the work of about six thousand authors. It is biased by what librarians have historically valued, which is by extension that which academics and library patrons have valued.
42. Assuming there was an actual rise in the use of SOC-like elements followed by a leveling off, one could explain the latter as part of a conscious rejection by both American and British writers of the previous decade's interest in modernist techniques and an embrace, in the shadows of the Great Depression, of explicitly outward political forms of writing. See Barbara Foley, *Radical Representations: Politics and Form in U.S. Proletarian Fiction, 1929–1941* (Durham, NC: Duke University Press, 1993); and Michael Denning, *The Cultural Front* (London: Verso, 1997).
43. This analysis, performed using standard logistic regression, is described in more detail in Long and So, "Turbulent Flow," 353.
44. Friedman, *Stream of Consciousness*, 255–62.
45. Arthur Power, *Conversations with James Joyce* (London: Millington, 1974), 75.
46. Jeffrey Farnol, *The Way Beyond* (Boston: Little, Brown, 1933), 30.
47. A list of all the novels analyzed in this experiment, ranked by their probability of being SOC or not, is provided in "US_NOVELS_SOC_predictions.csv," which can be found in the chapter 4 folder in the code and data repository.
48. Kawaguchi, *Shōwa shonen no* Ulysses, 98.
49. Hayashi Kazuhito, "Itō Sei to ishiki no nagare," *Kobe College Studies* 32, no. 2 (December 1985): 73.
50. See Kawabata Yasunari, *Shōsetsu nyūmon* (Yōshobō, 1952), 133–34; and Nakamura Miharu, *Shūjiteki modanizumu: Tekisuto yōshikiron no kokoromi* (Hitsuji Shobō, 2006), 255.
51. Ōta Saburō, "Joisu no shōkai to eikyō," in *Joisu kenkyū*, ed. Itō Sei (Eihōsha, 1955), 216.
52. Hojō, "Jeimuzu Joisu to Nihon kindai shōsetsu (I)," 35.
53. See Ōta, "Joisu no shōkai to eikyō"; Hojō, "Jeimuzu Joisu to Nihon kindai shōsetsu (I)"; Mebed Sharif, "Shōwa shoki ni okeru 'ishiki no nagare' juyō wo megutte," *Issues*

in Language and Culture, no. 4 (March 2003): 5–16; and Isogai Hideo, "'Suishō gensō,'" in *Shōwa shotō no sakka to sakuhin* (Meiji Shoin, 1980), 200–216.

54. Moretti, "World-Systems Analysis, Evolutionary Theory, *Weltliteratur*," 71, 75.
55. In addition to the previously cited articles, see also Ōta Suzuko, "Kawabata Yasunari 'Hari to garasu to kiri': ishiki no nagare no shuhō to teima to no kanren," *Gakuen* 577 (January 1988): 155–66.
56. Tsuchida Kyōson, " 'Ishiki no nagare' no bungaku wo megutte," *Shinchō* (February 1932), 35. Tsuchida's essay offers one of the more detailed accounts of the idea of consciousness that SOC seeks to represent, namely, as a flow of mental events simultaneously occurring at different levels of conscious awareness. Itō Sei also delves deeply into these matters, focusing on SOC's use for depicting the processual nature of consciousness. See, especially, Itō Sei, "Jemusu Joisu no metōdo 'ishiki no nagare' ni tsuite," *Shi•Genjitsu* 1 (June 1930): 170–75.
57. In the case of neologisms, the model simply identifies all words in a passage written in *romaji* or *katakana*, the latter being a distinct syllabary typically used to mark foreign loan words. These words will not always be neologisms, but in fiction of this period they do often connote things or concepts viewed as "new" or "foreign" to Japan. For the case of onomatopoeia, a list of more than one thousand *gitaigo* and *giongo* was extracted from the electronic dictionary developed by Jim Breen and is available at http://nihongo.monash.edu//enamdict_doc.html.
58. All but one of the features from the Anglophone model were replicated in the Japanese model. Although gerunds and adverbial phrases are grammatically possible in Japanese, they never occur at the beginning of a sentence. In the case of free indirect discourse, I identify nondialogue sentences in which the ending is marked by grammatical indicators of interior monologue or personal address. These can be questions, exclamatory statements, statements of supposition, or volitional phrases.
59. See, especially, Itō Sei, "Shin shinrishugi bungaku," in *Itō Sei zenshū* (Kawade Shobō, 1956), 1:311–18. Originally published in the journal *Kaizō* in March 1932.
60. Itō Sei, "Jemusu Joisu no metōdo 'ishiki no nagare' ni tsuite," 171.
61. Haruyama Yukio, " 'Ishiki no nagare' to shōsetsu no kōsei," *Shinchō* (August 1931): 49.
62. Cited in Seiji Lippit, *Topographies of Japanese Modernism* (New York: Columbia University Press, 2002), 30. Lippit provides a comprehensive overview of these emerging debates.
63. This threshold is determined based on the observed distributions of the prediction scores. Here nearly all passage-level scores fall to either side of the 0.5 mark. It is important to examine these overall distributions when determining this threshold.
64. Pierre Bourdieu, *The Rules of Art: Genesis and Structure of the Literary Field*, trans. Susan Emmanuel (Stanford, CA: Stanford University Press, 1996), 125.
65. Nagamatsu Sadamu, "Nihon ni okeru 'ishiki no nagare' shōsetsu," *Shinbungaku kenkyū* (April 1931): 264.
66. Gruesz, *Ambassadors of Culture*, 28.
67. Nagamatsu collaborated with Itō and Tsujino Hisanori on the first translation of *Ulysses*, the first eight chapters of which were serialized in the coterie journal *Shi genjitsu* from 1930 to 1931. Another team of translators led by Morita Sōhei serialized their translation in *Bungaku* between 1932 and 1935. Both versions were

subsequently published as complete volumes by publishers Daiichi Shobō and Iwanami Bunko, respectively.

68. Nagamatsu Sadamu, *Nagamatsu Sadamu sakuhin shū* (Gogatsu Shobō, 1970), 475–76.
69. Cited in Friedman, *Stream of Consciousness*, 255.
70. Moretti, *Modern Epic*, 134–35.
71. I have translated this passage from Nagamatsu's original Japanese translation to try to preserve his rendering of it and without correcting for any mistranslations. Italicized words are those that appear in *katakana* in his translation, as is true for all subsequent translated passages.
72. Nagamatsu's essay appeared in *Nihon gendai bunshō kōza*, vol. 8, alongside essays on Proust and Morand by Hori Tatsuo and Horiguchi Daigaku, respectively. Hatano cites Nagamatsu's own citation of Joyce in an essay from the September issue of *Shisō*, which became the preface to his treatise on the psychology of style, published in 1935. See Hatano Kanji, *Bunshō shinrigaku*, in *Hatano Kanji zenshū* (Shōgakkan, 1990–1991), 1:7–23.
73. Of the twenty-six SOC-designated works from which passages are drawn, nearly all the works by Itō and Hori fall in the top half of being most like SOC works when predicted scores are averaged across works. Only Itō's late *Yūki no machi* (Streets of Fiendish Ghosts, 1937), whose first chapter is a direct reimagining of a chapter from *Ulysses*, is left out. Of the two works by Kawabata, "Hari to garasu to kiri" (Needles, Glass, and Mist, 1930) and "Suishō gensō" (Crystal Fantasy, 1931), the former is the only one in the top half. A list of all SOC titles ranked by mean probability score can be found in the file "average_scores_SOC_vs_Inovel.csv," in the "Results" folder for this chapter.
74. Nagamatsu, "Nihon ni okeru 'ishiki no nagare' shōsetsu," 262–64.
75. Moretti, *Modern Epic*, 174.
76. A list of all SOC titles ranked by score is in "average_scores_SOC_vs_Popular.csv," in the "Results" folder for this chapter.
77. Titles are roughly evenly distributed across the period, ranging from thirty titles in 1926 to a high of seventy-four titles in 1934. For each year, I also subsampled serialized titles so only one work of any continuous series is included per year.
78. An alternative way to examine the results would be to classify works as SOC or not based on a probability threshold of 0.5. Doing so reinforces the distinctiveness of 1926 and 1929 because both years contain the highest percentage of SOC works (14 percent). Other years are consistently lower, ranging from 3 percent to 9 percent. In this case, I decided to retain the raw probability scores to better highlight the overall distribution. More granular analysis could be performed by comparing distributions at the passage level.
79. An analysis of Yokomitsu's contributions to this debate, and of the larger discursive context in which it played out, is given in Komori Yōichi, *Kōzō toshite no katari* (Shinchōsha, 1988), 455–506. See also Lippit, *Topographies of Japanese Modernism*, 30–31; and Gregory Golley, *When Our Eyes No Longer See: Realism, Science, and Ecology in Japanese Literary Modernism* (Cambridge, MA: Harvard University Asia Center, 2008), 145–49. Where Komori and Lippit read Yokomitsu's theories of the written word as antireferential, Golley reads them as decidedly realist in their insistence on the interaction of the text and the reader's physical body.

In his interpretation, writer, text, and reader "constitute a single field of interaction, comprehensible only as a network of relations" (146).

80. Itō, "Jemusu Joisu no metōdo 'ishiki no nagare' ni tsuite," 173.
81. Nakamura Murao, "Genka bundan no shosō to shosakka," *Bungaku jidai* 1, no. 3 (July 1929): 14–20.
82. "Tantei shōsetsu zadankai," *Bungaku jidai* 1, no. 3 (July 1929): 53. The writers Ōshita Udaru and Morishita Uson also participated in the roundtable, with Katō Takeo serving as moderator.
83. "Tantei shōsetsu zadankai," 62–63.
84. Inukai Takeru, "Arabia-jin Eruafi," Aozora Bunko edition, transcribed from vol. 62 of *Gendai Nihon bungaku taikei* (Chikuma Shobō, 1973), https://www.aozora.gr.jp/cards/001543/files/52219_41895.html. The story first appeared in the magazine *Chūō kōron* in January 1929. It was later revised in 1957. The revised version is the one included in the Aozora database, raising the question of whether the original version would be judged similarly by the model. The passage translated here, for example, does not contain the sequence of single noun sentences found in the original 1929 version. It does, however, preserve most of the longer noun-ending sentences from the first version.
85. Chiba Shunji, "*Oshie no kiseki* ron," *Kokubungaku: kaishaku to kyōzai no kenkyū* 36, no. 3 (March 1991): 98.
86. Yumeno Kyūsaku, "Shinamai no fukuro," Aozora Bunko edition, transcribed from vol. 6 of *Yumeno Kyūsaku zenshū* (Chikuma Shobō, 1992), https://www.aozora.gr.jp/cards/000096/files/2101_18783.html. The story originally appeared in the April 1929 issue of *Shin seinen*.
87. Although published in February, the original work indicates that it was composed in November of the previous year.
88. Cited in Kawabata Yasunari, "Hori-shi no 'Bukiyō na tenshi,'" *Bungei shunjū* 7, no. 4 (April 1929): 141–42. He uses their praise to mount his countercritique.
89. Kawabata, "Hori-shi no 'Bukiyō na tenshi,'" 142.
90. Hori Tatsuo, "Bukiyō na tenshi," Aozora Bunko edition, transcribed from vol. 1 of *Hori Tatsuo zenshū* (Chikuma Shobō, 1977), https://www.aozora.gr.jp/cards/001030/files/4819_30040.html. The story originally appeared in the February 1929 issue of *Bungei shunjū*.
91. Hori Tatsuo, "Jisaku ni tsuite," *Hori Tatsuo zenshū* (Chikuma Shobō, 1977), 4:202–3. These comments were originally published in January in the literary magazine *Bungaku*.
92. Nakamura Shin'ichirō argues for "Bukiyō na tenshi" as a new kind of psychological novel in Nakamura Shin'ichirō, *Akutagawa • Hori • Tachihara no bungaku to sei* (Shinchō Sensho, 1980). His argument is well summarized in Ishikawa Norio, "Genzai o kanki suru buntai—Hori Tatsuo 'Bukiyō na tenshi' ron," *Kokugakuin zasshi* 99, no. 10 (October 1998): 44–57. My description of the work's unique use of present-tense verb endings relies primarily on Ishikawa Norio and Watase Shigeru, "Hori Tatsuo 'Bukiyō na tenshi' no buntai ni okeru dōshi shūshikei," *Fuji fuenikksu ronsō* 8 (March 2000): 45–58.
93. These remarks come, respectively, from a 1954 essay by Yoshida Ken'ichi and a 1977 essay by Shibusawa Tatsuhiko. Cited in Totsuka Manabu, "Hori Tatsuo 'Bukiyō na tenshi' ron—hon'yaku kara shōsetsu he," *Nihon kindai bungaku* 81 (November

2009): 124; and Ishikawa, "Genzai o kanki suru buntai—Hori Tatsuo 'Bukiyō na tenshi' ron," 44.

94. All passages from 1929 that fall below the 0.5 threshold for being SOC are available in the file "1929_SOC_Passages.txt," included in the "Results" folder for this chapter.
95. Cited in Allan, *In the Shadow of World Literature*, 34.

5. DISCOURSE AND CHARACTER

1. Itō Sei, "Uchinaru koe to kasō," in *Shōsetsu no hōhō* (Iwanami Bunkō, 2006), 51. The essay was originally published in the journal *Gendaijin* (Modern Man) in January 1948.
2. Yokomitsu Ri'ichi, *Shanghai*, trans. Dennis Washburn (Ann Arbor, MI: Center for Japanese Studies, 2001), 75–76. Emphasis added.
3. Seiji Lippit says of the novel that "the Chinese bodies that inhabit the text are objects to be consumed" and often "represented at the edges of human existence." Seiji Lippit, *Topographies of Japanese Modernism* (New York: Columbia University Press, 2002), 109–10.
4. Abdul R. JanMohamed, "The Economy of Manichean Allegory," in *"Race," Writing, and Difference*, ed. Henry Louis Gates (Chicago: University of Chicago Press, 1986), 83.
5. Mary Louise Pratt, "Scratches on the Face of the Country," in *"Race," Writing, and Difference*, ed. Henry Louis Gates (Chicago: University of Chicago Press, 1986), 139–40.
6. Edward Said, *Culture and Imperialism* (New York: Knopf, 1993), 67.
7. Yokomitsu, *Shanghai*, 157.
8. Edward Said, *Orientalism* (New York: Vintage Books, 1979), 8.
9. Said, *Orientalism*, 8.
10. Said, *Culture and Imperialism*, xxii.
11. For an insightful reflection on the relation of Said's work, and of postcolonial studies more broadly, to the field of digital humanities, see Roopika Risam, *New Digital Worlds: Postcolonial Digital Humanities in Theory, Praxis, and Pedagogy*. Evanston, IL: Northwestern University Press, 2019, 25–32.
12. See Etienne Balibar and Immanuel Wallerstein, *Race, Nation, Class: Ambiguous Identities*, trans. Chris Turner (London: Verso, 1991); Ann Stoler, *Race and the Education of Desire: Foucault's History of Sexuality and the Colonial Order of Things* (Durham, NC: Duke University Press, 1995); and Michael Hardt and Antonio Negri, *Empire* (Cambridge, MA: Harvard University Press, 2001), 190–95.
13. See Chris Hanscom and Dennis Washburn, "Introduction: Representations of Race in East Asian Empire," in *The Affect of Difference: Representations of Race in East Asian Empire*, eds. Hanscom and Washburn (Honolulu: University of Hawai'i Press, 2016), 2–3.
14. Said, *Orientalism*, 71.
15. John Frow, *Character and Person* (Oxford: Oxford University Press, 2016), 114.
16. Stoler, *Race and the Education of Desire*, chap. 2. Emphasis added.
17. Pratt, "Scratches on the Face of the Country," 140.

18. See Robert Tierney, *Tropics of Savagery: The Culture of Japanese Empire in Comparative Frame* (Berkeley: University of California Press, 2010); Edward Fowler, "The Buraku in Modern Japanese Literature: Texts and Contexts," *Journal of Japanese Studies* 26, no. 1 (2000): 1–39; Kate McDonald, *Placing Empire: Travel and the Social Imagination in Imperial Japan* (Berkeley: University of California Press, 2017); and Hanscom and Washburn, "Introduction," 5.
19. Said, *Culture and Imperialism*, 62.
20. On the relation of ethnographic discourse to the literature of empire, particularly as this relation is inverted by decolonization, see Jed Esty, *A Shrinking Island: Modernism and National Culture in England* (Princeton, NJ: Princeton University Press, 2004). On the notion of empire as a formal narrative symptom, see Fredric Jameson, "Modernism and Imperialism," in *Nationalism, Colonialism, and Literature* (Minneapolis: University of Minnesota Press, 1990), 49.
21. Alex Woloch, *The One vs. the Many: Minor Characters and the Space of the Protagonist in the Novel* (Princeton, NJ: Princeton University Press, 2003), 14. Woloch treats these as narratological categories, defining "character-space" as "that particular and charged encounter between an individual human personality and a determined space and position within the narrative as a whole." The "character-system" is "the arrangement of multiple and differentiated character-spaces . . . into a unified narrative structure."
22. Particularly insightful on these counts are Oguma Eiji, *A Genealogy of 'Japanese' Self-Images*, trans. David Askew (Melbourne: Trans Pacific Press, 2002); Nayoung Aimee Kwon, *Intimate Empire: Collaboration and Colonial Modernity in Korea and Japan* (Durham, NC: Duke University Press, 2015); Cindi Textor, "Radical Language, Radical Identity: Korean Writers in Japanese Spaces and the Burden to 'Represent' " (PhD diss., University of Washington, 2016); Ying Xiong, *Representing Empire: Japanese Colonial Literature in Taiwan and Manchuria* (Leiden: Brill, 2014); and McDonald, *Placing Empire*.
23. Will Bridges, *Playing in the Shadows: Fictions of Race and Blackness in Postwar Japanese Literature* (Ann Arbor: University of Michigan Press, 2020), 7-8. Emphasis in original. Bridges goes on to write that "readers are quick to essentialize and rarely have time to regard the text…as a singular instantiation that *we* must work to connect to larger discourses, to ask it where it came from, how it got here, and where it is going" (7). He is interested in letting texts travel through a more deliberate "reconstruction" of the reading subject, whereas my interest is in refracting this subject through the lens of a scaled up encounter with the archive.
24. John R. Firth, "A Synopsis of Linguistic Theory, 1930–1955," in *Studies in Linguistic Analysis* (Oxford: Oxford University Press, 1962), 11.
25. Harris's argument is summarized in Magnus Sahlgren, "The Distributional Hypothesis," 2008, 2–3, http://soda.swedish-ict.se/3941/1/sahlgren.distr-hypo.pdf.
26. Using target words to predict context words is known as the Skip-Gram model and tends to produce better results for larger corpora. Using context words to predict target words is known as the CBOW model and is said to be more useful for smaller corpora. I use the former approach in my analysis. Several implementations of the word embedding model exist, including the "word2vec" algorithm, which is the one here. See Tomas Mikolov et al., "Efficient Estimation of Word Representations in Vector Space," 2013, https://arxiv.org/abs/1301.3781.

27. A good technical explanation of how these models work and their relation to previous attempts to leverage the distributional hypothesis is available in Dan Jurafsky and James Martin, *Speech and Language Processing*, 3rd ed. draft, chaps. 15–16, https://web.stanford.edu/~jurafsky/slp3/ed3book.pdf.
28. See Ryan Heuser, "Word Vectors in the Eighteenth Century," *Virtue and the Virtual* (blog), April 14, 2016, http://ryanheuser.org/word-vectors-1/; Ben Schmidt, "Vector Space Models for the Digital Humanities," *Ben's Bookworm Blog* (blog), October 25, 2015, http://bookworm.benschmidt.org/posts/2015-10-25-Word-Embeddings.html; and Michael Gavin, "Vector Semantics, William Empson, and the Study of Ambiguity," *Critical Inquiry* 44 (Summer 2018): 641–73. For applications to the study of race, see Richard Jean So and Edwin Roland, "Race and Distant Reading," *PMLA* 135, no. 1 (January 2020): 59–73, and Mark Algee-Hewitt, J. D. Porter, and Hannah Walser, "Representing Race and Ethnicity in American Fiction" (paper presented at the Annual Meeting of Alliance of Digital Humanities Organizations, Kraków, Poland, July 2016).
29. Examples of work in this vein include Sudeep Bhatia, "The Semantic Representation of Prejudice and Stereotypes," *Cognition* 164 (July 2017): 46–60; Aylin Caliskan et al., "Semantics Derived Automatically from Language Corpora Contain Human-Like Biases," *Science* 356, no. 6334 (April 2017): 183–86; and Nikhil Garg et al., "Word Embeddings Quantify 100 Years of Gender and Ethnic Stereotypes," 2017, https://arxiv.org/abs/1711.08412.
30. For instance, *heimin* (commoner) is not included under terms for "Burakumin" despite its use as a euphemism for members of this outcaste group in late Meiji. Although an argument could be made for including references to Ainu or Okinawans under the large umbrella of "Native," I decided that these were best analyzed as distinct terms and thus have not included them in my model.
31. For an example of the ways racial identity was left unmarked by Korean writers, even in a story set within a Korean farming village, see Chang Hŏkchu, "Gakidō" (Hell of Hungry Ghosts, 1932). For a discussion of the work and the strategies it adopts to mark "Koreanness" within a Japanese language text, see Christina Yi, *Colonizing Language: Cultural Production and Language Politics in Modern Japan and Korea* (New York: Columbia University Press, 2018), 6–7.
32. The test used is a Fischer's exact test (with Bonferroni correction to adjust for multiple testing) on the counts of clusters appearing within a specified window around each racial identifier.
33. See Leo Ching, *Becoming "Japanese": Colonial Taiwan and the Politics of Identity Formation* (Berkeley: University of California Press, 2001), 5–11; Rachael Hutchinson and Mark Williams, eds., *Representing the Other in Modern Japanese Literature: A Critical Approach* (London: Routledge, 2006), 1–5; Fowler, "The Buraku in Modern Japanese Literature," 7–8; Taylor Atkins, *Primitive Selves: Koreana in the Japanese Colonial Gaze* (Berkeley: University of California Press, 2010), 14–15; Xiong, *Representing Empire*, xix; Tierney, *Tropics of Savagery*, 1–37.
34. See McDonald, *Placing Empire*, 1–24; Oguma, *A Genealogy of 'Japanese' Self-Images*; and Komori Yōichi, *Posutokoroniaru* (Iwanami Shoten, 2001), 11–16.
35. Ching provides an excellent account of the difference between the more liberal assimilationist stance of *dōka* and the stricter *kōminka* and their interaction with both cultural and political identity formation in Taiwan. See Ching, *Becoming "Japanese."*

36. See, for example, Textor, "Radical Language, Radical Identity," 20; and Yi, *Colonizing Language*, 15.
37. See Tierney, *Tropics of Savagery*, 1; Ching, *Becoming "Japanese,"* 91; Hutchinson and Williams, *Representing the Other in Modern Japanese Literature*, 5; Faye Kleeman, *In Transit: The Formation of the Colonial East Asian Cultural Sphere* (Honolulu: University of Hawai'i Press, 2014), 9; and Hanscom and Washburn, "Introduction," 10.
38. An overview of the "Kindai Zasshi" corpus and the "Corpus of Historical Japanese," of which it is a subset, can be accessed at https://pj.ninjal.ac.jp/corpus_center/chj/overview-en.html. I am grateful to Ogiso Toshinobu for granting me full access to the corpus.
39. Prior to training the model, texts were lemmatized (i.e., words were converted to their base lemma forms) using Unidic, and high-frequency proper names were removed. Both steps help to reduce the dimensionality of the corpus lexicon and thus condense the total semantic space to be embedded. Model parameters for the word embeddings are specified in the "word2vec_bootstrap_kindai.py" and "word2vec_bootstrap_fic.py" files, contained in the "Code" folder for this chapter in the code and data repository.
40. On recommendations for bootstrap sampling word embeddings, see Maria Antoniak and David Mimno, "Evaluating the Stability of Embedding-based Word Similarities," *Transactions of the Association for Computational Linguistics* (February 2018): 6:107–19. For both the nonfiction and fiction corpora, twenty-word embedding models were created. When generating semantic clusters from seed terms, the most proximate terms were determined by averaging the similarity scores across all twenty models and keeping only those terms with averages above the specified threshold (e.g., 0.65). For example, for the seed term "beautiful," if "elegant" scored, on average, above this threshold across all models, the two were clustered together. Inevitably, when generating these clusters, one ends up with clusters that share some percentage of words in common. It is not useful to retain clusters in which most of the words are the same because this leads to double counting. But it is important to keep clusters that share only a small percentage of words because these may be capturing different semantic fields. For this analysis, I kept only clusters with 30 percent or fewer words in common.
41. "Burakumin" was excluded from these results due to its much lower frequency in the corpus. Also excluded were several generic or difficult to interpret categories including foreign countries and function words.
42. All statistically significant clusters are represented in this grid regardless of the strength of the underlying association. For clusters I discuss in the chapter, such as "photograph," I have extracted the relevant passages (context windows) and included them as a text file for further inspection. See the "ClusterContextsKindai" folder for nonfiction results and the "ClusterContextsFiction" folder for fiction results. Both can be found in the chapter 5 folder of the code and data repository.
43. This cluster co-occurs with "Native" 188 times, compared with 2,001 for "Japanese," 387 for "Chinese," 129 for "Korean," and 208 for "Westerner." As the frequency of "Native" is much higher overall, 188 is judged to be unexpectedly low.
44. The series *"Gaichi" no Nihongo bungaku sen*, 3 vols., ed. Kurokawa Sō, was published by Shinjuku Shobō in 1996.

45. Although more than double the size of the magazine corpus in terms of total number of lexical items, the fiction corpus contains just 116,525 unique items, about five thousand fewer than the magazine corpus.
46. Because of the extremely low number of texts published in the years before 1905, I have excluded them from this graph.
47. Oguma, *A Genealogy of 'Japanese' Self-Images*, chaps. 16–17.
48. As with the Kindai Zasshi corpus, preprocessing steps taken prior to training the word embedding model include lemmatization and removal of proper names. I also found it useful to remove character names from the texts because their frequent repetition in texts can interfere with the extraction of semantic clusters.
49. Fowler, "The Buraku in Modern Japanese Literature," 17–19.
50. When extracting clusters from the pretrained word embeddings for the fiction corpus, I again used the five thousand most frequent words. However, I increased the similarity threshold to .69 to increase the semantic coherency of the clusters and retained only those with 50 percent or fewer words in common.
51. Tierney, *Tropics of Savagery*, 32.
52. Future work might sharpen these signals by treating *naichijin* as its own identifier or by treating references to "Japanese" before and after 1945 as distinct lexical units. Tierney observes that "Japanese" in colonial discourse did not often distinguish between Japanese and Taiwanese (or Koreans), whereas *naichijin* specifically excluded the colonized. Tierney, *Tropics of Savagery*, 35.
53. Said, *Culture and Imperialism*, 52.
54. Code for extracting passages where the words in a semantic cluster appear in the same context window as a specified racial identifier is provided in "PrePostProcessing.ipynb," in the chapter 5 folder of the code and data repository.
55. To reiterate, each question deserves its own extended analysis and requires extracting the passages underlying the results. We can also go beyond comparisons with "Japanese." In fact, the procedure used to extract significant clusters does so for all possible pairings of racial identifiers, allowing us to observe how the system of racial discourse works at the level of distinctions between "Chinese" and "Korean," for instance, or "Chinese" and "Westerner." Such distinctions could themselves be a way to reflect on what it was to be "Japanese" or not. A list of significant semantic clusters for all pairwise comparisons can be found in the following file, in the "results_fic_bootstrap" folder: "kfree_thres0.69_numtest5000_window20_alpha0.05_overlap_percent0.50.txt."
56. The former appeared in *Shin shumi* (New Taste), which specialized in detective fiction and foreign translations; the latter appeared in *Chūgaku sekai* (Middle School World), which was more educationally focused. Both magazines were published by Hakubunkan, one of the largest commercial publishers at the time.
57. Sianne Ngai, *Ugly Feelings* (Cambridge, MA: Harvard University Press, 2005), 93.
58. Cited in Tierney, *Tropics of Savagery*, 12.
59. Ngai, *Ugly Feelings*, 91.
60. Currently, the model samples all racial identifiers in a document that are more than forty words apart (i.e., twice the selected window size).
61. Natsume Sōseki, *Kokoro*, Aozora Bunko, transcribed from *Kokoro* (Shūeisha, 1991), https://www.aozora.gr.jp/cards/000148/files/773_14560.html.
62. Tani Jōji, *Odoru chiheisen*, Aozora Bunko, transcribed from *Odoru chiheisen* (*ge*) (Iwanami Shoten, 1999), https://www.aozora.gr.jp/cards/000272/files/4363_8029.

html. Originally serialized in *Chūō kōron* in 1928–1929. Tani Jōji was one of the many pseudonyms of Hasegawa Umitarō, who also wrote historical and detective novels under the names Hayashi Fubō and Maki Itsuma.

63. Sakaguchi Angō, *Furenzoku satsujin jiken*, Aozora Bunko, transcribed from vol. 11 of *Sakuguchi Angō zenshū* (Chikuma Shobō, 1990), https://www.aozora.gr.jp/cards/001095/files/42626_60035.html.
64. Said, *Culture and Imperialism*, 51.
65. Said, *Culture and Imperialism*, 52.
66. Ngai, *Ugly Feelings*, 108. Ngai is here drawing on Stanley Cavell, "Types: Cycles as Genres," in *The World Viewed: Reflections on the Ontology of Film* (New York: Viking Press, 1971).
67. Woloch, *The One vs. the Many*, 19.
68. Woloch, *The One vs. the Many*, 26–32.
69. Phillip Brian Harper, *Abstractionist Aesthetics: Artistic Form and Social Critique in African American Culture* (New York: New York University Press, 2015), 127–30.
70. Deidre Lynch, *The Economy of Character: Novels, Market Culture, and the Business of Inner Meaning* (Chicago: University of Chicago, Press, 1998), 29.
71. Lynch, *The Economy of Character*, 76.
72. Lynch, *The Economy of Character*, 41. Ian Baucom connects this utility with the needs of speculative capital and its allegorization of enslaved bodies as commodities. See Ian Baucom, *Specters of the Atlantic: Finance Capital, Slavery, and the Philosophy of History* (Durham, NC: Duke University Press, 2005).
73. Tsubouchi Shōyō, *Nihon kindai bungaku taikei* (Kadokawa Shobō, 1974), 3:69–73.
74. Shōyō, *Nihon kindai bungaku taikei*, 3:65.
75. Natsume Sōseki, "Sōsakuka no taidō," in *Sōseki zenshū* (Iwanami Shoten, 1995), 16:242–44.
76. Yokomitsu Ri'ichi, "Junsui shōsetsuron," in *Gendai Nihon bungaku ronsō-shi*, ed. Hirano Ken, Odagiri Hideo, and Yamamoto Kenkichi (Miraisha, 2006), 3:110.
77. Kobayashi Hideo's famous response to the essay "Watakushi shōsetsu ni tsuite" (On the I-Novel, 1935) laid the blame squarely on Naturalist writers who failed to understand the "I" imported from European novelists as a "socialized I." As Atsuko Ueda points out, this became a standard line of criticism at the time. See Atsuko Ueda, *Concealment of Politics, Politics of Concealment: The Production of "Literature" in Meiji Japan* (Stanford, CA: Stanford University Press, 2007), chap. 6. For an in-depth review of the conversations that Yokomitsu's essay prompted, see Edward Mack, *Manufacturing Modern Japanese Literature: Publishing, Prizes, and the Ascription of Literary Value* (Durham, NC: Duke University Press, 2010), 168–74; and Kevin Michael Doak, *Dreams of Difference: The Japan Romantic School and the Crisis of Modernity* (Berkeley: University of California Press, 1994).
78. Yokomitsu, "Junsui shōsetsuron," 111.
79. Yokomitsu, "Junsui shōsetsuron," 112–13.
80. Masao Miyoshi, *Accomplices of Silence: The Modern Japanese Novel* (Berkeley: University of California Press, 1974), xi.
81. Yokomitsu, "Junsui shōsetsuron," 115.
82. Kwon, *Intimate Empire*, 51–54. The last quote comes from an advertisement blurb by author Satō Haruo. Kwon rightly notes a repetition of this double bind in Fredric Jameson's declaration that "all third world texts are necessarily . . . national

allegories." It is the "metropolitan critical encounter" itself that insists on this duality of particularity and generalizability. Kwon, *Intimate Empire*, 57–58.

83. Aoki Minoru, "Mannin mono ni tsuite," *Manshū bungei nenkan* 3 (1939): 52–56.
84. Kanō Saburō, "Gensō no bungaku," *Manshū bungei nenkan* 3 (1939): 42–46. Emphasis added.
85. See Ted Underwood et al., "The Transformation of Gender in English-Language Fiction," *Journal of Cultural Analytics* (February 2018), https://culturalanalytics.org/article/11035; Matthew Jockers and Gabi Kirilloff, "Understanding Gender and Character Agency in the 19th Century Novel," *Journal of Cultural Analytics* (November 30, 2016), https://culturalanalytics.org/article/11066; and Eve Kraicer and Andrew Piper, "Social Characters: The Hierarchy of Gender in Contemporary English-Language Fiction," *Journal of Cultural Analytics* (January 30, 2019), https://culturalanalytics.org/article/11055.
86. Andrew Piper, *Enumerations: Data and Literary Study* (Chicago: University of Chicago Press, 2018), 120–21.
87. The procedure, called BookNLP, is described in David Bamman, Ted Underwood, and Noah Smith, "A Bayesian Mixed Effects Model of Literary Character," *ACL 2014*, http://www.cs.cmu.edu/~ark/literaryCharacter/.
88. The technical challenge of resolving character name aliases and pronominal references is somewhat easier in Japanese because pronouns are less often substituted for character names. There are other challenges, however, in that subjects can be left implicit across many sentences once introduced. For my purposes, I identify prominent character names in a text by word counts and tag them as character references after manual verification.
89. When searching these texts, if two character names appear in a single context window, I inspect just one and skip ahead to the next character reference.
90. Naoto Sudo, *Nanyo Orientalism: Japanese Representations of the Pacific* (Amherst, NY: Cambria Press, 2010), 29–33.
91. Kikuchi Kan, "Shunkan," in *Kikuchi Kan bungaku zenshū* (Bungei Shunjū Shinsha, 1960), 3:397. Shunkan initially refers to his own language as *Yamato kotoba*, invoking the territory that is associated with the mythologized origins of the Japanese race.
92. Ching, *Becoming "Japanese,"* 102–5.
93. This and all page numbers in text that follow are from Kikuchi, "Shunkan"
94. Oguma Eiji, cited in Ching, *Becoming "Japanese,"* 109.
95. Ching, *Becoming "Japanese,"* 91.
96. Kleeman, *In Transit*, 19.
97. Tierney, *Tropics of Savagery*, 10.
98. Ching, *Becoming "Japanese,"* 81–86.
99. Cited in Chen Wan-Yi, "Yume to genjitsu—Oh Shō-yū *Honryū* shiron," trans. Tarumi Chie, in *Yomigaeru Taiwan bungaku* (Tōhō Shoten, 1995), 391. The story was originally published in *Taiwan shin-minpō* as "Eiki" (Decorated Return).
100. Oh Shō-yū, "Honryū," in *"Gaichi" no Nihongo bungaku sen* (Shinjuku Shobō, 1996), 1:235.
101. The work has been translated into English by Erin Brightwell, "A Torrent," *Japan Focus* 16, issue 1, no. 3 (January 2018), https://apjjf.org/2018/01/O.html.
102. Chen, "Yume to genjitsu—Oh Shō-yū *Honryū* shiron," 398–99, 399–400.

103. Tarumi Chie, *Taiwan no Nihongo bungaku: Nihon tōchi jidai no sakka-tachi* (Goryū Shoin, 1995), 117–18.
104. Cited in Chen, "Yume to genjitsu—Oh Shō-yū *Honryū* shiron," 394–95. The review, by Kubokawa Tsurujirō, appeared in the magazine *Taiwan kōron* (Taiwan Review) in February 1944.
105. All page numbers that follow are from Oh Shō-yū, "Honryū."
106. I follow Brightwell in translating *hontōgo* (lit., "language of the island") as "Chinese." It refers to the language of the Han Chinese in Taiwan, but it is not clear if characters are speaking Mandarin, Southern Min, or the indigenous Hakka.
107. Tierney, *Tropics of Savagery*, 87.
108. Baucom, *Specters of the Atlantic*, 43. Emphasis in original.
109. The full results of these comparisons were not analyzed for this study. They can be found in "kfree_thres0.69_numtest5000_window20_alpha0.05_overlap_percent0.50.txt," in the "results_fic_bootstrap" folder. Searching the fiction corpus for passages in which the voice cluster terms appear with "Korean" or "Chinese," I found twenty-two passages in the former case and fifty-two in the latter. Although less than the seventy-eight passages found for "Native," the difference is small enough that it does not register as statistically significant. The extracted passages for "Korean" and "Chinese" are in "KoreanVoice.txt" and "ChineseVoice.txt," in the "ClusterContextsFiction" folder.
110. Baucom, *Specters of the Atlantic*, 11, 21.
111. Itō Sei, "Uchinaru koe to kasō," 64.

EPILOGUE: DIFFERENCE IN NUMBERS

1. Fukuzawa Yukichi, *Bunmeiron no gairyaku*, trans. David A. Dilworth and G. Cameron Hurst (Sophia University, 1973), 47–51.
2. Ian Hacking, *The Taming of Chance* (Cambridge: Cambridge University Press, 1990), 123–28.
3. Fukuzawa, *Bunmeiron no gairyaku*, 52.
4. On Fukuzawa's ambivalence toward Buckle and his creative use of numbers to reason about social equality and difference, see Takeharu Ōkubo, *The Quest for Civilization: Encounters with Dutch Jurisprudence, Political Economy, and Statistics at the Dawn of Modern Japan*, trans. David Noble (Leiden: Global Oriental, 2014), 93–97; see also Hansun Hsiung, "Woman, Man, Abacus: A Tale of Enlightenment," *Harvard Journal of Asiatic Studies* 72, no. 1 (June 2012): 1–42, who further complicates the basic sketch provided here. It goes without saying that Fukuzawa's leveling efforts had their own limits, particularly with respect to "races" seen as lower in the world's civilizational hierarchy. In his own racial imaginary, he put the "primitive lands" of Africa below "advanced civilizations" such as America and "semi-developed" countries like Japan.
5. Karatani Kōjin, "Uses of Aesthetics: After Orientalism," trans. Sabu Kosho, *boundary 2* 25, no. 2 (1998): 148.
6. As cited in Karatani, "Uses of Aesthetics," 148, 151.
7. Johanna Drucker, "Humanities Approaches to Graphical Display," *Digital Humanities Quarterly* 5, no. 1 (Winter 2011), http://digitalhumanities.org/dhq/vol/5/1/000091/000091.html.

8. This holds true for North America as much as for Japan, where digital approaches to the study of modern literature have been very slow to take hold outside of linguistics. This contrasts with other humanistic fields, such as religious studies and history, where these approaches have been more actively adopted. To gain a sense of how digital methods are being applied to the study of culture and history in Japan, see the conference proceedings of the Japanese Association for Digital Humanities (JADH), https://www.jadh.org/node/8; and the longer running IPSJ SIG Computers and the Humanities, or *Jinmon Kagaku to Konpyūta Kenkyū Kai*, http://jinmoncom.jp/index.php?開催情報.
9. Jed Esty, *A Shrinking Island: Modernism and National Culture in England* (Princeton, NJ: Princeton University Press, 2004), 12, 6.
10. Esty, *A Shrinking Island*, 32.
11. Franz Fanon, *Black Skin, White Masks*, trans. Charles Markmann (New York: Grove Press, 1967), 152.
12. Fanon, *Black Skin, White Masks*, 111.
13. Fanon, *Black Skin, White Masks*, 170.
14. Fanon, *Black Skin, White Masks*, 189.
15. Karatani, "Uses of Aesthetics," 146–47.
16. Esty, *A Shrinking Island*, 15.
17. Benjamin defines the "New Jim Code" as "the employment of new technologies that reflect and reproduce existing inequities but that are promoted and perceived as more objective or progressive than the discriminatory systems of a previous era." See Ruha Benjamin, *Race After Technology: Abolitionist Tools for the New Jim Code* (Cambridge: Polity Press, 2019), 5-6. For some of the best critical work in this same vein, see Safiya Noble, *Algorithms of Oppression: How Search Engines Reinforce Racism* (New York: New York University Press, 2018): Virginia Eubanks, *Automating Inequality: How High-Tech Tools Profile, Police, and Punish the Poor* (New York: St. Martin's Press, 2018); Catherine D'Ignazio and Lauren Klein, *Data Feminism* (Boston: MIT Press, 2020); Roopika Risam, *New Digital Worlds: Postcolonial Digital Humanities in Theory, Praxis, and Pedagogy* (Evanston, IL: Northwestern University Press, 2019); and Cathy O'Neil, *Weapons of Math Destruction: How Big Data Increases Inequality and Threatens Democracy* (New York: Crown, 2016). The last few years have also seen a growing community of scholars in computer science and machine learning offering critical responses to the social use and abuse of algorithms. The organization FAT/ML (Fairness, Accountability, and Transparency in Machine Learning) has been particularly important in this regard. More recently, a group led by Marika Cifor and Patricia Garcia, who work in the field of information science, have authored the "Feminist Data Manifest-No" (https://www.manifestno.com/), a powerful statement refusing unethical practices of data extraction and the manipulation of data for profit maximization. Recognizing all the ways data science normalizes social inequities, they commit to a feminist data ethics that treats data as always situated, in-process, and co-constituted by communities who have a stake in its use.
18. Hayden White, *Tropics of Discourse: Essays in Cultural Criticism* (Baltimore, MD: Johns Hopkins University Press, 1978), 276–77.
19. White, *Tropics of Discourse*, 281.

20. Ruha Benjamin, *Race After Technology*, 195. For Benjamin, these settings represent the codes and environments "we have inherited from prior regimes of racial control, and how we can appropriate and reimagine science and technology for liberatory ends." Similarly, much of the best critical work in this vein is less about the total rejection of the tools and technologies of data science than about reimagining how they can be repurposed, hacked, and rebuilt by stakeholders in the name of equity and social justice.
21. Fukuzawa, *Bunmeiron no gairyaku*, 48.

WORKS CITED

Acker, Amelia, and Tanya Clement. "Data Cultures, Culture as Data—Special Issue of Cultural Analytics." *Journal of Cultural Analytics* (April 2019).

Akikusa Shun'ichirō. "Jutsugo toshite no 'sekai bungaku': 1895–2016." *Bungaku* 17, no. 5 (September 2016): 3–24.

Akiyama Shun, and Katsumata Hiroshi. Eds. *Watakushi shōsetsu handobukku*. Bensei Shuppan, 2014.

Algee-Hewitt, Mark, J. D. Porter, and Hannah Walser. "Representing Race and Ethnicity in American Fiction." Paper presented at the Annual Meeting of Alliance of Digital Humanities Organizations, Kraków, Poland, July 2016.

Allan, Michael. *In the Shadow of World Literature: Sites of Reading in Colonial Egypt*. Princeton, NJ: Princeton University Press, 2016.

Allen, Graham. *Intertextuality*. London: Routledge, 2000.

Allington, Daniel, Sarah Brouillette, and David Golumbia. "Neoliberal Tools (and Archives): A Political History of Digital Humanities." *Los Angeles Review of Books*, May 1, 2016. https://lareviewofbooks.org/article/neoliberal-tools-archives-political-history-digital-humanities/.

Allison, Sarah. *Reductive Reading: A Syntax of Victorian Moralizing*. Baltimore, MD: Johns Hopkins University Press, 2018.

Altmann, Gabriel, and Reinhard Köhler. *Forms and Degrees of Repetition in Texts*. Berlin: Walter de Gruyter, 2015.

Anderson, Mark. *Japan and the Specter of Imperialism*. New York: Palgrave Macmillan, 2009.

Anno Izumi, and Nichigai Asoshiētsu. *Kyōkasho keisai sakuhin 13000: yonde okitai meichō annai*. Nichigai Asoshiētsu, 2008.

Antoniak, Maria, and David Mimno. "Evaluating the Stability of Embedding-based Word Similarities." In *Transactions of the Association for Computational Linguistics* 6 (February 2018): 107–19.

Aoki Minoru. "Mannin mono ni tsuite." *Manshū bungei nenkan* 3 (1939): 52–56.
Apter, Emily. *Against World Literature: On the Politics of Untranslatability*. London: Verso, 2013.
Arishima Takeo. "*Omedetaki hito* o yomite." *Shirakaba* 2 (April 1911).
Atkins, Taylor. *Primitive Selves: Koreana in the Japanese Colonial Gaze*. Berkeley: University of California Press, 2010.
Baguley, David. *Naturalist Fiction: The Entropic Vision*. Cambridge: Cambridge University Press, 1990.
Balibar, Etienne, and Immanuel Wallerstein. *Race, Nation, Class: Ambiguous Identities*, trans. Chris Turner. London: Verso, 1991.
Bamman, David, Ted Underwood, and Noah Smith. "A Bayesian Mixed Effects Model of Literary Character." *ACL 2014*. http://www.cs.cmu.edu/~ark/literaryCharacter/.
Barthes, Roland. "Style and Its Image." In *Literary Style: A Symposium*, ed. Seymour Chatman, 3–15. London: Oxford University Press, 1971.
Baucom, Ian. *Specters of the Atlantic: Finance Capital, Slavery, and the Philosophy of History*. Durham, NC: Duke University Press, 2005.
Benjamin, Ruha. *Race After Technology: Abolitionist Tools for the New Jim Code*. Cambridge: Polity Press, 2019.
Berlant, Lauren. "On the Case." *Critical Inquiry* 33, no. 4 (June 2007): 663–72.
Bermann, Sandra, and Michael Wood. *Nation, Language, and the Ethics of Translation*. Princeton, NJ: Princeton University Press, 2005.
Bhatia, Sudeep. "The Semantic Representation of Prejudice and Stereotypes." *Cognition* 164 (July 2017): 46–60.
Bode, Katherine. *Reading by Numbers: Recalibrating the Literary Field*. London: Anthem Press, 2012.
——. "The Equivalence of 'Close' and 'Distant' Reading; Or, Toward a New Object for Data-Rich Literary History." *Modern Language Quarterly* 78, no. 1 (2017): 77–106.
——. *A World of Fiction: Digital Collections and the Future of Literary History*. Ann Arbor: University of Michigan Press, 2018.
Bourdaghs, Michael. "Introduction: Overthrowing the Emperor in Japanese Literary Studies." In *The Linguistic Turn in Contemporary Japanese Literary Studies: Politics, Language, Textuality*, ed. Michael Bourdaghs, 1–20. Ann Arbor, MI: Center for Japanese Studies, 2010.
Bourdieu, Pierre. *The Rules of Art: Genesis and Structure of the Literary Field*, trans. Susan Emmanuel. Stanford, CA: Stanford University Press, 1996.
Bowling, Lawrence. "What Is the Stream of Consciousness Technique?" *PMLA* 65, no. 4 (1950): 333–45.
Brennan, Timothy. "The Digital-Humanities Bust." *Chronicle Review*, October 15, 2017, https://www.chronicle.com/article/the-digital-humanities-bust/.
Bridges, Will. *Playing in the Shadows: Fictions of Race and Blackness in Postwar Japanese Literature*. Ann Arbor: University of Michigan Press, 2020.
Buurma, Rachel Sagner, and Laura Heffernan. "Search and Replace: Josephine Miles and the Origins of Distant Reading." *Modernism/Modernity Print +*, April 11, 2018. https://modernismmodernity.org/forums/posts/search-and-replace.
——. *The Teaching Archive: A New History of Literary Study*. Chicago: University of Chicago Press, 2020.

Caliskan, Aylin, et al. "Semantics Derived Automatically from Language Corpora Contain Human-Like Biases." *Science* 356, no. 6334 (April 2017): 183–86.
Carroll, John B. "Analysis of Verbal Behavior." *Psychological Review* 51 (March 1944): 102–19.
——. "Vectors of Prose Style." In *Style in Language*, ed. Thomas A. Sebeok, 283–92. Cambridge, MA: MIT Press, 1960.
Casanova, Pascale. *The World Republic of Letters*, trans. M. B. Devevoise. Cambridge, MA: Harvard University Press, 2004.
Cavell, Stanley. "Types: Cycles as Genres." In *The World Viewed: Reflections on the Ontology of Film*. New York: Viking Press, 1971.
Chatman, Seymour. *Story and Discourse: Narrative Structure in Fiction and Film*. Ithaca, NY: Cornell University Press, 1978.
Chen Wan-Yi. "Yume to genjitsu—Oh Shō-yū *Honryū* shiron," trans. Tarumi Chie. In *Yomigaeru Taiwan bungaku*, 389–406. Tōhō Shoten, 1995.
Chiba Shunji. "*Oshie no kiseki* ron." *Kokubungaku: kaishaku to kyōzai no kenkyū* 36, no. 3 (March 1991): 96–98.
Chikamatsu Shūkō. *Giwaku*. In *Gendai Nihon bungaku taikei*, Vol. 21, pp. 326–58. Chikuma Shobō, 2010.
Ching, Leo. *Becoming "Japanese": Colonial Taiwan and the Politics of Identity Formation*. Berkeley: University of California Press, 2001.
Clayton, Jay, and Eric Rothstein. *Influence and Intertextuality in Literary History*. Madison: University of Wisconsin Press, 1991.
Cohn, Dorrit. *Transparent Minds: Narrative Modes for Presenting Consciousness in Fiction*. Princeton, NJ: Princeton University Press, 1978.
Cryle, Peter, and Elizabeth Stephens. *Normality: A Critical Genealogy*. Chicago: University of Chicago Press, 2017.
Culler, Jonathan. *Structuralist Poetics: Structuralism, Linguistics, and the Study of Literature*. Ithaca, NY: Cornell University Press, 1975.
——. *The Pursuit of Signs: Semiotics, Literature, Deconstruction*. Ithaca, NY: Cornell University Press, 1981.
Da, Nan Z. "The Computational Case Against Computational Literary Studies." *Critical Inquiry* 45, no. 3 (Spring 2019): 601–39.
Dahl, Liisa. *Linguistic Features of the Stream-of-Consciousness Techniques of James Joyce, Virginia Woolf, and Eugene O'Neill*. Turku: Turun Yliopisto, 1970.
Dalton, Craig M., et al. "Critical Data Studies: A Dialog on Data and Space." *Big Data and Society* 3, no. 1 (January–June 2016): 1–9.
Dames, Nicholas. *The Physiology of the Novel: Reading, Neural Science, and the Form of Victorian Fiction*. Oxford: Oxford University Press, 2007.
Damrosch, David. *What Is World Literature?* Princeton, NJ: Princeton University Press, 2003.
Darnton, Robert. *The Forbidden Bestsellers of Pre-Revolutionary France*. New York: Norton, 1995.
Denning, Michael. *The Cultural Front*. London: Verso, 1997.
Derrida, Jacques. *Archive Fever: A Freudian Impression*, trans. Eric Prenowitz. Chicago: University of Chicago Press, 1998.
Desrosières, Alain. *The Politics of Large Numbers: A History of Statistical Reasoning*, trans. Camille Naish. Cambridge, MA: Harvard University Press, 1998.

D'Ignazio, Catherine, and Lauren Klein. *Data Feminism*. Boston: MIT Press, 2020.
DiLeonardi, Sean Michael. "Cryptographic Reading: Machine Translation, the New Criticism, and Nabokov's *Pnin*." *Post45*, January 17, 2019. http://post45.research.yale.edu/2019/01/cryptographic-reading-machine-translation-the-new-criticism-and-nabokovs-pnin/.
Doak, Kevin Michael. *Dreams of Difference: The Japan Romantic School and the Crisis of Modernity*. Berkeley: University of California Press, 1994.
Doi Kōichi. "Joisu no *Ulysses*." *Kaizō* 11, no. 2 (February 1929): 24–47.
Dombrowski, Quinn. "Preparing Non-English Texts for Computational Analysis." *Modern Languages Open* 1, no. 45 (2020). https://doi.org/10.3828/mlo.v0i0.294.
Dowdle, Brian. "Why Saikaku Was Memorable but Bakin Was Unforgettable." *Journal of Japanese Studies* 42, no. 1 (Winter 2016): 91–121.
Drucker, Johanna. "Humanities Approaches to Graphical Display." *Digital Humanities Quarterly* 5, no. 1 (Winter 2011). http://digitalhumanities.org/dhq/vol/5/1/000091/000091.html.
Edel, Leon. *The Modern Psychological Novel*. New York: Dunlap, 1964.
Eiji Noguchi, and Miyakawa Teruko. "Aozora bunko no monogatari." In *Aozora Bunko* (2005). http://www.aozora.gr.jp/cards/001739/files/55745_58656.html.
Emre, Merve. *Paraliterary: The Making of Bad Readers in Postwar America*. Chicago: University of Chicago Press, 2017.
Erlich, Victor. *Russian Formalism: History-Doctrine*. New Haven, CT: Yale University Press, 1955.
Esty, Jed. *A Shrinking Island: Modernism and National Culture in England*. Princeton, NJ: Princeton University Press, 2004.
Etō Jun. *Sakka wa kōdō suru*. Kōdansha, 1959.
Eubanks, Virginia. *Automating Inequality: How High-Tech Tools Profile, Police, and Punish the Poor*. New York: St. Martin's Press, 2018.
Fanon, Franz. *Black Skin, White Masks*, trans. Charles Markmann. New York: Grove Press, 1967.
Farnol, Jeffrey. *The Way Beyond*. Boston: Little, Brown, 1933.
Firth, John R. "A Synopsis of Linguistic Theory, 1930–1955." In *Studies in Linguistic Analysis*, 1–32. Oxford: Oxford University Press, 1962.
Fish, Stanley. "What Is Stylistics and Why Are They Saying Such Terrible Things About It?" In *Is There a Text in This Class?: The Authority of Interpretive Communities*, 68–96. Cambridge, MA: Harvard University Press, 1980.
Foley, Barbara. *Radical Representations: Politics and Form in U.S. Proletarian Fiction, 1929–1941*. Durham, NC: Duke University Press, 1993.
Fowler, Edward. *The Rhetoric of Confession: Shishōsetsu in Early Twentieth-Century Japanese Fiction*. Berkeley: University of California Press, 1988.
——. "The Buraku in Modern Japanese Literature: Texts and Contexts." *Journal of Japanese Studies* 26, no. 1 (2000): 1–39.
Freud, Sigmund. "Remembering, Repeating, and Working-Through" [1914]. *Standard Edition*, Vol. 12, pp. 145–57. London: The Hogarth Press and the Institute of Psycho-Analysis, 1953–1974.
Friedman, Melvin. *Stream of Consciousness: A Study in Literary Method*. New Haven, CT: Yale University Press, 1955.
Frow, John. *Character and Person*. Oxford: Oxford University Press, 2016.

Fucks, Wilhem. "On the Mathematical Analysis of Style." *Biometrika* 39, no. 9 (1952): 122–29.

Fujii, James. *Complicit Fictions: The Subject in the Modern Japanese Prose Narrative*. Berkeley: University of California Press, 1993.

Fukuzawa Yukichi. *Bunmeiron no gairyaku*, trans. David A. Dilworth and G. Cameron Hurst. Tokyo: Sophia University, 1973.

Galsworthy, John. *Shūto sono hoka*, trans. Ōtani Gyōseki. Dai Nihon Tosho, 1914.

Garg, Nikhil, et al. "Word Embeddings Quantify 100 Years of Gender and Ethnic Stereotypes." 2017. https://arxiv.org/abs/1711.08412.

Gavin, Michael. "Vector Semantics, William Empson, and the Study of Ambiguity." *Critical Inquiry* 44 (Summer 2018): 641–73.

——. "How to Think About EEBO." *Textual Cultures* 11, no. 1–2 (2019): 70–105.

Gemma, Marissa, Frédéric Glorieuz, and Jean-Gabriel Ganascia. "Operationalizing the Colloquial Style: Repetition in 19th-Century American Fiction." *Digital Scholarship in the Humanities* 32, no. 2 (June 2017): 312–35.

Geoghegan, Bernard Dionysius. "From Information Theory to French Theory: Jakobson, Lévi-Strauss, and the Cybernetic Apparatus." *Critical Inquiry* 38, no. 1 (2011): 96–126.

Gerring, John. "What Is a Case Study and What Is It Good For?" *American Political Science Review* 98, no. 2 (2004): 341–54.

Gigerenzer, Gerd, et al. *The Empire of Chance: How Probability Changed Science and Everyday Life*. Cambridge: Cambridge University Press, 1989.

Goldstone, Andrew. "The *Doxa* of Reading." *PMLA* 132, no. 3 (May 2017): 636–42.

Golley, Gregory. *When Our Eyes No Longer See: Realism, Science, and Ecology in Japanese Literary Modernism*. Cambridge, MA: Harvard University Asia Center, 2008.

Gordin, Michael. *Scientific Babel: How Science Was Done Before and After Global English*. Chicago: University of Chicago Press, 2015.

Gruesz, Kirsten Silva. *Ambassadors of Culture: The Transamerican Origins of Latino Writing*. Princeton, NJ: Princeton University Press, 2002.

Guillory, John. *Cultural Capital: The Problem of Literary Canon Formation*. Chicago: University of Chicago Press, 1993.

——. "Close Reading: Prologue and Epilogue." *ADE Bulletin* 149 (2010): 8–14.

Gunn, Edward. *Rewriting Chinese: Style and Innovation in Twentieth-Century Chinese Prose*. Stanford, CA: Stanford University Press, 1991.

Hacking, Ian. *The Taming of Chance*. Cambridge: Cambridge University Press, 1990.

Hadley, James. "The Beginnings of Literary Translation in Japan: An Overview." *Perspectives: Studies in Translation Theory and Practice* 26, no. 4 (2018): 560–75.

Haga Yaichi. *Haga Yaichi icho*. Fuzanbō, 1929.

Hammond, Mary. *Reading, Publishing, and the Formation of Literary Taste in England, 1880–1914*. Aldershot, UK: Ashgate, 2006.

Hanscom, Chris, and Dennis Washburn. Introduction to *The Affect of Difference: Representations of Race in East Asian Empire*, ed. Chris Hanscom and Dennis Washburn, 1–18. Honolulu: University of Hawai'i Press, 2016.

Hardt, Michael, and Antonio Negri. *Empire*. Cambridge, MA: Harvard University Press, 2001.

Harper, Phillip Brian. *Abstractionist Aesthetics: Artistic Form and Social Critique in African American Culture*. New York: New York University Press, 2015.

Harris, Richard. "As Artificial Intelligence Moves Into Medicine, the Human Touch Could Be a Casualty." *All Tech Considered*, April 30, 2019. https://www.npr.org/sections/health-shots/2019/04/30/718413798/as-artificial-intelligence-moves-into-medicine-the-human-touch-could-be-a-casual.

Haruyama Yukio. " 'Ishiki no nagare' to shōsetsu no kōsei." *Shinchō* (August 1931): 43–49.

Hasegawa Izumi. "Meiji·Taishō·Shōwa shishōsetsu sanjūgo sen." *Kokubungaku: kaishaku to kanshō* 27, no. 14 (1962): 77–90.

Hashimoto Motome. *Nihon shuppan hanbai-shi*. Kōdansha, 1964.

Hatano Kanji. *Bunshō shinrigaku <shinkō>*. Dai Nihon Tosho, 1965.

——. "Watashi no ayunda michi—shūjigaku to shinrigaku." *Nihongo-gaku* 3, no. 12 (December 1984): 110–17.

——. *Bunshō shinrigaku*. In *Hatano Kanji zenshū*, Vol. 1. Shōgakkan, 1990–1991.

Hayashi Kazuhito. "Itō Sei to ishiki no nagare." *Kobe College Studies* 32, no. 2 (December 1985): 73–81.

Hegel, Robert, and Richard Hessney. Eds. *Expressions of Self in Chinese Literature*. New York: Columbia University Press, 1985.

Herdan, Gustav. *Language as Choice and Chance*. Groningen: P. Noordhoff, 1956.

Heuser, Ryan. "Word Vectors in the Eighteenth Century." *Virtue and the Virtual* (blog). April 14, 2016. http://ryanheuser.org/word-vectors-1/.

Hibi Yoshitaka. *'Jiko hyōsho' no bungaku-shi*. Kanrin Shobō, 2002.

Hijiya-Kerschnereit, Irmela. *Rituals of Self-Revelation: Shishōsetsu as Literary Genre and Socio-Cultural Phenomenon*. Cambridge, MA: Harvard University Council on East Asian Studies, 1996.

Hill, Christopher. *National History and the World of Nations*. Durham, NC: Duke University Press, 2008.

——. "Exhausted by Their Battles with the World: Neurasthenia and Civilization Critique in Early Twentieth-Century Japan." In *Perversion and Modern Japan*, ed. Nina Cornyetz and Keith Vincent, 242–58. London: Routledge, 2009.

Hino Sukezumi. "Buntai kenkyū no ichi hōkō." *Kokugo kenkyū*, no. 12 (June 1961): 21–38.

Hirabayashi Hatsunosuke. "Iwayuru kagaku-teki hihyō no genkai." In *Hirabayashi Hatsnosuke ikōshū*, 75–86. Heibonsha, 1932.

Hockey, Susan. "The History of Humanities Computing." In *A Companion to Digital Humanities*, ed. Susan Schreibman, et al., 3-19. Malden, MA: Blackwell Publishing Ltd., 2004.

Hofmeyr, Isabel. *The Portable Bunyan: A Transnational History of* The Pilgrim's Progress. Princeton, NJ: Princeton University Press, 2004.

Hojō Fumio. "Jeimuzu Joisu to Nihon kindai shōsetsu (I)." *Publications of the Institute for Comparative Studies of Culture Affiliated to Tokyo Woman's Christian College* 41 (1980): 35–53.

Holstein, Arthur. "A Statistical Analysis of Schizophrenic Language." *Statistical Methods in Linguistics* 4 (1965): 10–14.

Hoover, David. "Another Perspective on Vocabulary Richness." *Computers and the Humanities*, 37, no. 2 (2003): 151–78.

Hoppé, A. J. *The Reader's Guide to Everyman's Library*. London: Dent, 1960.

Horiguchi Daigaku. "Shōsetsu no shinkeishiki toshite no 'naishin dokuhaku.'" *Shinchō* (August 1925): 6–9.

Hori Tatsuo. "Jisaku ni tsuite." In *Hori Tatsuo zenshū*, Vol. 4, pp. 202–3. Chikuma Shobō, 1977.

——. "Bukiyō na tenshi." Aozora Bunko. Transcribed from vol. 1 of *Hori Tatsuo zenshū*. Chikuma Shobō, 1977. https://www.aozora.gr.jp/cards/001030/files/4819_30040.html.

Hsia, Chih-tsing. *A History of Modern Chinese Fiction*, 2nd ed. New Haven, CT: Yale University Press, 1971.

Hsiung, Hansun. "Woman, Man, Abacus: A Tale of Enlightenment." *Harvard Journal of Asiatic Studies* 72, no. 1 (June 2012): 1–42.

Hsu, Raymond. *The Style of Lu Hsun: Vocabulary and Usage*. Hong Kong: Centre of Asian Studies, University of Hong Kong Press, 1979.

Humphrey, Robert. *Stream of Consciousness in the Modern Novel*. Berkeley: University of California Press, 1954.

Hutchinson, Rachael, and Mark Williams Eds. *Representing the Other in Modern Japanese Literature: A Critical Approach*. London: Routledge, 2006.

Ichikawa Takashi. "Buntai to buntairon." *Kokubungaku: kaishaku to kanshō* 21, no. 4 (April 1956): 107–11.

Igarashi Yohei. "Statistical Analysis at the Birth of Close Reading." *New Literary History* 46, no. 3 (Summer 2015): 485–504.

Ikeuchi Teruo. "Mushanokōji Saneatsu to 'Shirakaba'—'jibun' no seisei katei." *Kokubungaku: Kaishaku to kanshō* 64, no. 2 (February 1999): 44–49.

Iliadis, Andrew, and Federica Russo. "Critical Data Studies: An Introduction." *Big Data and Society* 3, no. 2 (July–December 2016): 1–7.

Inukai Takeru. "Arabia-jin Eruafi." Aozora Bunko. Transcribed from vol. 62 of *Gendai Nihon bungaku taikei*. Chikuma Shobō, 1973. https://www.aozora.gr.jp/cards/001543/files/52219_41895.html.

Ishihara Chiaki. *Kokugo kyōkasho no shisō*. Chikuma Shobō, 2005.

Ishii Jun. "1910 nendai ni okeru toshokan sentei jigyō—*Toshokan hyōjun mokuroku* o chūshin ni." In *Toshokan to shuppan bunka*, 55–68. Yayoshi Mitsunaga Sensei Kiju Kinenkai, 1977.

Ishikawa Norio. "Genzai o kanki suru buntai—Hori Tatsuo 'Bukiyō na tenshi' ron." *Kokugakuin zasshi* 99, no. 10 (October 1998): 44–57.

Isogai Hideo. " 'Suishō gensō.' " In *Shōwa shotō no sakka to sakuhin*, 200–216. Meiji Shoin, 1980.

Ito, Ken K. "Reading *Kokoro* in the High School Textbook." Paper presented at Sōseki's Diversity: A Workshop, University of California, Berkeley, CA, May 2015.

Itō Sei. "Jemusu Joisu no metōdo 'ishiki no nagare' ni tsuite." *Shi•Genjitsu* 1 (June 1930): 170–75.

——. "Shin shinrishugi bungaku." *Itō Sei zenshū*, Vol. 1, pp. 311–18. Kawade Shobō, 1956.

——. *Shōsetsu no hōhō*. Iwanami Bunkō, 2006.

——. "Uchinaru koe to kasō." In *Shōsetsu no hōhō*. Iwanami Bunkō, 2006.

Iwaya Daishi. *Nihon Bungeika Kyōkai gojūnenshi*. Nihon Bungei Kyōkai, 1979.

Jakobson, Roman. "Langue and Parole: Code and Message." In *On Language*, ed. Linda R. Waugh and Monique Monville-Burston, 80–109. Cambridge, MA: Harvard University Press, 1990.

Jameson, Fredric. *The Prison-House of Language: A Critical Account of Structuralism and Russian Formalism*. Princeton, NJ: Princeton University Press, 1972.

——. "Modernism and Imperialism." In *Nationalism, Colonialism, and Literature*, 43–68. Minneapolis: University of Minnesota Press, 1990.

——. "Foreword to *Origins of Modern Japanese Literature*, by Karatani Kōjin, ed. Brett de Bary, vii–xx. Durham, NC: Duke University Press, 1993.

JanMohamed, Abdul R. "The Economy of Manichean Allegory." In *"Race," Writing, and Difference*, ed. Henry Louis Gates, 78–106. Chicago: University of Chicago Press, 1986.

Jockers, Matthew. *Macroanalysis: Digital Methods and Literary History*. Urbana: University of Illinois Press, 2013.

Jockers, Matthew, and Gabi Kirilloff. "Understanding Gender and Character Agency in the 19th Century Novel." *Journal of Cultural Analytics* (November 30, 2016). https://culturalanalytics.org/article/11066.

Johnson, Wendell. *Language and Speech Hygiene: An Application of General Semantics, Outline of a Course*. Chicago: Chicago Institute of General Semantics, 1939.

Joshi, Priya. *In Another Country: Colonialism, Culture, and the English Novel in India*. New York: Columbia University Press, 2002.

Jurafsky, Dan, and James Martin. *Speech and Language Processing*, 3rd ed. draft. https://web.stanford.edu/~jurafsky/slp3/ed3book.pdf.

Kabashima Tadao. "Buntai no heni ni tsuite." *Kokugo kokubun* 30, no. 11 (November 1961): 23–38.

——. "Buntai no gogaku-teki kenkyū." In *Bunshō to buntai*, ed. Morioka Kenji et al., 221–37. Meiji Shoin, 1963.

——. *Hyōgenron*. Kyoto: Bunkōsha, 1964.

Kabashima Tadao, and Jugaku Akiko. *Buntai no kagaku*. Kyoto: Sōgeisha, 1965.

Kanō Saburō. "Gensō no bungaku." *Manshū bungei nenkan* 3 (1939): 42–46.

Karatani Kōjin. *Marukusu sono kanōsei no chūshin*. Kōdansha, 1978.

——. *Origins of Modern Japanese Literature*, ed. Brett de Bary. Durham, NC: Duke University Press, 1993.

——. "Uses of Aesthetics: After Orientalism," trans. Sabu Kosho. *boundary 2* 25, no. 2 (1998): 145–60.

Kawabata Yasunari. "Hori-shi no 'Bukiyō na tenshi.' " *Bungei shunjū* 7, no. 4 (April 1929): 141–42.

——. *Shōsetsu nyūmon*. Yōshobō, 1952.

——. "Gendai sakka no bunshō." In *Kawabata Yasunari zenshū*, Vol. 32, pp. 41–68. Shinchōsha, 1999.

Kawaguchi Kyōichi. *Shōwa shonen no* Ulysses. Misuzu Shobō, 2005.

Kikuchi Kan. "Shunkan." In *Kikuchi Kan bungaku zenshū*, Vol. 3, pp. 375–402. Bungei Shunjū Shinsha, 1960.

Kisaka Motoi. *Kindai bunshō seiritsu no shosō*. Osaka: Wazumi Shoin, 1988.

Kitchin, Rob. "Big Data, New Epistemologies and Paradigm Shifts." *Big Data and Society* 1, no. 1 (April–June 2014): 1–12.

Kleeman, Faye. *In Transit: The Formation of the Colonial East Asian Cultural Sphere*. Honolulu: University of Hawai'i Press, 2014.

Klein, Lauren F. "Dimensions of Scale: Invisible Labor, Editorial Work, and the Future of Quantitative Literary Studies." *PMLA* 135, no. 1 (January 2020): 23–39.

Kobayashi Hideo. "*Bunshō shinrigaku* o yomu." In *Gengo to buntai*, 120–27. Sanseidō, 1937.

Komori Yōichi. *Buntai toshite no monogatari*. Chikuma Shobō, 1988.
——. *Kōzō toshite no katari*. Shinchōsha, 1988.
——. *Sōseki o yominaosu*. Chikuma Shobō, 1995.
——. *Posutokoroniaru*. Iwanami Shoten, 2001.
Kōno Toshirō. "*Omedetaki hito* no 'jibun.' " *Kokubungaku: Kaishaku to kyōzai no kenkyū* 4, no. 6 (May 1959): 78–83.
Kontoyiannis, Ioannis. "The Complexity and Entropy of Literary Styles." *NSF Technical Report* 97 (June 1996–October 1997): 1–15.
Kraicer, Eve, and Andrew Piper. "Social Characters: The Hierarchy of Gender in Contemporary English-Language Fiction." *Journal of Cultural Analytics* (January 30, 2019). https://culturalanalytics.org/article/11055.
Krippendorf, Klaus. *Content Analysis: An Introduction to Its Methodology*. Thousand Oaks, CA: Sage, 2004.
Kurokawa Sō. Ed. *"Gaichi" no Nihongo bungaku sen*. 3 vols. Shinjuku Shobō, 1996.
Kwon, Nayoung Aimee. *Intimate Empire: Collaboration and Colonial Modernity in Korea and Japan*. Durham, NC: Duke University Press, 2015.
Lee, Haiyan. *Revolution of the Heart: A Genealogy of Love in China, 1900–1950*. Stanford, CA: Stanford University Press, 2007.
Lee, Leo Ou-fan. *The Romantic Generation of Modern Chinese Writers*. Cambridge, MA: Harvard University Press, 1973.
——. "The Solitary Traveler: Images of the Self in Modern Chinese Literature." In *Expressions of Self in Chinese Literature*, ed. Robert Hegel and Richard Hessney, 282–307. New York: Columbia University Press, 1985.
Lee, Vernon. *The Handling of Words and Other Studies in Literary Psychology*. London: John Lane, 1927.
Lee, Yeounsuk. *The Ideology of Kokugo: Nationalizing Language in Modern Japan*, trans. Maki Hirano Hubbard. Honolulu: University of Hawai'i Press, 2010.
Levelt, William. *A History of Psycholinguistics: The Pre-Chomskyan Era*. Oxford: Oxford University Press, 2013.
Levy, Indra. *Sirens of the Western Shore: The Westernesque Femme Fatale, Translation, and Vernacular Style in Modern Japanese Literature*. New York: Columbia University Press, 2006.
Lippit, Seiji. *Topographies of Japanese Modernism*. New York: Columbia University Press, 2002.
Liu, Alan. *Local Transcendence: Essays on Postmodern Historicism and the Database*. Chicago: University of Chicago Press, 2008.
——. "The Meaning of the Digital Humanities." *PMLA* 128, no. 2 (March 2013): 409–23.
Liu, Jianmei. "Shanghai Variations on 'Revolution Plus Love.' " *Modern Chinese Literature and Culture* 14, no. 1 (Spring 2002): 51–92.
Liu, Lydia. *Translingual Practice: Literature, National Culture, and Translated Modernity—China, 1900–1937*. Stanford, CA: Stanford University Press, 1995.
Long, Hoyt. "Fog and Steel: Mapping Communities of Translation in an Information Age." *Journal of Japanese Studies* 41, no. 2 (Summer 2015): 281–316.
Long, Hoyt, and Richard Jean So. "Literary Pattern Recognition: Modernism Between Close Reading and Machine Learning." *Critical Inquiry* 42, no. 2 (Winter 2016): 235–66.

——. "Turbulent Flow: A Computational Model of World Literature." *Modern Language Quarterly* 77, no. 3 (September 2016): 345–68.

Long, Hoyt, Anatoly Detwyler, and Yuancheng Zhu. "Self-Repetition and East Asian Literary Modernity, 1900–1930." *Journal of Cultural Analytics* (May 2018). https://culturalanalytics.org/article/11040.\

Lynch, Deidre. *The Economy of Character: Novels, Market Culture, and the Business of Inner Meaning*. Chicago: University of Chicago, Press, 1998.

Mack, Edward. *Manufacturing Modern Japanese Literature: Publishing, Prizes, and the Ascription of Literary Value*. Durham, NC: Duke University Press, 2010.

"Mandarin Ducks and Butterfly Literature." In *Yuanyang Hudie pai yanjiu ziliao*, ed. Wei Shaochang. Shanghai: Shanghai wenyi chubanshe, 1962.

Maeda Ai, and Katō Shūichi. Eds. *Buntai*. Iwanami Shoten, 1989.

Mani, B. Venkat. *Recoding World Literature: Libraries, Print Culture, and Germany's Pact with Books*. New York: Fordham University Press, 2017.

Marrow, Alfred J. *The Practical Theorist: The Life and Work of Kurt Lewin*. New York: Basic Books, 1969.

Matsuyama Yō, and Miyajima Yoshiko. "Hyōgen kenkyū to suryōka no mondai." *Keiryō kokugogaku*, no. 3 (1957): 28–34.

McDonald, Kate. *Placing Empire: Travel and the Social Imagination in Imperial Japan*. Berkeley: University of California Press, 2017.

McFarland, Daniel A., and H. Richard McFarland. "Big Data and the Danger of Being Precisely Inaccurate." *Big Data and Society* 2, no. 2 (July–December 2015): 1–4.

McVeigh, Brian. *The History of Japanese Psychology: Global Perspectives, 1875–1950*. London: Bloomsbury Academic, 2017.

Mebed, Sharif. "Shōwa shoki ni okeru 'ishiki no nagare' juyō wo megutte." *Issues in Language and Culture*, no. 4 (March 2003): 5–16.

Meiji·Taishō·Shōwa hon'yaku bungaku mokuroku, ed. Kokuritsu Kokkai Toshokan. Kazama Shobō, 1959.

Meiji-ki hon'yaku bungaku sōgō nenpyō. Vol. 51 of *Meiji hon'yaku bungaku zenshū*, ed. Kawato Michiaki et al. Ōzorasha, 2001.

Melas, Natalie. "Merely Comparative." *PMLA* 128, no. 3 (May 2013): 652–59.

Mikolov, Tomas, et al. "Efficient Estimation of Word Representations in Vector Space." 2013. https://arxiv.org/abs/1301.3781.

Miles, Josephine. *Major Adjectives in English Poetry: From Wyatt to Auden*. Berkeley: University of California Press, 1946.

Miller, George. *Language and Communication*. New York: McGraw-Hill, 1951.

Miller, J. Hillis. *Fiction and Repetition: Seven English Novels*. Cambridge, MA: Harvard University Press, 1982.

Mito Reed, Barbara. "Language, Narrative Structure, and the *Shōsetsu*." PhD diss., Princeton University, 1988.

Miyajima Tatsuo. "'Kanji no shōrai' sono ato." *Gengo seikatsu*, no. 436 (1988): 50–58.

Miyoshi, Masao. *Accomplices of Silence: The Modern Japanese Novel*. Berkeley: University of California Press, 1974.

Monroe, Burt L., Michael P. Colaresi, and Kevin M. Quinn. "Fightin' Words: Lexical Feature Selection and Evaluation for Identifying the Content of Political Conflict." *Political Analysis* 16 (2008): 372–403.

Montemurro, Marcelo A., and Damián H. Zanette. "Universal Entropy of Word Ordering Across Linguistic Families." *PLoS ONE* 6, no. 5 (May 2011): e19875. https://doi.org/10.1371/journal.pone.0019875.
Moretti, Franco. *Signs Taken for Wonders: Essays in the Sociology of Literary Forms*. London: Verso, 1988.
——. *Modern Epic: The World-System from Goethe to García Márquez*, trans. Quintin Hoare. London: Verso, 1996.
——. "Conjectures on World Literature." *New Left Review*, 121, no. 1 (January–February 2000): 54–68.
——. "World-Systems Analysis, Evolutionary Theory, *Weltliteratur*." In *Immanuel Wallerstein and the Problem of the World: System, Scale, Culture*, ed. David Palumbo-Liu, Bruce Robbins, and Nirvana Tanoukhi, 67–77. Durham, NC: Duke University Press, 2011.
——. *The Bourgeois: Between History and Literature*. London: Verso, 2013.
——. *Distant Reading*. London: Verso, 2013.
——. *Endoku: <Sekai bungaku shisutemu> e no chosen*, trans. Akikusa Shun'ichirō et al. Misuzu Shobō, 2016.
Morioka Kenji. *Buntai to hyōgen*. Meiji Shoin, 1988.
Mullaney, Thomas. *The Chinese Typewriter: A History*. Cambridge, MA: MIT Press, 2017.
Murphy, Joseph A. *Metaphorical Circuit: Negotiations Between Literature and Science in 20th Century Japan*. Ithaca, NY: Cornell University East Asia Program, 2004.
Mushanokōji Saneatsu. "*Omedetaki hito*." In *Gendai Nihon bungaku zenshū*, Vol. 40, pp. 5–27. Chikuma Shobō, 1973.
Nagamatsu Sadamu. "Nihon ni okeru 'ishiki no nagare' shōsetsu." *Shinbungaku kenkyū* (April 1931): 260–64.
——. *Nagamatsu Sadamu sakuhin shū*. Gogatsu Shobō, 1970.
Nagamine Shigetoshi. *<Dokusho kokumin> no tanjō*. Nihon Editā Sukuru Shuppanbu, 2004.
Nakamura Akira. "Kotoba no bi to chikara." In *Kotoba no kagaku*, Vol. 5, ed. Endō Yoshimoto et al., 2–36. Nakayama Shoten, 1958.
Nakamura Miharu. *Shūjiteki modanizumu: Tekisuto yōshikiron no kokoromi*. Hitsuji Shobō, 2006.
Nakamura, Miri. *Monstrous Bodies: The Rise of the Uncanny in Modern Japan*. Cambridge, MA: Harvard University Asia Center, 2015.
Nakamura Mitsuo. "Literature Under the Occupation," trans. Atsuko Ueda. In *The Politics and Literature Debate in Postwar Japanese Criticism 1945–1952*, ed. Atsuko Ueda et al., 257–68. Lanham, MD: Lexington Books, 2017.
Nakamura Murao. "Genka bundan no shosō to shosakka." *Bungaku jidai* 1, no. 3 (July 1929): 14–20.
Nakamura Shin'ichirō. *Akutagawa • Hori • Tachihara no bungaku to sei*. Shinchō Sensho, 1980.
Nakayama Shigeru. *The Orientation of Science and Technology: A Japanese View*. Folkestone: Global Oriental, 2009.
Natsume Sōseki. *Sōseki shiryō: Bungakuron nōto*, ed. Muraoka Isamu. Iwanami Shoten, 1976.
——. "Sōsakuka no taidō." In *Sōseki zenshū*, Vol. 16. Iwanami Shoten, 1995.

——. *Theory of Literature and Other Critical Writings*, trans. Michael Bourdaghs, Atsuko Ueda, and Joseph Murphy. New York: Columbia University Press, 2009.

——. *Kokoro*. Aozora Bunko. Transcribed from *Kokoro*. Shūeisha, 1991. https://www.aozora.gr.jp/cards/000148/files/773_14560.html.

Ngai, Sianne. *Ugly Feelings*. Cambridge, MA: Harvard University Press, 2005.

Noble, Safiya. *Algorithms of Oppression: How Search Engines Reinforce Racism*. New York: New York University Press, 2018.

Obi Toshito. *Shuppan to shakai*. Genki Shobō, 2007.

Oguma Eiji. *A Genealogy of 'Japanese' Self-Images*, trans. David Askew. Melbourne: Trans Pacific Press, 2002.

Oh Shō-yū. "Honryū." In *"Gaichi" no Nihongo bungaku sen*, Vol. 1, pp. 220–50. Shinjuku Shobō, 1996.

——. "The Torrent" trans. Erin Brightwell. *Asia-Pacific Journal: Japan Focus* 16, issue 1, no. 3 (January 2018). https://apjjf.org/2018/01/O.html.

Ōkubo Takeharu. *The Quest for Civilization: Encounters with Dutch Jurisprudence, Political Economy, and Statistics at the Dawn of Modern Japan*, trans. David Noble. Leiden: Global Oriental, 2014.

O'Neil, Cathy. *Weapons of Math Destruction: How Big Data Increases Inequality and Threatens Democracy*. New York: Crown, 2016.

Ong, Walter. *Orality and Literacy: The Technologizing of the Word*. London: Routledge, 1991.

Onoue Yukio. *Shuppan gyōkai*. Kyōikusha Shinsho, 1991.

Ōta Saburō. "Jeimuzu Joisu no shōkai to eikyō." *Gakuen* 175, no. 4 (April 1955): 14–38.

——. "Joisu no shōkai to eikyō." In *Joisu kenkyū*, ed. Itō Sei, 205–25. Eihōsha, 1955.

——. "Hon'yaku bungaku." In *Iwanami kōza Nihon bungaku-shi*, Vol. 14, pp. 3–44. Iwanami Shoten, 1959.

Ōta Suzuko. "Kawabata Yasunari 'Hari to garasu to kiri': ishiki no nagare no shuhō to teima to no kanren." *Gakuen* 577 (January 1988): 155–66.

Piper, Andrew. "The Wertherian Exotext: Models of Transnational Circulation." Paper presented at the Modern Language Association Annual Meeting, Chicago, IL, January 2014.

——. "There Will Be Numbers." *Journal of Cultural Analytics* (May 2016). https://culturalanalytics.org/article/11062.

——. "Think Small: On Literary Modeling." *PMLA* 132, no. 3 (May 2017): 651–58.

——. *Enumerations: Data and Literary Study*. Chicago: University of Chicago Press, 2018.

Pitarch-Fernandez, Pau. "Cultivated Madness: Aesthetics, Psychology and the Value of the Author in Early 20th-Century Japan." PhD diss., Columbia University, 2015.

Poovey, Mary. *Genres of the Credit Economy: Mediating Value in Eighteenth- and Nineteenth-Century Britain*. Chicago: University of Chicago Press, 2008.

Porter, Theodore M. *The Rise of Statistical Thinking, 1820–1900*. Princeton, NJ: Princeton University Press, 1986.

Posadas, Baryon Tensor. *Double Visions, Double Fictions: The Doppelgänger in Japanese Film and Literature*. Minneapolis: University of Minnesota Press, 2018.

Power, Arthur. *Conversations with James Joyce*. London: Millington, 1974.

Pratt, Mary Louise. "Scratches on the Face of the Country." In *"Race," Writing, and Difference*, ed. Henry Louis Gates, 138–62. Chicago: University of Chicago Press, 1986.

Průšek, Jaroslav. *The Lyrical and the Epic: Studies of Modern Chinese Literature*. Bloomington: Indiana University Press, 1980.

Pym, Anthony. *Translation Solutions for Many Languages: Histories of a Flawed Dream*. London: Bloomsbury Academic, 2016.

Radway, Janice. *Reading the Romance: Women, Patriarchy, and Popular Literature*. Chapel Hill: University of North Carolina Press, 1991.

Riffaterre, Michael. *Semiotics of Poetry*. Bloomington: Indiana University Press, 1978.

Risam, Roopika. *New Digital Worlds: Postcolonial Digital Humanities in Theory, Praxis, and Pedagogy*. Evanston, IL: Northwestern University Press, 2019.

Rubin, Jay. *Injurious to Public Morals: Writers and the Meiji State*. Seattle: University of Washington Press, 1984.

Sahlgren, Magnus. "The Distributional Hypothesis." 2008. http://soda.swedish-ict.se/3941/1/sahlgren.distr-hypo.pdf.

Said, Edward. *Orientalism*. New York: Vintage Books, 1979.

——. *Culture and Imperialism*. New York: Knopf, 1993.

Saitō Mineko. "Nihon bungaku zenshū to sono jidai (jō): Zenshū ga shuppan bunka o riido shita koro." *Bungei* 54, no. 1 (2015): 40-45.

——. "Nihon bungaku zenshū to sono jidai (ge): Kongon no rokujū nendai kara zenshū baburu no hōkai made." *Bungei* 54, no. 2 (2015): 348-354.

Saito, Satoru. *Detective Fiction and the Rise of the Japanese Novel, 1880–1930*. Cambridge, MA: Harvard University Asia Center, 2012.

Sakaguchi Angō. *Furenzoku satsujin jiken*. Aozora Bunko. Transcribed from vol. 11 of *Sakuguchi Angō zenshū*. Chikuma Shobō, 1990. https://www.aozora.gr.jp/cards/001095/files/42626_60035.html.

Sakimoto Kazuo. Ed. *Nihon gendai bunshō kōza*. Hōseikaku, 1934.

Sano Miki. *"Sangetsuki" wa naze kokumin kyōzai to natta no ka*. Taishūkan Shoten, 2013.

Sapiro, Giselè. "Globalization and Cultural Diversity in the Book Market: The Case of Literary Translations in the US and in France." *Poetics* 38 (January 2010): 419–39.

Schmidt, Ben. "Vector Space Models for the Digital Humanities." *Ben's Bookworm Blog* (blog). October 25, 2015. http://bookworm.benschmidt.org/posts/2015-10-25-Word-Embeddings.html.

Scholes, Robert, and Robert Kellogg. *The Nature of Narrative*. Oxford: Oxford University Press, 1966.

Seko Katashi. *Kindai Nihon bunshō-shi*. Hakuteisha, 1968.

Sherif, Ann. *Japan's Cold War: Media, Literature, and the Law*. New York: Columbia University Press, 2009.

Shih, Shu-mei. *Lure of the Modern: Writing Modernism in Semicolonial China, 1917–1937*. Berkeley: University of California Press, 2001.

Shore, Daniel. *Cyberformalism: Histories of Linguistic Forms in the Digital Archive*. Baltimore, MD: Johns Hopkins University Press, 2018.

So, Richard Jean. " 'All Models are Wrong.' " *PMLA* 132, no. 3 (May 2017): 668–73.

So, Richard Jean, and Edwin Roland. "Race and Distant Reading." *PMLA* 135, no. 1 (January 2020): 59–73.

So, Richard, Hoyt Long, and Yuancheng Zhu. "Race, Writing, and Computation: Racial Difference and the US Novel, 1880–2000." *Journal of Cultural Analytics* (January 11, 2019). https://culturalanalytics.org/article/11057.

Steinberg, Erwin. *The Stream of Consciousness and Beyond in "Ulysses."* Pittsburgh, PA: University of Pittsburgh Press, 1973.

Stoler, Ann. *Race and the Education of Desire: Foucault's History of Sexuality and the Colonial Order of Things*. Durham, NC: Duke University Press, 1995.

Sudo, Naoto. *Nanyo Orientalism: Japanese Representations of the Pacific*. Amherst, NY: Cambria Press, 2010.

Suzuki, Tomi. *Narrating the Self: Fictions of Japanese Modernity*. Stanford, CA: Stanford University Press, 1996.

Takashima Ken'ichirō. "Kadokawa shoten *Shōwa bungaku zenshū* no hanbai senryaku—sengo zenshūbon būmu to bungaku jōkyō o megutte (1)." *Kindai bungaku kenkyū* 21 (2004): 1–13.

Tanaka-Ishii Kumiko, and Shunsuke Aihara. "Computational Constancy Measures of Texts." *Association for Computational Linguistics* 41, no. 3 (2015): 481–502.

Tani Jōji. *Odoru chiheisen*. Aozora Bunko. Transcribed from *Odoru chiheisen (ge)*. Iwanami Shoten, 1999. https://www.aozora.gr.jp/cards/000272/files/4363_8029.html.

Tanizaki Jun'ichirō. *Bunshō tokuhon*. [1934]. Chukō Bunko, 2013.

Tannen, Deborah. *Talking Voices: Repetition, Dialogue, and Imagery in Conversational Discourse*. Cambridge: Cambridge University Press, 2007.

Tanoukhi, Nirvana. "The Scale of World Literature." In *Immanuel Wallerstein and the Problem of the World: System, Scale, Culture*, ed. David Palumbo-Liu, Bruce Robbins, and Nirvana Tanoukhi, 78–100. Durham, NC: Duke University Press, 2011.

"Tantei shōsetsu zadankai." *Bungaku jidai* 1, no. 3 (July 1929): 52–72.

Tarumi Chie. *Taiwan no Nihongo bungaku: Nihon tōchi jidai no sakka-tachi*. Goryū Shoin, 1995.

Textor, Cindi. "Radical Language, Radical Identity: Korean Writers in Japanese Spaces and the Burden to 'Represent.' " PhD diss., University of Washington, 2016.

Thoiron, Philippe. "Diversity Index and Entropy as Measures of Lexical Richness." *Computers and the Humanities* 20, no. 3 (1986): 197–202.

Thornber, Karen. *Empire of Texts in Motion: Chinese, Korean, and Taiwanese Transculturations of Japanese Literature*. Cambridge, MA: Harvard University Asia Center, 2009.

Tierney, Robert. *Tropics of Savagery: The Culture of Japanese Empire in Comparative Frame*. Berkeley: University of California Press, 2010.

Tokieda Motoki. *Bunshō kenkyū jyosetsu*. Yamada Shoin, 1960.

Tomasi, Massimiliano. *Rhetoric in Modern Japan: Western Influences on the Development of Narrative and Oratorical Style*. Honolulu: University of Hawai'i Press, 2004.

Tomita Michio. *Hon no mirai*. In *Aozora Bunko* (1997). https://www.aozora.gr.jp/cards/000055/files/56499_51225.html.

Tomita Michio, and Yamada Shōji. "Intabyū·Aozora Bunko ni tsuite." In *Komonzu to bunka: bunka wa dare no mono ka*, 180–201. Tokyodō Shuppan, 2010.

Totsuka Manabu. "Hori Tatsuo 'Bukiyō na tenshi' ron—hon'yaku kara shōsetsu he." *Nihon kindai bungaku* 81 (November 2009): 112–26.

Treat, John Whittier. "Japan Is Interesting: Modern Japanese Literary Studies Today." *Japan Forum* 30, no. 3 (2018). https://www.tandfonline.com/doi/full/10.1080/09555803.2018.1441171.

——. *The Rise and Fall of Modern Japanese Literature*. Chicago: University of Chicago Press, 2018.

Tsubouchi Shōyō. *Shōsetsu shinzui*. In *Nihon kindai bungaku taikei*, Vol. 3, pp. 39–166. Kadokawa Shobō, 1974.

Tsuchida Kyōson. "'Ishiki no nagare' no bungaku wo megutte." *Shinchō* (February 1932): 28–36.

Tsuchiya Noboru. "Bungeigaku ni okeru hōhō-teki jikaku." In *Nihon bungakuron kō*, ed. Tsubouchi Sensei Kanreki Kinen Kai, 16–32. Bungakusha, 1938.

Tuldava, Juhan. "Stylistics, Author Identification." In *Quantitative Linguistics: An International Handbook*, ed. Reinhard Köhler et al., 368–86. Berlin: Walter de Gruyter, 2005.

Tyler, William J. Introduction to *Modanizumu: Modernist Fiction from Japan, 1913–1938*, 1–48. Honolulu: University of Hawai'i Press, 2008.

Ueda, Atsuko. *Concealment of Politics, Politics of Concealment: The Production of "Literature" in Meiji Japan*. Stanford, CA: Stanford University Press, 2007.

——. "*Bungakuron* and 'Literature' in the Making." *Japan Forum* 20, no. 1 (February 2008): 25–46.

Underwood, Ted. "A Genealogy of Distant Reading." *Digital Humanities Quarterly* 11, no. 2 (2017). http://www.digitalhumanities.org/dhq/vol/11/2/000317/000317.html.

——. "The Stanford Literary Lab's Narrative." *Public Books*, November 2, 2017. http://www.publicbooks.org/the-stanford-literary-labs-narrative/.

——. *Distant Horizons: Digital Evidence and Literary Change*. Chicago: University of Chicago Press, 2019.

Underwood, Ted, David Bamman, and Sabrina Lee. "The Transformation of Gender in English-Language Fiction." *Journal of Cultural Analytics* (February 2018). https://culturalanalytics.org/article/11035.

Urbano, Julián, and Mónica Marrero. "The Treatment of Ties in AP Correlation." *ICTIR '17 Proceedings of the ACM SIGIR International Conference on Theory of Information Retrieval* (October 2017): 321–24.

Vaidhyanathan, Siva. *The Googlization of Everything (And Why We Should Worry)*. Berkeley: University of California Press, 2011.

Vincent, Keith. "Hamaosociality: Narrative and Fascism in Hamao Shirō's *The Devil's Disciple*." In *The Culture of Japanese Fascism*, ed. Alan Tansman, 381–408. Durham, NC: Duke University Press, 2009.

Wada Yoshie. *Chikuma Shobō no sanjūnen 1940–1970*. Chikuma Shobō, 2011.

Walker, Janet. *The Japanese Novel of the Meiji Period and the Ideal of Individualism*. Princeton, NJ: Princeton University Press, 1979.

Watase Shigeru. "Hori Tatsuo 'Bukiyō na tenshi' no buntai ni okeru dōshi shūshikei." *Fuji fuenikksu ronsō* 8 (March 2000): 45–58.

Wellmon, Chad. *Organizing Enlightenment: Information Overload and the Invention of the Modern Research University*. Baltimore, MD: Johns Hopkins University Press, 2015.

White, Hayden. *Tropics of Discourse: Essays in Cultural Criticism*. Baltimore, MD: Johns Hopkins University Press, 1978.

Wilden, Anthony. *System and Structure: Essays in Communication and Exchange*. London: Tavistock, 1972.

Williams, James. *Gilles Deleuze's Difference and Repetition: A Critical Introduction and Guide*. Edinburgh: Edinburgh University Press, 2013.

Winter, Thomas Nelson. "Roberto Busa, S. J., and the Invention of the Machine-Generated Concordance." *The Classical Bulletin* 75, no. 1 (1999): 3–20.

Woloch, Alex. *The One vs. the Many: Minor Characters and the Space of the Protagonist in the Novel*. Princeton, NJ: Princeton University Press, 2003.

Xiong, Ying. *Representing Empire: Japanese Colonial Literature in Taiwan and Manchuria*. Leiden: Brill, 2014.

Yang, Yoon Sun. *From Domestic Women to Sensitive Young Men: Translating the Individual in Early Colonial Korea*. Cambridge, MA: Harvard University Press, 2017.

Yasumoto Biten. "Bun no nagasa to kuten no kazu." *Keiryō kokugogaku*, no. 8 (1959): 13–22.

——. *Bunshō shinrigaku no shinryōiki*. Seishin Shobō, 1960.

——. "Bunshō shinrigaku." In *Bunshō to buntai*, ed. Morioka Kenji et al., 184–202. Meiji Shoin, 1963.

Ye Lingfeng. *Ye Lingfeng xiaoshuo quanbian*. Shanghai: Xuelin chubanshe, 1997.

Yi, Christina. *Colonizing Language: Cultural Production and Language Politics in Modern Japan and Korea*. New York: Columbia University Press, 2018.

Yokomitsu Ri'ichi. "Junsui shōsetsuron." In *Gendai Nihon bungaku ronsō-shi*, Vol. 3, ed. Hirano Ken, Odagiri Hideo, and Yamamoto Kenkichi, 103–15. Miraisha, 2006.

——. *Shanghai*, trans. Dennis Washburn. Ann Arbor, MI: Center for Japanese Studies, 2001.

"Yōrei saishū no tame no shuyō bungaku sakuhin mokuroku," ed. Kokugo Jiten Henshū Junbishitsu. Kokuritsu Kokugo Kenkyūjo, 1980.

Yoshida Morio. *Tantei shōsetsu to Nihon kindai*. Seikyūsha, 2004.

Yuanyang Hudie pai yanjiu ziliao, ed. Wei Shaochang. Shanghai: Shanghai wenyi chubanshe, 1962.

Yule, George Udny. "On Sentence-Length as a Statistical Characteristic of Style in Prose." *Biometrika* 30, no. 3–4 (1939): 363–90.

——. *The Statistical Study of Literary Vocabulary* [1944]. Hamden, CT: Archon Books, 1968.

Yumeno Kyūsaku. "Shinamai no fukuro." Aozora Bunko. Transcribed from vol. 6 of *Yumeno Kyūsaku zenshū*. Chikuma Shobō, 1992. https://www.aozora.gr.jp/cards/000096/files/2101_18783.html.

Zheng Boqi. Ed. *Zhongguo Xinwenxue daxi*. Shanghai: Liangyou tushu yinshua gongsi, 1981.

Zhang, Jingyuan. *Psychoanalysis in China: Literary Transformations 1919–1949*. Ithaca, NY: Cornell University Press, 1992.

Zhang, Yingjin. *The City in Modern Chinese Literature and Film: Configurations of Space, Time, and Gender*. Stanford, CA: Stanford University Press, 1996.

Zhou, Xiaoyi. "Salome in China: The Aesthetic Art of Dying." In *Wilde Writings: Contextual Conditions*, ed. Joseph Bristow, 295–316. Toronto: University of Toronto Press, 2003.

Zipf, George. *The Psycho-Biology of Language: An Introduction to Dynamic Philology*. Boston: Houghton Mifflin Company, 1935.

——. *Human Behavior and the Principle of Least Effort*. Cambridge, MA: Addison-Wesley Press, 1949.

Zuberi, Tukufu. *Thicker Than Blood: How Racial Statistics Lie*. Minneapolis: University of Minnesota Press, 2001.

Zwicker, Jonathan. *Practices of the Sentimental Imagination: Melodrama, the Novel, and the Social Imaginary in Nineteenth-Century Japan*. Cambridge, MA: Harvard University Asia Center, 2006.

INDEX

Page numbers in *italics* indicate figures or tables.

Printed in the USA
CPSIA information can be obtained
at www.ICGtesting.com
JSHW021437221024
72172JS00005B/40

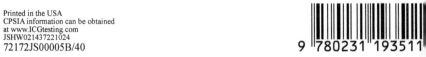